The Betsy-Tacy Companion

Maud Palmer Hart
about 1906

THE BETSY-TACY COMPANION

A BIOGRAPHY OF MAUD HART LOVELACE

SHARLA SCANNELL WHALEN

Portalington Press
Whitehall, PA

First Printing

Library of Congress Catalog Card Number: 91-66704.

Library of Congress Cataloging-in-Publication Data
Whalen, Sharla Scannell, 1960-
The Betsy-Tacy companion : a biography of Maud Hart Lovelace / by Sharla Scannell Whalen. -- 1st ed.
p. cm.
Includes bibliographical endnotes and index.
ISBN: 0-9630783-0-5 (hdbk.)
1. Lovelace, Maud Hart, 1892-1980. 2. Children's stories, American--History and criticism. 3. Authors, American--20th century--Biography. 4. Minnesota in literature. 5. Minnesota--Biography. I. Title.
PS3523.08356Z94 1995
813' .52--dc20 91-66704

The acid-free paper used in this book meets the minimum requirements of the American National Standard for Information Sciences - Permanence for Printed Library Materials.

Portalington Press
P.O. Box 695
Whitehall, PA 18052-0695
Listed in *Publishers in Print* at your local library.

Manufactured in the United States of America

For Two Saints
Margaret Scannell and Shaun Whalen
and Three Angels
Paul, Emily, and Patrick

CONTENTS

Preface

The real Betsy-Tacy companion is you, of course. You as a child, devouring *Betsy-Tacy and Tib* on a summer afternoon. You as a young teenager, turning to *Heaven to Betsy* on the night before your first day of high school. You as a college student, slightly embarrassed when friends see *Betsy and the Great World* on the bookshelf in your dorm room. You as a bride, incorporating forget-me-nots in your wedding flowers, for Betsy and Joe. You as a young mother, enjoying the escape to Deep Valley, which still brings such pleasure, and the even greater enjoyment of introducing *Betsy-Tacy* to your own children - and before you know it, your grandchildren.

With each rereading, you find something new to enjoy or admire. As your perspective changes, you appreciate even more, for instance, the Rays' parental love and wisdom. Perhaps you reread seasonally through the series, every fall or every spring. You also pick up a particular favorite in times of stress, disappointment, or illness. Through the years of your life, Betsy is a companion, always waiting between the covers of her books.

When Betsy begins piano lessons, her teacher says, "This is middle C," just as she had said to older sister Julia years before. "Betsy liked that. It gave her a warm feeling of the continuity of life."[1] The Betsy-Tacy books give us a sense of warm continuity. The rituals and traditions of the Ray family have evolved because the family knows how to <u>savor</u> life. Yet their happiness is never sappy, nor their optimism unrealistic. As one Betsy-Tacy fan said, *"Betsy learned not through severe moral trials, but through the ordinary dilemmas of life."*[2] The characters experience failure, rejection, guilt, and sorrow - to which they respond with healthy self-esteem and hardy common sense. Betsy, inevitably introspective, is undeniably whole as well as wholesome. The opportunity to share in her childhood and young adulthood is a gift.

Maud Hart Lovelace classified the ten books which take Betsy from age five to age twenty-five as "*main-line Betsy-Tacy,*" and noted that there were "*three more in which Betsy appears.*"[3] *Carney's House Party* and *Emily of Deep Valley,* though not Betsy-Tacy books, are tied much more closely to the series than is the third "other" Deep Valley book, *Winona's Pony Cart.* In *The Betsy-Tacy Companion,* one chapter is devoted to each of the ten main Betsy-Tacy titles. The *Companion*'s chapters on *Carney* and *Emily* have been placed between chapters on *Betsy and Joe* and *Great World* because the two "satellites" serve as a significant bridge between the two main-line books. Fewer pages have been devoted to chapters on the first four Betsy-Tacys, because the books about Betsy's childhood are more episodic and therefore less "documentable" than those about high school and young adult years.

The task of clearly delineating the many places, friends, and experiences which Betsy and Maud had in common is problematic. Confusion may be inevitable, but an attempt has been made throughout the *Companion* to provide consistency, at the very least. The name "Maud" has been used herein when referring to the author herself and when describing events which may not have occurred in the Betsy-Tacy books. When Maud's experiences are the same as those of her fictional counterpart, the name "Betsy" is most often used. (And, of course, "Betsy" is used when referring to something which may have happened to Betsy but not to Maud.) After the series had been written, Maud and her best friend Bick (the real-life Tacy) called each other "Betsy" and "Tacy" at times, so it seems fair for us to interchange the names, too!

Use of the affectionate "Maud" throughout this book, rather than the more respectful, but chilly, "Mrs. Lovelace" or the even chillier "Lovelace," seems an excusable familiarity in light of a letter the author wrote to a grown-up fan in 1964 that begins, "*Dear Susan, I address you as Susan because it seems that, thanks to Betsy, we have known each other for a long time.*"[4]

It should also be noted here that to distinguish quotations drawn from the Betsy-Tacy books from actual comments made by Maud herself (often taken from newspapers or letters), all non-series quotations have been italicized. Quotations culled elsewhere (both fiction and nonfiction) also appear in italics. The reader can thereby immediately see whether a reference is Betsy-Tacy or from another source.

Companion readers who experience difficulty correlating the fictional Deep Valley with the historic Mankato should keep in mind the words Maud wrote to a fan: "*I warn you right now that you are going to be CONFUSED. Not suspecting in the beginning that the books were going to turn into a series, I freely used the names of Mankato streets (but not the streets they really are) and of Mankato families, but not for people who belonged to those families. Carney, for example, was Marion Willard, before she became Mrs. Everett. And I picked the name Willard for Joe. You will leave completely bewildered but I do think you will have fun batting around.*"[5]

The confusion between fiction and reality arises because the Betsy-Tacy books are so very autobiographical. The lengths to which Maud went to achieve accuracy in the Betsy-Tacy series can be explained in part by the meticulous research she had earlier conducted to produce her works of historical fiction. So immersed had Maud been in the intense work on her novels, she later said, "*There was a time when I would have told you I was unlikely ever to write anything else.*"[6]

Reviewers of the 1920s and 1930s were impressed by Maud's attention to historical detail. Their praise for her ability to recreate the past in her historical novels anticipates the skillful backgrounds she would later create in the Betsy-Tacy books: "*One can but marvel at the great research that has preceded the writing of many of the descriptive passages, especially those relating to the styles of the day, the customs, the names and relations of the characters ... in the recreation of a life, long since vanished, with the quiet humor that seasons the narrative.*"[7]

One reviewer spoke of characters "*moving in their original settings as vividly and as realistically as though the reader were a part of those days.*"[8] Another admired "*that knack which Maud Hart Lovelace possesses of recasting a period by reviving its typical characters, scenes and incidents.*"[9] A third newspaper reporter predicted: "*Whatever historical periods Mrs. Lovelace chooses to depict in novels of the future, one thing is assured -- they will be authentic historically. She insists upon being faithful to historical reference, spending many long months in research before even attempting any work on a book.*"[10]

The novels of the future, the Betsy-Tacy books, were authentic historically; but Maud's admirers and reviewers alike were taken by surprise in 1940 with the publication of *Betsy-Tacy*, her first book for children. A reviewer actually called it an "historical novel" based on the author's childhood. This assessment would probably have pleased - or amused - Maud, who later explained, "*With all my historical novels, I did very thorough research, reading newspapers, magazines, and memoirs of the period ... to check costumes, furniture, popular music and so on. This procedure continued, in fact, even with the Betsy-Tacy books.*"[11]

It was certainly Maud's commitment to historical accuracy which produced the resounding authenticity of the Betsy-Tacy series. The books capture the feel of those halcyon days so powerfully, the reader feels almost as if she has gone through Deep Valley High School in another life! The dramatic content of the books rings true, even for readers who are unaware of the stories' autobiographical basis.

Maud saw herself as bringing to life a specific period of time, but she had not set out to tell the story of her life. Rather, Maud had immured herself in a method which obliged her to create something of an autobiography when once she had begun to write about life in her hometown. As she wrote, she would have been unable to represent her family, for example, as anything other than exactly the way they were. Yet Maud does not appear to have been entirely aware that what she was producing was autobiographical - the intensity of her method may not have permitted her to see the forest for the trees. While looking over her High School Scrapbook in the 1970s, Maud wrote that she had forgotten "*how many of my high school experiences I had put right into* [*Betsy Was a Junior*]."[12] Did she forget, or had she been blind to the fact that it was her own history she had researched as she sifted memorabilia in the 1940s and 1950s? It is known that Maud obtained story material not only from her Scrapbook, but, even more significantly, from her diaries (which she later burned).

Maud never denied that the Betsy-Tacy books were based on real life, but she was anxious that this be downplayed. She received a great volume of fan mail, and most letters asked about the people behind the series. "*Many of the characters are real people and I have found in speaking for children, teachers and librarians over the years, much interest expressed in that angle.*"[13] This interest seemed to have somewhat alarmed Maud, who replied coyly to questions in fan letters. "*Remember,*" she'd write, "*the books are fiction.*"

In a letter to a cousin, however, Maud was more candid. "*The invention sprang from fact, for in writing the high school books my diaries were extremely helpful. The Ray family is a true portrayal of the Hart family. Mr. Ray is like Tom Hart; Mrs. Ray like Stella Palmer Hart; Julia like Kathleen; Margaret like Helen; and Betsy is like me, except that, of course, I glamorized her to make her a proper heroine. The family life, customs, jokes, traditions are all true and the general pattern of the years is also accurate.*"[14] So while on one hand asserting that the books were fiction, on the other Maud took real satisfaction in their factual footing: "*It is a great joy to me to have that dear family between book covers.*"[15]

It should be emphasized that Maud was not writing from her own life in order to avoid inventing material. "*Of course, I could make it all up, but in these BT stories, I love to work from real incidents.*"[16] Maud certainly could and often did make things up - and masterfully. But working from real incidents not only gave Maud pleasure, it served an important purpose. Dr. Edward J. Cronin of the University of Notre Dame remarked: "*I see an interesting relationship between your Mrs. Lovelace and my James Joyce. You may recall that Joyce would send his poor Aunt Josephine scurrying about Dublin to get the exact measurement of things, their weight, their color, etc.... I think this almost obsession with accuracy is basically economic good sense, for it allows the author to use his imagination upon that which can be only imagined and not forced to 'think up' that which need not be imagined.*"[17]

It might be argued that the plots of the Betsy-Tacy books are largely fictional. For instance, Maud didn't quarrel with Delos when she was a senior in high school (as Betsy did with Joe in *Betsy and Joe*), because they hadn't yet met. For the most part, however, Maud's inventions were inconsequential, since the episodic plots of these books serve primarily to embody the themes, which are of more structural importance. Certainly the plots, such as they are, offer vital skeletal support. But the flesh and blood of the series, the pulsing life which quickens it, eliciting our laughter and tears, is found in the characters themselves and the relationships between them. The development and interaction of Maud's characters is pursued more through anecdote than plot. And the characters, relationships, and anecdotes were drawn carefully and lovingly from life. When asked by a group of school children why she made Tacy shy, rather than Betsy, Maud responded promptly, "*That is the way they were.*"[18]

A Betsy-Tacy fan once made a suggestion regarding the content of *The Betsy-Tacy Companion*. "*Don't tell everything* [about the real lives of the characters]. *Leave the magic!*" Perhaps realizing how faithful the stories were to Maud's own life will enhance that magic. Nothing the *Companion* relates is discordant with the spirit of the Betsy-Tacy books, since the counterparts were really as wonderful as the characters!

Some readers may feel somewhat nonplused by photographs of the real people and places, since these images may initially disrupt the mental pictures of Deep Valley and its inhabitants they have always treasured. However, it should be remembered that no matter how autobiographical these books are, they do remain fiction. And a fictional creation conjures unique images in each reader's mind, permeated by what each brings to the reading. The images that belong to you, and only to you, will ultimately remain your "true" Deep Valley. And if scrutiny of the real-life background alters your images, hopefully it will only embellish them. Some may find that the Betsy-Tacy books have been subjected to far too much thoroughness here, and that, as Jane Austen put it, "*Every view was pointed out with a minuteness which left beauty entirely behind.*"[19] Of course, it is my hope that this will <u>not</u> be the effect of *The Betsy-Tacy Companion*.

[1] *Betsy Was a Junior*, p. 69.

[2] Mary W. Atwell, "Betsy Ray: A Heroine Flourishes," p. 10.

[3] C.N. Richards, ed., *Minnesota Writers* (Minneapolis: T.S. Denison, 1961), p. 211.

[4] MHL to S. Thiets, 10-31-64.

[5] MHL to L. Demp, 7-23-58, p. 4.

[6] Richards, *Minnesota Writers*, p. 209.

[7] *St. Paul Dispatch*, 1-3-30.

[8] *Minneapolis T.*, 8-25-29.

[9] Ibid., 8-24-30.

[10] Ibid., 4-12-32.

[11] MHL to M. Freeman, 5-19-64.

[12] MHL to BECHS, 7-19-74.

[13] MHL to M. Flanagan, 9-26-64.

[14] MHL to M. Freeman, 5-19-64.

[15] Richards, *Minnesota Writers,* p. 211.

[16] MHL to M. Everett, 4-14-48, p. 2.

[17] Dr. Edward Cronin to SSW, 8-10-89.

[18] Lovelace Interview, University of Michigan.

[19] Jane Austen, *Pride and Prejudice* (London: Odhams Press Limited, n.d.), p. 155.

Introduction
by Johanna Hurwitz

One Saturday morning when I was about twelve years old, I woke with a wonderful plan. The evening before, I had finished rereading my very favorite library book. It was *Downtown* (later retitled by the publisher as *Betsy and Tacy Go Downtown*) by Maud Hart Lovelace. It was the third time I had borrowed the book from the library, and when the two-week lending period was over, I would have to part with this treasured book once again. Hence my plan: I would copy the words of the story for myself.

This was the era before inexpensive paperback editions of popular books for children. And this was the era before the existence of photocopy machines (and laws forbidding the copying of entire books). My father was an ardent bibliophile, and so I suppose I might have thought to ask for my own copy of *Downtown*. But my father's idea of going to a bookstore was browsing in dimly lit and dusty second-hand shops. I often went with him and had the thrill of buying one or two old books for a nickel or dime each. Yet, somehow, I could not imagine a copy of *Downtown* in one of those shops.

So I took a large notebook and a freshly sharpened pencil, and carefully, in my very best cursive writing, I began. The second paragraph that I wrote was less neat than the first. By the time I completed copying only the first page, my hand was very tired. I looked at my smudged paper and compared it to the clear print of the real book. I realized that even if I ever finished this monumental task which I had set for myself, it would not truly resemble the bound book I held in my hand. Nor would there be any of the charming drawings by Lois Lenski to accompany the text.

I tore the page from my notebook and gave up. I would just have to wait my turn and continue to borrow *Downtown* from the library whenever I could find it on the shelf.

Downtown was not my only favorite book. I loved the entire series about Betsy-Tacy. I had discovered them by chance on the library shelves and at once had fallen in love with Betsy (who was just like me!) and her friends. Betsy's friends were not like mine.

My friends squabbled constantly. Three was not a good number for best friends in the Bronx where I grew up. In fact, very little in the Bronx resembled the idyllic community of Deep Valley. Betsy's parents never lectured her about the dangers of speaking to strangers. In fact, some of Betsy's best adventures took place when she spoke to strangers. She even went inside their homes. But more than the refreshing vacation from my own city tenement life, the books offered me a new best friend who was myself and yet not myself.

At twelve, I already knew that I wanted to be a writer - just like Betsy. At twelve, I entertained my friends with original stories that I wrote out and tried submitting to magazines - just like Betsy. I didn't have freckles and my teeth weren't parted in the middle, but I was chunkily built like Betsy and I think I had her perky smiling face. That forty years separated my childhood from hers seemed immaterial. We were just alike in every important way.

I read the Betsy-Tacy books in order as they were published - with one important omission. The New York Public Library did not own *Heaven to Betsy* when I was growing up. This I later learned (when I was a children's librarian, working for NYPL myself) was because the matter of Betsy and her sister Julia changing religions was considered too controversial at that time.

I was in college and employed part time in the public library when the last book in the series was published. I happened to be browsing in the children's room when I discovered *Betsy's Wedding*. I stopped, stunned at the news. If my own sister had gotten married without telling me, I could not have been more surprised (or delighted). I grabbed the book from the library shelf and checked it out. If the children's librarian was amazed to see someone of my advanced age borrowing the book, she didn't say. Probably it happened all the time, anyhow.

The bond I felt with Betsy and Maud Hart Lovelace, her creator and alter ego, was strengthened by personal contacts over the years. In 1949, shortly after my eleventh birthday, I wrote a letter to Mrs. Lovelace. Writing letters to authors was not a classroom assignment in those days, and I don't remember how I figured out that if I wrote to her in care of her publisher, she might in time receive my letter. In any event, she did, and her response, written in her own hand, made me feel, more than ever, that we were personal friends. In time, I received several other handwritten notes from her.

Our bond was reinforced one evening when I was glancing at the newspaper. The *New York World Telegram*, a paper for which my father wrote, had recently merged with the *New York Sun.* I noticed an article written by Delos Lovelace. I recognized the name immediately because in the front of all the Betsy-Tacy books was a listing of other books by the author, including a couple which she co-authored with Delos Lovelace, her husband. I ran to my father to show him this wonderful new link with my favorite author.

He reported to his new colleague about my recognition of his name. And that year, at holiday time, I received a gift-wrapped and autographed copy of Maud Hart Lovelace's newest book, *Emily of Deep Valley.* I never found out if Mrs. Lovelace sent the book to me via my father or if my father purchased the book and asked her husband to have it signed for me. I think I preferred not knowing so I could pretend to myself that it was the former.

And now, after all those years of reading and rereading the stories of life in Deep Valley, here is a guide to help me see what really happened and how Maud Hart Lovelace shaped and borrowed from her real life. Over the years I have had occasion to study a Biblical concordance and use variorum editions of Shakespeare. I've read the *Annotated Alice* (in Wonderland) and the *Annotated Mother Goose.* Never did I dream that I would have access to a similarly detailed and fascinating explanation of the characters and situations in the Betsy-Tacy books. At one point, just as I was especially delighting in a particular comparison of details and contradictions, author Sharla Scannell Whalen wrote, "If I have to explain why it is amusing to analyze such trivia, you shouldn't be reading this book." I laughed aloud and knew that she had written this book just for me. Well, not just me. There are hundreds, no thousands, of other people out there who also read and loved the Betsy-Tacy stories.

Growing up in an era when creativity was not praised or fostered in schools, I know that Betsy/Maud was the mentor I needed to encourage me to continue writing. There must be hundreds of writers who can point to the Betsy-Tacy books as a source of inspiration. But it is not just writers who owe a debt to Maud Hart Lovelace. What about the librarians and teachers who grew up reading these books and went on to become as important to the young people they worked with as the librarian and teachers who encouraged Betsy and her friends. And what about the parents who aimed to make their homes as open, warm, and hospitable as that of the Rays. These books gave us goals, consciously and unconsciously.

I was among the first generation of readers, my daughter was part of the second, and now a third generation is starting out on this series. It is for all of us that Sharla has done this amazing job of research and reconstruction. She has found so many wonderful pieces of information and irony. What happened to the real Betsy, the real Tacy, the real Tib, the real Joe, etc. Finally, we can learn all the answers.

Let me mention one last thing: as an adult, I bought myself a copy of *Betsy and Tacy Go Downtown.*

"Began Betsy and Tacy.
Let's see what comes of it."

Maud Hart Lovelace diary notation
November 22, 1938

CHAPTER ONE
On the Early Years

The fictional world of Betsy-Tacy begins just before Betsy Ray's fifth birthday, for this is the setting on the first page of *Betsy-Tacy*. However, the history reported by Betsy's parents throughout the series takes us back another generation.

Through Ray family legends and anecdotes, Maud Hart Lovelace structures a historical framework which becomes as familiar to her readers as it was important in her own life. The framework of family history provides authenticity - so that the books ring as true as they in fact are. And our strong feelings about the characters are in part the result of the friendly intimacy of knowing about their parents and grandparents.

The avid Betsy-Tacy reader well remembers Mr. Ray's stories of his mother and the ten children (as well as the church) she raised on the Iowa prairie. Like Betsy and her sisters on the anniversary trips to Murmuring Lake, we know it all by heart, and we love hearing it over again.

Maud Hart Lovelace was the daughter of Thomas and Stella Hart, whom we know fictionally as Bob and Jule Ray. At age twenty, Tom Hart had come up to Mankato from Iowa. At first he drove a dray in town, then went on the road selling fiber ware, and later, nursery stock. He supplied seedling trees to homesteaders with tree claims all over western Minnesota and South Dakota. Decades later, he took pleasure in the sight of the fine groves which had grown from the seedlings he had supplied. After a few years, Tom went into the grocery business with A.H. Beebe at 510 S. Front.

Tom was rooming in Mankato with a tall, red-headed young man named Frank Palmer. It may have been through Frank that Tom met the lovely, red-headed Stella Palmer. Stella was living in Mankato at this time, rather than at the lake home of Chauncey Austin (her stepfather), since she was studying at the Normal School, preparing to be a teacher. Certainly Tom knew the Austins well by March of 1886, for when Chauncey's first grandchild was born, he was named Chauncey Hart Austin. Chauncey II was the child of Charles and Hattie Austin (Stella's stepbrother and his wife).

Tom and Stella signed each other's autograph albums. She wrote:

"*Friend Thomas,*
In contentment
Is true wisdom.
Truly your friend,
Stella M. Palmer."

He wrote:

"*Friend Stella,*
Friends may meet
And friends may part.
But distance cannot
Change the Hart."

He added in the lower corner, "*Pleasant memories of yesterday.*"[20]

An early resident of the area, Mrs. A.E. Larkin, knew Maud's mother when she was still Stella Palmer and teaching school in the country. When Stella was lonesome, she visited with Mrs. Larkin. Waxing lyrical, Larkin wrote of Stella: "*She was a beautiful girl at the age of seventeen when I first knew her. Tall, slender, active, she seemed to have no knowledge of her own attractions -- hair a bright auburn with dark shadows lurking above eyes that were dark and changeable, a smile that seemed born with her, and a charm that had nothing to hide.*"[21]

Stella went to see Mrs. Larkin after a weekend at home, during which she had quarreled with Tom. "*I know that we will never make it up. I know it, I know it. And I know that he will take some other girl out to the lake next Sunday. I know he will and if he does, it will kill me,*" Stella told Mrs. Larkin.

"*Oh no,*" Mrs. Larkin replied, "*it will not kill you, but I'll tell you what I will do. I'll take the horses and buggy and we will drive over to the lake next Saturday and you will talk it all out with him.*" "*Oh,*" said Stella, "*you are so good to do that.*"[22]

Stella and Mrs. Larkin drove the fifteen miles to Madison Lake, where Stella's mother and stepfather made their home at Austin Park (the fictional Pleasant Park). Stella set out in her boat. (Mrs. Ray's sailboat, "The Queen of the Lake," is mentioned on page 12 of *Betsy Was a Junior*.) "*Sure enough,*" Mrs. Larkin said, "*she found Tom out on the lake with another girl.*"[23] Stella no doubt returned to

Iowa State Historical Society

Arosamond Hart

"She was small and dark - she was Welsh, you know - and she had big eyes like Margaret's." (HTB p. 126)

Coll. of Mary Garbutt

James A. Hart

Betsy's paternal grandfather sent a silver dollar for her Christmas stocking. James Hart did the same.

MHL Archive

Tom Hart

Tom was attending the Breckenridge Institute when this photo was taken. He was about seventeen.

1895 Atlas

Mr. and Mrs. Chauncey Austin

Albertine Austin was Maud Hart Lovelace's maternal grandmother. Chauncey is mentioned fictionally as the peppery Grandpa Newton. He inspired a similar character in *The Black Angels.*

1895 Atlas

Austin's Shoe Store
Mankato

The girl with the muff, standing at the right side of this photo, may well be a young Stella Palmer (mother of Maud Hart Lovelace). The store was located at 107 S. Front Street.

the country in high dudgeon, but Tom followed a week later. He explained that he hadn't invited the girl into the boat - she had just "stepped in."

All was obviously forgiven, for Stella Palmer married Tom Hart on October 15, 1887. The Rays' fictional anniversary is celebrated in October. (The exact day, the fifteenth, is first vouchsafed on page 56 of *Betsy in Spite of Herself.*) The year is inaccurately reported in *Heaven to Betsy* as 1886. In *Heaven to Betsy,* Julia sings a solo at a Sunday church service on the Rays' twentieth anniversary. (In fact, October 15 fell on a Monday in 1906.) The Harts' anniversary was October 15, 1887, though that of their fictional counterparts, the Rays, may have been October 15, 1886!

Both fictional and real couples were married at the Austin home. Tom and Stella were married at noon on Saturday, the fifteenth, by the Reverend Henry Bowder, who had himself been married the year before to Flora Hart, Tom's sister.[24]

Maud wrote about her parents' wedding in a letter to a cousin. "*In Heaven to Betsy and also in later books, I describe our family custom of going out to Mother's old home on October 15th, Mother and Dad's wedding anniversary. I give a true picture of Grandpa Austin's beautiful place although I call Madison Lake, Murmuring Lake in the books. They used to show us children the very tree under which he had proposed; more accurately, two trees, the roots of which had grown together. He was camping with another young man on the lane which led along the lake to the wooded part of Grandpa Austin's land. The story was that he came to the Austins' door to borrow a cup of salt and then he and Mother went walking. They had been 'keeping company' for some years. And Mother would point out the second story window where she sat on her wedding day 'wearing a tea gown,' looking down the driveway and waiting for Tom's horse and buggy, a rented livery rig, to drive through the big, white gate. I don't doubt, Marjorie, that your parents attended that wedding.*"[25] Marjorie's parents definitely attended Tom and Stella's wedding, for Marjorie's mother, Hattie Austin, signed their marriage certificate, along with Zula Hart, Tom's sister.

Before it was described in *Heaven to Betsy*, Austin Park appeared in another Lovelace setting, "Cindy and the Family Treasures," a short story published in *Jack and Jill* magazine. "*A double row of evergreens led from the house to the arched gate.... The lawn, enclosed by its white picket fence, was like a little world.*"[26] The doll in that story was also "real." In 1899, Grandma Austin gave Maud a doll which had been Stella's. Maud was running down Center Street to show the fragile doll to a friend when she fell. Unfortunately, the doll could not be mended.

As portrayed in the Betsy-Tacy books, the Hart family was Baptist (until Maud and Kathleen became Episcopalians). "*As a matter of fact, Dad was a Methodist when he and mother were married, and she was a member of the Christian Church. I suppose they became Baptists as a compromise.*"[27]

At the time of the Harts' marriage, Tom was still in the grocery business in Mankato (though he'd moved the store from 510 to 521 S. Front). The next year, 1888, he joined the business of his father-in-law at Austin and Son, retail shoes, as traveling salesman. In 1892, Tom established his own shoe store at 306 S. Front.

On September 6, 1889, the Harts' first child, Kathleen A. Hart, was born at 515 S. Fourth Street. The middle initial "A" was for "Albertine" (Stella's mother), but the Harts' first daughter always went by "Kathleen Palmer Hart" before her marriage and "Kathleen Hart Foster" after - so the name "Albertine" was never used legally.

Two years later, Tom moved his family to 214 Center, where Maud was born on April 25 (sic), 1892. Tom's brother, Jim Hart, was living with them in this tiny house. Despite the cramped quarters, they must have been glad for his presence during Stella's confinement, since he would have provided help with Kathleen, who was then only two and a half years old. Stella's mother may not have come in from Madison Lake at the time Maud was born, since she had two young daughters of her own at home (Stella's half sisters).

Although every legal record reads "April 25," Maud Hart was actually born on the 26th. In the months during which Maud's birth was awaited, her Uncle Jim Hart fell in love with a young Center Street widow named Maud Fowler Maloney. They became engaged in April 1892, and Stella said that if her new baby were a girl and born on Maud Fowler Maloney's birthday, April 25, the baby should be named Maud. Stella went into labor on the 25th, and when the baby didn't come before midnight, she fudged.

Coll. of Mary Garbutt

Tom and Stella Hart

Tom and Stella are shown (seated) with Tom's sister, Emma, and brother, Jim.

MHL Archive

Birthplace of Maud Hart Lovelace

This tiny house stands at 214 Center Street in Mankato. Maud wrote, *"Betsy's first home, the Hill Street house in the books, is 333 Center Street. I was born actually two blocks away, also on Center Street."* (L.D. 7-23-58)

Mankato - Its First Fifty Years

John Wesley Andrews

In *The Black Angels,* Joe, the unmusical Angel, wished to become a doctor. John, an unmusical Andrews, became a doctor and brought many Mankatoans, including Maud Hart, into the world

Coll. of Minnesota Valley Regional Library

Center Street Neighbors in the Summer of 1892

The child is two-year-old Kathleen Hart. Stella Hart is standing behind her (third from left). Two of Tom Hart's sisters are pictured. Rhoda Hart is the fourth adult from the left. Minnie Hart is the second from the right. And Maud Fowler Hart (for whom Maud Hart was named) is third from right.

Maud didn't learn the true date until she was fifty years old. She had asked Stella about the hour of her birth, and Stella looked embarrassed as she answered, "*Well, it was pretty near midnight.*" After a moment she added, "*In fact, it was a little after. But only a teeny bit.*" Maud asked, "*You mean the 25th was just coming in?*" "*No,*" Stella answered, "*It was just over.*" Shocked, Maud wailed, "*Just over! You mean I was born on the 26th?*" Stella said, "*Well, I suppose so. It was after midnight, a half hour or so. But we all liked Aunt Maud so well ...*" After fifty years, it would be impossible to go back through the records and set her birthday straight. "*Why don't we put on the coffee pot,*" Stella suggested.[28]

When Maud was six months old, the family moved to a larger house at 333 Center, which became the fictional 333 Hill. Tom had purchased the property at 333 on April 19, 1892 (just the week before Maud's birth). It must have been the end of the summer before construction (or renovation) of the house was completed, since the Harts didn't move in until October 1892.

Tom's sister Minnie was often at the Hart home before her marriage. "*She used to recite and Kathleen, aged three, or so, used to stand behind her and imitate her gestures. Mother often told me how Aunt Minnie used to put Kathleen on the kitchen table and teach her to 'strike attitudes.' She would represent joy, sorrow, love or any other emotion upon request.*"[29]

Early in 1897, the Singer Sewing Machine Company at 514 S. Front hired a new manager named Patrick Kenney. The Kenneys (the fictional Kellys) packed up their large brood of children and moved from 16th Avenue South in Minneapolis to Center Street in Mankato. This brings us to the first page of *Betsy-Tacy*.

Birthplace of Frances Kenney (Tacy)

Frances (nicknamed Bick) Kenney was born at 2107 Milwaukee Avenue in Minneapolis on July 13, 1891.

First Mankato Home of the Kenney Family
309 Center Street

Patrick Kenney moved his family to this house in April 1897. In the autumn of the next year, the Kenneys moved one block up the Center Street hill, to a house directly across the street from the Hart home.

[20] Lovelace, *Living with Writing* (unpublished memoir), p. 13.

[21] Larkin (unpublished memoir).

[22] Ibid.

[23] Ibid.

[24] *Mankato Free Press*, 10-21-1887.

[25] MHL to M. Freeman, 5-19-64.

[26] *Jack and Jill*, August 1946, pp. 22-23.

[27] MHL to M. Freeman, 5-19-64.

[28] LWW, p. 12.

[29] MHL to R. Lee, 4-21-64.

CHAPTER TWO
On *Betsy-Tacy*
March 1897 to August 1898

The very first line of this first book in the series presents a telling reference point. "It was difficult, later, to think of a time when Betsy and Tacy had not been friends." This reference point, "later," gives us the immediate sense that autobiography is afoot.

All authors write with omniscience, but this one does so in a remarkably conspicuous way. Because Maud begins by telling us how we, and Hill Street, will feel "later," we experience her books on two levels: as very much part of Betsy's "now" (in this chapter, 1897) and also with the nostalgic sensation of looking back over someone's life. This effect is the result of the author's fidelity to her own history; for Maud's omniscience is not rooted in an invented reality but in truth. This is more than your average omniscience. This is testimony.

Betsy-Tacy finds us in a world which comprises only Hill Street. (This essentially remains true through *Betsy-Tacy and Tib*.) It is late March. Maud does not identify a calendar year until *Over the Big Hill*, but we know by working backward from the date given there (or forward from the year we know Maud Hart was born) that the spring Betsy first met Tacy was 1897.

Patrick Kenney worked for the Singer Sewing Machine Company in Minneapolis for almost ten years, starting out as a traveling salesman and ending up as city manager. Singer then sent him to run the Mankato store, "the office where Tacy's father sold sewing machines."[30]

Maud Hart and the Kenneys' fifth daughter, Frances Vivien, became friends at Maud's fifth birthday party, just days after the Kenneys arrived on Center Street. Maud wrote to Bick's granddaughter, "*Tacy certainly is your red-headed grandmother and has been my dearest friend ever since my fifth birthday party - the one I tell about in the first Betsy-Tacy book.*"[31]

Though the beginning of the girls' friendship coincides perfectly with the fictional account, the Kenneys didn't yet live across the street from the Harts, as the Kellys lived across from the Rays. The Kenneys had first lived at 309 Center, six houses down from the Harts, on the same side of the street. Patrick Kenney purchased 332 Center (directly across from the Harts) in October 1898. A floor plan can be found in Chapter 3 herein.

When the Kenney family moved to Center Street, it consisted of eight children, rather than the fictional eleven. In April 1897, Rose Kenney would have been eight months pregnant with child number nine, Ruth Kenney, who was Baby Bee in the books.

Betsy spends the day the Kellys move in with her nose plastered to the dining-room window, watching for a little girl her own size. Just as a wintry March darkness is falling, Tacy comes out the Kelly front door and runs up the hill to the bench. Donning her coat, mittens, overshoes, and pussy hood, Betsy pursues Tacy up the hill. Shy Tacy flees from Betsy, who calls, "What's your name?" Before disappearing into her storm shed, Tacy shouts her name at Betsy, but "It was such an odd one, Betsy didn't understand."[32] Young Maud might well have misunderstood if her future friend had shouted the name "Bick," by which Frances was known both as a child and as an adult. Her family and friends called her "Bickie." An explanation of how the mystifying nickname was derived is furnished by Bick's niece: "*Frances Kenney Kirch had very red hair as a child and was called 'Brick.' Not being old enough to pronounce it properly, she called herself 'Bick.'*"[33] Bick's brother John was mysteriously nicknamed "Bam." Younger brother Charles (Paul in the books) was called "Chick." Bick's sister Theresa Catherine (Katie in the books) was known as "Tess."

The source of the fictional name "Tacy" was unrelated to the Kenney family. "*I found the name 'Tacy' in a colonial newspaper in the Philadelphia Library when I was doing research for* <u>The Charming Sally</u> *in 1930. I wrote it down but it wasn't used in that book, so I carried it on (as I always carry on precious unused bits from one book to the next) to the notes for the next book. It didn't get into that book either and so the name 'Tacy' was carried on from novel to novel until I sat down to write the story of my childhood. It seemed the perfect storybook name.*"[34]

Bick's hair was, of course, really red. Tacy's new dress was navy, "because she had red hair."[35] She gets a navy Easter hat for the same reason.[36] And even in *Betsy's Wedding*, Tacy's hair must be considered when Betsy and Tacy discuss bridesmaids' dresses for Tib's wedding. They can't be pink "on account of"[37] Tacy's red hair! A character in Maud's novel *Gentlemen from England* also has red hair, and "*She should not wear pink, she knew.*"[38]

For her fifth birthday party, Betsy wears her first silk dress. "It was checked tan and pink, with lace around the neck and sleeves."[39] The real dress was just as described by Maud and drawn by Lenski. Maud said, "*Mother had made it especially for my birthday, checked silk in tan, rose, and cream. After the birthday party, I wore it every Sunday and did not doubt that the Baptist Sunday School was stunned by my beauty.*"[40] Brown or tan with pink must have been a favorite color combination, since the accordion-pleated dress Stella made Maud several years later was brown silk, piped with pink. (It was Maud who tore her accordion-pleated skirt - an incident she gave to the character Tib in *Over the Big Hill.*) Maud's accordion pleats make an appearance in *Winona's Pony Cart,* in which Betsy wears the dress to Winona's birthday party.[41] Stella did a good deal of sewing for her daughters. "*Once she turned a pair of my father's trousers into a school dress for me, a grey striped wool with a tucked red silk yoke. I wore it with red hair ribbons and considerable satisfaction until word of its origin leaked out in school.*"[42]

Tacy brought Betsy a little glass pitcher with a gold-painted rim. Though the gold-painted rim has worn away, this same pitcher (which really was Bick's gift on Maud's fifth birthday) can be seen in the Maud Hart Lovelace wing of the Minnesota Valley Regional Library in Mankato.

We meet the little boy named Tom at Betsy's birthday party. His real name was Tom Fox. He could not have been seated behind the girls on their first day of school, since he was a year older. (Tom graduated from high school in the class of 1909.) Maud wrote of him, "*He was a friend from my earliest days when we lived on Center Street. He really did say 'Let'th 'thppeak pietheth,' and spoke one, too, at my fifth birthday party. My mother never forgot it because it sounded so cute.*"[43]

To establish consistency in the Deep Valley world, Maud employs, among other things, careful repetition. Within the first two pages of many books in the series, she uses the same phrase to describe her beloved Hill Street: "It ran straight up into a green hill and stopped." (Compare *Betsy-Tacy* page 2, *Betsy-Tacy and Tib* page 2, and *Over the Big Hill* page 2.) By *Downtown*, the focus is shifting, as its title suggests, and the old Hill Street paradigms are no longer required.

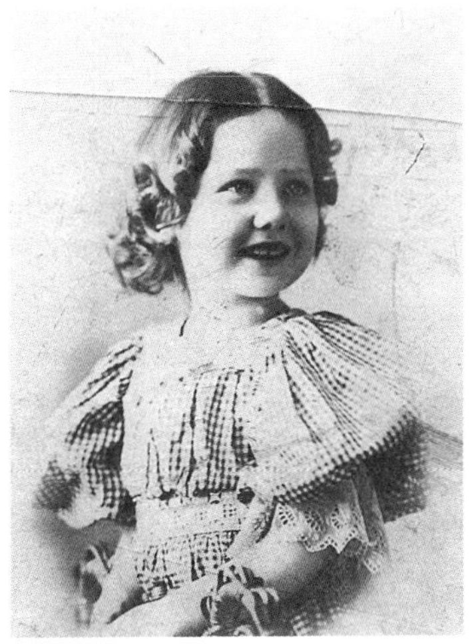

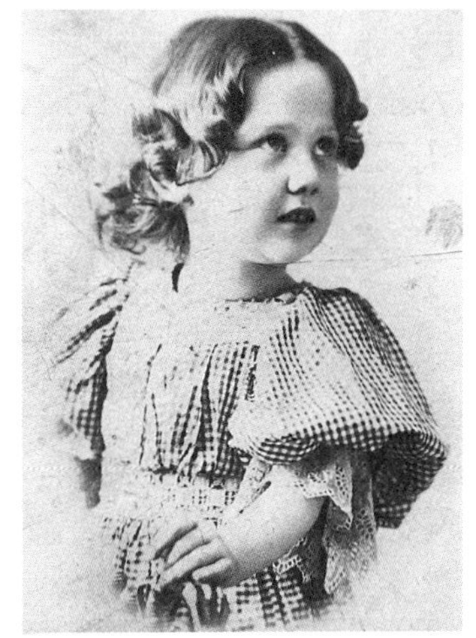

Coll. of Susan Ryder

Maud Hart, Aged Five Years

Maud's straight hair was curled for these photos - which may have taken some doing. Betsy's hair didn't take kindly to curls. This lament is repeated through the series, as first rags, then kid rollers, and finally Magic Wavers arrive!

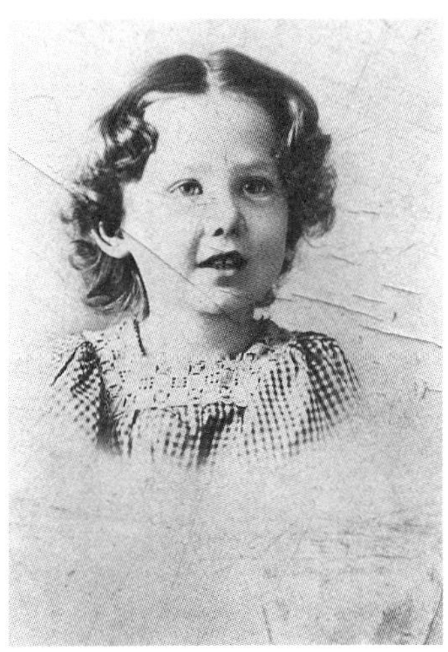

Coll. of Susan Ryder

More Maud

At least two sets of photo trios were done on the day these were taken. The other set is at the Minnesota Valley Regional Library in Mankato.

HarperCollins

Betsy Ray, Aged Five Years

Betsy is pictured in her tan-and-pink checked dress. The dress described in *Betsy-Tacy* was one Maud's mother had sewn on Center Street.

333 Center Street

On her return to Mankato in 1961, Maud commented: *"I could hardly believe that my father had planted those giant maples in front of 333 Center, but I've often heard him say he did."* (A.W. 10-23-61)

HarperCollins

333 Hill Street

In her illustration, Lois Lenski drew a "curlicue" under the front gable of Betsy's house. Maud's house really once had one. Stella asked Tom to put it up, as they were the latest thing.

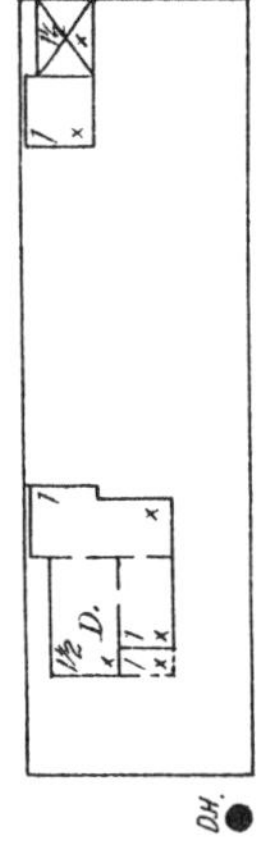

BECHS

333 Center

A 1908 insurance map reveals the barn and carriage shed at the rear of 333.

The Little Glass Pitcher

Bick Kenney gave Maud Hart this pitcher on April 25, 1892, at Maud's fifth birthday party. It is now at the public library in Mankato.

The claim that "Hill Street was rightfully named"[44] must have been written with tongue in cheek - since Maud herself gave it this name! "Hill" is certainly a more descriptive name than "Center." ("Deep Valley" might have been a better name than "Mankato," too.) Though she has rechristened the street, Maud retains the actual number of the house. The house number (333) is not provided until *Heaven to Betsy.*

The Hart and Kenney houses were the last on the block but not the last on the street. However, since access to the hills was from behind Betsy's house, the girls didn't pass other houses on their way to adventures on the Big Hill (until they reached the top and the Ekstroms'). The path up the Big Hill was a street called "Lewis." The Hart and Kenney houses stood on the northeast and northwest corners of Lewis and Center. Beyond Lewis (up the Hill Street Hill), there were several more houses on Center.

"You will be surprised to see that there are two or three houses beyond although in the story I said that Betsy's house and Tacy's, ended the street. There were always houses there, but since they had no children, they did not exist for us, so I left them out of the story. The Center Street hill - the hill which is an extension of Hill (Center) Street - used to be a grassy slope, incredibly lovely, but now it has a stone embankment. Just above that embankment and looking down on Center Street the Bench used to stand.... When I'm back some day, I'd like to build another one there."[45]

The bench had been placed by "some long-gone person."[46] This implies that the bench was already old by 1897. Gordon Kennedy, who was born at 323 Center Street in 1903, did not remember a bench at the top of Center. So we can be fairly sure that the bench was gone by 1906 or 1907. By this time, the girls were in high school and the bench had become less important.

"What I should like best of all is to have the old bench re-established at the top of Center Street. Cooks lived beyond us, and Sheldons and Fowles beyond Kenneys. The old bench (which I believe Mr. Fowles put up) used to stand just beyond the Fowles', between Fowles' and Cooks' lots. Do you remember it? I'm afraid there's a retaining wall there now."[47] (A memorial bench was placed at the top of Center Street in 1989.)

The two little girls really loved the bench, on which (Maud said), *"Bickie and I used to eat our suppers sometimes."*[48] One of the foods often on Maud's plate must have been fried potatoes.

The Big Hill
Cow Pasture
Road up the
Back Yard Maple
Betsy's Home
Hill Street
Hill Street Hill

This Lois Lenski map of the Hill Street neighborhood appeared on the endpapers of the first editions of the first four Betsy-Tacy books.

"A delicious smell of fried potatoes floated from the kitchen."[49] Stella was no doubt known for her fried potatoes! She's frying them again on page 59 of *Over the Big Hill.* In *Downtown*, Uncle Keith says that she fries potatoes extremely well. And "Sure enough, Mrs. Ray was frying potatoes."[50]

Mrs. Ray is also known for the violet scent she wears. In *Betsy-Tacy*, the handkerchief in Mrs. Ray's card case smells of violet perfume.[51] This is another thread woven through the fabric of the series. In *Betsy-Tacy and Tib*, Mrs. Ray is dressed up and "smelling of violet perfume."[52] Baby sister Margaret plans to buy Mrs. Ray violet perfume for Christmas in *Heaven to Betsy*.[53] In *Betsy in Spite of Herself*, Betsy wants to drench herself with perfume, always using the same kind, "so that whenever anybody smells that odor they will know it's me ... like Mama with violet perfume."[54] In *Betsy's Wedding*, "Mrs. Ray swept in, gleaming in satin, filling the air with Extreme Violet perfume."[55]

Mr. Ray, on the other hand, is known for his sense of humor. In *Betsy-Tacy*, we hear that "Betsy's father loved to joke."[56] It is the first thing we really hear about him, and we hear it repeatedly throughout the series. In *Betsy-Tacy and Tib*: "Betsy's father loved to joke."[57] In *Over the Big Hill*: "He was a great one to joke."[58]

The bench was Betsy and Tacy's first private spot. The second "and the dearest for years"[59] was the piano box. A neighbor remembered the piano box in the Hart backyard. Ray Wilcox, who was born in 1894, grew up at 229 Center. He was the good buddy of Chick (Paul Kelly) Kenney. Ray remembered the old wooden piano box behind 333 Center. He said it was finally carted away when it began to fall apart.[60]

In their purchase of a piano, the Harts were already manifesting their art-and-culture tendencies. They were later to make such unconventional choices as sending their daughters to hear opera in the Twin Cities and to Europe for study. Their home at 333 Center was small, and the Harts were a young family. Yet they bought a piano, because Kathleen had talent to be developed. This was a higher priority for them than furniture or the many other things they must have needed.

The piano box stood on the slope which was Betsy's back yard - the foot of the Big Hill. The description of the two hills (Big Hill

MHL Archive

332 Center Street - "Tacy's House"

A snowy Lewis Street runs down the left side of the photo. This was the street down which the neighborhood children rode bobsleds.

Coll. of Jane Kirch

Site of the Bench

Bick Kenney Kirch points to the spot at the top of Center Street where the bench which she and Maud loved once stood. A memorial bench was placed at the top of Center in 1989.

HarperCollins

Stories on the Bench

Lois Lenski's illustration captures a classic Betsy-Tacy moment. Maud told many stories on the bench, with Bick adding flourishes, just as Tacy did.

MHL Archive

Kathleen Hart

Kathleen was just the age of Julia in *Betsy-Tacy* when this photo was taken after school one day on Center Street.

HarperCollins

Julia Ray

In *Over the Big Hill,* Julia is pictured in a dress and hat which resemble those of Kathleen in the photo above.

MHL Archive

Stella Palmer Hart

This photograph was probably taken about 1888. Prior to her marriage, Stella was a school teacher in Minnesota and Iowa.

and Hill Street Hill) is a bit baffling, but it is consistent. Betsy and Tacy first climb the Big Hill at the age of five. Lewis Street was a dusty road up the Big Hill in those days. Apparently the city gave up on improving Lewis east of Center, since it was too steep. Today the Big Hill is corseted with a stone embankment, and thorny brush makes passage through the private property impossible (or at least unpleasant).

Beyond Betsy's garden, orchard, and barn, the girls come to "a ridge where wild roses bloomed in June."[61] These roses are mentioned again in the next two titles, as well as in the high school books. In *Betsy-Tacy and Tib*, "They came to a ridge where wild roses were in bloom."[62] Back to the ridge and roses in *Over the Big Hill*, "Flat, pink and golden-centered they clambered everywhere."[63] Gordon Kennedy remembered the roses and said they grew in exactly the location Maud described. He said that Maud's description of the road up the hill in *Betsy-Tacy* was also accurate: "On one side of the road, the hill was open. On the other it was fenced, with a wire fence which enclosed a cow pasture. A brindle cow was sleeping under a scrub oak tree."[64] Betsy wants to pretend they've gone so far up the hill that they "don't even know whose cow that is."[65] Tacy points out that it might be Mr. Williams' cow. (The same Mr. Williams whom they saw milking from their imaginary pink feather.) A Center Street neighbor, Mr. Edwards, pastured his cow on the hill. It seems likely that Maud remembered Mr. Edwards-with-a-cow, since her fictional cow-owning character also has a Christian-name surname. When Maud and Bick visited Mankato in 1940, just after the publication of *Betsy-Tacy*, they took a picnic lunch "*up to the Big Hill and ate under the thorn apple tree.*"[66]

In later years, Maud described some of the games she and Bick played. "*We used to color sand and put it in bottles and have sand stores and sell it. We cut our paper dolls out of the magazines. We dressed up in our mothers' long skirts. We went on picnics.*"[67] Betsy and Tacy too have a sand store, dress up, play with paper dolls, and go on picnics. Unless we find a reference in a letter or other memorabilia, however, we will not know such things as whether Betsy ever actually told a story about the girls floating on a feather. And yet, in a way, we know that she did. There are several layers of reality operating here. Maud (Betsy) invented that story at the age of forty-seven, when she wrote *Betsy-Tacy*. Whether she had also made it up at age five is perhaps immaterial. In any case, Maud had an impressive ability to stand in the shoes of a child, knowing what would capture her fancy. Children are entranced with this Feather Story as well as with the Milkman Story and the Easter Egg Tree Story later in the book.

When writing for children, it may be difficult to avoid sounding soppy, contrived, or patronizing. Maud avoids these pitfalls. She is able to enter into the world of a child naturally and directly. Her language is well chosen, with powerful simplicity, as in the phrase "the gray time called November,"[68] which effectively evokes the feeling of that month in words natural for a child to use.

Maud understood not only children's imagination, but children's logic. On the hill, Betsy and Tacy catch a hen. "And whenever we get hungry he can lay us an egg." The "he" is amusing - and as truly likely for a five-year-old child to come up with as the concept of a hen laying on demand! A child reader's hunger for resolution is satisfied when Betsy explains why the hen fails to produce the egg: "He isn't trained yet."[69]

As Maud said, "*The first four Betsy-Tacys are read aloud a good deal, and perhaps they help to draw parents and children together. Perhaps they help parents to remember the fresh exciting world in which children live. I do think I remember that better than most grown-ups.*"[70]

Parents find a great deal to chuckle over. For instance, when Betsy and Tacy see Tom on the first day of school, he is no longer lacking his front teeth. "Yes, I got them young," he says.[71]

The "First Day of School" chapter creates a few ripples in the parallel universes of Betsy's Deep Valley and Maud's Mankato. Pleasant Grove School (which Maud's mother had also attended) was on Pleasant Street (fictionally School Street). At age five, in 1897, Maud and Bick would have been starting kindergarten in the "Baby Room."[72] But Pleasant Grove had no kindergarten in 1897. Kindergartners went by horse-drawn bus to the Normal (Teacher Training) School (across the street from where Betsy's High Street house would be built). Pleasant Grove began to offer kindergarten in about 1901. So if Bick ran away on the first day of school, she would have had a long walk home.

BECHS

Pleasant Grove School

Maud Hart and her friends attended this school, which was built in 1871. It was "of red brick. A steep flight of steps led up to the door." (BTT 33) The school, which faced Pleasant Street, no longer stands.

HarperCollins

The Grade School

Betsy, Tacy, and Tib attended this school. Lois Lenski has again patterned her illustration after the actual building.

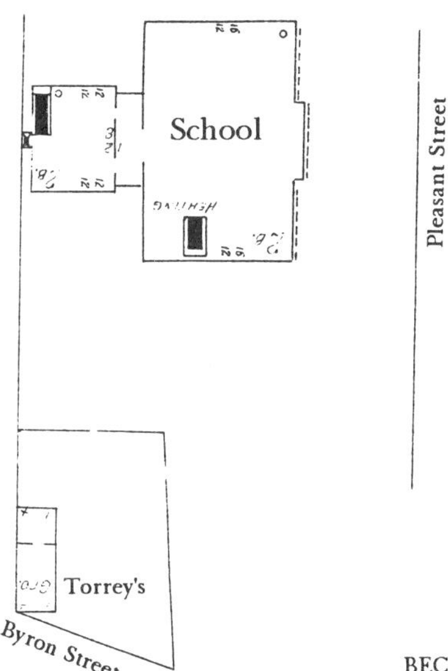

BECHS

School Zone

Torrey's candy store can been seen at the lower left of the map. The tiny building was later moved to the opposite side of Byron Street.

On the way to school, "They crossed the street and turned the corner and came to a little store."[73] This was Mrs. Chubbock's, from whom Betsy and Tacy each receive a chocolate man on page 38. The little grocer's was really called "Torrey's." Maud wrote, "*I remember Torry's* [sic] *Candy Store near the school with its marshmallow bananas and gum drops and all-day suckers and chocolate men with pennies inside.*"[74] She might have added to this list the "candy fried egg in a little tin pan ... one cent at Mrs. Chubbock's store"[75] which Julia gave to Betsy in *Over the Big Hill*. The store was sold to Frank Field shortly after Maud's days at Pleasant Grove. It originally stood at 414 Byron. The building has since been moved to 417 Byron, on the east side of the street.

Chubbock's also appeared in a Betsy story called "An Errand for Miss Canning," which was never included in a Betsy-Tacy book. "Betsy ran toward Mrs. Chubbock's ... to buy a chocolate man or a marshmallow banana or a handful of candy corn."[76]

One of only a handful of anachronisms in the series appears on page 3. We are told that Julia was eight years old (while Betsy is four). Kathleen Hart, Maud's older sister, would have been seven in April 1897. In later books, the age difference between the two is always referred to as two years.

We meet Katie Kelly on page 9. Like Julia, she was eight. Like Kathleen, Theresa Kenney would have been seven in the spring of 1897. She was always known as "Tess" or "Tessie." Maud probably chose the name "Katie" for the sake of Tess's real middle name, "Catherine." Katie "was the kind of person who never gave up."[77] This characterization is repeated throughout the series. It appears next in *Over the Big Hill*: "Square on her sturdy feet, her face scornful, she rattled without a mistake through the Gettysburg Address. She walked back to her seat and sat down hard. When she had to take bad medicine, Katie knew how to take it."[78] Her doggedness is a distinctive trait. Only Joe shows anything like it.

Tacy's brother, George Kelly (really George Kenney), is mentioned on page 48 and also on page 72, when he meets the girls in the vacant lot and convinces them that nine cents isn't enough to buy the chocolate-colored house. Later he wins Tacy a doll at the Street Fair, but after *Betsy-Tacy and Tib*, George is never again mentioned by name in the series.

Grown-up sister Mary is mentioned on page 76. This was probably the oldest sister, Rosemary, who was known as "Mame." She may also have gone by "Mary." The Kelly siblings are usually grouped together, anonymously, as on page 19 when "one or two of Tacy's brothers and sisters" are calling Tacy to come home. When she hasn't come home by page 20, "four or five" of them begin to call her. Later, in the high school books, an unnamed brother or two will appear to escort Tacy home from a party. Brother Paul is mentioned by name for the last time in *Heaven to Betsy*, after which he joins the miscellaneous throng.

Poor Mr. Kelly gets only one line in the entire series. "Thank you very much," he tells Mrs. Ray, "But Mrs. Kelly wants the children home."[79]

"Tacy's little sister Beatrice was sick. She was Bee, the baby, and she was very sick."[80] Ruth, the real Bee, was born May 26, 1897. At the time of Bee's death (Easter, April 10, 1898), Ruth was not quite one. Ruth did die as a young child but not until February 1901, when she was three years old. She was sick with the flu for several days and died of spinal meningitis. Maud wrote of her, *"She was the pet of all. Her voice was sweet and true and she knew whole songs like 'Just One Girl' which she sang for the Kenneys' delight. When she saw her father driving in at night, she would run to get out his slippers. But Mr. Kenney was away on a short trip when she fell ill and died. George, the oldest brother, was away too, in the Spanish-American war. He was a sweet-faced, dark-haired lad of eighteen, a great favorite with us children. The war lasted less than three months, but he was away for two years for he took ill with malaria. He was carried aboard the ship that brought him home. He reached Mankato in the early hours of a May morning. Joyfully intent on surprising the family, he walked home from the station. When he climbed the shady slope of Center Street, only the birds were awake, twittering in trees that were just leafing out, but the lilacs and snowballs were in bloom. As he walked up the hill, Gyp, the Kenney dog, barked at him, and when George spoke softly and told him to be quiet, he recognized him after two years and nearly turned himself inside out with joy. The baby had died in February but George knew nothing about it and after the family had come trooping from their beds to greet him, he missed her and started toward the downstairs bedroom asking, 'Where's the baby?' He sat on the couch all that morning and sobbed. ...The Betsy-Tacy sky is usually a cloudless blue, but of course we all know that rain must fall.*"[81]

In spite of the long Minnesota winter, there are numerous outdoor scenes in all the Betsy-Tacy books. Maud describes Betsy's surroundings, indoors or out, with care and accuracy. "The Ray house was small. But the sloping lawn was big, with maples and a butternut tree in front of the house, and behind it fruit trees and berry bushes and a garden, and Old Mag's barn, and the shed where the carriage was kept."[82]

The interior layout of the Ray cottage is somewhat confusing. We know that the dining room is at the front of the house because Betsy watches the Kellys move in from the dining room window. In *Over the Big Hill,* Mrs. Ray is sitting in the parlor (presumably the front parlor), which also looks down Hill Street.[83] In *Downtown*, it is clear that the back parlor looks out to Hill Street, too.[84] This back parlor window must have had a view down Hill from the side of the house.

Maud described the interior of 333 Center in this way: "*The front door went into the dining room and the side door into the parlor* [sic - she meant to say kitchen]. *The parlor had the piano, of course. The back parlor had a stove which warmed the whole house at first, a desk-book*[case] *combination, a cozy corner (when they were the fashion) and a very comfortable big couch.*"[85] This is the back parlor couch Betsy and Tacy climb while playing with paper dolls.

"*Kathleen, older sister, and I had the front bedroom,*" Maud recalled.[86] This corresponds to the description in *Over the Big Hill,* in which Betsy's bedroom window looks across to Tacy's house.

333 Center had no bathroom. "*There was a well-scrubbed privy in back of the house. There were decorated wash bowls, pitchers, and chamber pots in our bedrooms.*"[87] Baths were taken "*in the kitchen on Saturday night, one at a time.*"[88] Correspondingly, "Julia and Betsy had their baths in the tub set out before the kitchen fire."[89]

A fire in the stove "shone on the wild horses' heads which ran in a procession around the shining nickel trim. Up on the warming ledge the tea kettle was singing."[90] This same cozy hard coal heater had a previous existence in one of Maud's historical novels: "*From fall until spring a fire burned red behind the isinglass windows of its stove, and the horses' heads in the polished nickel trimming*

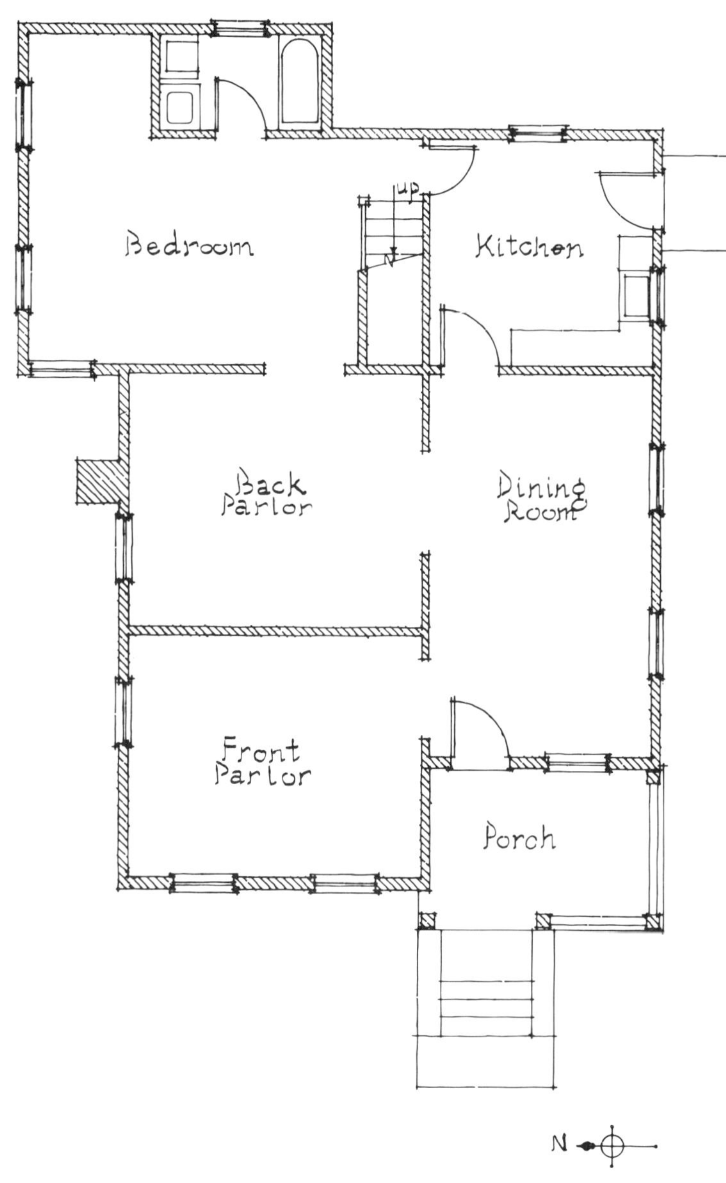

Plan by Philadelphia Architect Nancy Beckner Bastian

333 Center Street
First Floor

flung their wild manes in a warm glow."[91] The stove stood in the Halliday house in *Gentlemen from England* as well as in the Ray cottage!

"Green flowered carpet" makes its first appearance in *Betsy-Tacy*.[92] Throughout the Betsy-Tacy books, green is a favorite color for carpeting and wallcovering.

In the spring of 1898, Mr. Ray says, "What if our family should grow bigger? There's a bedroom for mother and me, and one for Julia and Betsy. But what about Robert Ray Junior, when he comes along?"[93] By May 1898, Stella Hart was seven months pregnant with Helen (Margaret Ray), and the Harts built a small addition on the back of the house to make more room. (In the illustration on page 8, Lois Lenski pictured the new addition poking out on the left side of the house - but it wasn't built until page 65!) The new bedroom was downstairs, in the corner between the back parlor and the kitchen. Maud wrote, "*When Daddy and mother knew another baby was coming, a bedroom was added - that had a door in front and back, the front one looked into the back parlor. It also looked into the kitchen and the stairs.*"[94]

In *Over the Big Hill*, "The rose bush under the dining-room window was covered with yellow roses which gave out a spicy smell."[95] Maud wrote, "*My father planted ... yellow rose bushes along the wall which passed the dining room windows and ended in the side kitchen door. There were lilacs on that wall too.*"[96]

The air was sweet from "the plumy purple lilacs by the side kitchen door."[97] Dooryard lilacs are an icon of spring. None of the action in *Betsy-Tacy and Tib* or *Downtown* takes place in the month of May, but in *Over the Big Hill*, "The lilacs had come into bloom by Betsy's kitchen door."[98] Even in *Betsy and Joe*, "Dooryards smelled entrancingly of lilacs."[99]

"That summer Julia and Betsy went for a visit to Uncle Edward's farm. They had a good time too."[100] Uncle Edward gets one other mention in the series - in *Over the Big Hill*, when Betsy remembers what fun she and Julia had on vacations at his farm. Uncle Edward couldn't have been Uncle Jim Hart (who now lived right around the corner in Mankato with his wife and children), since Uncle Jim didn't have a farm. (The only other uncle, Steve, was living with them at 333 Center as late as 1900. He didn't have a farm either!) Maud and Kathleen went to stay in the country with friends when Helen was born.

Betsy and Julia come home from the farm to find a big surprise. When Mr. Ray tells them about the baby, "he was smiling all over his face."[101] So he clearly wasn't disappointed that he didn't get his Robert Ray Junior! Helen Hart was born July 7, 1898, at 333 Center.

Betsy, feeling overwhelmed by the unexpected appearance of the new baby, retreats to the barn. "Tacy hadn't seen Betsy go into the barn. She just seemed to know that Betsy was in that barn, as Betsy had known that Tacy would come outdoors early the morning after Baby Bee's funeral."[102] This empathy the two had for each other was very real, and it lasted throughout their lifelong friendship. When Maud's husband died, Bick came out to spend two months with Maud in California.

Is it any wonder these children turned out so well, considering, as an example, the responses they get from their mothers (and Stella fewer than six weeks postpartum!) when they ask to climb the Big Hill all the way to the top? "All right," Betsy's mother says. "But you'd better take a picnic." "All right," Tacy's mother says. "What a good thing it is that I was just baking a cake!"[103] One Lovelace fan observed, "*From the age of five, when she was allowed to take her plate from the dinner table to go sit at the top of the hill with her friend Tacy, to the age of twenty when her parents sent her to Europe on her own, Betsy was encouraged to experience the good things of life on her own terms.*"[104]

Parents invariably respond positively in the Betsy-Tacy series. In *Betsy-Tacy and Tib*, when Tib's father tells the children they must dismantle the house they have built with firewood in the Muller basement, he suggests a game of the Three Little Pigs, and they huff and puff the house down happily. When the sisters quarrel in *Over the Big Hill*, Mr. Ray does not scold them for fighting and dismiss their disagreement as unimportant. He contrives the vote-gathering system to help them resolve the question of who will be Queen of Summer. The support the children receive in their endeavors is unfailing. Mrs. Ray uses the words "splendid" and "wonderful" to describe Betsy's poem in *Downtown*. "Mrs. Ray always thought that about her children's achievements."[105] As

Maud said, "*We girls were raised on praise and were as convinced as our parents that the Hart family was one in a million.*"[106]

A piece of loving portraiture appears at the end of *Betsy-Tacy*. "Betsy's mother was sitting on the porch, rocking the baby. She was laughing, and she looked very young and pretty, with her red hair (like Tacy's) flying around her face and the baby in her arms."[107] Betsy at age six would not have thought her mother "young." But Maud at forty-seven, writing this book, surely thought, "Mother was only thirty-two then," and called her "young."

Mrs. Muller comes to return Mrs. Ray's call, having found the calling cards which Betsy and Tacy left at the chocolate-colored house. Tib was all that Julia and Katie had promised (for they were home when Mrs. Muller called and had met Tib first). Tib was small and dainty with yellow curls and a lace dress. She could dance. All this was true of Marjorie Gerlach (pronounced "GRR-lock"). She was always called "Midge," being what Tacy's Irish father might have called "a slip of a girl."

Maud and Bick must have encountered Midge before the summer of 1898. Maud remarked, "*I have heard from my mother that I had known* (Midge) *since we were in our baby carriages, for our mothers knew each other.*"[108] Perhaps, though Maud and Bick knew of Midge earlier, they didn't become friends until the summer of 1898. The three-way friendship blossoms in *Betsy-Tacy and Tib*.

[30] *Betsy-Tacy and Tib,* p. 36.
[31] MHL to P. Kirch, 4-30-60.
[32] *Betsy-Tacy,* p. 6.
[33] Interview with M. Thuente, 2-19-91.
[34] MHL to L. Demp, 11-2-56.
[35] *Betsy-Tacy,* p. 31.
[36] Ibid., p. 58.
[37] *Betsy's Wedding,* p. 183.
[38] Lovelace, *Gentlemen from England* (New York: Macmillan Co., 1937), p. 138.
[39] *Betsy-Tacy,* p. 10.
[40] LWW, p. 2.
[41] *Winona's Pony Cart*, p. 75.
[42] LWW, p. 6.
[43] MHL to J. Ellen, 9-10-67.
[44] *Betsy-Tacy,* p. 2.
[45] MHL to L. Demp, 7-23-58.
[46] *Betsy-Tacy,* p. 4.
[47] MHL to T. Edwards, 4-12-50.
[48] MHL to A. Wiecking, 4-12-61.
[49] *Betsy-Tacy,* p. 6.
[50] *Downtown,* p. 174.
[51] *Betsy-Tacy,* p. 77.
[52] *Betsy-Tacy and Tib,* p. 55.
[53] *Heaven to Betsy,* p. 152.
[54] *Betsy in Spite of Herself,* p. 166.
[55] *Betsy's Wedding,* p. 57.
[56] *Betsy-Tacy,* p. 11.
[57] *Betsy-Tacy and Tib,* p. 46.
[58] *Over the Big Hill,* p. 14.
[59] *Betsy-Tacy,* p. 21.
[60] Interview with L. Erickson, 10-6-84.
[61] *Betsy-Tacy,* p. 23.
[62] *Betsy-Tacy and Tib,* p. 6.
[63] *Over the Big Hill,* p. 109.
[64] *Betsy-Tacy,* p. 24.
[65] Ibid., p. 24.
[66] *Mankato Free Press*, 8-26-65.
[67] Lovelace Interview, University of Michigan.
[68] *Betsy-Tacy,* p. 41.

[69] Ibid., p. 29.

[70] MHL to A. Brooks, 4-24-47.

[71] Ibid., p. 35.

[72] Ibid., p. 34.

[73] Ibid., p. 32.

[74] *Mankato Free Press*, 4-10-52.

[75] *Over the Big Hill,* p. 78.

[76] Lovelace, "An Errand for Miss Canning," *Woman's Day*, January 1944.

[77] *Betsy-Tacy,* p. 34.

[78] *Over the Big Hill,* p. 67.

[79] *Betsy-Tacy,* p. 58.

[80] Ibid., p. 57.

[81] LWW, p. 33-34.

[82] *Betsy-Tacy,* p. 10.

[83] *Over the Big Hill,* p. 80.

[84] *Downtown,* p. 109.

[85] MHL to B. Gardner, 7-14-75.

[86] Ibid.

[87] LWW, p. 18.

[88] MHL to B. Gardner, 7-14-75.

[89] *Betsy-Tacy,* p. 10.

[90] Ibid., p. 49.

[91] *Gentlemen from England,* p. 183.

[92] *Betsy-Tacy,* p. 49.

[93] Ibid., p. 65.

[94] MHL to B. Gardner, 7-14-75.

[95] *Over the Big Hill,* p. 107.

[96] MHL to B. Gardner, 7-14-75.

[97] *Betsy-Tacy,* p. 66.

[98] *Over the Big Hill,* p. 36.

[99] *Betsy and Joe,* p. 231.

[100] *Betsy-Tacy,* p. 91.

[101] Ibid., p. 92.

[102] Ibid., p. 95.

[103] Ibid., p. 100.

[104] Atwell, "A Heroine Flourishes," pp. 2-3.

[105] *Downtown*, p. 179.

[106] LWW, p. 7B.

[107] *Betsy-Tacy,* p. 102.

[108] LWW, n.p.

CHAPTER THREE
On *Betsy-Tacy and Tib*
June 1900 to August 1901

"Tib moved into [the Hill Street] neighborhood"[109] in 1898. In reality, the Gerlach family owned the property at 503 Byron by 1891, but they had been in Mankato for many years more. Tib's father, Henry Christian Gerlach, arrived in Mankato in 1883, after spending four years as an apprentice architect in his hometown of Milwaukee. Henry married Julia Lulsdorf in Mankato in 1885. She died the next year. Henry continued to reside in Mankato, but he certainly made periodic trips home to Milwaukee, for it was in Milwaukee that he married again, just after Christmas in 1889. Henry and his bride, Minnie Irasek (pronounced "EYE-ruh-sek"), returned to Mankato together. (For more details on Gerlach family history, see Chapter 7 herein on *Betsy in Spite of Herself*.)

Sadly, Henry and Minnie's first child, a boy, did not survive birth in the fall of 1890. Marjorie (Tib) came along March 6, 1892. She was born in an apartment at 113 N. Second. The block in which the building once stood (adjacent to the Veterans' Memorial Bridge) now contains a bank and a parking lot.

Tib's baby brother, Hobbie, appears on page 16. He was William Dewey Gerlach, born in Mankato on July 4, 1899. He was always called "Dewey."

Freddie, the middle brother, is first mentioned on page 45. "Like Tib he was good natured and easy to play with." Freddie was based on Henry Clay Gerlach, born December 29, 1893. Freddie was Paul Kelly's age. Henry was, in fact, only about eight months older than Chick Kenney, the real Paul.

The youngest Gerlach never appears as a Muller. Midge's baby sister, Dorothy Catherine, was born April 30, 1904. She would therefore not have entered the series until *Downtown*. By this time, the fictional Muller family seemed firmly established, and Maud was no doubt already receiving pressure from her publisher that there were "too many characters." Although Midge's sister never appears in the Betsy-Tacy books, her nickname will be familiar to readers: she was called "Dolly." Tib's Aunt Dolly is featured in *Betsy-Tacy and Tib*, *Betsy in Spite of Herself*, and *Betsy's Wedding*.

Betsy and Tacy are enthralled when they discover a photograph of Aunt Dolly: "This was certainly a most beautiful lady."[110] Betsy and Tacy imagine Aunt Dolly living in a "Mirror Palace." But Tib tells them, "My Aunt Dolly lives in a flat in Milwaukee."[111] Betsy will see Aunt Dolly in that Milwaukee flat in *Betsy in Spite of Herself*. (Midge's aunt wasn't the only target for the girls' imagination. They also made up glamorous stories about "Beadie," a young cousin of Bick's in St. Paul.)

Tib's house "sat like a big plump chocolate drop on the big square corner lot. There weren't many trees around it; just a green lawn with flower beds on either side of the white cement walk which led to the porch steps."[112] In *Betsy-Tacy* (circa 1898), Mrs. Ray calls it "that big new house."[113] The house was built some years before this, in about 1892. Henry Gerlach apparently designed it himself. There was no building on the lot in October 1891 when Henry bought the property. Presumably ground was broken the following spring, and perhaps the Gerlachs moved into the house late in the summer or in the fall, when Midge was about six months old.

Like Tib's house, 503 Byron is really a large corner house (now a duplex). The address is now given as 105 Bradley, and the door most frequently used faces Bradley (in Tib's day this would have been the side door). The oval decoration on the second story certainly inspired Lois Lenski in her artistic rendering, but the obvious feature which Lovelace fans look for and do not find is the tower. This house never had a tower. However, behind Midge's (there are now other structures in between) was a house with a most prominent and memorable tower. This is the Hickey house, which in Maud's time was painted barn red. According to the Mankato City Assessor's Office, the Hickey house was built in 1904. It was known as "the showplace of the neighborhood" and was not a house you could walk by without noticing. Maud, as a child, no doubt admired its tower and, as an adult, enhanced Tib's house by transferring the Hickey tower to 503 Byron. She so far succeeds that readers feel, when they view Midge's house, that there <u>ought</u> to have been a tower!

"To get to Tib's house from the place where Betsy and Tacy lived you went one block down and one block over. (The second block was through a vacant lot.)"[114] The vacant lot was directly behind Tib's. After the Hickey house was built on this lot, the girls would probably have kept to the sidewalks. On the other

1895 Atlas

Henry Gerlach

Tib's father was an architect. Henry Gerlach was a prominent Mankato architect. He worked on such projects as the high school, the Baptist church, and the State Normal School. Like Tib's father, Midge's father had a mustache.

Coll. of Bev Schindler

Minnie Gerlach

Mrs. Muller "was short and chunky and had yellow hair like Tib's and earrings in her ears." Perhaps the earrings in the photograph were really the gift of Mrs. Gerlach's father-in-law. (BTT p. 110)

Colored Glass

Colored glass can be found over many of the doors and windows in the former Gerlach home.

Coll. of SSW

503 Byron Street - "Tib's House"
Circa 1911

This photograph shows the house in a light-colored coat of paint. According to Maud, the Gerlach house was originally painted chocolate brown. It never had a tower!

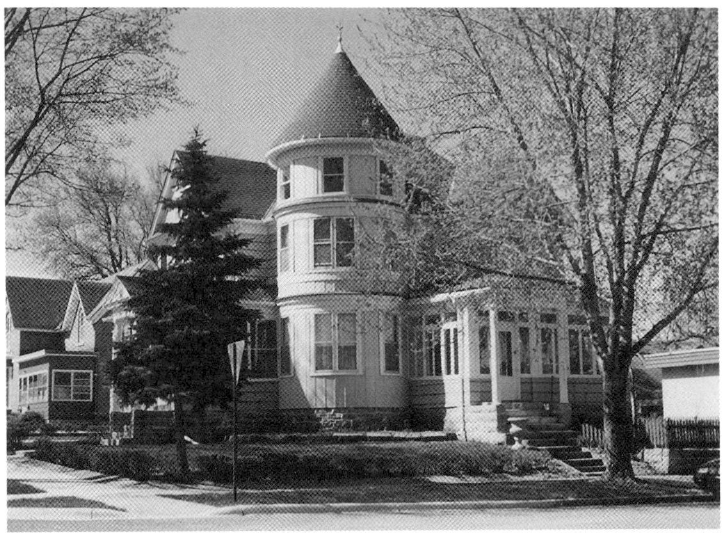

Tower House
Corner of Center and Bradley

This house, once the home of the Hickey family, was painted red when Maud lived on Center Street. Maud does not represent the Hickeys or their house in the Betsy-Tacy series, but it is likely that their tower inspired her to invent one for Tib's house.

503 Byron Street - "Tib's House"
Circa 1988

Like many homes, this one has had its porch enclosed. The interior has been changed more drastically than the exterior, as walls have been moved to create apartments.

HarperCollins

Tib's House

Lois Lenski has added an oval decoration to the second story - which can be seen on the photograph of Midge Gerlach's house (above). Puzzlingly, the decoration does not seem to appear on the photo from 1911. Perhaps this was simply because at that time it was not painted in a contrasting color.

hand, Bick and Maud's speediest route to Midge's house would have been by way of Bick's back fence and down the alley which split the block in two (a tiny street called "Grace").

Betsy and Tacy are impressed to find that Tib's house has "front stairs as well as back stairs!"[115] The house really has two staircases, but the interior has been changed rather drastically (having been converted at one time into a fourplex). No living person can remember the interior room arrangement as it was in the Gerlachs' time, so no floor plan is offered here.

The porch of 503 Byron is now enclosed, so the front door is not visible from the street. There is no colored glass "in" the front door, as per page 3 of *Betsy-Tacy and Tib.* But *Betsy-Tacy* makes it clear that the glass was <u>above</u> the front door: "'Tacy and I like that colored glass,' said Betsy. ...'That colored glass over your door.'"[116] And though there really <u>is</u> a pane of colored glass over the front door (like a transom), none of the ornamental stained glass in the house is red. Perhaps the current faded burned-orange color was bright red a hundred years ago.

Rather unfortunately, 503 Byron was painted brown for only a short period of its history. Emma Wiecking lived across the street from the Gerlach house from the time she was born in 1894 until her death in 1992. She remembered it only as white. However, in 1906, when the Gerlach family sold it, the house was yellow. And according to Maud, it was still painted brown about the time she and Bick started school (1897). "*Bick and I discovered* (Midge's) *chocolate colored house with colored glass over the front door which was to us a mansion of all glories.*"[117]

With her yellow curls and pretty clothes, Tib was as magical to the girls as her house was. Though she looked like a fairy, she was very down to earth. Tib's frankness causes affectionate "but we like her anyway" smiles to appear on Betsy and Tacy's faces in nearly every book in the series. The phrase "but Betsy and Tacy liked her just the same" appears for the first time on page 6 of *Betsy-Tacy and Tib.* This characteristic is not tempered as Tib grows up. In *Betsy's Wedding,* when Tib sees Betsy in bridal array, she says, "'Betsy! You look so pretty! Much prettier than you are!'[118] Betsy and Tacy twinkled at each other. 'Just like Tib!' their glances said."

At the beginning of *Betsy-Tacy and Tib*, the girls are eight. Maud, Bick, and Midge would, in fact, have been eight years old in June 1900. We learn that they will begin third grade in the fall.

Tacy's brother Paul is now a more substantial character than the baby he was in *Betsy-Tacy* - old enough to trot from house to house asking permission for the girls to climb the hill. Bick's younger brother Chick was born in Minneapolis in 1894. By the second book in the series, Chick/Paul would have been going on six. "He was playing with a cart" on page 16. "Paul was always playing with carts." He's at it again on page 91. It is no coincidence that Chick worked for the Ford Motor Company for forty-seven years.[119]

Tacy's house is described as rambling, but Maud provides little description of the interior. On page 121 of *Betsy-Tacy and Tib*, they go up to the "little room Tacy shared with Katie." There were only two small slant-roofed rooms upstairs at the Kenney house - no doubt one for the boys and one for the girls. The parents probably used the back parlor as their bedroom.

We get our best peek at the Kelly home in *Betsy and Joe*. Mrs. Kelly "sat with her mountain of darning in the window of the dining room. This big bow window was the heart of the house. Here Mr. Kelly sat in the evening with his newspaper, here on Sunday he played his violin. Here Betsy and Tacy used to cut out paper dolls, looking up at the overhanging hills."[120]

A few of the episodes from *Betsy-Tacy and Tib* can be documented. The three girls go begging, learn to fly, have a Flying Lady show, build a house in Tib's basement, make Everything Pudding, play in a Mirror Palace, cut their hair, find the Secret Lane, and meet Aunt Dolly.

Describing a Thanksgiving dinner reunion with Bick, Maud wrote, "*We talked about old days and laughed very hard about the time we made Everything Pudding and cut off one another's hair.*"[121] In 1961, "*One little boy asked 'Did you really make everything pudding,' a pudding with such ingredients as bacon grease, raisins and baking powder. 'Yes, we really did,'* Maud replied."[122] Modern readers may not know that "saleratus" (put in Everything Pudding on page 60) is baking soda. (Oddly, Tib had already added "soda" on page 59.)

"We may have to pretend we're beggars,"[123] Betsy tells her hungry friends. Maud used the same begging scene in a piece of

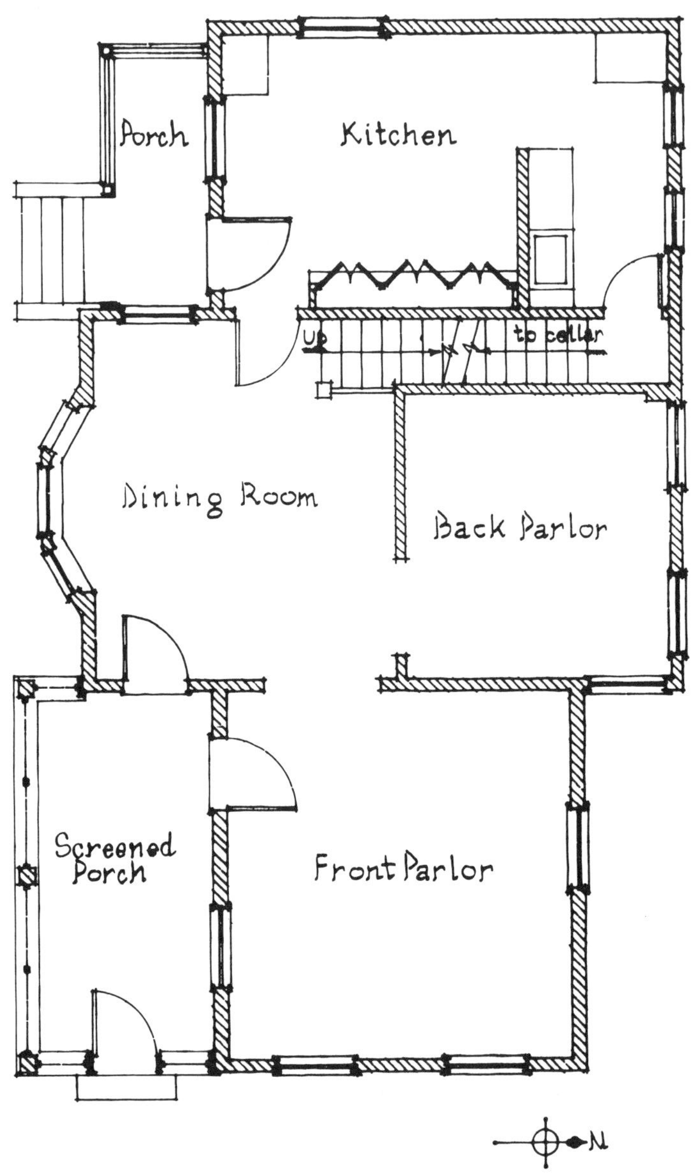

Plan by Architect Nancy Beckner Bastian

Floor Plan of 332 Center
First Floor

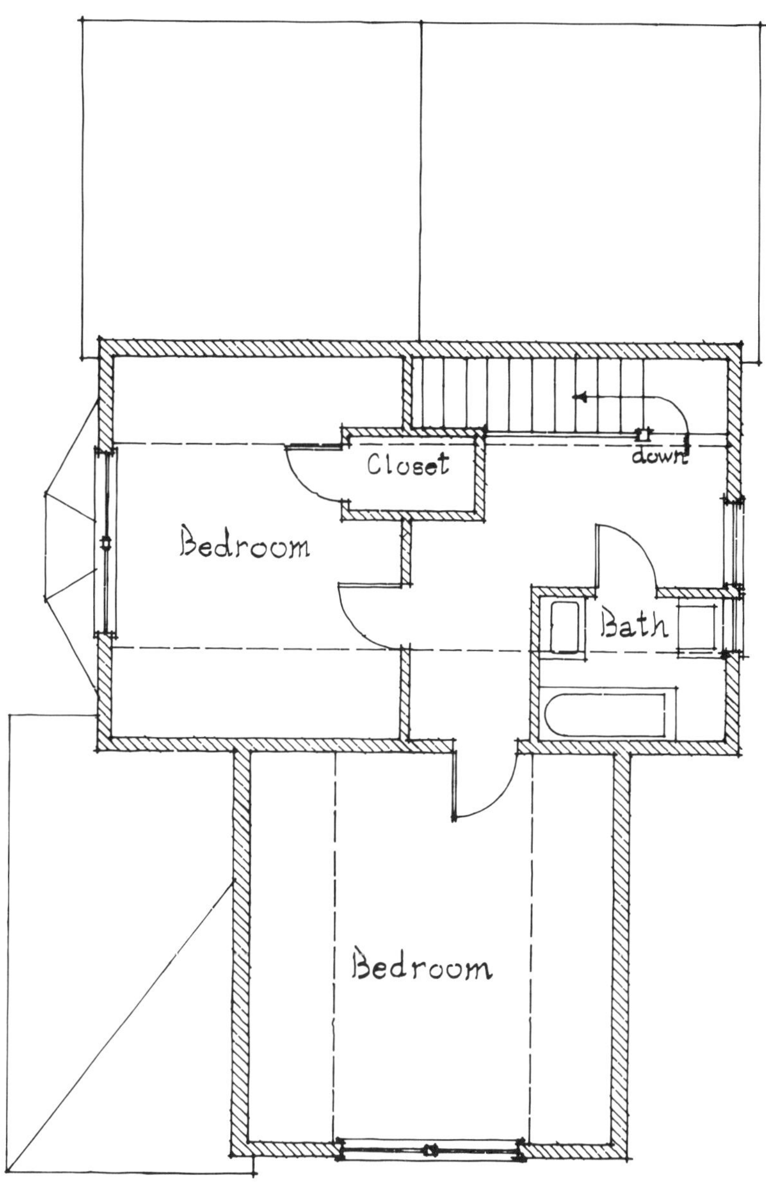

Plan by Architect Nancy Beckner Bastian

Floor Plan of 332 Center
Second Floor

much earlier fiction. It appears in "Carmelita, Widow," one of her best short stories: "*Carmelita, as a child, had once snarled her hair, splashed her face with mud, discarded shoes and stockings, and, to the delight of her playmates, begged from door to door, drawing pennies, bread, and even tears from kindly housewives.*"[124]

Mrs. Ekstrom is the kind lady who had just baked sugar cookies when the three hungry beggars arrived at her door. She lived in the only house on the top of the Big Hill. Mrs. Ekstrom was blond and small with a "thin tired face," we learn on page 10.

The Big Hill was known as "Prospect Heights" in Maud's time. Now called "Sumner Hills," it is covered with 50s-era houses. There was once only one house on the top of the hill. It was apparently built by architect Frank Thayer before the turn of the century. Thayer sold his house to John Asplund, who had arrived from Sweden only a few years earlier. Asplund lived in the house on the hill (527 Prospect Avenue) with his wife Anna (the fictional Mrs. Ekstrom) and their four children - three of whom were from Anna's previous marriage. Anna's first husband's young sister and brother, Annie and Erik Lindman, also lived with the Asplunds. In 1900, Annie (then seventeen) was a clerk in Mr. Kenney's sewing machine store.

Maud described the top of the Big Hill on page 6. It was "flat and there were oak trees scattered about. The white house stood in the middle.... Behind the Ekstroms' house was a ravine, with a spring of water in it, and a brook.... The grass was full of red and yellow columbine."

Another native of the Big Hill was Judge Edward Freeman. He and his friends played on the Big Hill four or five years before Maud was born. He said, "*Prospect Heights has shrunk. It isn't nearly as high as I remember it. It was a natural playground for all the children in our neighborhood. On the other side of the hill was a ravine with a small creek, and on the other side of the creek was Bunker Hill. On the hill and in the ravine, the wild flowers grew in abundance. The May flowers, bloodroots, the jack-in-the-pulpits, Lady Slipper, the blue and yellow violets and the honeysuckles.*"[125]

An outing downtown opens new vistas when Mrs. Muller takes the girls to the Front Street carnival. After seeing the Flying Lady, they adjourn to Heinz's, which is across the street. This is the first of many, many visits to Heinz's for ice cream. (Chapter 7 herein contains information about the real Heinz's.) Eleanor Wood Lippert (the inspiration for the character Dorothy, introduced in *Over the Big Hill*) remembered that "*the street carnival was just as it is in the book, flying lady and all.*"[126] Maud recalled Bick playing the part of the Flying Lady on the end of a seesaw in the Hart woodshed. As in the Betsy-Tacy books, admission was paid in pins. "*She yelled once that she was falling off, but no one asked a pin back.*"[127] Maud and Bick also held a circus parade in which little Helen, pulled along in a wagon, was the star attraction. "*She's wonderful! She's marvelous. She combs her hair with her feet!*"[128]

Julia ventures beyond the Hill Street neighborhood for music lessons. "Julia will be taking her music lesson, and she is going to stay late to practise [sic] for the recital,"[129] Mrs. Ray remarks in *Betsy-Tacy and Tib*. In *Over the Big Hill,* Julia's music teacher was a neighbor, Miss Williams. In *Downtown,* we learn that Julia has begun to go downtown for music lessons, because the Williamses have moved away. But later, Miss Williams seems never to have existed. When Julia thinks back to her first music lesson (on page 55 of *Betsy Was a Junior*), she remembers "sitting down before the key-board and having Miss Cobb show me where middle C was."

Miss Cobb was based on Kate Robb. Paul Hoerr (who graduated from Mankato High School in 1911) wrote, "*Miss Robb was a very popular music teacher and always had a large number of students. I took piano lessons from her when I was a small boy. On April 2, 1901, her students gave a recital at her home and I took part in it. I still have a copy of the program in her hand-writing.*"[130] Mr. Hoerr is now deceased, and the program has been lost.

Like *Betsy-Tacy*, *Betsy-Tacy and Tib* has some humorous moments for the reading parent. Tib protests that since they haven't been bad, they can't punish themselves in the "Christian Kindness" club. "We were born bad," said Tacy. "Everyone is. Go on, Betsy."[131]

"Betsy was a Baptist, and Tacy was a Catholic, and Tib was an Episcopalian."[132] The three girls were really of these three respective denominations. From a demographic standpoint, it is interesting that in 1908 there were 300 members of the First Baptist Church, 185 members of St. John's Episcopal, and 3,000 parishioners at St. Peter and Paul Catholic Church, where baptisms were held every Sunday. The pastor was assisted by six priests and four brothers. This church was on the same street as the Rays' High Street house. The Kellys would have attended St. John's Catholic Church on Broad Street, which had 450 members.

"They loved to sit on Tacy's back fence and talk about God. Tacy's back fence was a very good place for such talk."[133] Maud later wrote that Tacy's house looked much the way it once did, *"except for the fact that ... homes have been built on what was once the long slope of the Kenney back yard, with its pump and buggy shed and barn, and fence on which we used to sit and watch the sunset."*[134]

Attempting to earn a stone for her Christian Kindness "penance bag," Tib "jumped into the seat of the baker's wagon ... while the baker's boy offered his tray of jelly rolls and doughnuts at Mrs. Benson's back door."[135] The baker's boy appears again in *Over the Big Hill*, again with jelly rolls and doughnuts. "He was a fat boy with red cheeks; they knew him well."[136] He also appears in the Betsy-Tacy short story "An Errand for Miss Canning." *"Mr. Hanna ran the bakery, and the children of Deep Valley called the boy who drove the wagon the Hanna boy. He was fat with red cheeks and he was good-natured."* Once again he was delivering *"jelly rolls and doughnuts."*[137]

Betsy and her friends are third-graders in "An Errand for Miss Canning." Nearly ten years after writing this short story, Maud used the name "Miss Canning" again - in *Winona's Pony Cart* (in which the girls are also third-graders).

The change in seasons is introduced with subtlety. Maud doesn't tell us that the summer is drawing to a close (and along with it, the book), but the illustrations begin to show the girls wearing their black stockings. Sumac is soon reddening, and in chapter X, the girls pick a bouquet of "goldenrod and asters" - fall flowers which are featured in many Lovelace books. They certainly symbolized autumn in Maud's mind. In 1914, while in Europe, she wrote home, pining to go on a picnic with Bick *"when the sumacs are turning red and the asters and golden rod blooming and make a fire in one of our old places."*[138]

These symbols of autumn appear in nearly every Betsy-Tacy book. In *Betsy-Tacy*, the girls pass through goldenrod and asters in the vacant lot on their way to the first day of school.[139] And at the end of *Betsy-Tacy*, "It was a late summer day. Goldenrod and asters were coloring the hill."[140] *Over the Big Hill* never sees the end of summer, but *Downtown* does, and goldenrod and asters are there in the seventh-grade classroom: Miss Paxton has "a bouquet of purple asters and goldenrod"[141] on her tidy desk. In *Heaven to Betsy*, Carney, Bonnie, and Betsy eat stolen apples in a field with goldenrod and asters.[142] In *Betsy in Spite of Herself*, Betsy and Tacy take a picnic up the hill and sit in "the goldenrod which rolled in a green-gold flood to the depths of the valley."[143] And when Tony and Cab bring Betsy a thank-you bouquet for teaching them *Ivanhoe*, in it she finds "golden rod and asters."[144] Betsy and Tacy take Tib back to the slope for a picnic with smoky cocoa at the beginning of *Betsy Was a Junior*, and the "goldenrod and asters"[145] get their due. They return for a third late-summer picnic in *Betsy and Joe*, where the hillside was "a slanting coppery sea of golden rod."[146] (Note that "goldenrod" is sometimes one word, sometimes two, even in the same Betsy-Tacy book!) They follow us to New York, with Carney arriving at Vassar for her junior year. She walks to her favorite bench, and "on the lower slopes the grasses were full of goldenrod and asters."[147] *Betsy and the Great World* takes place in winter, spring, and summer but not fall. *Betsy's Wedding* takes us to September and Betsy's honeymoon, complete with bouquets of "goldenrod and starry asters."[148] Sometimes sumac and sometimes thistles accompany the flowers. They even appear in Maud's adult fiction. In *The Black Angels*, "*goldenrod, asters*" are "*banners of autumn*."[149] In *The Charming Sally*, "*the Commons was yellow with goldenrod*."[150] And in *Gentlemen from England*, "*the Queen Anne's lace of summer was mingled with autumn's goldenrod and asters*."[151] Goldenrod and asters appear likewise in "Mademoiselle Waffles," a short story set in the fall, which Maud wrote in 1920.

Dependably recurring flowers become a formula for autumn. The mechanics of the Betsy-Tacy books never clink or clank. They are silent and subtle, with a power as pervading as the goldenrod and asters.

[109] *Betsy-Tacy and Tib,* p. 1.
[110] Ibid., p. 69.
[111] Ibid., p. 71.
[112] *Betsy-Tacy,* p. 80.
[113] Ibid., p. 102.
[114] *Betsy-Tacy and Tib,* p. 2.
[115] *Betsy-Tacy,* p. 109.
[116] Ibid., p. 110.
[117] LWW, n.p.
[118] *Betsy's Wedding,* p. 58.
[119] C. Kenney to L. Erickson, 10-30-84.
[120] *Betsy and Joe,* p. 29.
[121] MHL to Miss Gilland, 5-22-42.
[122] *Minneapolis Star,* 10-8-61.
[123] *Betsy-Tacy and Tib,* p. 4.
[124] M.H. Lovelace, "Carmelita, Widow," *Catholic World,* October 1924, p. 14.
[125] *Mankato Free Press,* 11-25-52.
[126] E.W. Lippert, unpublished memoirs, p. 9.
[127] LWW, p. 26A.
[128] Ibid., p. 26B.
[129] *Betsy-Tacy and Tib,* p. 54.
[130] P. Hoerr to M. Marshall, 8-10-77.
[131] *Betsy-Tacy and Tib,* p. 100.
[132] Ibid., p. 96.
[133] Ibid., p. 97.
[134] *Mankato Free Press,* 4-10-52.
[135] *Betsy-Tacy and Tib,* p. 103.
[136] *Over the Big Hill,* p. 97.
[137] Lovelace, "An Errand for Miss Canning."
[138] MPH to Hart Family, p. 185.
[139] *Betsy-Tacy,* p. 32.
[140] Ibid., p. 99.
[141] *Downtown,* p. 32.
[142] *Heaven to Betsy,* p. 77.
[143] *Betsy in Spite of Herself,* p. 14.
[144] Ibid., p. 42.
[145] *Betsy Was a Junior,* p. 29.
[146] *Betsy and Joe,* p. 31.
[147] *Carney's House Party,* p. 236.

[148] *Betsy's Wedding,* p. 68.

[149] M.H. Lovelace, *The Black Angels* (New York: John Day Co., 1926), p. 57.

[150] M.H. Lovelace, *The Charming Sally* (New York: John Day Co., 1932), p. 188.

[151] *Gentlemen from England,* p. 74.

CHAPTER FOUR
On *Over the Big Hill*
January 1902 to June 1902

"Betsy, Tacy, and Tib were nine years old, and they were very anxious to be ten."[152] Tacy would turn ten first, in January. Tib's birthday was next, in March. And of course, Betsy's birthday was in April. In late winter, 1902, Maud and Midge were indeed on the verge of turning ten. But Bick had been ten since the previous July. Had Maud used Bick's real birthdate (July 13, 1891), these chapters wouldn't have worked. (A child reader would have thought, "How could Tacy be the oldest? July comes <u>after</u> April, doesn't it?") Moving Bick's (Tacy's) birthday to January was a simple but wise choice. With a single change in actual dates, Maud creates several very effective chapters.

Maud saw the process of turning ten as the central theme of the book. The original title she gave it was *Betsy-Tacy and Tib are Ten*. Thomas Y. Crowell Company, the publisher, did not approve. Maud renamed the book *Over the Big Hill,* the title by which it was originally published. Thomas Y. Crowell later decided that "Betsy-Tacy" should be included in the title, so that the book would be identified with the growing series. With "and" replacing the hyphen, the final and current title, *Betsy and Tacy Go Over the Big Hill,* was produced. (The original title of *Downtown* was likewise changed to *Betsy and Tacy Go Downtown*.)

At the end of *Betsy-Tacy and Tib,* Betsy points out, "You have two numbers in your age when you are ten."[153] She says exactly the same thing on page 1 of *Over the Big Hill*. Maud harkens back to the traumatic climax of *Betsy-Tacy and Tib,* reassuring us that the girls' hair has indeed grown back. The girls have grown on the inside, too. They had cut their hair when they were only eight "and didn't know any better."[154] Now they are nearly ten and have learned a thing or two. (A. A. Milne and A.E. Houseman employed the same literary motif.)[155]

To celebrate coming of age, the girls call each other by their full first names: Elizabeth, Anastacia, and Thelma,[156] rather than by the nicknames Betsy, Tacy, and Tib. The real three probably would have had a good time with this. Instead of Maudie, Bickie, and Midge, they would have been Maud, Frances, and Marjorie. They no doubt would really have rolled when they said "Frances," a far cry from "Bick."

The closest we get to the date of Betsy's birthday is "late April." Maud never mentions the 25th, her actual birthday, in any of the Betsy-Tacy books. On the morning of her tenth birthday party, Betsy wonders why Tacy and Tib aren't invited to supper. "You know Friday's cleaning day,"[157] Julia explains (to cover up the impending surprise party for Betsy). April 25, 1902 was a Friday.

On the evening of her birthday, Betsy is asked to return an egg to their neighbor, Mrs. Rivers. "Mrs. Rivers lived next door, and she was very nice. She had a little girl just Margaret's age, and a still smaller girl, and a baby."[158] The Federal Census for 1900 reveals a "Brooks" family (note the two "waterway" names) living at 331 Center. The parents were Walter and Margaret. Their daughter Katherine was the little girl just Margaret's age. There was also a younger girl, and the baby would have been Freeman Brooks, who later became a doctor.

At Betsy's tenth birthday party, we are introduced to Alice and Dorothy, who both "lived down on Pleasant Street."[159]

Alice was Ruth Williams, who lived in the house which once stood at 613 Byron. This was originally the property of her great-grandfather, for whom nearby Wickersham Street was named. Ruth didn't live in this house until 1902 (she had previously lived with her grandparents on Broad Street). It makes sense that Alice didn't enter the Betsy-Tacy series until 1902 (*Over the Big Hill*).

The house in which Ruth grew up has been moved from the spot it occupied when Maud lived on Center Street. The house was set far back from the street, rather than with its elbows up to the sidewalk in the conventional manner. The Williams house was the first one built on the five acres at the south end of Byron Street. The move was made to align the house with other houses on the street and to facilitate the sale of land to the north. The house was moved forward and slightly south. The number was changed from 613 to the current 621.

Ruth was the child of Theodore and Fallie Welsh Williams. Fallie died when Ruth's younger brother Wheaton was several months old. When Ruth was eight, her father remarried. A new half-brother, Howard, was born in 1904. Neither brother appears in the Betsy-Tacy books. Howard Williams provided assistance to Maud in researching the Syrian colony described in *Over the Big*

Hill. Maud wrote to him in 1942, "*Bick and Ruth and I played in the hills behind our houses when you were a baby. I don't know whether your memory reaches back to the swing on your hillside in which we blissfully endangered our bones.*"[160] Wheaton Williams remembered the swing, too. "*Up at our house we had a single rope swing that was the most dangerous one I have ever seen kids use. We would climb a tree to a platform, put the broom handle that was tied in the rope between our legs and jump off the platform and soar way up over our barn. When Harry Miller would deliver ice to our house he would stay and watch us until his conscience drove him back to work. I suspect he wanted to be there when one of us got hurt, but we never did.*"[161]

Ruth told her daughter Fallie that Maud loved to make up plays when they were children, and that Ruth herself demurred from the speaking parts. "*I'll be the audience,*" she would say.[162] This was characteristic of Ruth (and of the Alice, shy and quiet, whom we know). "She was an earnest little girl with fat yellow braids."[163] The fictional name "Alice" may not have been an arbitrary choice. Ruth's aunt, Alice Williams, was a kindergarten teacher at the Normal, and Maud may well have been in her class.

Ruth Williams has another incarnation, in a short story called "The AHOPs Club," which Maud wrote for *Jack and Jill* magazine in 1944. And in this case, "Ruth" is Ruth's fictional name! "*Ruth was ... tall and quiet with thick yellow braids and calm blue eyes.*"[164] This short story also features a park with "*a view over the town, and picnic tables with benches, and two high swings,*" which sounds suspiciously like the Page Park of the high school books. The four girls in the story want a club with initials for a name, just as Betsy, Tacy, and Tib do in *Betsy-Tacy and Tib* and *Over the Big Hill.* (AHOP stands for "Ancient and Honorable Order of Peacocks.") One of the AHOPs, Babs, sounds much like Betsy. "*Babs was Secretary, as usual. She liked to be Secretary and write things down in her notebook.*" Babs also supplies the group with "rocks," the same variety of cookie Rena bakes on page 42 of *Downtown*. In real life, Maud, Bick, and Ruth made up a club called the P.O.F. (Pledge of Friendship).[165]

Dorothy's fictional surname, Drew, is not supplied until *Heaven to Betsy*. Her real name was Eleanor Wood. "*She was a very close friend of the sister I called Julia ... much more so than you would think*

"Alice's House"
621 Byron

"Mrs. Benson's" House

Mrs. Benedict, who lived in this house at 324 Center, was a good friend to Maud, Bick, and Midge. She no doubt purchased jars of colored sand from the girls. (She did not ride a motorcycle.)

Coll. of Elizabeth Miller

Eleanor Wood

Eleanor is shown here doing a Highland Fling. As Dorothy, she "was one of the little girls' favorite big girls, with brown curls and eyes and a very sweet voice." (OBH p. 95)

Coll. of Elizabeth Miller

528 Byron circa 1905

Dr. Milton B. Wood (a dentist) and his family lived at 528 Byron.

528 Byron circa 1990

Maud wrote of the Woods that *"the whole family was dear to us."* (MFP 4-10-52) *from the books. Having 'typed' Katie, Tacy's sister, as Julia's friend - and the books being already crowded with too many characters - I never could develop 'Dorothy' and the good times she and Julia had together.*"[166]

Dorothy's "father and mother played with Betsy's father and mother in the High Fly Whist Club."[167] They really did. According to Maud, Eleanor Wood's parents "*belonged to the Hi-Fly* [sic] *Whist Club along with my parents and the Charlie Macbeths, and the Sam Wilsons and the Plummer* [sic] *Pitchers and others. They were gay young-marrieds.*"[168] Sam Wilson was a lawyer who lived nearby on Clark, and Plumer Pitcher was the uncle of Tom Slade (the brother of Tom's mother, Grace).

Having turned ten, the girls' heads were turned by Alphonso the Thirteenth of Spain. He was crowned on May 17, 1902, his sixteenth birthday. May 17 was a Saturday, as reported by Maud. It is not possible to trace the exact newspaper photos mentioned in *Over the Big Hill*, since we cannot be sure which newspapers the girls were looking at. The Harts could easily have received their Sunday paper from Minneapolis or St. Paul, and we know from *Betsy-Tacy and Tib* that Mr. Muller's paper came from Milwaukee.

The school Entertainment approaches and everyone is preparing. Betsy and Tacy will sing a "Cat Duet." The "Cat Duet" is described in Chapter 9 of this *Companion*. Tib announces that her mamma is making her a white accordion-pleated dress in which she will dance her Baby Dance at the Entertainment.

The Baby Dance was difficult. "There were five different steps and she did each one thirty-two times ... a slide, a kick, a double slide, a jump step, and then a Russian step which was done in a squatting position kicking out first one foot and then the other. It was hard but Tib could do it."[169] Maud later wrote that Mankato folk knew Midge "*for her dancing, especially the Baby Dance. She danced this for years for school and church and lodge entertainments, and kept outgrowing the dress she danced it in, so that her mother made one after another, identical except in size ... white, accordion-pleated, trimmed with insertion and lace and streamers of white satin ribbon. Midge ran out on the stage holding the skirts wide and the dance ended with the difficult 'Russian step' which unfailingly brought down the house.*"[170]

The Entertainment opened with "Men of Harlech" on page 66. This same song was also noisily rendered on page 66 of *Betsy Was*

MHL Archive

A Tale of Two Picnics

"The Woods were always close to the Harts. Our two families, often with the Macbeths, used to take picnics out. I have a darling picture of one in 1898 which shows Eleanor, Kathleen, Flossie Macbeth (later the famous opera singer, Florence Macbeth) and me, all of us having fun." (I.V. 8-23-66) Maud and Kathleen, wearing matching dresses, are seated between their parents.

Coll. of Elizabeth Miller

On this occasion, the Harts and Woods were joined by the Fox family. Front row, left to right: Kathleen Hart, Eleanor Wood, Flossie Macbeth, Maud Hart, Tom Fox (Tom Slade). Stella Hart is leaning her elbow on the shoulder of Dr. Wood (who is reading a dental journal). Tom Hart is holding baby Helen. The three women at the right side are Mrs. M.B. Wood, Mrs. Grace Fox, and Grandma Pitcher (the fictional Grandma Slade).

Coll. of Berg Family

Midge Gerlach

Her accordion-pleated dress "was made of fine white organdie trimmed with rows of insertion and lace. A sash of pale blue satin was tied high in princess style." (OBH p. 63)

HarperCollins

Tib Muller

Tib and Midge were both famous for their Baby Dance, which consisted of a series of difficult steps.

Newspaper File

The King of Spain

Betsy, Tacy, and Tib all fell in love with the sixteen-year-old King of Spain. They sighed over pictures like this one.

Coll. of Elizabeth Miller

Flossie Macbeth, Eleanor Wood, and Kathleen Hart

Florence Macbeth wrote: "*The Hague was not my first public appearance. I have a picture of Eleanor Wood Lippert, Kathleen Hart Foster and myself each done up in crinoline and spangles. What roles the three of us played, I cannot remember, but we look very elegant in our spangles.*" (MFP 4-8-52) They danced a Kermiss. Kathleen's dress was green. Eleanor's was in probably a dark red - her counterpart's trademark color!

HarperCollins

Kathleen

"Her feet loved a platform as Betsy's loved a grassy hill. Whether she was playing the piano, singing, or reciting, Julia was happy so long as she had an audience."
(OBH p. 62)

a Junior. The Hallidays, too, sing "The March of the Men of Harlech" on page 102 of *Gentlemen from England.* Julia recites "Queen of the May." "Her feet loved a platform as Betsy's loved a grassy hill. Whether she was playing the piano, singing, or reciting, Julia was happy so long as she had an audience."[171] Kathleen Hart loved to recite, play the piano, sing ... and dance. One of her fellow dancing pupils was Florence Macbeth, a Chicago and New York opera star who grew up in Mankato. (Her parents were the Charlie Macbeths who were members of the High Fly Whist Club.) Though not represented fictionally in the Betsy-Tacy books, Flossie Macbeth was an old friend, not only of Kathleen's, but of Maud's as well.

Kathleen had "airs" which annoyed Maud in their early years as much as Julia's annoyed Betsy. Maud remembered that when Kathleen was a little girl, she discovered the phrase, "I beg your pardon." When callers came to the Center Street house, Kathleen would pass in front of them several times just for the opportunity to ask their pardon. *"Isn't just 'excuse me' good enough?"* Maud grumbled to her mother.[172]

On page 29, we hear that the Entertainment will be on the last day of school. But on page 76, after the Entertainment is over, we learn that "as soon as school was over, they intended to plan that game in which Tib would be queen." School is already over! Such small slip-ups might well have been the fault of an editor.

After a trip downtown, Julia and Katie come toiling up Hill Street in the June heat. There <u>were</u> sidewalks on Center. They are mentioned in *Betsy-Tacy,* when Betsy runs up the hill to the end of the sidewalk, going to meet Tacy for the first time.[173] Around 1906 the wooden sidewalks on Center and other residential streets were replaced with concrete. Emma Wiecking remembered the day the old wooden sidewalks in front of her house on Byron were torn up. She said the neighborhood children all came to look for lost nickels and pennies.

When the girls all set out down Hill Street for votes, we get a wonderful overview of the homes in the neighborhood. Maud describes seven houses on the east side of Hill Street. Following is a summary of these seven, showing fictional names (if provided) and actual house numbers: House One - 309, no name given;

House Two - 313, no name given; House Three - 317, Granger; House Four - 323, Williams; House Five - 327, Hunt; House Six - 331, Rivers; House Seven - 333, Ray. (The current homes at 301, 305, 311, 315, and 321 were not there in Maud's day. Between 309 and 323 were two houses that are now gone: 313 and 317.)

Children live in the first two houses, 309 and 313, but no other details are offered. The next house, 317 (which no longer stands), was "a neat light tan house with brown trimmings ... the Granger daughters were grown up. But Betsy and Tacy knew the house well, for here they often borrowed *Little Women*. They had borrowed it almost to tatters."[174] Maud later described some of the houses in the neighborhood of her childhood. "*Wreathed in glory in my memory is the neat tan house with brown trimmings where one borrowed Little Women. I used to borrow it, read it through, reluctantly return it, and if it were returned on Monday, by Wednesday I was back on the doorstep, bright and smiling, to borrow it again.*"[175]

The Williams house is still standing at 323 but is no longer blue frame. Betsy, Tacy, and Tib "called there sometimes to borrow the Horatio Alger books."[176] Maud never commented on the real family who lived at 323. But she wrote of the house, "*I remember the blue frame house with a wide porch, halfway down our hilly street, from which one borrowed the Horatio Alger books.*" [177] Gordon Kennedy was born in this house in 1903. His family had moved there in 1901. Mr. Kennedy could not remember the time when Maud lived at 333 (since he was three years old when she moved). The members of the Kennedy family do not correspond with the fictional Williamses.

Fictionally, 323 Center belonged to "Ben who walked home from school with Julia. His sister, Miss Williams, was Julia's music teacher."[178] The 1900 census shows a Yates family at 323. The Yates family may have been the fictional Williams family. Gertrude was nineteen, old enough to be giving music lessons if so inclined. Her brother Warren was fourteen, and perhaps escorted twelve-year-old Julia home from school. The name "Ben Williams" may have been selected because it was the name of the proprietor of a popular Mankato restaurant at 308 S. Front. This Ben Williams sold the restaurant in 1910. As a final wrinkle on the subject, there was a music teacher named Williams in Mankato.

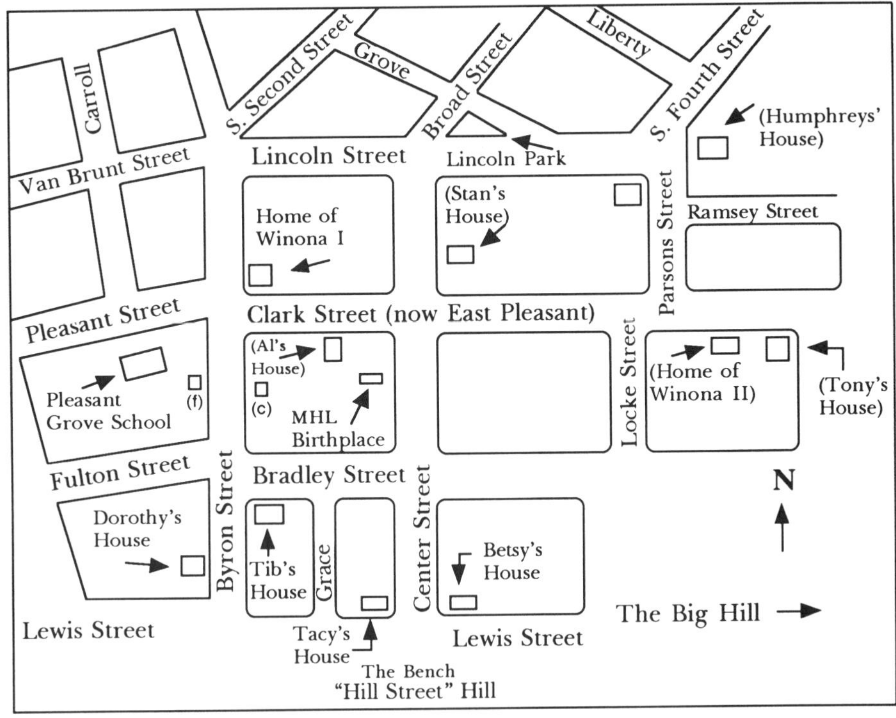

The small buildings on either side of Byron, near the school, represent the former (f) and current (c) locations of the candy store.
The homes of high school characters shown on this map are marked with parentheses. This map is not drawn to exact scale.

Maud Hart (Betsy): 333 Center.
Bick Kenney (Tacy): 332 Center.
Midge Gerlach (Tib): 503 Byron.
MHL birthplace: 214 Center.
Eleanor Wood (Dorothy): 528 Byron.
Beulah Hunt (Winona I): 327 Byron.
Henry Lee (Al): 133 Clark.
Herman Hayward (Stan): 123 Center.
Eleanor Johnson (Winona II): 325 Clark.
Mike Parker (Tony): 339 Clark.
Helmus and Rupe Andrews (the Humphreys boys): 645 S. Fourth.
Jim Baker (E. Lloyd Harrington): 104 Parsons.
Ruth Williams (Alice): just off the map, 621 Byron.
Mildred Oleson (Irma): off the map, 405 Pleasant.
Pleasant Grove School is no longer standing.

This was Ethel, who taught at 326 Broad, but with no evidence of a brother to match up with Ben. The threads of fiction and reality are snarled here. Only Maud could have untangled them for us.

The girls were collecting votes on sheets of "foolscap." Foolscap was a writing paper about 13 x 16 inches, becoming 13 x 8 inches when folded. This variety of paper was originally impressed with a watermark of a fool's cap with bells. Julia and Katie take their sheet of foolscap up the west side of the street. The only house mentioned is Mrs. Benson's, which is opposite the Williams' (323). The house across from 323 was 324 Center, which actually belonged to the Benedict family. The similarity between "Benson" and "Benedict" is telling, and it is very likely that Mabel Benedict was the woman Maud had in mind when she described Mrs. Benson. However, unlike her fictional counterpart, Mrs. Benedict was not childless. She had a son three years younger than Maud and a daughter five years younger. Therefore, in 1897 (in *Betsy-Tacy*), Mrs. Benedict may well have been saving fashion magazines for Maud and Bick, since her own little girl had not yet arrived - or was much too young for paper dolls!

At the time of *Over the Big Hill,* only one house stood between the Benedict and Kenney homes (the house currently beside Tacy's had not been built by 1902). When Julia and Katie sneak away, Betsy says, "They've cut through lots somewhere."[179] There were many more vacant lots and fewer houses in the neighborhood when Maud and her friends were children.

North of the Benedicts was the Walker home (which later belonged to the Lewis family), the only brick house on the block. Maud remembered "*the red brick house with arched windows where one borrowed Toby Tyler.*"[180] A house which once stood between the former Benedict (324) and Walker (312) homes was torn down long ago to make way for two "new" houses (numbered 314 and 318 Center).

The last house on Tacy's side of the street, standing on the southwest corner of Center and Bradley, was the towered Hickey house, built on the vacant lot which had been behind Midge Gerlach's house. "*I must not forget the red brick* [sic] *Hickey home back on Center Street. That was not only glamorous, with its round tower-room, but hospitable and child-loving."*[181] (The Hickey house was not brick - perhaps Maud wrote "brick red" and the newspaper typed "red brick"!)

The girls are not allowed to collect votes beyond Lincoln Park. So School Street must have been south of Lincoln. Since School Street cannot have been Bradley (the street on which Tib's house sits, at the corner of Bradley and Byron), School must have been Clark Street. In *Downtown*, we find supplementary evidence that Clark must be the fictional School Street, for now Betsy, Tacy, and Tib have a friend living there - Winona - and the real Winona did live on Clark Street.

For some baffling reason, the city of Mankato has changed the time-honored name of Clark Street to "East Pleasant." This was obviously not done to commemorate the Betsy-Tacy books, since Byron was the fictional Pleasant, not Clark! Maud no doubt chose the name "School" for Clark because Pleasant Grove School stood on this street, west of Byron. Here the name of the western continuation of Clark Street was always "Pleasant" (now "West Pleasant"). It may be necessary to read this paragraph three times before proceeding.

The Humphreys house was "a large yellow stone house that overlooked the Park."[182] Was this Herbert Humphreys' house? The Humphreys boys are not mentioned until *Downtown* (1904); but the Andrews family, upon whom the Humphreys were based, lived near Lincoln Park, at 645 S. Fourth, by 1900. Maud wrote that *"The C.N. Andrews family moved to Mankato about that time; they lived opposite the General Bakers. They were a great addition to this merry group* [of parents] *as their sons were to the high school crowd."*[183] The Baker family mentioned above lived at 104 Parsons. Their son James became a character in the Betsy-Tacy high school books (see Chapter 8 herein).

The Andrews house, though nearby and within view, did not immediately face Lincoln Park. When Maud described the yellow stone house, she was probably thinking about 810 S. Broad, known for many years as "the Rose house." Elsewhere Maud spoke of this *"yellow brick house with a cupola."*[184] (The Rose house is no longer painted yellow.) Like the fictional Humphreys house, the Rose house is directly opposite Lincoln Park.

The description of the hills is also accurate, though the geography of the Big Hill becomes more complex as the girls explore it more thoroughly. When they climb to the top and turn left, they come out on a rim overlooking Deep Valley. When they turn right, they come to the Secret Lane, with beech trees in two rows. Maud wrote, "*Behind Betsy's house, of course, rises the Big Hill, now spoiled in the lower stretches by a stone embankment; and on the top where once the sun came up behind a lone white house, there are scores of beautiful homes. But the view from the top is the same. The Secret Lane is still there but you will be smart if you find it. (The trees are not beeches.) ...and walking along south you will find the crest with the view of Little Syria on which Betsy, Tacy and Tib had so many picnics.*"[185]

Betsy, Tacy, and Tib discover Naifi, the girl from Little Syria, during a picnic on the hill. The valley Maud calls "Little Syria" was known as "Tinkcomville," named for the man who bought the land and sold lots to the Syrians. The name "Naifi" may have been suggested to Maud by information sent to her by Howard Williams: "*Naiff Abdo was probably the first Syrian to come into this community, having left Syria in 1892.*"[186] Naiff opened a grocery store at 127 James Avenue. He was the unofficial leader of the Syrian group and, Gordon Kennedy adds, "*also probably the operator of high stakes poker games!*"[187] It is with an air of authority that Naifi's father tells Betsy, Tacy, and Tib that "the Syrians will sign your paper,"[188] so perhaps he was patterned after Naiff - and this real name almost certainly inspired the fictional diminutive.

On page 152, the girls learn, to their surprise, that Naifi's last name is "Bushara" and that her grandfather was the frightening "Old Bushara." Howard Williams supplied Maud with an inspiration for this name in his letter of January 15, 1942. Mr. Williams told Maud that one of the colorful Syrians who "*stands out in my mind more than any other was one called Bushadi.*"

Betsy, Tacy, and Tib are also surprised to learn that Naifi is an *emeera*, a Syrian princess. There is, unfortunately, no trace of a Syrian princess in Mankato. Maud stated in *Heaven to Betsy* that Naifi moved away "long ago." So Naifi had probably left Mankato by about 1904. It is not surprising that no living person can remember her. And even if no *emeera* actually resided in Mankato, what remains important is that <u>Maud</u> thought there was a Syrian princess in Tinkcomville. "*From spring to fall we children picnicked and roamed on the hills. We loved to invade Tinkcomville, fascinated by the colorful Syrian colony. There was a rumor which used to enthrall us that one Syrian child was a princess. Many years later in New York I discovered that she was, indeed, a Syrian Emeera.*"[189]

The Syrians of Mankato, however, were actually Lebanese, since at the end of the last century, Lebanon was part of Syria. Lebanon became a country in its own right in 1948. Maud knew that the Syrians were Lebanese. In *Emily of Deep Valley*, she wrote: "They were talking about Syrians. He knew where they came from. It was the Lebanon district, he said."[190] At the turn of the century, the immigrants living in Tinkcomville called themselves "Syrians," which for our purposes is what matters.

In the center of Little Syria stood one big brick house and a row of tiny houses. The brick house is Mr. Meecham's mansion. The story the girls had heard their fathers tell about Mr. Meecham went like this: "He had come from the East and had bought all the land in this valley, calling it Meecham's Addition. He had tried to sell lots there, but none of his American neighbors had wished to live so far from the center of town. At last he had sold his lots to a colony of Syrians, strange dark people who spoke broken English and came to Hill Street sometimes peddling garden stuff and laces and embroidered cloths."[191]

There was an early settler in Mankato named Harvey Meacham, whose name probably inspired Maud's choice of "Meecham." The character Mr. Meecham was based on James Ray Tinkcom. (Maud made use of the name "Tinkcom" in her first novel, *The Black Angels*.) Mr. Tinkcom really came from the East (New York). He bought all the land in the valley in 1873, calling it "Tinkcom's Addition." Tinkcom sold his lots to the Syrians in the 1890s. The row of houses Maud describes were on James Avenue (though other Syrian families lived on Fairfield Avenue).

Tinkcom lived at 204 James Avenue (on the corner of James and Fairfield) with his only child, Mary Lilly. Tinkcom named one of the streets in Tinkcomville after his daughter and, of course, the main street after himself, but he did not name a street after his absent wife, Laura. They had married in Pennsylvania five years before he departed for the West. Apparently Laura wasn't the pioneer type, since she remained in the East. Mary joined her father and lived with him until his death, but unlike Miss Meecham, Mary Tinkcom was not a spinster. She married Olaf G. Lundberg of Mankato.

Maud describes Mr. Meecham's "team of white horses" on page 8. It "was the finest in the county; and it was driven by a coachman. Mr. Meecham and his daughter came to town in style." Anna Wiecking, in her book about Mankato, *As We Once Were*, remembered Mr. Tinkcom and his horses. He "*was a well-to-do man. He had a fine open carriage pulled by two fine horses. Two people could sit facing the front and two facing the back. The coachman sat up high in front. The horses, the carriage and the people seemed very elegant to us. If we saw the carriage coming up or down our street we ran out to watch them go by our house. Usually there were two ladies in beautiful dresses. They had plumes on their large hats, or carried parasols if it were sunny. We were sure they must be princesses. A friend about my age and I were reminiscing about the Tinkcoms. She said, 'Don't you remember the beautiful snow-white horses with the long white tails?' And I said, 'Do you remember white horses? I remember they were shiny coal-black horses with long black tails.' Then we talked with a man much older than we, and he laughed at us. 'Those horses were neither white or black.... They were bays.' So much for memory*!" [192] Perhaps all three were right, since over the course of forty years in the valley, Tinkcom no doubt owned a number of different teams! The two fine ladies in the carriage would have been Mary Tinkcom Lundberg and her daughter, Stella (who became an actress).

Mr. Tinkcom was definitely Mr. Meecham. But Tinkcom's house, though large and brick, was <u>not</u> Mr. Meecham's mansion. The home Maud had in mind once stood on the hillside above James Avenue. The *Mankato Free Press* stated: "*The new school* [Jefferson] *is on the site of Mr. Meecham's house which is mentioned in the Betsy-Tacy books.*"[193] This was the home of the Ibach family, who owned a brewery built in the valley in 1878. Their house was probably built at the same time.

A complication: Maud thought that James Tinkcom had lived in the Ibach house. Maud once told a Betsy-Tacy fan that the Tinkcom house was not the house she had written about in *Over*

Mr. Tinkcom's House but Not "Mr. Meecham's Mansion"

James Tinkcom's house stands at the corner of James Avenue and Fairfield. Though Mr. Tinkcom appears fictionally in *Over the Big Hill*, his house does not. When she described Mr. Meecham's mansion, Maud had in mind the Ibach property, which stood on the opposite side of Fairfield, set well into the hill.

HarperCollins

Mr. Meecham

"He was a tall old man with a flowing white beard and a proud scornful bearing." (OBH p. 8)

Mankato, Its First Fifty Years

Mr. Tinkcom

Mr. Tinkcom studied to be a doctor in his early years.

Coll. of Lillian Leftault

The Ibach House - "Mr. Meecham's Mansion"

"An avenue of evergreen trees led the way to the house." (OBH p. 112) They weren't evergreens, but a row of trees lined the Ibach drive. Jefferson School now stands on this part of the hill.

Coll. of Lillian Leftault

Ibach House

"The gray brick house had tall arched windows which looked like suspicious eyes." (OBH p. 113)

Coll. of Lillian Leftault

Brewery Ruins

The Ibach brewery burned in 1887, but its ruins remained for many years. This may have been where Katie and Julia had their club meetings in *Betsy-Tacy and Tib*. The little girl pictured is Lillian Leftault. The dog was named Oley and had a very bad reputation.

the Big Hill. "*I think you would like to know that I feel positive about the location of the rich man's house ... it was on the hillside.*"[194] Tinkcom's house was not on the hillside - but Ibach's was. Many other Mankato old-timers also thought that the Ibach house was Tinkcom's home.

The Ibachs' brick house was as grand as Tinkcom's, though without stables. It faced James, but the address was 136 Fairfield. The house was on the hillside, so that you looked up to it from James Avenue. It is clear from *Over the Big Hill* and from *Emily of Deep Valley* that Mr. Meecham's Mansion is on the hillside above James Avenue.

Art Ibach had a notorious dog, Oley (named after Mary Tinkcom's husband!). Oley was known to kill sheep and was kept on a chain. He sounds like Mr. Meecham's scary hound.

Naifi's patriotic coronation was an appropriate celebration for the summer of 1902. It was the fiftieth anniversary of the founding of Mankato. As Maud writes, "*I remember the Semi-Centennial of 1902. My father owned the volume which was issued in celebration of that affair. As a child I loved its pictures of the bearded pioneers and the views of Mankato in the early days.*"[195] The interest in the history of Minnesota which had begun to develop would affect Maud's career profoundly.

[152] *Over the Big Hill,* p. 1.

[153] *Betsy-Tacy and Tib,* p. 128.

[154] *Over the Big Hill,* p. 3.

[155] Ed. note, Laura Vadaj.

[156] *Over the Big Hill,* p. 19.

[157] Ibid., p. 15.

[158] Ibid., p. 22.

[159] Ibid., p. 24.

[160] MHL to H. Williams, 1-13-42.

[161] *Mankato Free Press*, 1952.

[162] Interview with F. Beers, 1-26-86.

[163] *Over the Big Hill,* p. 95.

[164] M.H. Lovelace, "The AHOPs Club," *Jack and Jill*, November 1944, p. 2-8.

[165] LWW, p. 25.

[166] MHL to L. Demp, 7-23-58.

[167] *Over the Big Hill,* p. 95.

[168] *Mankato Free Press,* 4-10-52.

[169] *Over the Big Hill,* p. 63.

[170] *Mankato Free Press*, 2-4-65.

[171] *Over the Big Hill,* p. 62.

[172] LWW, p. 4.

[173] *Betsy-Tacy,* p. 5.

[174] *Over the Big Hill,* p. 94.

[175] M.H. Lovelace, "A Child's Reading and Libraries in Mankato During the Early Twentieth Century," *Minnesota Libraries*, December 1955.

[176] *Over the Big Hill,* p. 93.

[177] Lovelace, "A Child's Reading."

[178] *Over the Big Hill,* p. 93.

[179] Ibid., p. 100.

[180] Lovelace, "A Child's Reading."

[181] Ibid.

[182] *Over the Big Hill,* p. 101.

[183] *Mankato Free Press*, 4-10-52.

[184] Ibid.

[185] MHL to L. Demp, 7-23-58.

[186] H. Williams to MHL, 1-15-42.

[187] G. Kennedy to SSW, 5-5-90.

[188] *Over the Big Hill,* p. 121.

[189] *Mankato Free Press*, 4-10-52.

[190] *Emily of Deep Valley,* p. 209.

[191] *Over the Big Hill,* p. 8.

[192] Anna Wiecking, *As We Once Were*, (Mankato, MN, 1971), p. 29.

[193] *Mankato Free Press*, 10-7-61.

[194] MHL to K. Reuter, 2-3-75.

[195] *Mankato Free Press*, 4-10-52.

CHAPTER FIVE

On *Betsy and Tacy Go Downtown*

September 1904 to January 1905

The focus of the Betsy-Tacy series shifts in *Downtown* from Hill Street to the world beyond Lincoln Park (the boundary of Betsy's neighborhood). Maud suggests this change symbolically on the first page. Betsy is sitting in her office in the backyard maple. (Betsy's aerie was based on Maud's childhood office: "*I had a desk made from a cigar box up in our backyard maple.*"[196]) Betsy's view "did not look toward the Big Hill where she and her friends Tacy and Tib had had so many adventurous picnics. It looked towards the town."[197] Maud recalled: "*As we grew older we made more trips downtown.*"[198] Picnics on the Big Hill no longer satisfy the wanderlust of Betsy, Tacy, and Tib; and Maud's readers are ready for a change, too.

The Betsy-Tacy books evolve as their reader matures. As Betsy and her friends gradually grow up, the language and subject matter of Lovelace's books become more sophisticated. At age six, a child may not be ready for *Downtown.* At eight she may love it, but perhaps will be appalled by her first sight of *Heaven to Betsy.* Not only are the familiar drawings gone, but Betsy has her hair up and her skirts down. What the heck do Betsy and Tacy think they're doing, the traitors?! Later, *Heaven to Betsy* becomes the same child's ideal of high school life, and she longs to look like one of Vera Neville's illustrations!

To accommodate the expanding perimeters of the Betsy-Tacy world, the size of the print in *Downtown* decreases dramatically. And with each series title, the length of the text has been increasing. (*Betsy-Tacy* is 113 pages, *Betsy-Tacy and Tib* is 128 pages, and *Over the Big Hill* is 171 pages.) Not only is *Downtown* 180 pages, but with smaller type, there are many more words per page. All these details are indications that, as she begins to grow up, Betsy's life is becoming more complicated.

It is September 1904, and the girls are twelve years old. In *Over the Big Hill*, they were finishing fourth grade. Now they are entering seventh, and Maud puts up another mile marker: "When Betsy and Tacy and Tib were only ten years old and didn't know any better, they had written a letter to the King of Spain."[199] Though they may know a thing or two more, Betsy, Tacy, and Tib are still "kids." But we have a glimpse of the long skirts and hair bows that lie in store for them through Julia and Katie, who are in high school now.

On more than one occasion Julia and Katie have provided convenient foreshadowing of changes to come. The two big sisters ask for permission to go down to Front Street in *Over the Big Hill.*[200] This is the first we hear of any of the children going downtown alone. Betsy, Tacy, and Tib are still busy and content in the Hill Street environs, but Maud has shown us the rite of passage ahead.

For the fourth book in a row, Maud plants a seed early in the story which sprouts later into a theatric climax. In *Betsy-Tacy,* the two girls admire Tib's house on their way to school. Later, their admiration for it leads them to a new friend, Tib. In *Betsy-Tacy and Tib,* they discover a photo of Aunt Dolly and, at the end of the book, enjoy the excitement of meeting her. In *Over the Big Hill,* the girls discover Little Syria in the first chapter. Little Syria later yields Naifi and the final "coronation" chapter. And in *Downtown,* the seed is planted on page 10: Betsy writhes when Julia mentions the play she saw at the Opera House. It is Betsy's "sorest grievance" that she had not gone. "She had never even been inside the Opera House."[201] She will be, by the end of the book - on the stage itself, where a dramatic reunion will take place.

The Rays now have a hired girl. "Rena had come from a farm to help Mrs. Ray. She was young and good-natured, not like Tib's mother's hired girl, Matilda, who was old and cross."[202] But Rena has something in common with a Gerlach (Muller) hired girl. Her name is suspiciously similar. A girl named Lena Jenden was living with the Gerlachs in 1900, presumably as a hired girl. She was only eighteen, so she doesn't fit Matilda's description; however, it would be typically Lovelacean for the fictional name (Rena) to have come from a real name (Lena).

Rena was based on Abby Cragun. Maud wrote, "*When Abby Cragun was going through high school she lived with my parents, Thomas and Stella Hart, at 333 Center Street, Mankato. She was fondly remembered by my family.*"[203] Abby admitted to being a "hayseed,"[204] but she did graduate from Mankato High School in 1898. We can be sure that the girls read Abby's dime novels, for Maud wrote, "*I started borrowing from our red-cheeked, country-bred hired girl. Her treasures were paper-backed novels, Lady Audley's Secret, and that ilk. Some instinct told me to read them in strict seclusion but, as I have related in Betsy and Tacy Go Downtown, my secret, like Lady Audley's, was discovered.*"[205] Abby was married in 1902 and living in Indian Lake, however, so she was not with the Harts during the era of *Downtown* (1904).

Betsy now shares the little front bedroom with both Julia and Margaret. For "Rena slept in the little back bedroom that had once been Margaret's."[206] Describing the sleeping arrangements in the Hart house on Center, Maud wrote that "*the hired girl had the back room.*"[207]

Another Kelly sibling appears in *Downtown* for the first time: Celia. When Tacy's father discovers *Lady Audley's Secret*, he asks first Mary, then Celia, then Katie, then Tacy to whom the book belongs. "Mary and Celia were typewriter girls now and away from home all day."[208] As already noted, Mary Kelly was probably Rosemary Kenney. Celia Kelly was most likely based on Margaret Kenney. The last we hear of Tacy's grown-up sisters is on page 114 of *Downtown*, when Tacy borrows a piece of sister Mary's good stationery.

Betsy, Tacy, and Tib are on the verge of growing up themselves. With our foreknowledge of *Heaven to Betsy*, we can see all the changes which will be taking place so soon. Maud described one change which did not occur in the series. "*We girls grew up calling our parents 'papa' and 'mamma,' but about the time I was twelve or so, mother gathered us together and asked us to change to 'mother' and 'daddy.' (I suspect that the mother-daddy combination was the rage just then.) Helen was amenable to the change but Kathleen and I disliked it.*"[209] Maud gradually adapted to the change. Kathleen eventually switched to 'mother,' but she called her father 'papa' all her life. Betsy and her sisters use 'mamma' and 'papa' throughout the series.

"'I like Herbert Humphreys,' said Tib. It was just like Tib to like a boy and say so."[210] We understand that Herbert had moved to Deep Valley from St. Paul. Herbert Humphreys "was a handsome boy with thick blond hair, a rosy skin, and lively blue eyes."[211] As already explained, the Andrews family, with sons

Duplicated in several sources

Lincoln Park

"Lincoln Park was a pie-shaped wedge of lawn with a giant elm tree and a fountain on it. Hill Street turned into Broad Street there." (OBH p. 98) This description is still accurate, except that the elm and fountain are now missing.

Coll. of Tom Fox

George Fox

Fictionally, George Fox was known as "Jerry." He is pictured here in the uniform of Shattuck School (Cox Military).

BECHS

Lincoln Park

There was a statue atop the red stone fountain, but we don't hear about it fictionally until *Emily of Deep Valley*: "The statue of a Union soldier surmounted a sparkling fountain." (EDV p. 47)

Duplicated in several sources

St. John's Catholic Church

This church once stood on Broad Street at Hickory. St. John's built a new church in 1961, four blocks south of the one pictured above. Bick Kenney's family belonged to St. John's parish.

Duplicated in several sources

First Baptist Church

Betsy's father was a deacon here. The Harts really attended this church.

BECHS

Tom Hart's Shoe Store
403 S. Front Street

Betsy "loved visiting the store, riding the movable ladders from which he took boxes from the highest shelves, helping herself to the advertising tablets, talking to customers." (DT p. 86)

Helmus (Herbert) and Rupert (Lawrence), were in Mankato by 1900. But it was a few more years before boys were of even peripheral importance to Betsy and Tacy. The Humphreys therefore have made no appearance until now. The newly emerging boy-girl sociability in *Downtown* contributes further evidence that the girls are growing up: "They weren't quarreling. The boys thought it was fun to be talking to the girls. And the girls felt as old as Julia and Katie."[212]

The high school world is beginning to encroach. Jerry, Julia's beau, introduces the first taste of high school slang. He is afraid Mrs. Ray will tell him "to go way back and sit down."[213] Jerry attends Cox Military. He is musical, and he sings the song about "Brown October Ale" on page 12. Jerry was based on the brother of a character with whom we are already familiar (and with whom we also associate both slang and Cox Military!). Jerry's real name was George Fox, which means he was a Slade! In other words, Tom Fox and George Fox were brothers in real life, but to the best of our fictional knowledge, Tom Slade is not related to Jerry! Jerry appears only in *Downtown*, and no last name is provided. Perhaps Maud thought it would add confusion to explain that he was Tom's older brother.

"Tom's brother George was Jerry in Betsy and Tacy Go Downtown. He was the boy who used to come to see my older sister Kathleen (Julia in the books) and walk home from school with her and sing beside our piano. He was the one who used to give Tacy and Tib and Betsy nickels to get us out of the way. He was very good to us little nuisances, and the whole Hart family was fond of him. He was a handsome boy."[214]

Shattuck has no record of George Fox's graduation. The only record of his attendance on file is a letter written to the school in 1937 by Fanny Pitcher, George's aunt. *"I have been asked by a former 'Shad' to send you a letter regarding George Fox, a nephew of mine who attended Shattuck in 1901-02. George Talfourd Fox was there but the one year."*[215] George was, therefore, not at Shattuck the year his fictional self was at Cox Military, 1904-1905. Nor did George attend West Point (as stated on page 79 of *Heaven to Betsy*), though his brothers Tom and Milo did. But significantly, George did attend the military school, and Jerry was based on this real person who inspired his uniform-wearing, nickel-giving self.

Having acquired some loose change from Jerry, Betsy, Tacy, and Tib head downtown, about a mile's walk from their neighborhood. We get our first look at Deep Valley's business district. Like Deep Valley, Mankato was "a thriving county seat"[216] with a population of about 11,000. Maud retains many of its actual street names. Broad Street, Second Street, and Front Street are all described in accurate detail. Broad Street did have the church steeples. The Rays' First Baptist Church is on the east side of Broad between Jackson and Cherry. Tacy's St. John's Catholic Church once stood on the southwest corner of Broad and Hickory. Tib's St. John's Episcopal was on the southeast corner of Broad and Warren. The original First Presbyterian Church building (which we later know through Bonnie and Carney in *Heaven to Betsy*) is on the northwest corner of Broad and Hickory. The Carnegie Library is also on Broad, between Main and Walnut, on the west side.

The train depot was at the foot of Jackson Street, and the Big Mill (the Hubbard Mill) was at 308-328 N. Front. (There was a cooper shop on Van Brunt which blew a loud whistle, but the Big Mill whistle Maud describes was more likely that of the Hubbard Mill.) The Opera House was on Second Street (between Hickory and Walnut). Front Street boasted the stores and the Melborn Hotel (on Front at Main).

The Melborn was actually the Saulpaugh Hotel, built in 1889 by Thomas Saulpaugh and, shortly after, run by his portly son, Clarence. The designer of the Saulpaugh was Minneapolis architect W.H. Dennis. The hotel's ballroom, overlooking the river, was considered the height of luxury around the turn of the century. The four-story hotel was demolished in 1974.

On their trip to Front Street, Betsy, Tacy, and Tib buy a nickel's worth of jaw breakers at Schulte's Grocery Store. There were a number of grocers on Front. Those closest to Maud's father's shoe store (to which the girls always seemed to gravitate) were Draper & Pettersen at 429 S. Front, Hansen & Nelson at 408 S. Front, and Eckhardt's at 221 S. Front.

Designation of the real-life Cook's Bookstore, to which the girls were headed (and to which they gave much business in the high school books), also presents a choice. There were two bookstores

BECHS

Beulah and Friend

"Winona had black hair that hung in long straight locks on either side of a somewhat sallow face. She had gleaming black eyes and very white teeth which she showed almost constantly in a teasing smile." (DT p. 15) The dog is featured prominently in *Winona's Pony Cart.* His real name was Peter.

HarperCollins

Winona Root

We are first introduced to Winona when she appears on a bicycle in *Downtown.*

Coll. of Bonnie Bond

Beulah Hunt

Beulah is at the corner of Clark and Byron, in front of her house.

Coll. of Bonnie Bond

"Winona's House" - 327 Byron circa 1902

Frank Hunt, Beulah's father, stands at the left side of the photo. Beulah's pony cart can be seen at the right.

327 Byron circa 1984

Fire escapes have been added, as the house was divided into apartments. The address was changed to 102 Clark at one point. And Clark Street has been renamed East Pleasant.

on South Front, both within a block of Hart's Shoe Store. Warwick's was at 305 S. Front. Stewart & Holmes was at 321 S. Front. There were two additional bookstores in Mankato, but the significant ones were on Front (as was the fictional Cook's). Perhaps Mr. Cook of the silky toupee was William Warwick, whose house was on Byron, between Tib's and Alice's, but on the other side of the street. (John Stewart and Clark Holmes are also possible Mr. Cooks.)

Coming out of Cook's, the girls find Front Street in an uproar and, in this boisterous setting, come upon Winona Root.

Winona "lived on School Street in a white-painted brick house with a terrace and a beautiful garden."[217] This was Beulah Hunt, who lived at 327 Byron Street. Her non-brick white house is at the corner of Byron and Clark (by 1910, the house had been renumbered as 102 Clark, and in fact, the front door does face Clark {East Pleasant}, the fictional School Street).

Beulah's father was Frank W. Hunt, editor and owner of the *Mankato Free Press* Printing Company on Jackson Street. Maud may have chosen the fictional name "Root" because she associated it with newspapers. Her uncle Steve Hart worked for the Root Newspaper Association of St. Louis, Missouri, until 1910. She later remembered that "*sometimes, if we were lucky, we went to a matinee at the Opera House; on passes, since Beulah's father was editor of the Free Press.*"[218]

On their way to see the horseless carriage, Betsy, Tacy, and Tib run past the office where Mr. Kelly sold sewing machines (514 S. Front), Mr. Ray's shoe store (403 S. Front), then the Melborn, where they turn the corner to go up to the Opera House. Actually, they would have turned right on Walnut, rather than overshooting to Main and backtracking on Second to Walnut. (A map of downtown Mankato is provided in Chapter 8 herein.)

"Sunny Jim worked in the livery stable next door to the Opera House."[219] Phillips' livery stable was nearby, on Walnut at Front. There was also a "horseshoer," Foley's, at 222 S. Second, but Phillips' is most likely the livery stable Maud was remembering, since she uses the name "Phillips' Livery Stable" on page 178 of *Carney's House Party*. Sunny Jim probably worked at Phillips', but he is lost in the murky depths of time and fiction.

Tib's ride in the auto, however, is much closer to the surface. While writing *Downtown*, Maud wrote to Tom Edwards, a Mankato friend and newspaperman. "*I would like to bring in Mr. Bennett ... or Mr. Saulpaugh's automobile.... I feel sure it was about that date (1903-04) that Midge took her famous ride.*"[220] The first automobile in Mankato which Maud remembered "*belonged to a Mr. Bennett. Midge Gerlach was given a ride in it, to the envy of the rest of us. I am quite sure we were in Pleasant Grove School at the time, so it must have been before 1905.*"[221] Maud hoped to verify the correct date of the arrival of an auto in Mankato. Mr. Patterson of the Blue Earth County Historical Society assured Maud, via Mr. Edwards, that Mr. Bennett's was one of the first automobiles in town, in 1903. Maud responded: "*I am not using Mr. Bennett (whom I did not know at all) in the story; but I am using the incident of his giving Midge a ride. And I am glad to know that the date was 1903, for that's the year I'm using.*"[222] Maud obviously changed her mind at some point before completing *Downtown*, for if the girls are twelve, as she says, it is 1904.

Another Mankatoan remembered the appearance of the Bennett auto. C.E. Wise wrote, "*One evening a buggy-like thing without a horse chugged and bumped along. I believe the man guiding it was a Mr. Bennett. It broke up the ball game that night for we all crowded around the 'horseless carriage.' As it rattled along, the watchers commented. Someone said, 'Everybody will have one of those things some day.' That was around 1902.*"[223] There had been an auto in town even earlier, however - a Stanley Steamer, which came to Mankato in 1897.

Clarence Saulpaugh (Melborn Poppy) had an early auto, too (a Reo), and since the main focus of *Downtown* was to be the Opera House, which the Saulpaughs owned, the Poppys were the perfect characters to give Tib her memorable ride.

Mr. and Mrs. Poppy, those models of elegance, the owners of hotel and Opera House, first appear on page 18. Maud originally intended to spell the name "Poppe." Fearing that children would give it an ecclesiastical pronunciation, someone at Thomas Y. Crowell apparently suggested changing the spelling to "Poppy."

Clarence and Roma Saulpaugh, the counterparts of the Poppys, were married in Minneapolis in 1893 and set up housekeeping in

Coll. of J. Allen

The Saulpaughs in their Auto

Clarence Saulpaugh is shown at the wheel of his auto. He was one of the earliest auto drivers in Mankato. Mrs. Saulpaugh is the woman on the right in the back seat. The other woman is her sister.

HarperCollins

The Poppys in their Auto

"With a burst of vapor and a clanking ... the horseless carriage moved. It actually moved. It went ahead without pushing or pulling. It ran right along behind nothing. The crowd sent up a tremendous cheer." (DT p. 23)

BECHS

The Saulpaugh (Melborn) Hotel

This hotel once stood at the corner of Front Street at Main. A Holiday Inn was built in its place.

Coll. of J. Allen

Clarence Saulpaugh

Maud described Melborn Poppy as "three hundred pounds of suave sophistication." (BSH p. 63) Clarence inherited the hotel from his father. He also leased the Opera House.

Coll. of J. Allen

Roma Saulpaugh

"Blonde and radiant, she was said to look like the famous beauty and actress, Lillian Russell ... except that she was stouter, of course." (DT p. 18)

Coll. of Tom Hagan

Saulpaugh Hotel Lobby

The girls "inspected the red leather chairs in the lobby." (CHP p. 148) Two rows of the leather chairs can be seen facing each other in the center of the lobby in the photo above.

BECHS

Saulpaugh Hotel Lobby

"She looked at the grand staircase rising at the end of the lobby." Is that the *Winged Victory* standing in the shadows on the landing? (DT p. 91)

Mankato at the Saulpaugh Hotel. Like Mrs. Poppy, Roma was decidedly Junoesque. Before a photograph could be located, evidence of Mrs. Saulpaugh's size was found only in a dubiously delightful newspaper account: "*Sunday morning while enjoying a walk on North Second Street, Mrs. C.H. Saulpaugh had the misfortune to slip and fall. As she is a large, heavy woman the result was a fracture of a bone in one of her legs. At last accounts she was resting easy but it will be some time before she can be about again.*"[224] Mrs. Saulpaugh probably didn't appreciate the reporter's unnecessary reference to her size (a very slender person could also break a leg from a fall on ice!).

It is perhaps not surprising that the Saulpaughs were such a well-padded couple. The printed menu (from the collection of the Blue Earth County Historical Society) for a Saulpaugh Hotel breakfast from Sunday, February 19, 1899, is an eyeful: "*Clam broth with salted wafers, baked apples, fruit, Shredded Wheat with cream, boiled or broiled salt macherel* [sic], *broiled sirloin steak (plain or with mushrooms), ham, bacon, mutton chops, broiled quail en canape, fried oysters, sausage, baked pork and beans, hot Boston brown bread, eggs as you like, French fried potatoes, baked potatoes, dry and buttered toast, hot rolls, corn muffins, doughnuts, plain bread, rye bread, graham bread, buckwheat and wheat cakes with maple syrup, tea, coffee, chocolate, milk, Ceylon tea.*"[225] One can picture the Saulpaughs sampling it all!

Like Mrs. Poppy, Mrs. Saulpaugh was not only big, but also on the fair-haired side. There is no evidence, however, of any dramatic or singing career before her marriage. Maud must have had some other town lady in mind when she created the theatrical side of Mrs. Poppy's character, and there was, in fact, a decidedly Poppyish woman in Mankato. She was Nettie Snyder, married to Fred Snyder, who managed the hotel for the Saulpaughs.

Mrs. Snyder was remembered by composer Clara Edwards: "*A very remarkable woman came to Mankato, who I feel personally had an important influence on the musical life there, and I am sure many agree with me. She was Nettie Fuller Snyder, the wife of Fred Snyder who ran the Saulpaugh Hotel at that time. She opened a vocal studio in the hotel. She brought with her the glamour that comes with having lived and studied in a foreign city - namely Florence, Italy. She had a very beautiful voice, with good looks and a compelling personality. She knew many of the great artists before the public at that time, having sung with them and to them. She was instrumental in bringing the Minneapolis Orchestra to Mankato on several occasions.*"[226] (Clara Edwards was the composer of "By the Bend of the River" and the aunt of the real-life Phil Brandish.)

Kathleen Hart did indeed go to the Saulpaugh Hotel for singing lessons, as Julia did. Her teacher was Nettie Snyder. Nettie Snyder also ran the Moorish Cafe in the Saulpaugh, so perhaps it was she who joined the Harts at an anniversary dinner there (as Mrs. Poppy did in *Betsy in Spite of Herself*). Mrs. Poppy, we might conclude, is a composite of Roma Saulpaugh and Nettie Snyder.

Betsy had often heard that "when Mr. Poppy built the Opera House, he had two special seats made for Mrs. Poppy and himself. Extra wide, extra deep, and extra comfortable."[227] Clarence Saulpaugh did not actually build the Opera House. It was built in 1872 by beer-baron Bierbauer (whose name Maud gave to a fictional bakery). The theater was called "Harmonia Hall" for ten years - until it burned down. After being rebuilt, the theater was renamed the "Opera House." In 1893 Clarence Saulpaugh took over the lease of the theater, and it was renovated and renamed again - as the "Mankato Theater." Townsfolk seemed to prefer "Opera House," since this is the name many continued to use. The Opera House stood on a section of the street now occupied by the building at 209 S. Second.

Perhaps when Saulpaugh renovated the interior of the Opera House, he had two of its 1,000 seats custom-sized. "Where the dress circle met the parquet, in the very center of the house, were two wide, well-padded seats,"[228] for two wide, well-padded bottoms! This description from *Downtown* is repeated, word for word, on page 179 of *Betsy and Joe*. With the exact repetition of the sentence, we have, for Lovelace, what amounts to historical evidence. Maud wouldn't entrench this image in the lore of Deep Valley unless it were also the lore of Mankato. There was, in fact, an extra-wide seat in the Opera House, but it belonged to 340-pound John C. Wise Sr., who published the *Mankato Review*. Could there have been two sets of such seats? Or was Maud thinking of Wise's seat? Wise died in 1900, so his wide seat coincided with the era of Mr. and Mrs. Poppy. Perhaps it became Mr. Saulpaugh's seat after Wise's death. Since the Opera House was razed in 1931, persons with memories of the wide seats have remained elusive.

Clarence Saulpaugh hired Charles H. Griebel as resident manager of the Opera House. Griebel was the manager Maud knew, for she wrote: "[The name] *Charley Griebel evokes the very feeling produced by the old opera house. His name, I think, was on the bill board and program advertisements.*"[229] Maud was thinking of Griebel when she described Winona greeting a "Mr. Kendall"[230] at the Opera House.

Maud describes the curtain in the Opera House, "on which a gentleman in a sedan chair and beautiful ladies in hoop skirts were transfixed in a gay romantic moment. There was a flower booth behind them."[231] Maud related that "*in the art gallery at the New York Public Library I ran across the painting from which the curtain of the Mankato Opera House was copied. Do you remember the sedan chair and the flower booth?*"[232] Unfortunately, this painting, called "May Festival in Spain," by Luis Alvarez, can no longer been seen at the New York Public Library. It must have been in their art gallery as part of a traveling exhibition or was otherwise on loan there during the 1930s or early 1940s.

Julia's first visit to the Opera House was to see *Robin Hood.*[233] Kathleen's was to see *The Prince of Pilsen.* Like the Rays, Mr. and Mrs. Hart felt that Maud was too young to attend and "*it had never ceased to rankle.*" But she was soon to go to the Opera House herself, quite unexpectedly. "*Dick Carle was coming in The Tenderfoot, a musical show. Mr. and Mrs. Gerlach had seats in the dress circle for an evening performance. They were dressed, as was usual in Mankato, for the theatre in gala attire and were ready to depart. I was at their house with Midge. Our faces must have shown how we were longing to go. At any rate, on a sudden impulse, they took us along. I was dizzy with joy. The Gerlachs had only two seats, but we sat in their laps ... turn and turn about, I hope - for although Midge was light as a fairy, I was a chunky little girl. Our foursome may have looked a little odd to the opera cloaks and full dress suits around us, but Mr. and Mrs. Gerlach weren't the kind to care. In a blissful daze, Midge and I listened to Richard Carle sing his famous song, 'I Lost My Heart on the Alamo.'*"[234]

Coll. of SSW

Opera House

"The Opera House was a large brick structure. It was a fine theatre for a town the size of Deep Valley.... The expectant four stood under the canopy." (DT p. 57)

BECHS

The Big Mill

When the Big Mill whistle blew, Mankatoans knew it was time to go home for supper. The mill, which opened in 1878, was owned by R.D. Hubbard in Maud's time. It was sold to Cargill in 1984.

HarperCollins

The Brand New Carnegie Library

"This small white marble temple was glittering with newness." (DT p. 83)

Carnegie Library/Arts Center

Mankato's Carnegie Library opened its doors in 1904.

Before long, the girls attended *Uncle Tom's Cabin*. "Tom shows," as they were called, were common around the turn of the century. After the performance viewed by Betsy, Tacy, Tib, and Winona, Little Eva and her mother/escort "proceeded up Front Street to the Deep Valley House. This was the place farmers stayed when they came to town."[235] There had been a rustic Mankato House on Front Street which, like the Deep Valley House, was a "low wooden structure." But the Mankato House had been torn down about 1890. The most modest accommodation in Mankato about 1904 was likely to be found at the St. Paul House, 330 N. 4th. Maud and her friends probably did follow a child actress back to her hotel. Maud writes of Little Eva: "The children did not see her again. But none of them was ever to forget her."[236] When Maud's perspective, as omniscient author, overtly postdates the setting of her story (as it does in only a handful of cases), you can strongly suspect that she is writing from specific experience.

As in *Downtown*, Maud and her friends gave plays themselves. Maud wrote many of them. "*We gave The Repentance of Lady Clinton in Midge's back parlor. I repented so hard and to such good effect that I made a little boy in the audience cry. We had to stop the show to soothe him.*"[237]

Another exciting event in Maud's life transpired at about this time - Tom Hart's election to the position of Blue Earth county treasurer in November 1904. Here Mr. Hart and Mr. Ray part company. Mr. Ray continues in the shoe business throughout the series, and his only involvement in politics is his identification of himself as a Republican.

In *Betsy-Tacy*, Maud mentions that the library was on Broad Street.[238] But according to *The History of Blue Earth County* by Thomas Hughes, Mankato's first library was housed in second-floor rooms in the Meagher Building on Front Street. The fine, new Carnegie Library was built on Broad Street a few years later, as per *Downtown*. "*In February 1901, Andrew Carnegie, the great Pittsburg* [sic] *philanthropist, offered $40,000 to build a public library, provided a site was furnished and the city guaranteed $4,000 a year in perpetuity for its maintenance. The conditions were accepted.*"[239]

The Carnegie Library was not "almost" ready to open in November 1904, as stated on page 78 of *Downtown*. It had been open since the year before. The cornerstone had been laid July 2, 1902, with C.N. Andrews, the father of the Humphreys boys, presenting an address. The building opened its doors in June 1903.

Maud remembered that "*The world, before the coming of Library Children's Rooms, was a world for book borrowers. A fascinating dining room cupboard, in the home of my Best Friend across the street, contributed the boys' stories of the lovable Father Finn. Although a Protestant, I read avidly, along with Tacy.*"[240] (The Kellys' Father Finn books are mentioned on page 3 of *Downtown*.) "*Our mother read the popular novels of the day ... When Knighthood was in Flower.*"[241] Mrs. Ray is reading that title on page 77 of *Downtown.*

Mrs. Ray makes a writing desk for Betsy out of Uncle Keith's theatrical trunk. Though this is the first we hear of the trunk, the brown shawl Mrs. Ray brings out to cover it is familiar. We saw it in *Betsy-Tacy* on page 26 and in *Over the Big Hill* on page 36. "*Betsy-Tacy fans want to know whether I really kept my writings in his trunk. That is one of those legends which is both true and untrue. I did sometimes. I also had a bottom drawer of a certain chest.*"[242] And though Betsy clung to the trunk through high school, Maud got a new desk in the fall of 1907 (sophomore year).

After Betsy's mother discovers that the girls have been reading the turn-of-the-century equivalent of Harlequin Romances, she talks with Mr. Ray, and the two devise a plan to send Betsy to the library for books every other Saturday. Mr. and Mrs. Hart came up with exactly the same plan for Maud. They "*conferred together upon my love for reading and my often announced intention of becoming an author, and conceived between them a truly beautiful plan.... The new temple of reading was far away from our hillside home. My father's plan was to let me take out a library card, and then, every other week, go down to the Library and spend the day. I was to go out for lunch ... all by myself ... at a nearby bakery and in the late afternoon bring home a load of books to be returned on the next library visit.*"[243]

Betsy starts out one gray November day, the day of the first snowfall. "*I started these wonderful trips in the winter, I think, for I recall a fire in the fireplace of the Children's Room.... And I recall snow sifting past the windows as I read at one of the low comfortable tables ... after browsing blissfully along the so-accessible shelves.*"[244]

The librarian, Miss Sparrow, "had a cozy little face, with half a dozen tiny moles. Her eyes were black and dancing. Her hair was black too, curly and untidy."[245] Maud remarked that "*the first Mankato librarian, according to the records, was a Minnie McGraw. The librarian of my memory and the Betsy-Tacy books is doubtless a composite of her and the Miss Maud Van Buren who followed,*" Maud wrote.[246] Minnie McGraw was appointed librarian when the library was established in 1894. She held the position through the transition to the new building. On April 3, 1906, Miss McGraw resigned and was succeeded by Miss Maud Van Buren.

"*The fireplace in the children's room used to have hanging above it that painting called The Isle of Delos which I mentioned in Downtown. But it's gone now, and no one knows where it is.*"[247] The pleasant irony of the name of this painting was not lost on Maud. In 1960, she wrote: "*It was on a snowy day that I made the acquaintance of the Mankato Public Library with its children's room and the (for me) prophetic painting of Delos (but, alas, only the island!) above the mantle-piece.*"[248]

"*I was guided to Lamb's Tales from Shakespeare and recall ... Tanglewood Tales, Gulliver's Travels.*"[249] These are among the titles which Miss Sparrow recommends to Betsy on page 85.

While working on *Downtown*, Maud wrote to the librarian in Mankato to request a photo of the Carnegie Library. "*In a letter received recently from Mrs. Lovelace by Mrs. C.C. Bordwell, city librarian, the former requested a picture of the library here and stated her intention of using it in her next book.*"[250] This not only establishes additional evidence of Maud's efforts to "real-ize" her work, it also explains how it is that the illustrations look so much like the real Mankato buildings. Maud simply kept her illustrators supplied with photos of the appropriate homes and public buildings. Among her research papers is a note Maud wrote to remind herself to look over her old photos with a magnifying glass![251]

After her morning in the library, Betsy goes to Bierbauer's Bakery for a bologna sandwich, milk, and ice cream. The actual location of this bakery presents another subject for speculation. The Bierbauers ran a brewery in Mankato, but there was no bakery or eatery connected with it. (An odd aside: Oscar Bierbauer was something of an unsavory character. In 1907, the

Mankato Free Press reported that Mr. Bierbauer had disappeared from town "somewhat mysteriously."[252] And when Maud was a senior in high school, Oscar Bierbauer was arrested by the sheriff for forgery![253])

Maud might have been picturing Heinze's when she sent Betsy out for lunch on page 86. Known as "Heinze's Bakery and Confectionery," it wasn't just an ice cream parlor, as one might gather from the description in *Betsy-Tacy and Tib*. Heinze's also had a small restaurant at the back which served sandwiches and hot meals. That Betsy had ice cream at the "bakery" is perhaps significant in light of the fact that Heinze's was one of the few manufacturers of ice cream in town. However, there is another possible location: Musser's. Maud wrote that after excursions downtown, the girls "*always visited Heinze's Ice Cream parlor, or Musser's*."[254] Musser's, at 324 S. Second, was about two blocks closer to the library than Heinze's. If Maud had meant Heinze's, she would have used the fictional Heinz's (with which her reader was already familiar), rather than introducing a new name. Bierbauer's, therefore, was probably Musser's.

Another memorable November event, in addition to Betsy's historic first trip to the library, was her first bobsledding party. Jerry "and his friend Pin were taking Julia and Katie out coasting the night after Thanksgiving night."[255] Betsy, Tacy, and Tib teased to be allowed to come, and permission was reluctantly granted. This was a dangerous recreation.

Bobsledding took place down the Big Hill. Tom Edwards, a native of the area, a few years older than Maud, recalled, "*How we skied and slid down the hill on Lewis Street. Dangerous as it was crossing Byron Street, this made it all the more inviting.*"[256] (As a boy, Carney's real-life father broke his leg sledding down the Byron Street hill.)

Pin was the expert on bobsleds. He was adept at other winter sports, too. In *Heaven to Betsy*, we learn that Pin was a skillful skater. "Tall and thin, Pin looked like a dragon fly as one long leg after another swung easily through the air."[257] There was, in fact, a boy in Mankato High School whose nickname was "Pin." He was in the class of 1909, with Carney. Pin's full name was C. Ernest Jones. He <u>was</u> very tall and thin!

After their spill, the bobsledding group is entertained at the Rays' with buttered popcorn, singing at the piano, and dancing to Mrs. Ray's tunes. This is an introduction to the kind of gatherings which become commonplace in the high school books. In February 1904, the *Mankato Free Press* reported that twelve-year-old "*Miss Maud Heart* [sic] *entertained a number of her young friends at a five o'clock dinner last evening. Four courses were served. The evening was spent in playing cards and dancing.*"[258]

Betsy stays home from school to rest her ankle following the bobsled accident. Maud once said that the quiet of the apartment after her marriage was good for her writing. This effect is also articulated in *Betsy and Joe*: "She wanted to be a writer, and she had already discovered that poems and stories came most readily from the deep well of solitude."[259] It is therefore characteristic that the quiet, snowbound solitude of 333 inspired young Betsy to write "Flossie's Accident."

Betsy has been telling stories since the first book, but this is the first time she writes one down. Tib later prints it out on a piece of pink stationery, and they send it to the *Ladies' Home Journal.* Though twelve-year-old Maud Hart may not have written "Flossie's Accident," one of her stories was really printed carefully on pink paper and submitted to a magazine. The first of Maud's short stories, "*written, it is said, on a brilliant pink paper, was never heard from.*"[260]

In *Heaven to Betsy,* Mrs. Ray recalls that Betsy "has been writing since she could hold a pencil. I remember her when she was five years old asking me how to spell 'going down the street.'"[261] Maud later said that "*I started writing stories as soon as I could hold a pencil. My mother said I used to follow her around with that pencil, before I started to go to school, asking her, 'How do you spell going down the street?'*"[262]

Maud's ambition was, like Betsy's, a lifelong blessing. "*I cannot remember back to a year in which I did not consider myself to be a Writer, and the younger I was the bigger that capital 'W.' Back in Mankato, I wrote stories in notebooks and illustrated them with pictures cut from magazines. When I was ten my father, I hope at not too great expense, had printed a booklet of my earliest rhymes.*"[263]

Mr. and Mrs. Ray do not agree on the source of Betsy's talent for writing. Mr. Ray is sure it was inherited from her mother's side. "I never write anything but checks myself," he says. Mrs. Ray protests, "Bob! You wrote the most wonderful letters to me before we were married. I still have them, a big bundle of them. Every time I clean house I read them over and cry."[264] Stella Hart did indeed have a bundle of letters from Tom. She must have kept them upstairs and near a crack in the floor or wall, for several of them slipped down into a wall of the house, where they remained in the darkness for some eighty years. The owners of the house discovered them while doing renovation work. One of the letters is dated April 16, 1885, and reads: "*Dear Friend Stella, Why not write to you this morning? It is raining. Just the kind of day that I always am thinking about you the most. Why is that I wonder. Perhaps it is because it always rains when you and I are together. If it don't* [sic] *rain again till you and I are together I am afraid we will have some dry weather! Your last letter was splendid. I am so sorry that I am not capable of writing you a good one in return. But perhaps you can imagine it is good!*" The letter is signed, "*Lovingly, Tom.*"[265]

As an aspiring writer, young Maud was very sensitive to dramatic scenes - and Christmas at the Hart house afforded many. Tom and Stella Hart obviously knew how to "do" holidays. "*We had so many festivals, anniversaries, and traditions. The year was strung with them like lights on a Christmas tree.*"[266]

Downtown is the first book which features a description of Ray Christmas festivities, but Maud brings us up to date on page 117 with the information that Betsy, Tacy, and Tib have been making their annual Christmas shopping trip "for years." She even tells us what ornaments Betsy selected in the previous years, 1902 and 1903, which do not fall into the span of a Betsy-Tacy book.

The reader's sensation that the books represent genuine experience is increased by the knowledge that Betsy and her friends have not only an interesting present but an interesting past, a history, some of which the reader already knows, and some of which she has yet to learn. If Betsy, Tacy, and Tib can refer to a past that wasn't in a previous book, it must really have happened. This may not be entirely logical, but its effect on the reader is nevertheless potent. Another such case is the pact that Betsy, Tacy, and Tib made to always believe in Santa Claus. They tell Winona about it on page 121. This is the first we hear of it. Such references give one a faint sense of regret, as though we've been somehow left out!

Front Street at Christmas time features "displays of tempting merchandise in all the store windows."[267] One year something in particular caught Maud's eye and fancy. *"I remember one Christmas season when I was a little girl, I conceived a mad longing for a chatelaine in Martin and Hoerr's show window. A silver pencil and a pad of paper were attached to a chain which would swing, presumably from one's belt. I thought it would be just the proper equipment for a little girl who wished to be an author and plastered my nose against the window admiring it every time I went downtown. Mary Wood, probably a high school girl then, bought it and put it in my Christmas stocking."*[268] Mary, not mentioned in the Betsy-Tacy books herself, was the older sister of Eleanor Wood, the character Dorothy.

Christmas shopping starts at Cook's, where Betsy chooses *Little Men*; "I got *Little Women* last year."[269] In fact, Maud did receive *Little Women*, but it was for the Christmas when she was ten, rather than eleven. *"The volume had been worn to tatters (it still survives tied up with red ribbons).... I stopped reading it finally, perhaps when I gave up hope that sometime, by some miracle, Jo would relent and marry Laurie."*[270]

Shopping continues next door to Cook's, at the harness and saddle maker's. The harness shops on Front were Schmidt Saddlery at 226 S. Front (where it had stood since 1861) and Walker's at 521 S. Front. (It is of passing interest that both Front Street bookstores were in the 300 block, so neither could have been "next door" to the harness shop.) Schmidt's had a wooden horse, like the one Tib rode on page 122 of *Downtown*. Schmidt's was a Mankato institution, the harness and saddle maker's shop - so very likely the one Maud was remembering. (Four generations of Schmidts succeeded to the business before the stores were closed in 1986.) On the other hand, Walker's had a wooden horse too, and perhaps tellingly, Maud used the name "Walker's Harness Shop" on page 207 of her novel *Gentlemen from England*. It may be that the fictional harness maker's shop was a combination of Schmidt's and Walker's.

The girls' next stop is the hardware store to try out the

horseless carriage. Lulsdorff's hardware store at 115 S. Front was owned by the father of a family friend, Lora (Dodie) Lulsdorff. But the hardware store which first sold autos was J.A. Lewis & Son at 501 S. Front. They sold Reos.

Betsy, Tacy, Tib, and Winona sniff perfume at a drugstore. This was probably either Laack's Drug Store at 325 S. Front or Lamm's at 307 S. Front. Jewelers in this same block were Crandall's at 302 S. Front and Palmer Brothers at 311 S. Front.

The final stop, the toy shop, is less easy to identify. There were no toy shops *per se* in Mankato at this time. The girls may have looked at toys and bought ornaments at a number of general merchandise stores, such as Brett's at 327 S. Front or Kruse's at 417 S. Front.

This year Betsy bought a large red ball.[271] We know then that the red ball was from 1904, the harp (bought "last year") from 1903, and the angel (from the "year before") from 1902.[272] But on page 155 of *Heaven to Betsy*, "Betsy put on the golden harp from this [1906] year's shopping expedition with Tacy. She hung the red ball she had bought last year [1905], the angel from the year before [1904]." There appear to be several inconsistencies in this account. In the first place, the red ball could not have been from "last year," unless she bought red balls two years in a row. We don't know whether Betsy bought a red ball in 1904 (as per *Downtown*) or an angel (as per *Heaven to Betsy*). And it seems unlikely that Betsy would have chosen a harp in both 1904 and 1906. In 1909, she buys a silver ball, according to *Betsy and Joe*. ...That's the last we hear of ornament purchases. If I have to explain why it is amusing to analyze such trivia, you shouldn't be reading this book.

After they complete their Christmas shopping, the four girls go to Betsy's father's shoe store, since it was closest to Heinz's. Between 1900 and 1902, Tom Hart moved his store from 306 S. Front to 403 S. Front. Heinze's was right next door, at 405 S. Front. Maud reminisced about trips downtown with friends. "[We] *usually called on one of our fathers for a ride home behind the family horse*."[273] And, of course, "you can't call on four fathers without being invited out to Heinz's restaurant for ice cream."[274]

Coll. of Gail Palmer

Schmidt's Saddlery

The horse Tib used to sit on at the harness and saddle maker's is standing just outside the door of the shop.

Coll. of Gail Palmer

Brett's Department Store

This is probably the store Maud had in mind when she described the Lion Department Store - although the lion actually stood before a different store.

Coll. of Colleen Smith

Richards Department Store

A decorative golden lion once stood in front of this store.

On Christmas morning, the Ray girls unpack their stockings down to the "dollar from Grandpa Ray that [was] always found at the bottom."[275] Maud wrote to a cousin: "*When my sisters and I were very tiny there used to be a silver dollar from him (Grandpa Hart) in the toe of each Christmas stocking.*"[276] Grandpa James A. Hart visited Maud's family in Mankato as late as the summer of 1908. He passed away in Canada in October 1913 at the age of eighty-one.

"Uncle Keith was Mrs. Ray's brother, and no one knew where he was. Betsy had never seen him, but she had heard about him all her life. He had run away to go on the stage when he was only seventeen. Like his sister, he was redheaded, spirited, and gay, and he had quarreled with their stepfather, a grim man who had not approved of the boy's lightheartedness. He had gone with a *Pinafore* company and had never come back."[277]

Mrs. Ray tells Betsy that Uncle Keith "doesn't know that our stepfather has gone out to California with mother."[278] (We aren't given the stepfather's fictional name, "Newton," until page 124 of *Heaven to Betsy*.) Chauncey Austin (Grandpa Newton) had in fact moved his extended family to California in 1899.

Uncle Keith was based on Frank Palmer, Maud's uncle, her mother's only brother. Frank had an earlier fictional self in Alex from *The Black Angels*, Maud's first novel. "*The plot idea had sprung from the family legend of Uncle Frank, who did not get on well with his stepfather, running away from home with an opera troupe and marrying an actress as old as his mother. The character I call Alex was based on Uncle Frank, and mother's memories of his looks and temperament as a boy were helpful to me, as were the yarns he himself had told me in California about his barn-storming days.*"[279]

The singing troupe Maud called the "Angels" was based on the Andrews Opera Company. "*Uncle Frank did, actually, sing with this company for a time.*"[280] "The Andrews Family Swiss Bell Ringers," as they were first called, began performing in 1874. After a performance at the Mankato Opera House in 1882, their bells were lost in the fire which destroyed the building. Their luck changed with the arrival of a backer, Johnnie Colston (represented fictionally as the man in the coon coat in *The Black Angels*), and they became the Andrews Opera Company. Frank Palmer was most likely involved with the troupe in the 1880s.

MHL Archive

Frank Palmer
and Stella Palmer Hart

Uncle Frank "was tall and thin with a pompadour of red wavy hair. ... He had the gayest smile I ever saw." (DT p. 70) This photo was taken in 1915.

MHL Archive

Libby Palmer

Like Alex in *The Black Angels*, Frank married an actress old enough to be his mother. "Aunt Libby" came to visit at the Harts' Center Street home every year.

Frank probably patched up the feud with his stepfather by 1899, for he moved to California that year with all the Austins. But Frank was involved in another family quarrel - and this one was with Tom Hart. In the early 1890s, one of Tom's pretty sisters was living at 333 Center. Frank fell madly in love with her, and he took umbrage when Tom pointed out that he was already married. According to Maud, the quarrel was "*explosive, for Tom was truculent where his womenfolk were concerned and Frank disappeared again. I believe my father always felt a wrench in his heart about that quarrel, although it was basic in his philosophy not to brood over any situation in which he had done his best. He had promised his mother to look after his young sisters... But quarrels were rare with him; he was a man of peace.*"[281] Frank and his first wife, Libby, were eventually divorced. Aunt Libby visited every summer and was loved by the family. She brought old opera scores from her singing career for Kathleen. One of the pieces was called the "Cat Duett" (sic). Maud and Bick would make good use of it!

"Betsy, Tacy, and Tib made many trips downtown that winter but none equaled or even approached in excitement the one they made on Saturday to act in *Rip Van Winkle*."[282] Two of the most powerful moments in the Betsy-Tacy books are the discovery of Uncle Keith in *Rip Van Winkle* and the appearance of Joe's ad in the Agony Column (in *Betsy and the Great World*). And both were apparently pure fiction. Uncle Frank actually did run away from home. And he was very likely to have acted on the stage of the Mankato Opera House with the Andrews Opera Company. (If this occurred, however, it would have been before Maud was born - she didn't meet Uncle Frank until she was grown up.) Though Uncle Frank was not on the playbill, Maud and her friends did see *Rip Van Winkle* at the Opera House. Maud created a vivid, powerful fictional scene from a few bright paint pots in her memory.

A prophesy appears on the last page of *Downtown*. "Some day in her maple or on Uncle Keith's trunk, she would write something good."[283] She sure did.

[196] MHL to E. Deike, 8-25-66.
[197] *Downtown,* p. 1.
[198] *Mankato Free Press,* 4-10-52.
[199] *Downtown,* p. 117.
[200] *Over the Big Hill,* p. 79.
[201] *Downtown,* p. 10.
[202] Ibid., p. 4.
[203] MHL to BECHS.
[204] A.B. Cragun, "Spanish American War," unpublished memoir.
[205] Lovelace, "A Child's Reading."
[206] *Downtown,* p. 11.
[207] MHL to B. Gardner, 7-14-75.
[208] *Downtown,* p. 39.
[209] LWW, p. Ia.
[210] *Downtown,* p. 6.
[211] Ibid., p. 58.
[212] Ibid., p. 58.
[213] Ibid., p. 106.
[214] MHL to J. Ellen, 9-10-67.
[215] F. Pitcher to Shattuck School, 7-27-37.
[216] *Downtown,* p. 57.
[217] Ibid., p. 15.
[218] *Mankato Free Press,* 4-10-52.
[219] *Downtown,* p. 19.
[220] MHL to T. Edwards, 7-25-42.
[221] MHL to T. Edwards, 7-20-42.
[222] MHL to T. Edwards, 9-15-42.
[223] *Mankato Free Press*, 9-10-52.
[224] *Mankato Ledger*, 2-3-03.
[225] *Companion* editor, Laura Vadaj, adds, "*What? No kielbasi*??!!"
[226] *Mankato Free Press*, 8-9-52.
[227] *Downtown,* p. 18.
[228] Ibid., p. 60.
[229] MHL to T. Edwards, 7-25-42.
[230] *Downtown,* p. 59.
[231] Ibid., p. 61.
[232] MHL to T. Edwards, 10-13-42.
[233] *Downtown*, p. 9.
[234] LWW, p. 26.

[235] *Downtown,* p. 68.

[236] Ibid., p. 68.

[237] LWW, p. 26.

[238] *Betsy-Tacy,* p. 87.

[239] Thomas Hughes, *The History of Blue Earth County* (Chicago: Midwest Publishing Co., 1909), pp. 217-218.

[240] Lovelace, "A Child's Reading."

[241] Ibid.

[242] LWW, n.p.

[243] Lovelace, "A Child's Reading."

[244] Ibid.

[245] *Downtown,* p. 84.

[246] Lovelace, "A Child's Reading."

[247] MHL to L. Demp, 7-23-58.

[248] Lovelace, *Library Views and Reviews*, Academy of the Holy Angels, February 1960.

[249] Lovelace, "A Child's Reading."

[250] *Mankato Free Press*, 1-28-43.

[251] CA C.V. file.

[252] *Mankato Free Press,* 11-25-07.

[253] *Mankato Free Press*, 11-17-09.

[254] *Mankato Free Press,* 4-10-52.

[255] *Downtown,* p. 103.

[256] *Mankato Free Press*, 9-4-41.

[257] *Heaven to Betsy,* p. 189.

[258] *Mankato Free Press*, 2-18-04.

[259] *Betsy and Joe,* p. 4.

[260] From *The Black Angels*, Author Bio.

[261] *Heaven to Betsy,* p. 247.

[262] Lovelace Interview, University of Michigan.

[263] Richards, *Minnesota Writers*, p. 209.

[264] *Downtown,* p. 77.

[265] From a private collection.

[266] LWW, p. 7b.

[267] *Downtown,* p. 120.

[268] *Mankato Free Press,* 4-10-52.

[269] *Downtown,* p. 121.

[270] *Mankato Free Press,* December, 1953.

[271] *Downtown,* p. 127.

[272] Ibid., p. 129.

[273] *Mankato Free Press,* 4-10-52.

[274] *Downtown,* p. 126.

[275] Ibid., p. 134.

[276] MHL to R. Lee, 8-1-63.

[277] *Downtown,* p. 47.

[278] Ibid., p. 69.

[279] MHL to M. Freeman, 5-19-64.

[280] Ibid.

[281] LWW, p. 16.

[282] *Downtown,* p. 153.

[283] Ibid., p. 180.

CHAPTER SIX
On *Heaven to Betsy*
July 1906 to June 1907

Betsy has changed! And the difference between the Betsy of *Downtown* and the Betsy of *Heaven to Betsy* is made tangible by a change in illustrators, from Lois Lenski to Vera Neville. Betsy is pictured differently, and she is different, with long skirts, curled hair, and a new interest in boys. Betsy is only a year and a half older, but she has entered a new world.

Betsy's world is also about to change geographically, since the Rays are moving from their little yellow cottage on Hill Street to a wind-swept corner on High Street. The seeds were sown in *Downtown* for the transition to High Street and high school: "The house was getting crowded," Mr. Ray says.[284] Mrs. Ray tells Betsy that they can't afford a desk "yet."[285] A change is in store. In 1904, Tom Hart had been elected Blue Earth county treasurer, so by 1906 they could afford the new house ... and a new desk. (His position paid $4000 a year. Maud's allowance was $6 per month.)

Maud recalled: "*My father's shoe store had become Wood and Sterling's and he had become County Treasurer. We moved up to Fifth Street in order to be nearer the Court House and the high school which Kathleen and I attended.*"[286] The shoe store had first become "Wood and Baker" when Lea Wood (the real-life brother of the character Dorothy) and Warner Baker purchased it from Tom Hart in 1904. In 1911, Wallace Sterling bought out Baker, and the store became "Wood and Sterling," by which name it was known until closing in 1954. Mr. Hart's election to the position of county treasurer and the sale of the store are not mentioned in the Betsy-Tacy books.

Even by the time the girls are twelve, in *Downtown*, Hill Street seemed to belong more to the younger children than to Betsy, Tacy, and Tib. "She thought of herself and Tacy and Tib going into their 'teens. She even thought of Tom and Herbert and of how, by and by, they would be carrying her books and Tacy's and Tib's up the hill from high school."[287] In fact, they would be going up to the high school building the very next year. Pleasant Grove School only accommodated children up through grade seven. (In *Over the Big Hill,* we read that the seventh-grade room was the school's largest.) Eighth-graders from all grade schools met together for classes in the high school building every day. Since the eighth-graders were taught and administered separately from

BECHS

General Store in Butternut

Maud may have passed through Butternut (fictionally known as Butternut Center) on her way home from a farm visit. She may even have seen a handsome young clerk at the general store there - but it wasn't Delos Lovelace (who inspired the character Joe Willard). Delos lived in Michigan during his high school years.

Duplicated in several sources

Union Depot, Mankato

In *Betsy Was a Junior,* the Rays have coffee at the depot because Mrs. Ray won't stir until she hears Julia's Epsilon Iota story, and Mr. Ray wants to rest his feet. The Chicago, St. Paul, Minneapolis, and Omaha Railway passenger depot in Mankato was called "Union Depot" and stands at the foot of Main Street. There **was** a coffee shop at the depot in 1907, run by the Shaver News Company.

Newspaper File

Tom Hart

Maud's father used this photo in his campaign when he ran for Blue Earth County Treasurer. He held the office for three terms.

1895 Atlas

Blue Earth County Court House

The Court House was only two blocks from the Hart family's new home on Fifth Street.

Coll. of SSW

Bird's Eye View

The County Court House is at the right edge of the photo. The high school Maud attended is at the left side. The spire of the Presbyterian church can be seen behind and to the left of the Court House.

the high school students, Betsy's excitement on the first day of high school was genuine - there was a big difference (new teachers, new classrooms, "high school" status).

As much as Betsy has changed, she is certainly not yet "grown up." Maud handles the subject of adolescence in *Heaven to Betsy* with gentle humor: "Julia, Betsy often heard, had never had an awkward age. Betsy never heard this said about herself and suspected strongly that she was in the midst of one."[288]

Over the course of the four high school books, Betsy matures gradually - which her evolving reactions to heartache illustrate. In *Heaven to Betsy*, she retreats to her bed when Bonnie steals Tony. In *Betsy in Spite of Herself*, she faces the break-up with Phil Brandish more doughtily, for "the powerful arm of pride stretched out to steady Betsy."[289] By *Betsy and Joe*, she faces a painful breach with Joe bravely for the sake of her family: "All the careful planning in the world, the nicest presents, wreaths in the windows, and candy canes in the doorways would not make Christmas Eve a happy time in any house unless the people in that house were happy. If Betsy's eyes were red no forced gaiety would make the hearts of the others light."[290] Betsy's motivation has evolved from self-pity, to pride, to consideration for others.

Maud's reader is growing up, too - and Maud keeps pace. Not only does the subject matter of the high school books become more sophisticated, but the vocabulary is increasingly recondite. Maud deliberately inserts words for her reader to look up in the dictionary. (Of course, most of us kids continued to reread the books for years before we finally looked up "physiognomy" {page 3} and "acumen" {page 67}, but we do eventually learn what they mean and always have a good feeling when we see them elsewhere, for Betsy's sake!) There are other elements in the series which are similarly over the heads of most young readers - such as the unflagged reference to a Gilbert and Sullivan lyric in *Betsy Was a Junior*: "We'll just have to find more flowers in the spring. That's when they bloom, tra la."[291] (Those flowers that bloom in the spring {tra la}, come from *The Mikado*.)

Like Betsy, Tacy too has changed. Now grown tall, "her ringlets were gone, and thick auburn braids were bound about her head."[292] Unlike Betsy, however, Tacy is uninterested in boys, and she makes an unknowingly ironic remark on page 74: "Don't worry about getting a boy for me, Betsy." Betsy certainly doesn't have to worry about it after Harry Kerr comes along in *Betsy and Joe*!

So much a part of Deep Valley does the reader feel, that she almost resents having been kept in the dark during this period of change between January 1905 and July 1906 (the lapse between *Downtown* and *Heaven to Betsy*)! One important event we missed, never mentioned in the series, was a Hart family trip to Canada.

A great loss has also occurred during the gap: Tib is gone. Somehow it seems less painful to hear about her removal after the fact. We are consoled by the fat letters flying back and forth between Deep Valley and Milwaukee. Tib moved in eighth grade (1905), we learn on page 5 of *Betsy Was a Junior*. Correspondingly, Midge's family disappeared from the Mankato city directory in 1905, and in 1906 they appeared in the Milwaukee city directory.

Heaven to Betsy begins with a homesickness-plagued visit to the Taggarts' farm. We are told on page 1 that Mrs. Taggart is baking, because it is a Wednesday - baking day. The postmark on the letter from Tacy which Betsy receives there is July 25, 1906. July 25, 1906, <u>was</u> a Wednesday. Apparently the mail was either delivered very quickly (if it was postmarked and delivered on the same day) - or it took a whole week (if the Wednesday Betsy received it was August 1st). One of the grandiloquent names Tacy lavishes on the envelope is "Rosemond." This was Maud's unofficial middle name. Legally she had no middle name, but in her early years, she was called "Maud Rosemond" (after her grandmother, Arosamond Hart). When she was ten, Maud's father had a booklet of her poems printed, and her mother convinced him to print "Maud Palmer Hart" on the cover. Rosemond was never used again.

The name "Butternut Center" was probably based on Butternut Valley, also called simply "Butternut." (The name was suggested by an early settler, Colonel Shaw, because in his hometown in New York "*butternuts were thick.*"[293] But Butternut has no butternut trees!) This village is twenty miles west of Mankato. Maud doesn't mention crossing the river when Mr. Taggart drives Betsy out to the farm - rather, they climb Pigeon Hill, which makes it sound as though Butternut Center is east of Deep Valley. Maud does mention crossing the river when Betsy comes home from the Beidwinkles' farm in *Betsy and Joe*. Butternut Valley had a church, a creamery, and a station for the Chicago, St. Paul, Minneapolis, and Omaha Railway. It also had a store - the Lake Shore Mercantile Company, run by the Laingen family.

If Maud had a flirtation with someone at the general store in Butternut, we may never know. She certainly didn't meet Joe Willard there. Joe Willard was Delos Wheeler Lovelace, though he neither worked in Butternut Valley nor attended Mankato High School. As Maud said, "*Delos came into my life much later than Joe Willard came into Betsy's, and yet he is Joe Willard to the life.*"[294]

Delos attended high school in Detroit. He was two years Maud's junior and would have been three classes behind in school. Maud and Delos didn't meet until three years after her trip to Europe, but the only difference between Joe and Delos is time and place. Maud once said, "*I think that as far as Joe's personality goes, I did a wonderful job.*"[295]

"She was struck by the way he walked, with a slight challenging swing. He had very light hair brushed back in a pompadour, blue eyes under thick light brows and healthy red lips with the lower one pushed out as though seeming to dare the world to knock the chip off his shoulder."[296] Before beginning work on the high school books, Maud first asked Delos to give her "*a description of his boyhood and then gave it to Joe*."[297] This explains the accuracy of the tidbit on page 179 of *Betsy Was a Junior*. Joe tells Betsy that he was born in Brainerd (where Delos was born in December 1894).

Betsy returns home from the Taggarts' farm to find that her family has purchased a new house. The Rays' move to High Street would have been a good literary device, even had it not been historically accurate, since the new house serves as an effective backdrop for the "new" high school aged Betsy. At first the reader feels as mournful as Betsy about the move, but we get used to it (and grow to love it) just as she does.

The dramatic manner in which Betsy is introduced to the new house would also have been a good literary device ... but it too was based closely on reality. While visiting with "*some farmer friends of my father's, I received a phone call from Kathleen telling me to come home because the family had a surprise for me. When I reached 333*

Center Street (of course, I took the hack), I ran into a mystery indeed. A folded handkerchief was laid across my eyes and tied tightly in back. I was led into the surrey and dad, mother, Kathleen, Helen, and Bick all crowded in. We drove up hill and down dale, and when we landed at last, I was led up steps and a door was opened and there was smell of new paint. My blindfold was taken off and I discovered myself in the hall ('Music Room' Kathleen called it) of a spanking brand new house. Daddy had bought it while I was gone."[298]

The fictional address of the new house is given only once, in *Betsy in Spite of Herself*: 400 High Street.[299] The actual address was 428 South Fifth Street. 428 stood at the corner of Fifth and Cherry until August 17, 1966, when it was demolished to make way for a parking lot.

We readers become far better acquainted with the High Street house than we had been with the Hill Street cottage. The layout is described painstakingly: inside the front door was the small hall which Julia had christened "the music room." The staircase went up at the right (along the north wall). To the left, through an archway, was the parlor with the bay window, which later boasted the brass bowl. The room behind it, to the west, was the dining room, where, Maud explains, "There was a fireplace in one corner." (The fireplace was, in fact, literally in the corner.) From here, "they pushed through a swinging door into a pantry, into a kitchen, empty and smelling of newness. Returning by a small door to the music room they climbed the golden oak stairs. There were two bedrooms at the front. Margaret rushed into the right-hand room."[300] This was Mr. and Mrs. Ray's. Julia's was the left-hand room with a window seat. The room at the head of the stairs was Betsy's. Down the hall was the bathroom and Margaret's room, "a small room at the end of the hall."[301] Helen Benham Day, who herself grew up in this house and provided the information for the floor plans here, was surprised that the tiny room at the end of the hall had ever been used as a bedroom. And in fact, Maud and Helen shared a room.[302]

Helen Day has an interesting association with the Betsy-Tacy books. Her mother was Louise Oleson, Maud's Sunday school teacher and the real-life sister of the character Irma Biscay (Mildred Oleson). Helen's father was Dr. Benham, whose first wife

Coll. of Helen Day

428 S. Fifth Street
The "High Street" House

Betsy's family moved from the yellow cottage on Hill Street to the lofty corner of High Street and Plum. The Harts' new house was on the lofty corner of Fifth Street and Cherry. Mr. Hart's vine looks very luxuriant on the porch of 428 in this photo.

BECHS

State Normal School
The "German Catholic College"

Across the street from the Harts' new home was the State Normal, as Gothic as Betsy's German Catholic College. The building pictured here burned to the ground in 1922. It was replaced with "Old Main," built in 1924.

MHL Archive

The Music Room

The Harts' piano was placed in this entry hall, which Maud's sister grandly called the "Music Room." Maud is at the foot of the stairs. The photos on this page were taken about 1906.

MHL Archive

Maud and Helen Hart

The photograph in the square frame on the wall above Maud's head is the campaign photo of Tom Hart which appears on page 119.

MHL Archive

Tom and Stella Hart

"It's wonderful how much in love papa and mamma are," Julia remarks. (HTB p. 125)

Coll. of Minnesota Valley Regional Library

Helen and Anna

The Harts really had a hired girl named Anna - but only for a short time.

MHL Archive

428 South Fifth

This photograph was taken in 1940. The house was no longer painted green, but Tom Hart's vine was still flourishing.

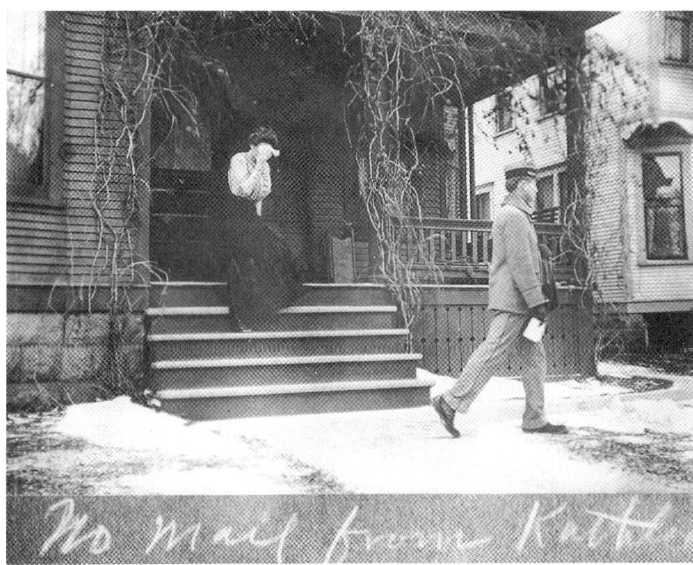

MHL Archive

428 South Fifth

In 1909, the Harts pasted a series of photos of the family and home into a book, as a Christmas gift for homesick Kathleen in Berlin. This photo shows Stella Hart weeping as the mailman walks away. The inscription reads "No mail from Kathleen."

MHL Archive

Interior of 428 South Fifth - Music Room

Maud, now a senior in high school, is descending the stairs. Helen is no doubt playing "Little Birdie is Dead," as Margaret did in *Betsy and Joe*. The inscription reads, "Helen in Kathleen's footsteps."

MHL Archive

Interior of 428 South Fifth - Parlor

Grandma Austin, Stella, Tom, and Helen are enjoying the parlor on a Sunday afternoon. The brass bowl Mr. Ray didn't (sic) buy for Mrs. Ray stands on a table in the foreground. Helen is holding General Baker, the cat, on her lap.

MHL Archive

Interior of 428 South Fifth - Music Room

Mr. Hart is carrying up a breakfast tray for his wife - just as Mr. Ray did for Mrs. Ray. The family coffee pot (always put on in a crisis) is on the tray.

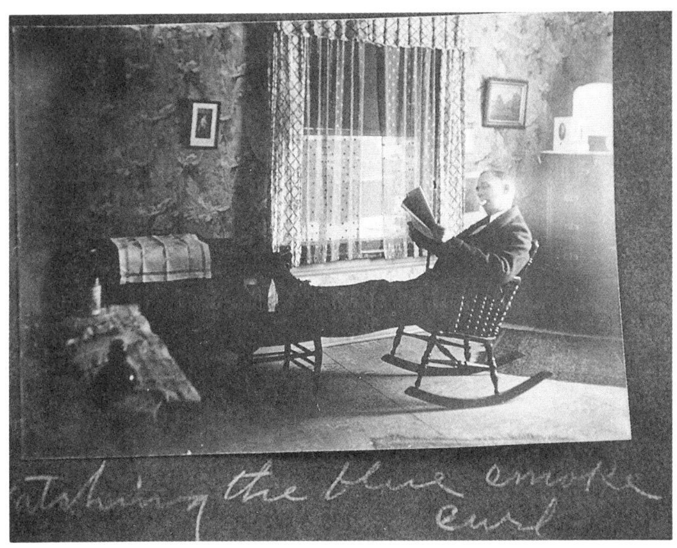

MHL Archive

Interior of 428 South Fifth - Master Bedroom

Mr. Hart is enjoying his paper in the quiet of his bedroom (to which Mr. Ray retreated from the noise of his daughters' teen-age guests). According to the inscription, he is "watching the blue smoke curl."

MHL Archive

Interior of 428 S. Fifth - Master Bedroom

Mrs. Hart is sitting at her dressing table, much like Mrs. Ray on page 55 of *Betsy in Spite of Herself*. Grandma Austin is at the door. Note the framed "Don't Worry" motto on the wall.

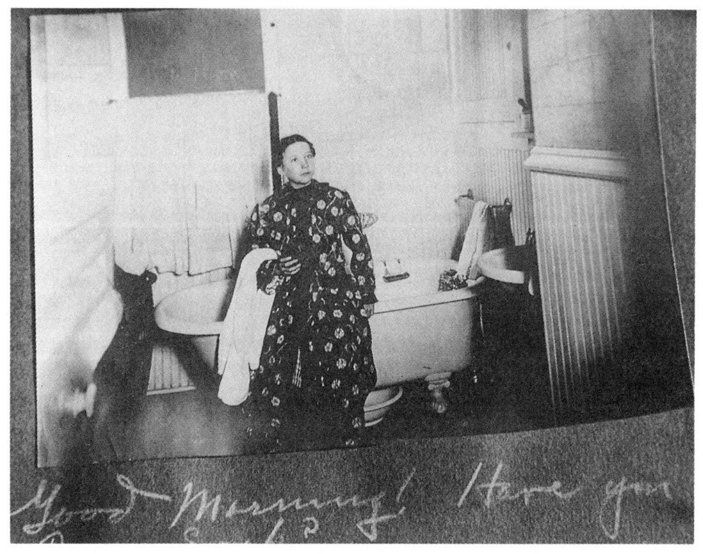

MHL Archive

Interior of 428 S. Fifth - Bathroom

Helen Hart is enjoying the new bathroom. The inscription asks: "Have you used Pear's soap?"

MHL Archive

Interior of 428 South Fifth - Maud's Room

Is Maud pretending to sew? She didn't enjoy needlework any more than Betsy did. We recognize the pattern of large flowers clambering up vines and can only assume they were blue and white, like Betsy's. Some of the photographs behind Maud appear in this book. The one at the left edge of the bulletin board is of Mike Parker (Tony).

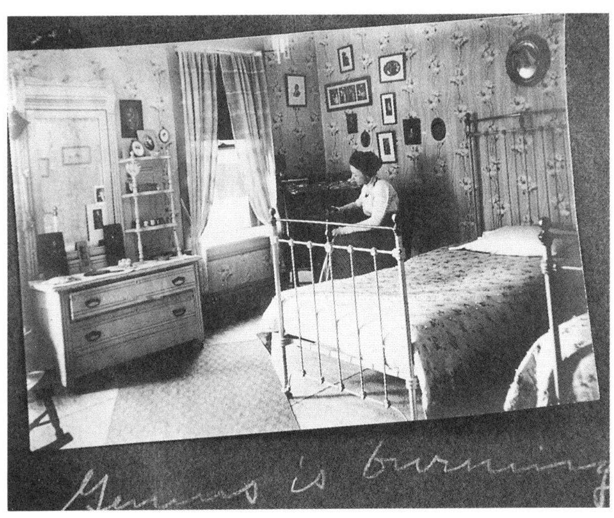

MHL Archive

Interior of 428 South Fifth - Maud at Her Desk

Maud and her younger sister shared this room (see twin beds at right). The campaign photo of Tom Hart (on the wall above her desk) has been moved upstairs from the parlor (where it hung in the photo taken three years previously). The inscription reads "Genius is burning."

MHL Archive

Interior of 428 S. Fifth - Music Room

Maud and Helen are ready for school. Helen had only to cross the street to the Normal. And Maud had just two blocks to walk to high school. The inscription reads: "School Days, School Days."

MHL Archive

Interior of 428 S. Fifth - Dining Room

This is the scene of the consumption of countless sandwiches on Sunday nights. The inscription: "Where is now the merry party?"

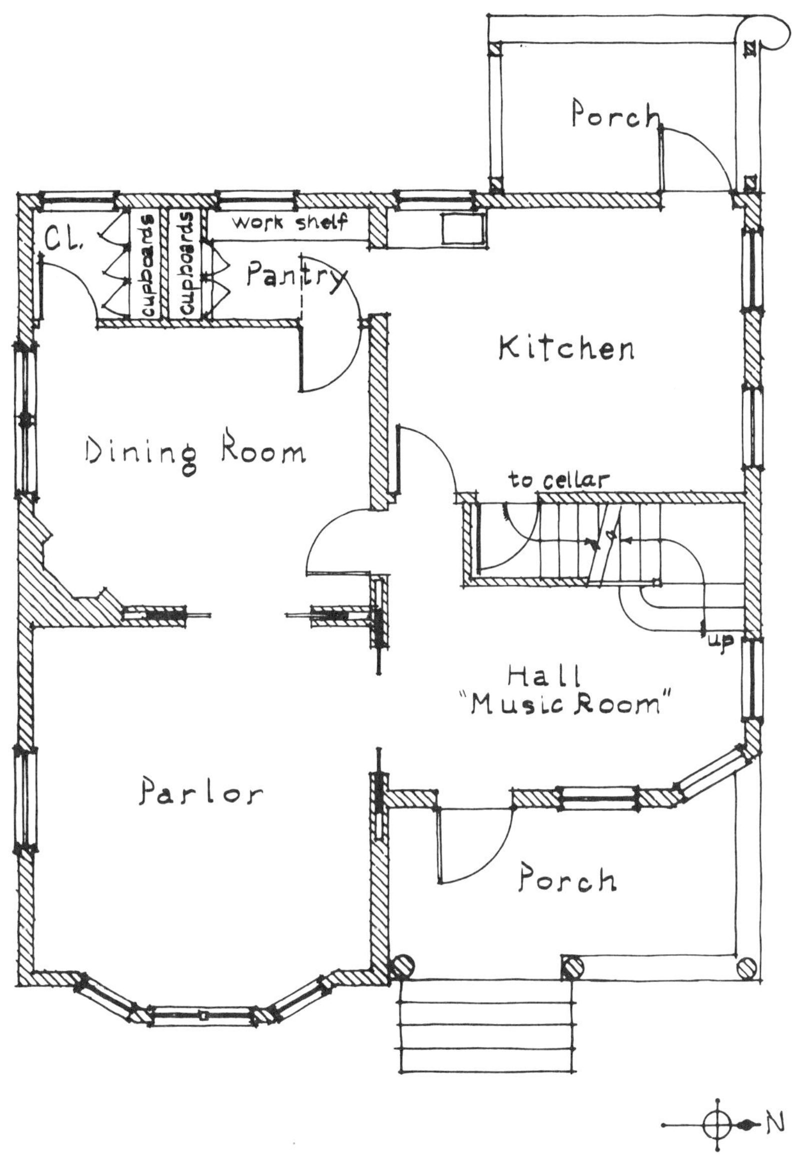

Plan by architect Nancy Beckner Bastian

428 S. Fifth Street
First Floor

Helen Benham Day, who grew up in this house, provided the sketches from which these floor plans were drawn.

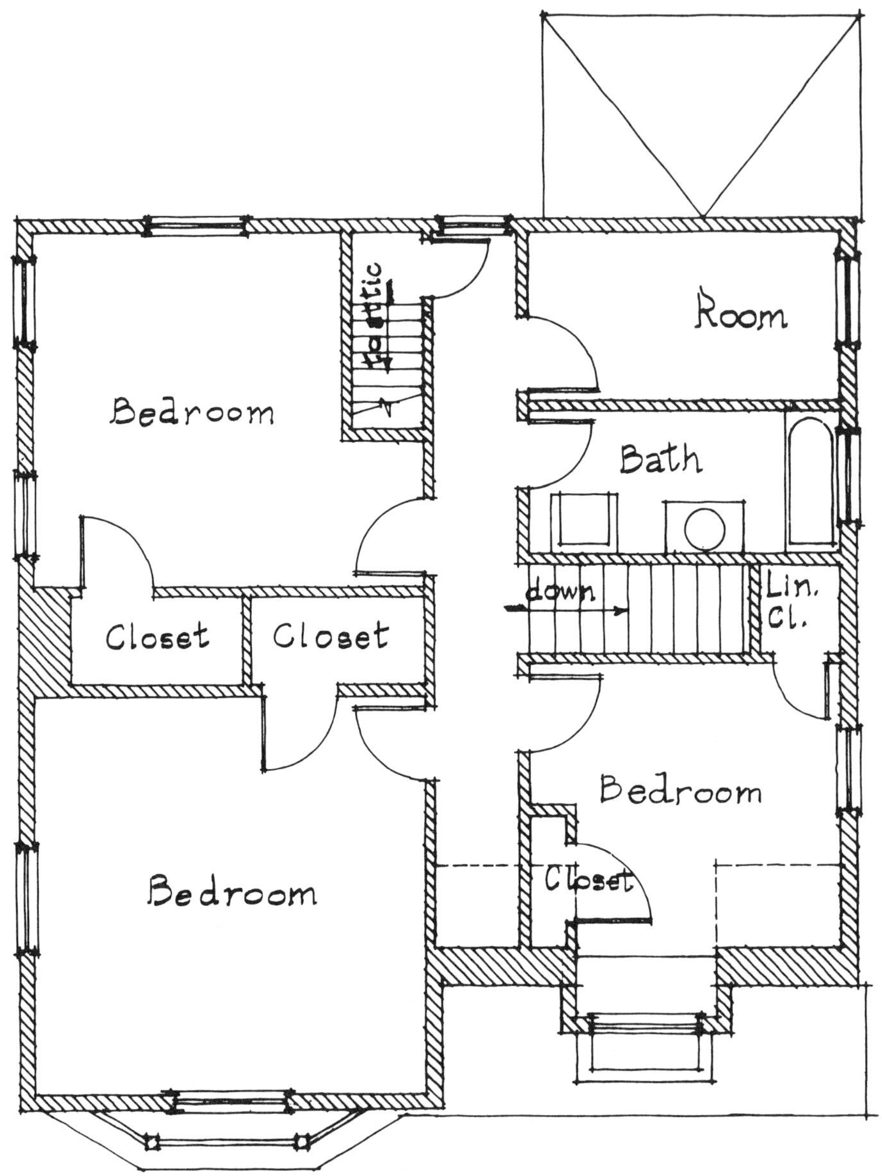

Plan by architect Nancy Beckner Bastian

428 S. Fifth Street
Second Floor

There were really only three bedrooms in use. The fourth was apparently too small for Helen Hart, who moved into Maud's bedroom.

was Maud's Aunt Flora. Flora was not hearty and died young (so family legend had it) from practicing the piano too much! After Flora's death, Dr. Benham boarded for a time with the Harts, in hired-girl Anna's attic room, no doubt. (The attic did have a window, looking east, as described in *Heaven to Betsy*.) When the Harts moved to Minneapolis in 1910, Dr. Benham and his new wife Louise bought the "High Street house." According to Helen Day, the house really was painted forest green.

Descriptions of wall dressings and furnishings are supplied in *Heaven to Betsy* and *Betsy and Joe*. The music room was wallpapered with dark green leaves in gold panels. The parlor was "in lighter green with loops of roses for a border." The dining room had "a plate rail, papered above with pears and grapes."[303] (Maud calls it a "dark fruity pattern" in *Betsy and Joe*.) "A glittering gold-fringed lamp was suspended by a gold chain from the ceiling."[304] The parlor had the bay window with lace curtains, a leather sofa, a green-shaded gas lamp on a mission oak table and a mission oak bookcase. The detailed descriptions were certainly based on Maud's memories of her girlhood home. A friend of the family remembered, "*The Harts had solid mission oak furniture in their living room.*"[305]

Betsy's room "was papered in a pattern of large blue and white flowers clambering up vines. There were blue ruffled curtains at the windows, blue matting on the floor, a blue, white-tufted bedspread on the white iron bed. The furniture was Mrs. Ray's old Hill Street bedroom set, freshly painted white."[306] This is probably exactly the way the room looked, for when Maud sought to describe Carney's bedroom in *Carney's House Party*, she wrote to Marion Willard Everett (upon whom the character was based), asking for a description of her girlhood bedroom and furnishings, including the accurate wallpaper color. (See Chapter 10 herein.)

The Rays delighted in their new bathroom. "No more baths in a tub in the kitchen," Julia says on page 26. (Back on Hill Street, Betsy and Julia had had their baths in the tub by the kitchen fire, as on page 10 of *Betsy-Tacy*.) The Harts loved their new tub, too. "*We didn't have a bathroom in the first house. We took our baths in the kitchen on Saturday night, one at a time. When we moved to Fifth Street we had a beautiful bathroom and how we enjoyed it!*"[307]

The Harts had not actually purchased the new house on Fifth. They rented it from a farmer named Marion Hills, who lived in North Mankato. Just prior to their move to Minneapolis, Tom bought the house from Hills for $4,500, and the following day he sold it to Dr. Edward Benham for the same amount. The Harts didn't sell 333 Center until August 16, 1915.

Betsy still lives on a hilly street, but instead of running up the hill, as does Hill Street (and Center Street), High Street runs across the hill. "Above them rows of rooftops indicated layers of streets, all the way to the top of High Street's hill, where the sun came up behind a German Catholic College."[308] Since Fifth is essentially the highest of these layers of streets, "High" was a more descriptive name (just as "Hill" was more appropriate than "Center," which isn't particularly in the center of anything but is certainly hilly).

On the opposite side of Fifth Street from the Harts', slightly to the north, reposed the State Normal or "Teachers' College." (Now called "Mankato State University," its campus sprawls across a different hill.) A German Catholic School (St. Peter and Paul's) stands on Fifth Street, five blocks north of the Hart home. The "German Catholic" part of the fictional institution was no doubt contributed by St. Peter and Paul's, and the "College" by the State Normal.

Katie enrolls at the German Catholic College ("the College on the hill") in *Betsy Was a Junior*. In fact, Bick's sister Tess took courses at the Normal. Tacy, too (we hear in *Betsy and Joe*), will attend the College on the hill to study "Public School Music."[309]

The name "Normal" was derived from a teacher-training college in Paris - the *Ecole Normale Superieure*, which was established in 1794. The first teacher-training college in America was formed in 1839, and it took the French name, the use of which became widespread in this country as "Normal."

After Betsy's first visit to the new house, the Rays and Tacy go downtown to a restaurant for supper. The closest restaurants to the house were W. M. George's at 318 S. Front, Bennett Williams' at 308 S. Front, and the Ideal Restaurant at 126 S. Front. The Harts sometimes dined at the Clifton House, and once again, Heinze's is always a possibility in affairs comestible.

Mr. Ray transplanted vines from the Hill Street house to the new house on Fifth. There really were vines at 333 Center. "*My father planted ... the vines around the front porch.*"[310] The vines were also transplanted to both the Fifth Street house and the Harts' Minneapolis house. The Hart home in Minneapolis is gone, but the Canoe Place cottage is still standing - and although no vines climb the house, a very old vine grows at the back fence. (See Chapter 13 herein.)

In *Downtown,* we learn that "Mrs. Ray loved to fix things up around her house,"[311] so we are not surprised to find her tiptoeing across a muddy yard with a towel on her head and a hammer in her hand, to get the effect of the new curtains on page 32. Mrs. Ray doesn't get a brass bowl to put in that window for 124 more pages, but by planting the idea in our minds early on, Maud enhances our enjoyment of the final, satisfying "brass bowl" denouement. Mrs. Ray was a clever wife, as well as a loving one.

Was Mrs. Ray actually younger than most mothers, as we are told on page 20? In 1906, Stella Hart was 40 years old. To use the fictional names for the real women, Mrs. Kelly and Mrs. Root (I) were already 52, while Mrs. Andrews was 46, Mrs. Edwards was 44, Mrs. Slade was 44, Mrs. Muller was 43, and Mrs. Biscay was 42. Mrs. Sibley was 39, however, and Mrs. Root (II) and Mrs. Morrison were only 38. Therefore Mrs. Ray was younger than most of the other mothers but not significantly so. Eleanor Wood wrote of Stella Hart, "*She was always interested and understanding with the young people who frequented their home, full of fun and music just as Mrs. Ray in the story.*"[312]

Betsy's relationship with Julia has changed drastically since *Downtown*. Betsy is no longer a pest: "During the last year all big-sister, little-sister friction had miraculously melted away."[313] We now hear Julia use the affectionate nickname "Bettina" for the first time. Maud's only nickname appears to have been "Maudie." She was, however, called "Maudina" at least once. Among Maud's literary papers was a card sent from Kathleen to "Maudina." The card was not dated, so we cannot know whether this nickname inspired the fictional "Bettina" or vice versa. Kathleen, meanwhile, was always "Kath" when the girls were young, and "Katie" in later years. In high school, Maud called her mother "muvver" or "muv." Bick was sometimes "Frankie" and Midge was occasionally "Pickles."

Julia has a new beau, "solid, sober, well-dressed" Fred.[314] Fred "had a fine voice and liked to sing."[315] Fred was probably based on new neighbor Dick Wood. Dick graduated from high school in 1908, the same year as Kathleen and Tess. Emma Wiecking remembered that *"all the girls were crazy about Dick Wood."*[316] He was musical and sang at high school functions. And he lived just across from the Harts' new house, at 421 E. Cherry, where the Heritage Center now stands.

Margaret, meanwhile, "was starting at a new school and unlike Betsy was not sure that she was going to like it."[317] After the move to Fifth Street, Helen Hart attended school at the Normal (though her year was interrupted when she came down with measles in October 1906). The Normal would truly have been a "new school" to her in 1906, since unlike her sisters, she had not attended kindergarten there. By the time Helen began school, kindergarten was offered at Pleasant Grove. "Miss Parry" really was the name of one of Helen's favorite teachers.

Mrs. Wheat, the neighbor on whom Margaret called almost every day, was Mrs. Moore, who lived at 420 S. Fifth.

Other new neighbors are introduced. "The Rays' back lawn ended in an alley, and across the alley was the Edwards' barn. Their house looked the other way, fronting on the street below High Street, but it was as close as Tacy's had been."[318] Maud chose the fictional Christian name "Edwards" because the real new neighbors had a Christian-name surname. The Edwards family was based on the Lloyds, who lived at 427 S. Fourth Street, on the northeast corner of Fourth and Cherry. Just as Maud wrote, the Lloyd house fronted on the street below Fifth. There was an alley between the Harts' and the Lloyds' homes. But the Harts didn't own the two lots on their "back lawn," and while Maud was in high school, two houses were built on this slope (on the east side of the alley). The Lloyds owned all the property on their side of the alley, so they had a large backyard.

"There was an Edwards boy just about her age named Caleb. People called him Cab."[319] The Lloyd boy Maud's age was named Jabez. People called him Jab. "He was about her own height, which was tall for a girl but not for a boy. He was thin and wiry

MHL Archive

Kathleen Hart
(Julia)

Julia's hair "waved in a high pompadour above a truly beautiful face ... arched brows, violet eyes, classic nose, and a delicate pink and white skin." (HTB p. 20)

MHL Archive

Kathleen with Parasol

Kathleen is walking up Cherry Street with her parasol - very much the way Betsy must have looked when she walked down to the Majestic Theater.

Coll. of SSW

Front Street, Mankato
Looking South from Jackson Street

When this photograph was taken (1907), Mr. Hart was no longer in the retail shoe business. His former store is the second one from the corner on the left side of the photo. (The word "shoes" can just be made out on the raised awning.) The next store is Heinze's. (Its sign is just beside the pole.) On the right side of the photo, at the end of the block, the small oval sign for the Majestic Theater can be found.

with black hair, snapping green eyes and a dark monkeyish face which was not handsome but undeniably attractive, especially when, as now, he grinned."[320] Cab is Welsh Calvinistic Methodist;[321] Jab Lloyd's family was Welsh Presbyterian. Jab was born in Mankato on August 4, 1891, probably at 115 Clark Street (now called East Pleasant). He was the fifth of eight children.

No longer the unfailingly gregarious little girl of Hill Street, Betsy initially holds herself a little aloof from Cab. This makes the end of the summer lonelier than ever for Betsy. Mrs. Ray takes pity on a restless daughter and sends Betsy to her brown purse to get two nickels for a movie and ice cream. The Majestic Theater had in fact "been just a short time before an ordinary Front Street store."[322] In 1906, the Majestic Theater really opened at 426 S. Front.

Before setting out for the Majestic, Betsy runs her mother's chamois skin over her face. "It isn't really powdering."[323] There is a related note in Maud's High School Scrapbook. The anonymous author wrote (presumably of Maud): "*So young! So fair! Such curly hair! Too bad she powders.*"[324]

Betsy starts down Plum (Cherry) on her way to the Majestic Theater. Two blocks down the hill, she would have reached Broad Street, but with trees in summer leaf in August of 1906, Betsy wouldn't have been able to gaze at the Willard (Sibley) house, one long block down from the corner of Broad and Cherry. However, here was a handy way for Maud to whet the reader's appetite for information about this new character, Carney Sibley. (Betsy doesn't <u>really</u> think Carney is a "stick.")[325] Similar poetic license was taken after the Christmas party at Alice's. Betsy is to stay with Bonnie that night "to avoid the late walk home."[326] The longer part of the walk would have been from Alice's to Bonnie's. If she were to avoid a late walk, she should have stayed with Tacy. But the writer's purpose was to give Bonnie an opportunity to sound Betsy out on the subject of Tony - our first hint that Bonnie is setting her sights for him.

The end of the summer becomes more lively for Betsy when Anna Swenson comes to work for the Rays. There really was an Anna who once worked for the Harts, but her last name does not appear to have been "Swenson." Perhaps the real maid was Anna

Gustafson, a "domestic" in Mankato at the time. In any case, Anna did not stay with the family through the years as did the Rays' Anna. The real-life Anna was probably with the Harts for only a short time. Family friend Eleanor Wood could not remember a maid at the Fifth Street house.[327]

Maud confirmed that the maid's name was Anna when asked by a fan where she had gotten the ideas for the freckle-removing cream and Magic Wavers which appear in *Heaven to Betsy*: "*Our hired girl Anna told me about them, just as I said in the story. I tried them, too, but I never lost the freckles and there was really nothing magic in those curlers, for a sprinkle of rain took my curls away.*"[328] Since the cream and wavers came freshman year, Anna must have been with the Harts in 1906. Magic Wavers (really popular hair curlers of the era) appear in all the succeeding titles, including *Betsy's Wedding*, in which Betsy waits until Joe goes to work before rolling up her "lamentably" straight hair.

After Maud's freshman year, the Hart attic had no room for a maid, since Dr. Edward Benham was rooming with them. The 1910 Federal Census shows Dr. E.W. Benham still with them as a lodger (and, as we know, soon-to-be owner).

Stella Hart probably had regular help with housework, though not a live-in maid. On October 24, 1910, the *Mankato Free Press* chronicled an injury she incurred while doing the dishes: "*While Mrs. T.W. Hart was working in the kitchen Saturday evening, a pan of boiling water that she was carrying slipped and the contents ran down over her left arm, scalding it badly from the elbow to the wrist and hand. The skin peeled off and it will be two or three weeks before Mrs. Hart will recover fully.*" Surprisingly, Stella was well enough to travel to Minneapolis two days later to visit Maud at college.

Soon after Anna joins the Ray household, further end-of-summer excitement is provided by the arrival of Miss Mix, the dressmaker. The reticent, rouge-wearing Miss Mix makes her first appearance in *Heaven to Betsy*. (An earlier embodiment of Miss Mix was Miss Meade, the sewing woman who visited the Ray cottage in *Betsy-Tacy*.[329]) There were many dressmakers in Mankato between 1906 and 1910. Probably a number of them did sewing for the Harts. Eleanor Wood revealed that "*Miss Mix the dressmaker was Miss Amelia Rausch. She wore rouge long before other women in the city*."[330] Miss Rausch lived at 326 S. Broad. In 1908, she attended the dressmakers' convention in St. Louis, no doubt "bringing back the latest styles ... not only in fashion books but on her person."[331] It is amusing that in *Emily of Deep Valley,* when Maud is not writing about her own household, we hear that "Miss Mix sewed for all the 'best' families of Deep Valley."[332]

The first day of high school would have been Tuesday, September 4, 1906. When Betsy and Tacy arrive for the first day, the high school doors are opened by the "grizzled janitor."[333] This was probably Frank Barnard, who lived on Glenwood Avenue. There was a door on High (Fifth), but the main entrance of the high school faced Hickory.

Betsy and Tacy run into Winona in the cloakroom. But this is no longer Beulah Hunt. This Winona was based on Maud's high school friend Mary Eleanor Johnson, known as "El." Maud's editors, as we know, felt that too many characters were being introduced into the series. Since Beulah Hunt belonged to a different high school group, Maud reused the name "Winona" for her friend Eleanor. (Maud had no idea of the confusion this would eventually cause readers fascinated with the real-life world hidden within the stories.) From *Heaven to Betsy* forward, it is Winona II (El) on the scene, rather than Winona I (Beulah).

Maud said this of the two Winonas: Beulah Hunt "*is still a friend but in high school we went with different crowds. When I started* Heaven to Betsy *I was trying not to add too many new characters and I gave the name Winona to a girl who did go with my crowd and who had the same gay spirit. She was a blonde but the grade school Winona was dark and black eyed, as described*."[334] Naturally, having established in *Downtown* that Winona's coloring was dark, Maud had to stick with it. Like Beulah, Eleanor was tall and angular - and thankfully, both were fond of scuffles!

Beulah (Winona I) was in the class of 1911, a year behind Maud, but this small difference in age doesn't explain why they went their separate ways, for other major Betsy-Tacy characters graduated later than Maud. Eleanor (Winona II), on the other hand, was in the class of 1909.

On the first day of school, Winona hangs up a red hat. All the brunettes in the Betsy-Tacy books wear red. Winona wears a red

HarperCollins

Deep Valley High School

The high school building, really just two blocks down from the Harts' new house, was very much as described and almost exactly as illustrated.

1895 Atlas

Mankato High School

"The red brick building with its tall arched windows and doors and the cupola that made an ironical dunce's cap on top of all." (EDV p. 2)

Coll. of Tom Hagan

View Looking South on Fifth Street
(From the Court House Block)

The turret on the high school looks impressive from this angle. No wonder the principal was severe when the Zetamathians climbed it. The high school was built in 1891 and burned down fifty years later.

Coll. of SSW

Miss Comstock
(Miss Clarke)

"She wore glasses, but she was pretty, with dark wings of hair and soft white skin." (HTB p. 62)

Coll. of SSW

Miss O'Rourke
(Miss O'Donnell)

Miss O'Rourke had "curly hair and smiling eyes and looked trimly lovely in a white shirtwaist and collar." (HTB p. 62)

Coll. of Bonnie Bond

Beulah Hunt
(Winona I)

In high school, Maud and Beulah were in different crowds. Therefore, after *Downtown*, Beulah no longer "played the role" of Winona.

Coll. of Paul Ford

Eleanor Johnson
(Winona II)

Maud said that El had the same mischievous spirit as Beulah. This spirit was Winona's distinctive characteristic.

dress the day Betsy, Tacy, and Tib try to hypnotize her on page 32 of *Downtown*. On page 119 of the same book, Winona is looking like "a cardinal" in a red coat and hat on the day she joins the trio for their Christmas shopping trip. In *Over the Big Hill*, "Dorothy, who had dark curls, wore a red dress" on page 160, notwithstanding the fact that in the same paragraph, when the girls "stood together they made a bouquet of light summer tints." Tony wears a red tie on a number of occasions. He has on "a most becoming red tie" at Bonnie's Christmas party on page 162 of *Heaven to Betsy*. The next year, on page 144 of *Betsy in Spite of Herself*, he has on a "red Christmas tie" which "looked well with his black eyes." And Betsy even buys him a red tie in *Betsy and Joe* (page 130). This consistency is typical of Maud and is worth noting from an artistic point of view. Brunettes <u>do</u> look good in red - and our friends from the turn of the century did not require a "color analysis" to know it!

Freshman-year classes include algebra with Miss O'Rourke, Latin with Mr. Morse, ancient history with Miss Clarke, and composition with Mr. Gaston.

The real Miss O'Rourke, Emma C. O'Donnell, was mathematics instructor, as well as assistant principal - and later, principal of Mankato High School. Miss O'Donnell received a bachelor of science degree from the University of Minnesota and began teaching at Mankato High in 1899, where she remained until her retirement in 1940. Because of her initials, she was sometimes called "ECOD."[335]

General Everett S. Hughes was the older brother of Bob Hughes, who appears in the Betsy-Tacy series as Dave Hunt (see Chapter 8 herein). General Hughes attributed his admission to West Point to Miss O'Donnell's teaching. *"I have many a time blessed Miss O'Donnell for the solid start she gave me and for all she did for me. I owe her much."*[336]

Miss Clarke "was gentle; she trusted everyone."[337] In *Betsy In Spite of Herself*, Miss Clarke is described in a similar way: "Her manner in class was timid and appealing, but out of class she had an innocent girlish gaiety."[338] This was Grace E. Comstock, who did teach history. Miss Comstock came from an old Mankato family. She received her bachelor of arts degree from the

University of Minnesota. She left Mankato to teach in St. Louis in the 1920s.

Miss Clarke had her pupils' names "written on cards stacked alphabetically. Miss Clarke sat down each morning with the neat pile before her, lifted a card, peered at it mildly through her eye-glasses, and asked the pupil named thereon a question.... Knowing exactly when his card would come up, a student had no difficulty in figuring out beforehand just which paragraph it was advisable to study. It was not considered sporting to study anything else."[339] Eleanor Wood remarked of Miss Comstock that *"the author's description of her is very good. Her card method was just as described and taken advantage of as in the story."*[340] During her trip to Europe in 1914, Maud wrote home to her family: *"Cardinal Richelieu's tomb, with his statue lying on it, and his hat suspended from the ceiling over it, really brought him to me as an historical personage, while hitherto he and his policy had been a paragraph heading to be glanced at hastily amid note writing and cartoon drawing while awaiting my turn in Comstock's history class."*[341]

Mr. Gaston may have been based, in part, on Cleon Headley. "He was a dark, sardonic-looking young man with thick, unrimmed glasses."[342] He even made a "sardonic" Santa Claus on page 133 of *Betsy and Joe*. Maud uses the word "sardonic" almost every time she mentions this teacher. Mr. Headley taught science and physics - however, Mr. Headley's first year at the high school was Maud's senior year, and he never taught English.

Mr. Gaston falls for Julia at the faculty/senior picnic in *Betsy in Spite of Herself*. A teacher from the high school did fall for Kathleen but not until some years after the Harts left Mankato. Dr. E.C. Stakeman was then (about 1913) at the University of Minnesota, and he renewed his acquaintance with the Hart family in Minneapolis. Kathleen (who was engaged at the time!) didn't give him any encouragement, however, and apparently Dr. Stakeman gave up after calling a time or two. He taught at Mankato High School during Maud's first years there. Dr. Stakeman acted as Santa Claus for the 1907 Christmas festivities on the last day before vacation.[343] Mr. Gaston plays Santa in *Betsy Was a Junior,*[344] and as previously mentioned, he does so again "as usual" in *Betsy and Joe.*[345]

Deep Valley High School students were divided into two literary societies, Philomathian and Żetamathian. The societies "competed in athletics, in debate and in essay writing as the three cups testified."[346] The two-society system had been established the year before Maud Hart began high school. Such societies were common in turn-of-the-century high schools.

The Mankato High School yearbook from 1912 describes the function of the Zetamathean (sic) Society in this way: "*The purpose is to give the students a literary training, and all students must belong to this society or to the Philomathean* [sic]. *The members of the society must attend the meetings unless excused by the teacher in charge. The meetings are held the fourth Friday in each month, when a literary program is given. Miss Grace Comstock is the society teacher.*" Miss Emma O'Donnell was the Philomathean Society sponsor, just as described in the Betsy-Tacy books. The two societies were reorganized, however, and the charming names were dropped in 1916.

It is pleasant for the reader to see some familiar faces in the bewildering new high school world. Alice Morrison from the Hill Street neighborhood, now in high school too, was "a tall blonde girl with glasses."[347] Ruth Williams, her real-life equivalent, was actually an eighth-grader in 1906.

Tom Slade was off to Cox Military School on page 53. There is no record of his attendance in the files of Shattuck School, but thanks to a Lovelace letter, we know that Tom Fox did in fact attend Shattuck for at least a portion of his high school years: "*Tom came often to the Hart house, both on Center Street (Hill Street) and Fifth Street (High Street). We were still on Center Street, I feel sure, when he went to Shattuck. When he went there, we missed him and I wrote him a letter in rhyme.*" Maud remembered Tom bringing his violin when he came up to the Fifth Street house. "*When he was not at Shattuck, he was a frequent visitor at the Hart 'Sunday night lunches,' so often described in the high school stories.... He and Kathleen liked to play piano and violin duets.*"[348] We can therefore conclude that Tom Fox went to Shattuck in 1905, as a freshman. This may have been his only year there. Tom and his family lived in Minneapolis for a time during his high school years. They returned to Mankato in the summer of 1907, and Tom graduated from Mankato High School in 1909. Fictionally, Tom Slade went to Cox for all four years. Maud may have chosen the fictional name "Cox" because it rhymed with "Fox."

Tom may be gone, but many new friends now come into Betsy's life. Soon after school begins, Betsy gets to know Carney Sibley better. This was Marion (Marney) Willard, whose real surname became Delos' fictional surname (which, perhaps, shows how much Maud thought of Marney Willard). Marney was born at 810 S. Broad Street on June 24, 1891. This is the same house discussed in Chapter 4, which Maud may have had in mind when mentioning the Humphreys house on Lincoln Park in *Over the Big Hill* (though it was not the same house the Andrews {Humphreys} boys lived in). In 1892, the Willards moved to 306 Byron Street (where their three sons were born). In 1903, at the cost of $8000, they purchased 609 Broad Street (Carney's house, as we know it in the Betsy-Tacy books).

The sense of autobiography we experience when reading the Betsy-Tacy series manifests itself potently when we are told that Carney will look like her mother when she reaches maturity. (We find a similar case in *Betsy in Spite of Herself* when the author tells us that Betsy will "never forget" the moonlight drive on Christmas night through Milwaukee.)

The W.D. Willard house is still standing, but the interior has been greatly altered. Walls and even staircases were moved when the house was converted into four studio apartments. The big porch that once curved all the way around the house on the south side has been drastically abbreviated, leaving only a dab at the front door. The downstairs window seat has been walled in.

The interior of the house is described on pages 132-133 of *Heaven to Betsy*. "At the end of the Sibleys' hall were dining room and kitchen. At the right in a row were front parlor, back parlor, and a library. The rooms could be closed off with folding doors." The library had "the fireplace, and a window seat full of cushions and Mr. Sibley's armchair."

Carney's three brothers are all in grade school when introduced in *Heaven to Betsy*. This impression persists throughout the series, although Grant Willard (Hunter Sibley) was only one year behind Maud in high school. Maud probably enjoyed the opportunity to bring Grant onto the scene as Hunter in *Carney's House Party*.

Coll. of Robert Cahill

Tom Fox
(Tom Slade)

"Not even his uniform could make him handsome, but he was an original and interesting boy." (HTB p. 142)

BECHS

Shattuck School
(Cox Military)

Cox Military was based on Shattuck School (now Shattuck/St. Mary's School) in Faribault, Minnesota. Tom Fox was not a Shattuck graduate - but, like his counterpart, he attended West Point.

Coll. of Louise King

Marion Willard
(Carney)

This photograph of Marion as a young girl was probably taken about 1904.

Coll. of Louise King

Connie Davis
(Bonnie)

"Bonnie had calm blue eyes [and] a soft, chuckling laugh that flowed continuously through the conversation." (HTB p. 66) Might Connie be wearing the locket which the Crowd presented to Bonnie as a going-away gift?

MHL Archive

Marney and Connie
(Carney and Bonnie)

Marney and Connie were photographed together shortly before Connie's departure for St. Paul (not Paris).

Coll. of Louise King

Marion and her Brothers

Carney's "straight brown hair was parted and combed smoothly back to an always crisp hair ribbon." (HTB p. 66)

Coll. of Louise King

The Sibley Boys
(Grant, Harold, and John Willard)

In *Carney's House Party*, we earn the names of Carney's brothers: Hunter, Jerry, and Bobby (from l to r in photo).

BECHS

Cartoon of Marney

This cartoon of Marion Willard was pasted into Maud's High School Scrapbook. The artist is unknown.

Coll. of Louise King

609 S. Broad circa 1908

"The high school crowd had the most indoor fun at the Ray house and the most outdoor fun at the Sibleys' ... on the wide, trampled side lawn, and the porch running across the front and around the side of the house. The porch was unscreened and shaded by vines, now turning red." (HTB p. 65)

609 S. Broad circa 1988

The house has been relieved of most of its gracious porch and the turret has been blinded. (Downstairs, where its windows remain, the turret now contains a closet.) The former Willard home was converted to a fourplex.

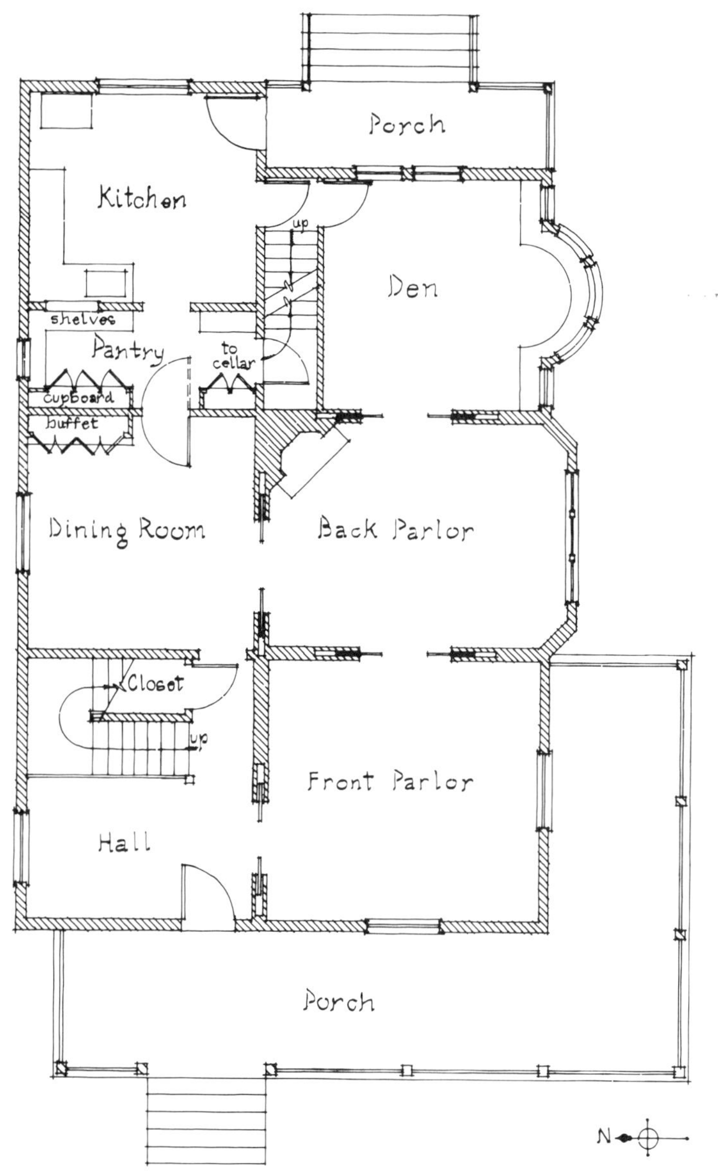

Plan by architect Nancy Beckner Bastian

609 S. Broad
First Floor

Margery Ertsgaard, granddaughter of W.D. and Louise Willard, provided the sketches from which these floor plans were drawn. She cleaned the house for her grandfather when she was a teenager and knew it well.

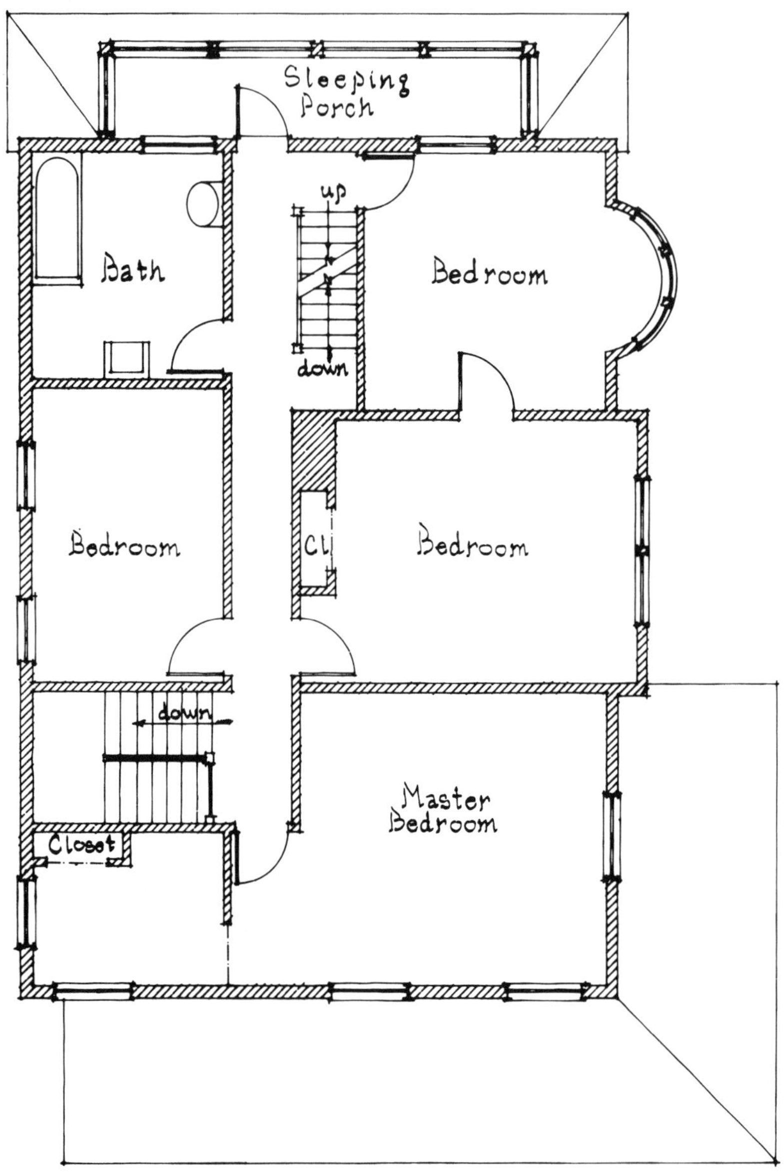

Plan by architect Nancy Beckner Bastian

609 S. Broad
Second Floor

The sleeping porch on the rear of the house was built by W.D. Willard and his sons. See Chapter 10 for photo.

Other members of the future Triumvirates and eventual Crowd are introduced one by one. Bonnie Andrews was based on Constance Emily Davis, called "Connie." Bonnie's father is "the new minister at the Presbyterian Church. She's the reason all the boys have started going to Christian Endeavor."[349] This makes it sound as though Bonnie has recently moved to Mankato, from Paris. But Connie's father had assumed the Presbyterian pastorate in Mankato in 1901.

Later on, in *Carney's House Party,* one gets the feeling that Carney and Bonnie have been friends longer than since tenth grade. Carney and Bonnie talk about when they were "little girls," rather than just when they were teenagers. Bonnie, we hear, is a very old friend.

"For years the two little girls had played together and had gone to Sunday School together. Later they had belonged to the same high school crowd. Once, Carney remembered, they had had their best dresses made alike."[350] This description in *Carney's House Party* is not in sync with Bonnie's introduction in *Heaven to Betsy*, but it reflects the actual facts. Marney and Connie had been friends for several years before they reached high school age.

"Dr. Andrews, impressive in a beard, came in to welcome them."[351] Mrs. Andrews had curly dark hair. Like Mrs. Andrews, Mrs. Davis (Sarah Emily Grinshaw) was English, but she had met her husband in England, not France. Dr. Davis was also English. Bonnie tells Betsy that her family had lived in Paris for four years[352] - the Davises really lived there for only two.

It is not surprising that Dr. Andrews has a book-filled library and is able to tell his daughter the meanings of "Zetamathian" and "Philomathian" ("Investigator" and "Lover of Learning"). Dr. George W. Davis was an extremely erudite man. He had been an undergraduate at Victoria University in England, then a post-graduate at Yale in Semitic languages. He was regarded as a brilliant minister and scholar. His journals are peppered with remarks in Greek and Latin. On October 19, 1891, the day his only daughter was born, Dr. Davis noted: "*This morning Emily gave us a plump, broad-backed daughter at 6:45 a.m. Both are doing well thank God. Very wet today and only a few to service.*" And the next day: "*Emily, I am very thankful to say, may probably nurse the youngster.*

I had had constant visions of night scenes with bottles & rubber tubing & etc. & etc.!!!!" The family was living in Connecticut at the time of Connie's birth.

The Davis house, at 628 S. Broad, was opposite the Willard house, set back from the road beside Hubbard's Creek (between the Hubbard and Patterson homes on the west side of the street). The Davis house and the creek are both gone, however. The house was demolished about 1943, and the creek was directed underground.

"Herbert, in vacation tan, blonder, bigger and brawnier than ever, was outstandingly good looking."[353] Herbert confides to Betsy that he stops being crazy about Bonnie until Sunday night comes around again and he sees her in action at Christian Endeavor, or "so he had told Betsy one day in a confidential moment." Later they would become "C.F.s," confidential friends.

"Lawrence Humphreys was as dark as Herbert was light, as big or bigger, and equally handsome."[354] Herbert and Larry Humphreys were Helmus and Rupert (or Rupe) Andrews. Maud has chosen another fictional Christian-name surname for a real one ("Humphrey" for "Andrew"). And confusingly, Maud gave this family's real surname to her character Bonnie Andrews. Helmus, known as "Hal" in later years, was really blond. Rupe was darker but not bigger. Their parents, Mr. and Mrs. Humphreys, were good friends of Mr. and Mrs. Ray, and at the end of the book, Betsy asks the Humphreys to be her godparents. Maud wrote that "*Mrs. A. was my godmother*."[355]

The Andrews children were all born in Wells, Minnesota. Rupe and Helmus had two older sisters, never mentioned in the Betsy-Tacy books. They were Alice (born 1883) and Lois (born 1887). Their father, Charles Nathaniel Andrews, an attorney, moved his family to Mankato from Wells in 1899. In 1907, the Andrews family moved to San Diego, just as the Humphreys did.

The appearance of Tony is presaged on page 95: "When I feel romantic about a boy, he'll be somebody dark and mysterious, a stranger." Betsy's description reminds Tacy of the "Tall, Dark Strangers" in Rena's novels. The real Tony wasn't tall, but he was dark and a stranger, having moved to Mankato in 1906. "He might almost have walked out of her conversation with Tacy."[356]

Coll. of Louise King

Connie's Mankato Home

The Andrews' house, at 608 S. Broad, was "opposite the Sibleys', a sprawling old house, set back from the road." (HTB p. 88) This house was demolished in the 1940s. It stood directly across from the Willard home, set well back from the street. The Davis family lived in Mankato from about 1901 to 1907.

Connie's St. Paul Home

The Davis family lived at 547 Ashland Avenue in St. Paul from 1908 to 1911.

BECHS

Jab Lloyd
(Cab Edwards)

Coll. of Billie Andrews

Helmus Andrews
(Herbert Humphreys)

Coll. of Robert Cahill

Earl King
(Squirrelly)

Coll. of Robert Cahill

Pin Jones
(Pin)

One wonders if Tony did indeed walk out of Maud's mind. If any character in the Betsy-Tacy series were pure fiction, surely it would be this fairy-tale "TDS." Consider the scene at the freshman party on page 116: "He had surveyed the room and his eyes had come to rest on her.... Betsy didn't feel frightened. She had known that he would come." This is so romantic, "knowing" that he would come, and there's Betsy, waiting in her becoming blue silk mull! In fact, it sounds so delicious that one might be inclined to think Tony is too good to have been real. On the other hand, the affectionate way in which Maud describes Tony's closeness to her family does not feel manufactured: "From the first step across the threshold he felt at home in the Ray house. He fell in love with the family, and they with him."[357]

Tony was very real indeed. His name was Clarence Lindon Parker. When asked about Clarence, his niece responded: "*Do you mean Uncle Mike*?" She did not know why the family had given Clarence a nickname so ostensibly unrelated to his real name. He does look more like a Mike than a Clarence, and he certainly looks the part of Tony.

Like Tony, Mike Parker was gifted musically. Like Tony, he was an Episcopalian. The Parkers lived at 339 Clark Street (now called East Pleasant), and by the time Maud graduated from high school, they had moved to 620 S. Fourth.

Bonnie's new beau was a junior boy to whom Julia had introduced her, "a tall, thin, freckled boy nicknamed Pin, who had gone around with Katie."[358] We remember him from *Downtown*. Though only one class ahead in school, C. Ernest "Pin" Jones was four years older than Maud. He lived at 114 N. Fourth Street with his older sister and mother.

Hank Weed is mentioned once - an apple was snapped for him on page 134. There was a John Weed on the Mankato High football team, but he was not a senior when Maud was a freshman. John was only one year ahead of Maud. He was apparently, at some point, one of Maud's beaux. (Consult Chapter 8 herein.)

After beginning high school, Betsy and her friends become telephone addicts. Phone numbers are never mentioned specifically, but on page 105, Betsy "gave the Kellys' number" to the operator. The Kenneys did not have a telephone in 1906, but the Harts' phone number was 230. Other phone numbers for the Crowd were as follows: Bonnie, 305; Winona, 226; Carney, 147; Irma, 698; Alice, 445; Herbert and Larry, 358. (Fictional names have been used for clarity. The phone numbers are those assigned to the real-life families in 1906.)

Maud's choice of fictional names which rhymed with real names was frequent: Carney/Marney, Cab/Jab, Bonnie/Connie, Cobb/Robb. Mark(ham) and Park(er) almost rhyme. A look at the "Characters and Counterparts" list reveals other similarities. A fictional name often begins with the same letter or sound as the actual one. The old Mankato family names of Bangerter, Meacham, and Thumler resemble the fictional Bangeter, Meecham, and Thumbler.

Carney suggests that the girls go riding. "All our horses are named Dandy," she says. "All our horses are named Old Mag," Betsy responds, "whether they're girls or boys."[359] Eleanor Wood remembered that the Harts' horse was indeed named "Old Mag"[360] but that Old Mag had died or was sold before the Harts moved to Fifth Street. The Willard family really had a horse named "Dandy." W.D. Willard, Marion's father, wrote, "*We always had a horse ... Dandy with whom the children grew up and whose laziness became a family joke.*"[361] And Ruth's horse was really "Rex," just like that of her counterpart, Alice.[362]

When Carney, Bonnie, and Betsy take their ride out with Dandy, "They left Broad Street at the Episcopal Church and took the road leading to Cemetery Hill. They passed the watering trough ... and the road began to climb."[363]

Which was Agency Hill? We hear that Joe Willard lived both "under" Agency Hill and on the north side of town. If Agency Hill was Main Street Hill, then houses north of the road up the hill would have been on the north side of town (Main Street being a dividing line).

Maud's fictional geography is often confusing, though usually accurate. We are told that Betsy's bedroom looks south - towards Hill Street, as Maud's really did (compare floor plan). Fifth Street does fork, with jogs that lead to Center. This route is described in *Betsy in Spite of Herself*, when Betsy "set off for Hill Street, up side streets that climbed gently at first, then more and more steeply."[364] The description is more specific in *Betsy and Joe*: "She ran out of

Coll. of Peg Barnard

Andrews House circa 1908

Helmus and Rupert (Herbert and Larry) lived with their sisters and parents in this house at 645 S. Fourth Street.

Andrews House circa 1988

This house has undergone major changes through the years. It appears, however, to be the same basic structure as the original.

BECHS

Presbyterian Church ... Then ...

This was the church Marion Willard and her family attended. The building dates to 1896.

... And Now

The church once had a "Hope Mission" like the one described in *Carney's House Party*.

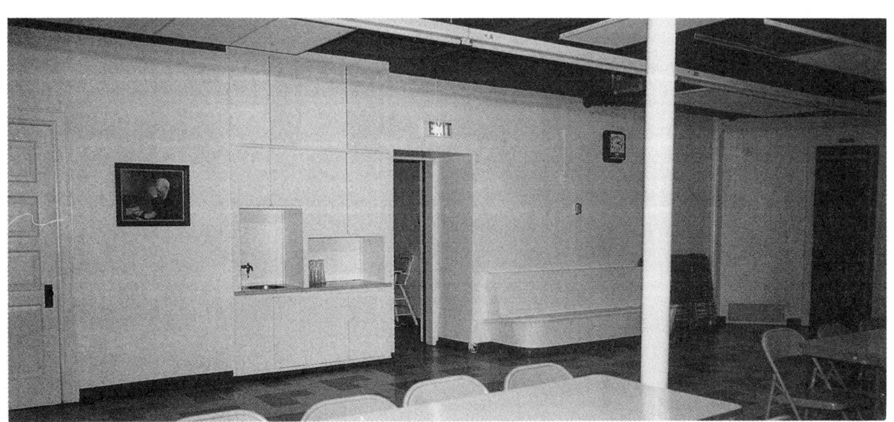

Church Basement

The Presbyterian church basement is still used as a social hall. In *Heaven to Betsy*, we hear that there is a kitchen, to which the hospitality committee repairs to prepare steaming cups of cocoa.

the house, in the direction opposite the school house, down the hill to the corner where a watering trough, now frozen, and rimmed with icicles, marked the junction with Cemetery Road."[365] Cemetery Road would have been Glenwood Avenue. This is the "eastern" route. Most of the time, Betsy and her friends seem to take a "western" route to Hill Street, via Plum (Cherry) to Broad, then over to Lincoln Park. When Phil Brandish drove Betsy home in *Betsy in Spite of Herself*, he took the western route. "The car bounced along down Hill Street, down Broad Street, and up the Plum Street hill."[366] Betsy may have preferred this route, since she was able to stop by Carney's on Broad, en route to Tacy's.

The Crowd walks to the Presbyterian church on Broad for Christian Endeavor meetings. The Presbyterian church in Mankato does have "a pointed steeple and a round stained glass window on one side."[367] It stands on the corner of Broad and Hickory. The Sunday School room was in the basement.

Herbert teases Betsy about her writing at Christian Endeavor. "He and Larry started calling her The Little Poetess."[368] Apparently Rupe Andrews (the real-life Larry) called Maud just that. There is a poem handwritten by Rupert in Maud's High School Scrapbook:

Maude was a little poetess
So every body said,
But if she was, then that is all
That was ever in her head.
And that is a grave mistake,
For if you will only come
By pounding on her head you'll see
It is filled with vacuum.[369]

The Humphreys boys often come to Betsy's for Sunday Night Lunch. "Sunday night lunch was an institution at the Ray house."[370] This is the first we read of it, but we are told that Sunday Night Lunch is an established routine. "The meal was prepared by Mr. Ray. This was a custom of many years' standing.... He used slices of mild Bermuda onions, sprinkled with vinegar and dusted with pepper and salt."[371]

Maud explained that Sunday Night Lunch began after Helen was born, to give Stella a break from cooking. When Delos joined the family, he presented Tom with a knife which bore a silver plate on the handle reading: "*Tom Hart's Sunday Sandwich Knife*."[372]

A year before the Sunday Night Lunch descriptions in *Heaven to Betsy* were written, Maud wrote a short story in which "*Grandfather always made sandwiches for Sunday night supper. He made good ones too*."[373] Tom Hart appears as the Grandfather in this Lovelace story, called "The Scrappies' Club," from *Jack and Jill* magazine. He had "*silvery hair which lay close to his finely shaped head. He had hazel eyes full of kindliness and wisdom, and he had a big, strong nose. He stood very straight*."[374]

"*Grandfather made very good suggestions, which he called 'snoggestions,' for a joke*."[375] Mr. Ray first uses this expression in *Betsy in Spite of Herself* when he "snoggests" their anniversary dinner at the Moorish Cafe. Like Sunday Night Lunch, it really was an invention of Tom Hart. Writing home in 1914, Maud referred to "*Papa's far-famed snoggestions*."[376]

Maud once said, "*I loved to put down how many boys came to Sunday Night Lunch each week. You would think from my diary that they came to see me, but that was far from being the case. I wasn't the attraction. To this day when I meet some of those boys, grandfathers now, of course, they look at me dreamily and say, 'Oh Maud, I can still remember your father's onion sandwiches*.'"[377]

In a 1981 article, "Making Pancakes on Sunday: The Male Cook in Family Tradition," Thomas A. Adler writes: "*...the male cook typically establishes sovereignty over a given weekend meal for which he always prepares the same foods. The diminishment of choice then marks the meal quickly as a family tradition constructed around Dad's preparation of his specialty*."[378]

After sandwiches, friends and family would sing with Julia at the piano or dance to Mrs. Ray's tunes. "*After supper, my sister who was like Julia would play the piano and everyone would gather around it and sing. My mother loved to have young people around, just as Mrs. Ray did. Do you remember in the high school Betsy-Tacy books how Mrs. Ray sometimes used to let the youngsters roll up the rugs and dance? And she would play for them to dance, and she knew only two tunes, a waltz and a two-step? Well, that was the way my mother used to do*."[379]

With all the making of fudge at home and eating of banana splits at Heinz's, it is a wonder that these girls were so willowy thin. Many Betsy-Tacy fans may identify more with an only-glimpsed woman in *Over the Big Hill.* On page 78, one of the women whose doorbell the girls ring is "plump" and happens to have just made some fudge. (She was probably sitting inside with a Betsy-Tacy high school book.) The power of suggestion is very strong in all the Betsy-Tacy books, because the food always sounds so good! Even one of Maud's reviewers got hungry, remarking that the description of Sunday Night Lunch "*almost compels the reader to raid his own icebox.*"[380]

There are wonderful culinary descriptions even in the first book in the series. The alfresco dinners on the bench in *Betsy-Tacy* are simple but sound delicious. The picnic which Betsy invents for the imaginary trip to Milwaukee in the surrey sounds very appetizing and is a forerunner of menus to come: "Chicken sandwiches and hard-boiled eggs and potato salad and watermelon and chocolate cake and sweet pickles and sugar cookies and ice cream."[381] A picnic menu from Maud's 1937 novel, *Gentlemen from England*, is similar: "*sandwiches, hard-boiled eggs, cold broiled prairie chicken, potato salad, pickles, apple pie, a frosted cake.*"[382]

September events included Julia's seventeenth birthday (Kathleen Hart turned seventeen on September 6, 1906). Also in September, "Chauncey Olcott came to Deep Valley in his play, *Aileen Asthore* [sic]."[383] The Ray family went together in the evening. This was actually on Monday night, September 10, 1906. The title was *Eileen Asthore*.

Of course, there really was a Chauncey Olcott. Ralph Hammett, a Mankato native of Maud's vintage, remembered "*plays by Chauncey Olcott who always opened the theater season in September with the latest of his Irish plays and songs. It was Chauncey Olcott who wrote and introduced 'When Irish Eyes Are Smiling,' and many others that have become near classics.*"[384] Chauncey Olcott wrote "When Irish Eyes Are Smiling" with two other songwriters, Graff and Ball, in 1912. Maud certainly remembered the singer best for "My Wild Irish Rose," which Olcott wrote in 1899.

In *Betsy in Spite of Herself*, Maud comments that the Olcott plays were so alike that "the name didn't matter much."[385] But the names of the plays obviously did matter, since Maud never fails to get them right. The Olcott plays which she describes in the Septembers of 1906, 1907, and 1908 all really came to Mankato those respective Septembers. (1906, *Aileen/Eileen Asthore*; 1907, *O'Neill of Derry*; 1908, *Ragged Robin.*)

September also brought the first football game. The town of Red Feather was probably Red Wing, though it would have been a fair distance for the teams to travel. The girls wore streamers of maroon and gold on their coats. (There are some faded maroon and gold streamers in Maud's Scrapbook.) Mankato High School's first game in 1906 was against Lake Crystal. Mankato won 34-0, unlike Deep Valley, which lost its first game 40-0.

Since Betsy didn't attend dances yet, the freshman party was the social highlight of the season. Herbert's note of invitation comes almost word for word from a note typed by Helmus Andrews and pasted into Maud's High School Scrapbook.

The note in *Heaven to Betsy* reads:

Dear, dear Betsy,

It makes no difference to me which way you take the following. Will you accompany me to the High School this evening? My mother is going to serve punch, and I'm glad because then you can't flirt with me. Of course, you'll have to pay your own way. If you answer this, and if affirmative, tell me when to call. I remain

Yours very truly

Herbert W. Humphreys.[386]

The real note reads:

Dear, Dear Maud;

It makes no difference to me which way you take the following. Will you accompany me to the High School this evening? My mother said she was going along too and I am glad because then you cant [sic] *flirt with me. Of course you will have to pay your own way. If you will answer this and if affirmmative* [sic] *tell me when to call. I remain*

Yours truly,

Helmus W. Andrews[387]

HarperCollins

Tony, Herbert, and Cab

When the Rays return from the lake, they find the lights blazing in their home and a savory aroma coming from the kitchen. Tony, Herbert, and Cab's fried-egg welcome may really have occurred.

Duplicated in several collections

Mike, Henry, and Clayton?

The handsome young man on the left side is certainly Mike Parker (Tony). But the other two are apparently not Helmus Andrews (Herbert) and Jab Lloyd (Cab). They appear to be Henry Lee (Al Larson) and Clayton Burmeister.

Austin Park

Maud wrote of Stella's girlhood home: "*A twin row of spicy-smelling evergreens led from the house to that gate and the property was enclosed by a white fence.*" (MHL to M. Freeman, 5-19-64)

The Former Austin Home

Tom and Stella Hart were married in this house, standing in the bay window, on October 15, 1887. This side of the house faces Madison Lake.

Helmus' note is folded and marked "Maude Hart -- Important." Maud's actual response is not available, but it was no doubt as witty as Betsy's.

Herbert and Betsy set out for the party and find Cab waiting for them at the corner. Herbert says that Cab is "horn[ing] in on me and my girl."[388] Many years later, Helmus' wife, Billie Andrews, reported that Helmus was guilty of doing just this himself. When the Lovelaces and Andrews got together for dinner in the 1950s, they laughed over the crush Helmus had had on Maud about 1906. He used to follow her around, even when she was out with another boy![389]

The whole Ray family attends services at the Episcopal church one Sunday in mid-October, for Julia is singing a solo. The "event fell fortuitously upon the Rays' twentieth wedding anniversary."[390] But in 1906, it was the Harts' nineteenth anniversary, not their twentieth.

The Rays always celebrate their anniversary with a drive to Murmuring Lake. As discussed previously, Pleasant Park was really called "Austin Park" after Stella's stepfather, Chauncey Austin. The name was naturally changed after Austin sold the park in 1900 to Frank Hoehn (whose gracious daughter-in-law, Violet, has opened her home to many Lovelace pilgrims). The farmer's wife who "seemed to enjoy the annual October visit from the Rays"[391] would have been Katie Hoehn (suitably enough, her maiden name was "Farmer").

The interior of the former Austin home is mentioned in *Betsy and Joe*. "They show us the bay window where they were married ... it looks down a long avenue of evergreens to the big front gate. Mamma's room was just above it and she says that on her wedding day she sat in an upper window and looked down that avenue, waiting for Papa to come. She was wearing a tea gown, she says."[392] (In actuality, the bay window does not look down the avenue of evergreens, since this window is on the opposite side of the house, facing the lake.)

The Inn at Murmuring Lake was "a favorite vacation ground." Madison Lake had and still has a resort called Point Pleasant Inn. "The Inn with its flock of cottages looked like a hen surrounded by chicks."[393] Maud used almost the same simile in *Over the Big*

Hill. "Mr. Meecham's Mansion with the little houses in a row looked like a hen followed by chicks."[394] (See Chapter 8 herein for more Inn details.)

Maud did not have to embellish the relationship between her parents. As Julia says, "It's wonderful how much in love papa and mamma are."[395] When Mrs. Ray puts her arms around Mr. Ray, asking with a smile if he ever regretted his errand to borrow a cupful of salt, and he answers "Not for a second," then kisses her, we feel the magic, too. The affection Mr. and Mrs. Ray feel for each other is represented in all of the books. At Betsy's surprise tenth birthday party in *Over the Big Hill,* "Betsy's father stood there with his arm around Betsy's mother and both of them were smiling."[396]

Maud wrote to a cousin, "*My father was so very, very gallant. Do you remember at all how he carried my mother around on a cushion? He brought her breakfast to bed to her on weekend mornings, even when she was perfectly well. (My husband sometimes does the same.) He, daddy, coddled us girls, also.*"[397]

As Christmas approaches, Mrs. Ray asks Mr. Ray for the big brass bowl in the window of Dodd and Storer's. Stella Hart did acquire a brass bowl, probably in exactly the way described (Mrs. Ray bought it for herself). The bowl stands on three little legs. This story, perhaps more than any other, captures the love between these parents, and the humor and charm of their lives together.

Dodd and Storer's was almost certainly Martin and Hoerr's at 111 S. Front, opposite the Saulpaugh - though Tom Hart would not have walked past it on the way to his shoe store (as Bob Ray passed Dodd and Storer's every day). Martin and Hoerr sold jewelry, china, cut glass ... and brassware. The firm remained in business in Mankato until 1990. There was another store on Front Street which sold brassware - Palmer Brothers at 311 - but Mr. Hart wouldn't have passed this on his way to the shoe store, either. This is all beside the point, because by this time, Mr. Hart was working at the Court House on Fifth Street, and he didn't pass <u>any</u> stores on his way to work.

One of Betsy's Christmas gifts is a Ouija board, and the fact that it plays a role in the story is puzzling. Betsy, despite her romanticism, is "a balanced, capable person"[398] (upon whom Julia always relies for common-sense advice). Yet Betsy seems to believe in the power of the Ouija board. When Betsy asks it what lies ahead for her in Christmas week, the table responds, "Trouble." Betsy is sure that Tacy, who was running the board with her, would not have engineered such a response. Julia suggests that some inner dramatic impulse caused Betsy to push it unconsciously. Betsy "pretends" to be satisfied with this explanation. And "trouble" is definitely ahead. What is the reader meant to deduce? The Ouija board seems to have the last word. Of course, when Bonnie asks the board for the name of Carney's future husband, it tells them "Lawrence!"[399] (A Ouija-oops, since Carney doesn't marry Larry.)

A similar instance occurs in *Carney's House Party*. When Betsy tells Carney the "wishing well" story, Carney challenges Betsy: "You don't believe in wishing wells!" "Don't I?" is Betsy's cryptic response.[400] Maud probably felt she had good reason to believe. The wish she made at Ramona's Wishing Well (near San Diego) really was that she might sell a story, and very soon after, she sold her first one. When Grandma Austin heard what Maud had wished for, she said, "*I should think a girl of your age would be wishing something about a young man or to be married.*"[401] Carney's response to Betsy is similar: "What a silly thing to wish for. I should think you'd have wished something about Joe."[402]

Cathy Halliday, the heroine of *Gentlemen from England*, takes astrology very seriously. Her face assumed "the expression of mystic abstraction that it always wore when she studied the science of the stars."[403] Moreover, her charts and predictions prove to be very accurate as the plot unravels. The Ouija board, wishing well, and astrological prognostications may reflect a streak of superstition in Maud - but more likely, they just make for a good story.

The mistletoe at Bonnie's party probably had a real-life osculatory counterpart. Maud wrote "*Oh you mistletoe*!" in her High School Scrapbook under a clipping (presumably from her sophomore year) which reads: "*Mr. and Mrs. Hayward gave an informal dance at their home on Saturday evening to twenty of the girls and boys of the younger set. Miss Constance Davis of St. Paul being the honor guest."*[404] Perhaps the party from *Heaven to Betsy* was really at the home of Herman Hayward (the inspiration for the character Stan Moore), rather than at Bonnie's - but the mistletoe was obviously as pleasantly mischievous for Maud as it was for Betsy.

One of the Crowd's Christmas week outings freshman year is the winter picnic, to which they walk through Little Syria. Sophomore year, the Crowd acquires a member who, in real life, lived in Tinkcomville (Little Syria). The young man appears as Squirrelly in the Betsy-Tacy books. Tinkcomville was home to many families which did not belong to the Syrian (Lebanese) community; "Squirrelly's" family is one example.

Tony lights up a cigarette during another Crowd event - the skating party. Both girls and boys are shocked by this, but Tony was headed for even worse trouble. In *Betsy Was a Junior*, Tony says on page 158, "You ought to try to keep boys away from the pool hall, Betsy. It's a den of iniquity, Miss Bangeter says." (The town's pool hall was located at 103 S. Front.) By page 207 of *Betsy Was a Junior*, things have gotten much worse. "I hate to say it, but I believe he came to school when he'd been drinking." This is a pretty severe charge, since alcohol is almost never mentioned in the Betsy-Tacy books.

Christmas was on Tuesday, we learn in *Heaven to Betsy*, and sure enough, Christmas <u>did</u> fall on a Tuesday in 1906. Was there actually a full moon looking down on Tony and Betsy as they walked home from Bonnie's party (on December 26)? Very nearly, since the moon was full on December 30, 1906.

The week of holiday activities follows the actual 1906 calendar. Tuesday was Christmas, so the following Monday was December 31, New Year's Eve (which was celebrated at Tacy's). On New Year's Day, Betsy and Julia plan to tell their father about their desire to become Episcopalians. Betsy says, "We go back to school a week from tomorrow. Let's talk to him a week from today."[405] But then, "the Sunday before school resumed ... she said to Julia: 'Today is the day we talk to papa.'"[406] If New Year's Day was Tuesday, one week later would not have been a Sunday.

Early in *Heaven to Betsy*, we hear that Julia has joined the choir of St. John's Episcopal Church. This was the real name of the Episcopal church whose choir, and eventually congregation,

BECHS

St. John's Episcopal Church

Maud and her older sister became Episcopalians, just as Betsy and Julia did. St. John's was first built in 1866. The old building was replaced by a modern church (on the same site) in 1967.

Coll. of Elizabeth Miller

Mike Parker
(Tony Markham)

"His hair, parted at the left side, stood up on the right side in a black curly bush. He had heavy eyebrows and large sleepy dark eyes and full lips." (HTB p. 103)

Mike's House
(Tony's House)

The Parker family was living in this house at 339 Clark Street (now East Pleasant) around the time Maud met Mike.

1912 Otaknam

Interior of High School
First Floor Hallway circa 1910

1912 Otaknam

Interior of High School
Assembly Room circa 1910

Maud and her friends usually attempted to secure back-row seats in the Assembly Room.

Kathleen joined, followed by Maud. (Both had been confirmed as Episcopalians before Maud began high school.) After a particularly powerful sermon in October of her sophomore year, Maud wrote in her high school diary, "*The Bishop of Porto* [sic] *Rico almost made me a missionary.*"[407]

No doubt Mr. Hart responded to his daughters in much the same way Mr. Ray did. In his brilliant armchair speech, Mr. Ray says that the Baptists respect the Rays, though they enjoy dancing and playing whist, activities frowned upon by the Baptist Church. "They even asked papa to be a deacon."[408] Tom Hart really was a deacon of the Baptist church in Mankato. "The most important part of religion isn't in any church," Mr. Ray said. "It's down in your own heart. Religion is in your thoughts, and in the way you act from day to day, in the way you treat other people. It's honesty, and unselfishness, and kindness. Especially kindness."[409]

Mr. Ray says that everything is settled, until the day Margaret comes to them and says she wants to be a Mormon. Of course, he was kidding. And Helen Hart never became a Mormon, but Alice Dunnell (Louisa from *Betsy's Wedding*) related that she and Helen had dabbled in the Church of Christ Scientist in Minneapolis. Later in life Helen became a devout Christian Scientist. So none of the Hart girls remained Baptist.

During the talk with Mr. Ray, "Julia's eyes filled with tears, although she didn't cry as easily as Betsy did."[410] In a letter to her family written in 1909, Kathleen confided, "*I wish I were the kind of a woman who can cry easily because it is much simpler. I always fight it some other way. So I walked around alone until it* [her problem] *was most all gone and I wanted to sleep.*"[411] This is the way Julia dealt with the blow from the Epsilon Iotas in *Betsy Was a Junior.* "I was walking all that evening. I walked all the way to downtown Minneapolis and back. I had to keep walking to keep going."[412]

With the holiday season behind them, the members of the Crowd buckle down to prepare for exams. At the end of the first semester, Betsy "squeezed through algebra by a breath, through Latin by a hair. Her history mark was fair." In English Betsy earned a 96.[413] The following are actual grades for Maud Hart's first semester of high school: *algebra, 76; Latin, 76; ancient history, 93; English, 90.*

After examinations, the Crowd goes on a sleighing party. It is described in far less detail than most Crowd excursions - in only a handful of sentences. Yet in few words, Maud is able to convey a feeling of real wretchedness. With Tony's arm draped along the back of the seat behind Bonnie, "it was a horrible party for Betsy."[414] There was an equally horrible sleighing party for Emily in *Emily of Deep Valley*. Surely Maud must have experienced a memorably unpleasant sleigh ride. These two were pretty awful for the protagonists. In both cases, the man of the heroine's dreams has chosen to sit beside another woman! Fictionally, Maud calls the sleigh the "Blue Jay"[415] or "Bluejay,"[416] and Mankato newspapers of the time refer to sleigh rides on the "blue jay." Merian Lovelace Kirchner remarks: "*Well, she'd never have been at her best on a sleigh ride. She really did hate the cold!*"[417]

The Rays attend the annual St. Patrick's Day supper at the Catholic church. They are waited on by "Katie and Tacy with shamrocks on their shirtwaists, green bows in their hair."[418] St. John's Catholic Church really held an annual St. Patrick's Day dinner - a tradition begun in 1885.

March also brought Bonnie's departure. Connie Davis really left Mankato on March 23, 1907. Though her father was not called back to Paris, the family did make a trip to Europe before Dr. Davis joined the faculty of Macalester College in St. Paul. He taught in the department of Social and Political Science from 1907 until 1933. The reader is somewhat glad to see Bonnie go, though Maud must not have been - Connie spent the following Thanksgiving (1907) as a guest of the Hart family.[419]

The next to go are, of course, the Humphreys. The Andrews family did move to San Diego in 1907. Betsy and Herbert are consoled by plans for Betsy to visit him when she eventually travels to San Diego to see her grandparents. This is exactly what Maud did in 1911. By this time, her grandmother was a widow, but her Uncle Frank was living there, too. (Consult Chapter 12 herein for more particulars.)

When Betsy and Tacy reminisce about events from previous books, their fictional world and our experience of it blend intangibly. Those Hill Street memories are in our memory banks, too. Those who read (or were read) the first books at an early

Duplicated in several collections

Half a Dozen Peaches

"The girls went down to the Photographic Gallery and had their pictures taken with Bonnie." (HTB p. 234) The name of the photographer is not given fictionally, but in *Betsy and Joe*, Betsy's graduation pictures are taken at Snow's. Snow's was on the second floor at 313 S. Front. He took this photo of the six peaches.

JUST AT THE THRESHOLD
of the lovliest period of her life, what mother does not wish to perpetuate her daughter's beauty at sweet sixteen.
A LIFE SIZE PHOTOGRAPH
in sepia or colors, is just the thing. We do fine work in this line.
JOHN R. SNOW, Photographer

Mankato Free Press

History of Blue Earth County

Mr. Snow

John R. Snow was a prominent Mankato photographer.

Duplicated in several collections

Two Triumvirates
(Minus Cab)

Eating ice cream in the Hart dining room, left to right: Jim Baker, Marion Willard, Helmus Andrews, Maud Hart, Rupert Andrews, Connie Davis. About 1907.

Duplicated in several collections

Hot Dog!

Connie Davis (Bonnie), Herman Hayward (Stan), and Marion Willard (Carney) are roasting weenies, as Betsy's Crowd so often did.

age, may have had the dyed-sand-store episode in memory for six or more years before coming to *Heaven to Betsy* and finding Betsy and Tacy reminiscing about it. It is by this time an event in our childhood almost as much as it was in theirs. "I can even remember when you were little girls,"[420] Margaret boasts. So can we, and it gives us the same sense of pleasure and even pride that Margaret feels.

As Betsy travels to Milwaukee in *Betsy in Spite of Herself,* Maud retells the story of "one summer afternoon when Betsy and Tacy were five years old."[421] (In fact, they were six at the end of *Betsy-Tacy*!) Betsy can only remember the first verse of the song she and Tacy made up about going to Milwaukee in "that distant roseate past."[422] It is roseate for the reader too, but not distant. We have only to pick up a well-worn copy of *Betsy-Tacy* to reread the Milwaukee song in its entirety.

The idea of a character set in her own high school days had begun to ferment in Maud's mind as early as 1938, when she wrote a short story in which the protagonist "*thought she looked skippy in a blue and white sailor suit* [which] *belted trimly at a small swaying waist and swirled about slender ankles.*"[423] This character also wore an "*airy regiment of puffs,*" which is, word for word, just what Tib created for Betsy on page 153 of *Betsy Was a Junior.*

Our high school Betsy soon began to take even more dramatically distinct form, in another short story, "I Am Curly." This story, written in the first person, is told by a young girl with such stubbornly straight hair that her friends teasingly call her "Curly." Her big sister "Nannine" has naturally curly hair and sings soprano. Her baby sister is "Pussy" and the family horse is "Old Mag." Curly's red-haired mother is from a strict background and likes to see her own daughters have fun. Her father teases her about all the boys who come to the house. "*He says he wouldn't mind the sugar bills if only the fudge hardened once in a while.*"[424] Many of the Betsy-Tacy high school characters are described. Tacy appears as "Bee for Beatrice," Tib as "Gretchen," Carney as "Dot," Winona as "Peg," and Irma as "Erma." Tony appears as "Bill Burgess." Mr. Thumbler is "Buzz Hickey" and Mamie Dodd is "Lizzie Cross."

Coll. of Elizabeth Miller

Eleanor Wood (Dorothy)
As a Young Lady

Dorothy was a member of Julia's small circle of friends.

Newspaper File

Anna Held

Starched ruffles pinned across her chest may have given Betsy an Anna Held curve - but Anna Held's curves were surely the product of the sturdiest Victorian whalebone.

Coll. of Fallie Beers

Ruth Williams (Alice)
As a Young Lady

Alice, Betsy's friend from Pleasant Street, has lost her fat blond braids. In *Heaven to Betsy*, she appears as a "tall blonde girl with glasses." (HTB p. 75)

Miss Clarke explains the Essay Contest: "The Philomathians and Zetamathians compete every year for the essay cup. Each society chooses one senior, one junior, one sophomore and one freshman to make up a team. A subject is assigned, and the two teams are excused from all homework in English in order to have time for library study."[425] Miss Clarke points out that by spring of '07, the Zetamathians hold the athletics cup and the Philomathians the debating cup. This is historically accurate. May 11th was a Saturday that year, as reported, but the Zets won the essay cup.

Members of the chorus, Betsy and Tacy sing "My Heart's in the Highlands" at commencement. A "Program of Scotch and Irish Songs" was given by the high school chorus on December 6, 1907, at eight p.m. Kathleen Hart sang "Comin' Thro' the Rye." Tessie Kenney (Katie) sang "Killarney." And a group of "eight boys" sang "My Heart's in the Highlands."[426]

At the end of *Heaven to Betsy*, Maud provides the second semester grades: "algebra, 75; Latin, 78; ancient history, 91; composition, 92."[427] These are close to the actual second semester results but not exact. The real grades were these: *algebra, 76; Latin, 80; ancient history, 89; English 85.*

On the last day of the book, Betsy wears her pink lawn jumper walking to meet Tacy at Lincoln Park - the same jumper she had worn on the day she was so out of sorts, before high school began. So much changed. So much the same. As always with Lovelace, the circle is unbroken.

[284] *Downtown,* p. 11.

[285] Ibid., p. 71.

[286] *Mankato Free Press,* 4-10-52.

[287] *Downtown,* p. 180.

[288] *Heaven to Betsy,* p. 20.

[289] *Betsy in Spite of Herself*, p. 257.

[290] *Betsy and Joe,* p. 137.

[291] *Betsy Was a Junior,* p. 123.

[292] *Heaven to Betsy*, p. 21.

[293] *Mankato Free Press,* 4-7-10.

[294] MHL to L. Demp, 11-2-56.

[295] *Minneapolis Tribune*, 8-25-65.

[296] *Heaven to Betsy*, p. 13.

[297] MHL to L. Mayotte, 2-19-76.

[298] LWW, n.p.

[299] *Betsy in Spite of Herself*, p. 8.

[300] *Heaven to Betsy,* p. 26.

[301] *Betsy Was a Junior,* p. 162.

[302] HHF to MHL, 8-11-46.

[303] *Heaven to Betsy,* p. 26.

[304] Ibid., p. 26.

[305] A. Brown to SSW, 3-29-91.

[306] *Heaven to Betsy,* p. 58.

[307] MHL to B. Gardner, 7-14-75.

[308] *Heaven to Betsy,* p. 30.

[309] *Betsy and Joe,* p. 125.

[310] MHL to B. Gardner, 7-14-75.

[311] *Downtown,* p. 72.

[312] Lippert memoirs, p. 20.

[313] *Heaven to Betsy,* p. 20.

[314] Ibid., p. 31.

[315] Ibid., p. 44.

[316] Interview with E. Wiecking, 8-14-85.

[317] *Heaven to Betsy,* p. 48.

[318] Ibid., p. 33.

[319] Ibid.

[320] Ibid., p. 35.

[321] Ibid., p. 90.

[322] Ibid., p. 26.

[323] Ibid., p. 35.

[324] Maud Hart, unpublished High School Scrapbook, p. A'.

[325] *Heaven to Betsy,* p. 34.

[326] Ibid., p. 168.

[327] Lippert memoirs, p. 19.

[328] Lovelace Interview, University of Michigan.

[329] *Betsy-Tacy,* p. 48.

[330] Lippert memoirs, p. 19.

[331] *Heaven to Betsy*, p. 45.

[332] *Emily of Deep Valley,* p. 8.

[333] *Heaven to Betsy,* p. 50.

[334] MHL to Gretchen, et al., 5-29-65.

[335] Editor Laura Vadaj notes that "ECOD" was a euphemistic exclamation used in Goldsmith's *She Stoops to Conquer.*

[336] *Mankato Free Press*, 9-10-52.

[337] *Heaven to Betsy,* p. 62.

[338] *Betsy in Spite of Herself,* p. 80.

[339] *Heaven to Betsy,* p. 140.

[340] Lippert memoirs, pp. 21-22.

[341] MPH to Hart Family, p. 283.

[342] *Betsy in Spite of Herself,* p. 30.

[343] *Mankato Free Press,* 12-20-07.

[344] *Betsy Was a Junior*, p. 138.

[345] *Betsy and Joe*, p. 133.

[346] *Heaven to Betsy,* p. 53.

[347] Ibid., p. 75.

[348] MHL to J. Ellen, 9-10-67.

[349] *Heaven to Betsy,* p. 61.

[350] *Carney's House Party,* p. 36.

[351] *Heaven to Betsy,* p. 89.

[352] Ibid., p. 70.

[353] *Heaven to Betsy,* p. 58.

[354] Ibid., p. 67.

[355] MHL to J. Tessari, 8-11-73.

[356] *Heaven to Betsy,* p. 103.

[357] Ibid., p. 118.

[358] Ibid., p. 98.

[359] Ibid., p. 69.

[360] Lippert memoirs, p. 7.

[361] W.D. Willard, unpublished memoirs, p. 25.

[362] RWW to MHL, 5-31-48.

[363] *Heaven to Betsy,* p. 75.

[364] *Betsy in Spite of Herself,* p. 10.

[365] *Betsy and Joe,* p. 171.

[366] *Betsy in Spite of Herself,* p. 252.

[367] *Heaven to Betsy,* p. 100.

[368] Ibid., p. 90.

[369] High School Scrapbook, p. B, attach. b.

[370] *Heaven to Betsy,* p. 92.

[371] Ibid., pp. 92-93.

[372] LWW, n.p.

[373] "The Scrappies' Club," *Jack and Jill*, April 1944, p. 21.

[374] "The Scrappies' Club," *Jack and Jill*, November 1943, p. 4.

[375] Ibid., p. 3.

[376] MPH to Hart Family, p. 240.

[377] Lovelace Interview, University of Michigan.

[378] The Adler article appeared in *Western Folklore* 40 (1981):45-54. The above citation was first made by Debbie Hanson in her essay "To Thine Own Traditions True: Folklore and Adolescent Romance in Maud Hart Lovelace's Betsy-Tacy Series."

[379] Lovelace Interview, University of Michigan.

[380] *Mankato Free Press*, 11-20-46.

[381] *Betsy-Tacy,* p. 87.

[382] *Gentlemen from England*, p. 77.

[383] *Heaven to Betsy,* p. 96.

[384] *Mankato Free Press*, 4-16-52.

[385] *Heaven to Betsy,* p. 48.

[386] *Heaven to Betsy,* p. 111.

[387] High School Scrapbook, p. B, attach. a.

[388] *Heaven to Betsy,* p. 113.

[389] Interview with B. Andrews, 11-3-90.

[390] *Heaven to Betsy,* p. 120.

[391] Ibid., p. 124.

[392] *Betsy and Joe,* p. 89.

[393] *Heaven to Betsy,* p. 123.

[394] *Over the Big Hill,* p. 10.

[395] *Heaven to Betsy,* p. 125.

[396] *Over the Big Hill,* p. 23.

[397] MHL to R. Lee, 7-25-65.
[398] *Heaven to Betsy,* p. 147.
[399] Ibid., p. 168.
[400] *Carney's House Party,* p. 120.
[401] CA C.V. file, p. 8.
[402] *Carney's House Party,* p. 120.
[403] *Gentlemen from England,* p. 116.
[404] High School Scrapbook, p. F'.
[405] *Heaven to Betsy,* p. 206.
[406] Ibid., p. 206.
[407] M. Hart, Diary Outtakes., p. 5.
[408] *Heaven to Betsy,* p. 210.
[409] Ibid., p. 212.
[410] *Heaven to Betsy,* p. 210.
[411] KPH letters, p. 13.
[412] *Betsy Was a Junior,* p. 196.
[413] *Heaven to Betsy,* p. 216.
[414] Ibid., p. 215.
[415] *Betsy Was a Junior,* p. 147.
[416] *Emily of Deep Valley,* p. 156.
[417] MLK to SSW, 11-15-91.
[418] *Heaven to Betsy,* p. 227.
[419] *Mankato Free Press,* 11-29-07.
[420] *Heaven to Betsy,* p. 237.
[421] *Betsy in Spite of Herself,* p. 114.
[422] Ibid., p. 114.
[423] M. Hart, "Rendez-Vous with Fame," p. 1.
[424] M. Hart, "I Am Curly," p. 2.
[425] *Heaven to Betsy,* p. 228.
[426] High School Scrapbook, p. B', innards b.
[427] *Heaven to Betsy,* p. 262.

CHAPTER SEVEN
On *Betsy in Spite of Herself*
September 1907 to June 1908

Since this book, the sixth in the series, begins with a quotation from Betsy's journal, the reader is naturally curious about Maud's high school diaries. A promotional booklet about Maud and the series produced by Thomas Y. Crowell, the original publisher of the Betsy-Tacy books, sheds some light on those diaries. The cover of the first edition, printed in 1949, pictured the Vera Neville drawing from the dust jacket of *Carney's House Party*. According to the booklet, the Betsy-Tacy series "*might never have been written if Mrs. Lovelace were not, among other things, one of the most unflagging diarists since Pepys....* [Maud's] *diaries are well-thumbed, well-worn copy books with marbled-paper backs and blue-lined pages packed full of young Maud Hart's adventures with her teachers, girl friends, boy friends, parents, aunts, uncles, train acquaintances, hack drivers and even, yes, Santa Claus.*"

Maud told an interviewer that she began a new diary each high school year, "*entitling the first 'Comedy of Errors,' then 'Much Ado About Nothing,' 'As You Like It,' and finally, 'All's Well That Ends Well.'*"[428] (All four diaries were subtitled, "Monkeyshines of a Mankatonian.") It is of interest that in Maud's sister Helen's high school yearbook (the 1917 *Hesperian*), the four classes are labeled the same way. The caption under the photo of the freshmen reads, "Comedy of Errors"; the sophomores, "Much Ado About Nothing"; the juniors, "As You Like It"; and the seniors, "All's Well That Ends Well." All four, of course, are titles of Shakespearean comedies. After Maud had first used them on the covers of her journals, Helen, rightfully thinking the idea a clever one, borrowed it. Helen was on the *Hesperian* board as a senior.

The second edition of the Crowell promotional booklet provides some of the few existing quotations from Maud's diaries. "*Just a few lines to open the record of my sophomore year. Isn't it a little mysterious to begin a new journal like this? I can run my fingers through the fresh clean pages, which I am going to write upon. But I cannot tell what the writing will be! It is almost as if I were ushered into the winding hall of fate, but next day's destiny was just hidden behind a turning and I could not reach it until the day was over.*" This will sound familiar to Betsy-Tacy readers, for it appears, almost verbatim, on the first page of *Betsy in Spite of Herself*.

Maud shared with a fan one amusing diary entry which never made it to a Betsy-Tacy book: "*Mother and Kathleen and I sat up until midnight, eating ice cream and discussing leprosy.*"[429]

The short story "I Am Curly" begins with a good chunk of Betsy's entry on page 2 of *Betsy in Spite of Herself.* Whether Maud took both sections from her real diary or applied to Betsy what she had written for Curly is anyone's guess. "*I am Curly. They call me Curly because my hair is straight, and I have to put it up on kid curlers, which I despise, because what am I going to do when I get married? But on the other hand, if I* <u>*don't*</u> *put it up on curlers, I probably never* <u>*will*</u> *get married. That's the way I look at it. It's all right, it's fine for the kids to tease me and call me Curly, because it's no joke to sit around all day on the day of a party with my hair up on kid curlers and then in the evening have it rain and my hair go straight as a string. I can't see why Edison and all these people who go around inventing autos and things can't concentrate on something important like how to make a girl's hair stay curled in rainy weather.*"[430]

A number of diary quotations appear throughout *Betsy in Spite of Herself*, and they were very likely borrowed from, or at least inspired by, the real sophomore-year diary. Journal entries can also be found in *Betsy and Joe* on pages 51, 150, and 244. Another journal excerpt might be cloaked as a response from Mr. Ray in *Betsy and Joe*. He asks Betsy what she did on her last day of school. She responds, "Oh, finished my physics notebook, practiced my oration for Miss O'Rourke, opened presents, and wept."[431] These <u>feel</u> like Maud's own words at age eighteen.

Similarly, the two times Maud quotes Betsy's letters to Herbert in California, they seem particularly authentic. One is on page 148 of *Betsy Was a Junior*: "'Now,' she wrote to Herbert, 'will I show an unparalleled exhibition of courage, steadfastness, self-denial, etc. !!!!!!'" It may be the six exclamation points - for whatever reason, this feels suspiciously like a quotation, taken perhaps word for word from Maud's diary.

Maud certainly did correspond with Helmus Andrews (Herbert). In the fall of 1909, Kathleen wrote home from Germany: "*Give up Helmus ... and write your poor homesick sis.*"[432] Maud herself commented, "*For years Helmus and I corresponded. No romance; we both just liked to write.*"[433] According to his wife, Billie

Andrews, Helmus had not saved Maud's letters through the years, so they could not have been returned to her for use as research material when she was writing *Betsy in Spite of Herself* in 1945. And since it is very unlikely that Maud would have kept copies of her letters to Helmus, the excerpts from Betsy's letters must have been from Maud's diary, if they in fact represent real quotations.

Maud donated her High School Scrapbook and many portrait-style photographs to the Blue Earth County Historical Society in Mankato. It is regrettable that Lovelace, like Pepys, did not bequeath her diaries to a college or literary collection. Unfortunately, Maud decided the diaries were too silly to withstand the scrutiny of posterity, and she burned them.

It is not entirely surprising that Maud destroyed her diaries. (It may have been while doing so that she accidentally singed her marriage certificate, which has mysteriously charred edges.) By the second half of the 1950s, the Betsy-Tacy books had all been written, and Maud suspected that there would not be another. Meanwhile, she was receiving many letters from fans asking about real-life counterparts to Betsy-Tacy characters and events. Maud surely found this curiosity rather daunting. Her diaries had yielded chunks of plot, and even some phrasing for the high school books, but the diaries were written when Maud was a young teenager who probably sounded pretty frivolous and silly at times. For example, in *Heaven to Betsy*, we hear that Tony came to the Ray house seven times one day during Easter vacation.[434] Maud had probably found in her diary that a young man (possibly the real Tony) had paid seven calls one day. As she herself said, the diaries "*were full of boys, boys, boys.*"[435] Did Maud want to go down in history as the author with the silliest diaries? Who among us can read over a diary written at age fourteen without a blush? Maud's decision is understandable, though unfortunate. We must respect the author's privacy - or rather, we must respect her decision. Her privacy, to a certain extent, she forfeited by writing more than ten magically autobiographical books. By virtue of our dedication to Maud's books, we have a "need to know"!

Maud made an unknowingly prophetic comment after she had completed *The Charming Sally*. She remarked that children cannot begin to write too young, and that they should keep diaries of everyday events, of their school days. Such early memoirs will provide invaluable assistance to them as adults, should they choose to pursue a career in writing. When she made this comment in 1932, Maud had no idea just how invaluable her own diaries would be to her, that Betsy's lifeblood would flow from them!

The day Betsy begins her sophomore-year diary is the day before school starts. If school begins the day after Labor Day, as in *Heaven to Betsy,* this date would be September 3, 1907. The Ray family has just returned from a summer at the lake. Last year (in *Heaven to Betsy*) we heard that the Rays enjoyed visits to Murmuring Lake at all seasons, but this is the first evidence of any visit other than the October anniversary trip. Perhaps the Rays didn't have the means to stay at the lake in the Hill Street days. Tom Hart's new job and status brought a real lifestyle change, as well as a new house.

The Harts did spend the entire summer of 1907 on the lake - but it was at Lake Crystal rather than Madison Lake (Murmuring Lake). They rented the Gilbert Guttersen residence and returned to Mankato on August 28, 1907. In the summer of 1908, the Harts spent the better part of July at Point Pleasant, Madison Lake. In 1909, they spent several weeks of the summer visiting relatives in Willmar and a short time at Madison Lake.

The Harts no doubt enjoyed their yearly return to Mankato as much as the Rays enjoyed getting back to Deep Valley. Autumn brings, as usual, the Rays' wedding anniversary - but this year, rain prevents the pilgrimage to Murmuring Lake. However, we feel more than compensated (as do the Rays) by the anniversary dinner at the Moorish Cafe. "The Cafe was on the ground floor. One could enter it from the street or from the lobby. Mr. Ray had told Julia to enter from the lobby."[436] An insurance-company floor plan reveals that the cafe did have two doors. "The long narrow room was mysteriously dim, lighted only by small brass lamps studded with red and green and purple glass. When she grew accustomed to this colored dusk, Betsy saw rich rugs and hangings."[437] Tom Edwards of Mankato provided a description of the Moorish Cafe which was of a piece with Maud's: "*If some diva or world renowned traveler came to town, Mrs. F.K. Snyder would entertain them in the Moorish room, furnished with Oriental rugs and lamps made of brass, studded with red and purple glass.*"[438] As discussed in Chapter 5, Mrs. Poppy may have been partly inspired by Nettie Fuller Snyder. This theory seems increasingly likely, given the fact that Mrs. Poppy was associated with the visit to the Moorish Cafe and that Mrs. Snyder was in fact the proprietor of the cafe (while her husband ran the hotel itself).

An advertisement for the Saulpaugh ("Minnesota's Best Country Hotel") appears in the 1910-1911 Mankato Directory: "*At the Hub of the Business Center. RATES: $2 to $3.50. Now thoroughly modernized by installation of running water, local and long distance phones and Tungsten electric lights in each room. Our Moorish Cafe the finest in Southern Minnesota. Headquarters for all automobilists.*"[439]

The twenty-first wedding anniversary gift Mrs. Ray receives at the Moorish Cafe is "a dish, gold-rimmed, hand-painted with sprays of green leaves and reddish colored berries."[440] The dish, really Mr. Hart's gift to his wife, is exactly as described.

Another festive celebration in the fall of 1907 is Julia's eighteenth birthday party. "Betsy and Carney, assigned to serve the refreshments, were hilariously inspired to wear their fathers' dress suits."[441] The *Mankato Free Press* described Kathleen's eighteenth birthday party as follows: "*A very pleasant event occurred last evening, when Mr. and Mrs. T. W. Hart entertained a party of young people at a six o'clock dinner for their daughter, Miss Kathleen. The rooms were decorated in pink and white. The dinner was a delicious one, in seven courses, and was served by Misses Maude Hart and Marion Willard.*"[442] The newspaper doesn't mention that Maud and Marney were wearing their fathers' dress suits! The two really wore the dress suits to serve at Kathleen's eighteenth birthday party, as described in *Betsy in Spite of Herself*. Maud noted in her diary, "*I look so sporty in my dress suit, I hate to take it off.*"[443]

The girls hold a mock wedding at Julia's birthday party. The guests write the names of seven boys on seven slips of paper to put under their pillows with a piece of "wedding" cake. (Tacy is right, by the way - there was a Mrs. Olcott {Rita O'Donovan Olcott}.) This cake ritual, with variations, is chronicled in the *Frank C. Brown Collection of North Carolina Folklore*.

Maud plays on two prophetic strains here. "What if you haven't met your future husband yet? I hope I haven't," Tacy says.[444]

MHL Archive

Maud Hart, Aged 16

The bracelet on Maud's right arm is presumably the one Betsy received for her sixteenth birthday.

Duplicated in several collections

Tess and Bick Kenney (Katie and Tacy)

Bick is wearing the coronet braids for which Tacy was famous. The Kenney sisters look very much the way the reader might picture the Kelly sisters.

Minnesota Valley Regional Library

Helen Hart

Margaret's braids "were short, but that didn't matter, for they were almost completely concealed by giant hair bows behind each ear, yellow tonight, to match the sailor suit." (BWJ p. 18)

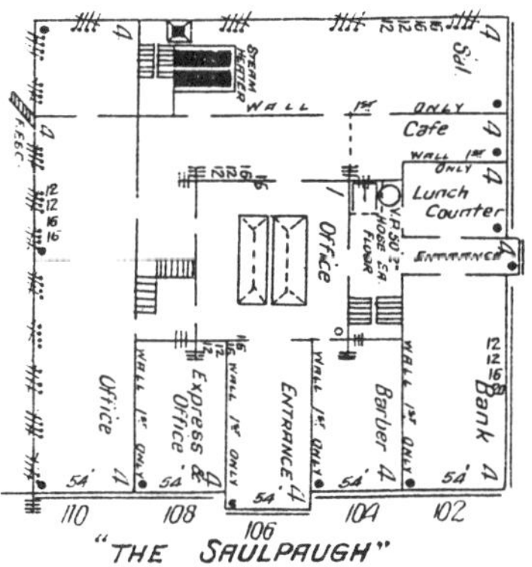

BECHS

Saulpaugh Hotel Floor Plan

The Rays celebrated their anniversary in the hotel's Moorish Cafe.

Coll. of Louise King

Carney and Al

Al is "Carney's chief escort since Larry Humphreys had moved away." (BWJ p. 44)

Coll. of Paul Ford

Winona II

"Winona was tall, thin, angular, yet jauntily graceful." (HTB p. 52)

Duplicated in several collections

Bick and Maud A-Halloweenin'

"There's no one I can be so silly with as I can with you," Tacy tells Betsy. (HTB p. 262)

(And she hasn't yet met him. Two books to wait.) Betsy, meanwhile, lists seven boys, and after four days, the remaining three are swept away by Anna, who doesn't know what's going on. Betsy "was stranded by Fate not knowing whom she would marry ... a Stranger, Phil Brandish, or Joe."[445] It was calculated of Maud to leave Phil in the running - thus maintaining the interest level she is slowly building for him as a new character.

Betsy's diary mentions Irma, another new friend. Irma was based on Florence Mildred Oleson, who was called "Mil" or "Billie." She was the middle daughter of Carl and Hattie Oleson. All three daughters, Louise, Mildred, and Loretta, were born in Howard, South Dakota. Mildred's father became president of the National Bank of Commerce after the family moved to Mankato in about 1901. Mildred's nieces, who often visited the Oleson house at 405 Pleasant Street while Mildred's parents were alive, remember no diamond-shaped flowerbeds (which Irma's house had). We learn that Irma is an Episcopalian.[446] Mildred Oleson was an Episcopalian, until she became a Catholic upon her marriage.

Irma was not the only newcomer to the Crowd. "Before Hallowe'en a curly-headed Irish boy named Dennis started going around with Cab. Cab brought him to the Ray house, and Betsy asked him to her party. And she asked a football hero named Al who had started going with Carney, and a boy nicknamed Squirrelly who had a case on Irma."[447]

Dennis Farisy is "Dennie" by page 83 of *Betsy in Spite of Herself.* (His name appears as both "Dennie" and "Denny" on page 99 of *Betsy and Joe.*) Dennie was really Paul Gerald Ford and he was Irish and he did like to sing.

We learn Al's surname (Larson) on page 181, with another reminder that he was a "football hero." (He was.) He was also a "good-natured Dane."[448] Al was based on Henry Lee. Henry was born in Massachusetts - not Denmark. (His father, Ole, came from Norway.) Henry moved from Sleepy Eye, Minnesota, to Mankato in 1904 with his parents and his four brothers. At the time the Crowd was in high school, the Lees lived at 133 Clark Street (East Pleasant).

Squirrelly was Earl ("Squ-EARL") King who lived in Tinkcomville at 119 James Avenue. Maud's Scrapbook contains a

Coll. of Robert Cahill

Mildred Oleson

"She's nice; she's very sweet, with a figure like Lillian Russell's. The boys are crazy about her." (BSH p. 4)

Coll. of Robert Cahill

aka Mil

These photos were taken during an Oleson family vacation at Lake Washington, not far from Mankato.

Coll. of Robert Cahill

aka Billie

Mildred's high school friends sometimes called her "Billie."

Coll. of Robert Cahill

aka Irma (fictionally)

Mildred is getting the mail to take back to her family's lake cabin.

1910 Annual

Herman Hayward
(Stan Moore)

Stan was class president for two years.

Coll. of Robert Cahill

Paul Ford
(Dennie Farisy)

"He was an ingratiating Irish boy with a curly tangle of hair, fuzzy eyebrows and a dimple in his chin. He liked to sing." (BWJ p. 122)

Coll. of Robert Cahill

Henry Lee
(Al Larson)

Al was a football hero who had started going around with Carney. Henry was a prominent member of the high school football team.

Coll. of Louise King

Clayton Burmeister

Clayton (nicknamed Scid) was an important part of Maud's high school Crowd.

Mankato, Its First Fifty Years

Ferdinand Heinze

"Mr. Heinz [sic] was indulgent. He appreciated the devotion ... and the nickels ... of high school boys and girls." (BSH p. 34)

1895 Atlas

Heinze's

The rear room originally housed the restaurant, while baked goods and candy were sold at the front of the store. "Repairing to Heinz's [sic], to the small mirror-walled room in back of the bakery which was labeled Ice Cream Parlor ... *Ivanhoe* was forgotten in Banana Splits and Deep Valley Specials." (BSH p. 34) note written by Marion Willard (Carney) which reads: "*Look here girls - don't you think this looks like 'Squirrell King.'*"[449] Earl's name also appeared on a list of the eight boys entertaining the Oktw (sic) Deltas. In *Betsy Was a Junior*, he is described as "a senior with a headful of tight curls, high color and a deceptively bashful air. He was one of the stars of the football team."[450] Earl graduated in 1909, like Squirrelly, but he doesn't appear to be in the football team photos shown in Chapter 8 (herein).

We meet two members of a more peripheral group of high school friends on page 187. The sophomore class president was Stan Moore. Stan was tall and relaxed and "conducted a meeting admirably."[451] This was Herman "Pinkey" Hayward. When he danced with Maud, he wrote his nickname on her dance card.

"Cab was vice-president, and a nice freckle-faced girl named Hazel Smith was treasurer." In *Betsy Was a Junior,* Hazel "was a friendly, freckle-face girl whom Betsy liked." Later she is described as "mirthful and breezy." She was "just coming into the group" as of autumn 1909.[452] Who was this likeable freckle-girl? See Chapter 8 (herein) for clues.

The Crowd often adjourns to Heinz's after school, "to the small mirror-walled room in back of the bakery which was labeled Ice Cream Parlor." The Crowd "sang, banged, whistled, shouted from one small table to another as though across a football field. Mr. Heinz was indulgent. He appreciated the devotion ... and the nickels ... of high school boys and girls. *Ivanhoe* was forgotten in Banana Splits and Deep Valley Specials."[453] By spring it will be Merry Widow Sundaes.

Mr. Heinz was Ferdinand Heinze, who was born at Bottendorf, Germany, in 1848. He was two years old when his family immigrated to America. Ferdinand opened his Mankato bakery and grocery business in 1879, which after 1890 was operated at 405 S. Front. After bearing him three children, Ferd's first wife died in 1883. Ferd then married her sister and had seven children more.

In the spring of 1908, Heinze renovated the entire interior and converted the back room into an ice cream parlor with a $3,000 soda fountain. The ice cream parlor was, as Maud described, a mirrored room. "*Each wall has three large panel mirrors, four by eight feet, and one four by six feet. The woodwork is all in mahogany, the rich color of which contrasts handsomely with the alabaster of the fountain, and the soft green tints of the walls and ceiling. Numerous electric lights, reflected back in the mirrors, make the scene one of brilliance. New tables and chairs provide accommodations for sixty people at one time.*"[454] With the restaurant section converted to ice cream parlor, Heinze's no longer served lunches and dinners, but an expert soda mixer was hired to create "*angels' delight, silver cremo, heavenly twin, devil's dream, Coney Island, pineapple soufile, tutti fruitti, maple nut, Buffalo, crushed fruit and numerous other sundaes. Others even more rare and beguiling will be supplied later. Then there are egg drinks galore, phosphates, mineral waters and lemonade, plain and fancy.*"[455]

Frequent visits to Heinz's afford a respite from the rigors of school. Sophomore classes include Latin with Mr. Morse, geometry with Miss O'Rourke, modern history with Miss Clarke, and rhetoric with Mr. Gaston. Maud's actual sophomore curriculum consisted of Caesar (Latin), plane geometry, modern history, and English II.

Miss Bangeter's Shakespeare class for seniors was "an institution at Deep Valley High School."[456] Betsy read the plays along with Julia, and Maud probably read the plays along with Kathleen, who was a senior. Maud wouldn't have known much about the class otherwise. The real Caroline[457] Bangeter was Caroline Fullerton. Miss Fullerton retired in 1908, at the end of Maud's sophomore year. From Maud's description of Miss Bangeter, we can conclude that Miss Fullerton was a memorable principal, well worth keeping on for two additional fictional years!

Betsy is elected secretary of her class this year. In fact, Maud was elected class treasurer during her sophomore year.

Miss Clarke suggests that the two Rays work together on a presentation for November Rhetoricals, since this is their last year in school together. Betsy is to write new words to a song for Julia to sing. "I'd thought of that 'Same Old Story' everybody's singing."[458]

"So Betsy went home and wrote new words for 'Same Old Story.' There were verses about the Freshman Girl, the Sophomore Girl, the Junior Girl and the Senior Girl, and after each verse the same refrain:

Parody on "Same old Story".

(1) I am going to sing a ditty-
Of the little freshman Maid,
Timid, fearful, and retiring,
Flirtacious I'm afraid.
Faithfully she learns her lessons,
And she never, never, cheats
Never sticks a pin into her neighbor,
Or carves initials on the seats.

cho. Same old story, same old High.
Same old bunch of gigglers,
As the years pass by.
She's a hummer, shining light,
Hurrah for 'Kato's Highschool girl,
For she's alright.

(2) But in constrast comes the sophmore,
She's no longer sweet and shy,
Maiden coyness has departed,
In her one year at the High,

Maud's Lyrics for "Same Old Story"

She disports herself at wink 'em
When the sophomores celebrate—
Post office her naughty soul delights in—
She fears not to stay out late
cho.

(3) Next in order comes the junior,
To descend from sophmore flight,
She's in love with some young senior,
Mourns and weeps at night,
From her lips fall words of wisdom,
Shakespeare, Chaucer, Milton too,
She holds learned discourse with (the teachers
Till the very air turns blue.
cho.

(4.) Tremble as you name the senior,
She fills the freshman heart with dread.
Youth, do not approach her lightly,
She's a brainy head.
She will work you to a finish,
Rope you in for all the shows,
Be warned by trophies she exhibits,
She's experienced, goodness knows!
cho.

Same old story,
Same old High,
Same old bunch of gigglers
As the years pass by.
She's a hummer,
A shining light,
For she's Deep Valley's High School Girl
And she's all right."[459]

"Same Old Story" gets Betsy into trouble with Mr. Gaston. He is annoyed by the success of the parody and attacks her about the color of apple blossoms in a short story she writes for his class. (Mr. Gaston claims that they are white.) Three years before writing *Betsy in Spite of Herself*, Maud described apple blossoms in *Over the Big Hill*: "An apple orchard made a patch of grayish pink."[460] Joe, of course, coming to Betsy's rescue, puts it best. "I think Betsy's word 'rosy' is excellent. They're colored just enough to make the effect rosy."[461]

In her senior class play, Kathleen Hart sang a solo which she had written called "In the Jolly Social Room." Maud probably helped out with the lyrics, as she did with "Same Old Story."

Late in the fall, the Episcopal church puts on a talent play and "through November the entries in Betsy's journal were all about *Wonderland*: 'Rehearsal for *Wonderland*.' 'Homework and *Wonderland*.' 'Practiced the Scarf Dance for hours. My feet are killing me.'"[462] Maud's fictional *Wonderland* was based on a play called *Puss in Boots*, really a benefit for the ladies of the Episcopal church, and really given in November 1907. Maud writes of *Wonderland* in *Betsy in Spite of Herself*: "It was to be given in the Opera House, and Julia was asked to play the leading part, the princess. Betsy's crowd of girls was in the chorus. They were to dance a Scarf Dance."[463] *Puss in Boots* was given at the Opera House, and Kathleen did play the part of a princess. The scarf dance, however, was not performed in *Puss in Boots*. It was in fact a number from the actual *Up and Down Broadway*, described fictionally in *Betsy and Joe*.

The talent play brings Julia together with a new beau, Harry, much to the dismay of last year's beau, Hugh. In the opinion of Eleanor Wood, Hugh was based on Alan C. Fleischbein, who boarded at 220 S. Broad. Harry seems to have been based on a young man named Jay J. Flachsenhar. Jay played the male lead, Florinet, in *Puss in Boots*, and like Harry, he was "not a high school boy." Harry worked "in his father's bank."[464] Jay was the manager of the collections department at the First National Bank of Mankato.

When Mr. Ray grumbles about Harry, he complains that Harry is a Democrat. "Mr. Ray was a Republican."[465] Tom Hart was, of course, a Republican. The *Mankato Free Press* reported that Tom *"has always been a staunch Republican, supporting the principles of the party while others have wavered in their faith."*[466]

Julia manages to elude Hugh's invitation to see Rose Stahl in *The Chorus Lady* and accepts Harry's. Betsy and her friends attend the play, too. *The Chorus Lady* with Rose Stahl actually came to Mankato that fall. It was performed at the Opera House on Monday night, September 23, 1907. The Chauncey Olcott play, *O'Neill of Derry* (mentioned on page 48 of *Betsy in Spite of Herself*) had been performed in Mankato on September 18, 1907.

Thanksgiving dinner is at the Slades' in 1907. This is the first we hear of the story-telling powers of Tom's grandmother. "She was a very old lady, wizened and small, with thin white hair and sunken lips. She could remember Indians going on the warpath in the valley."[467] This was Mary Warren Pitcher. (Warren Street in Mankato was named for her father.) Grandma Pitcher was born in 1840, so she was therefore only sixty-seven in Betsy's sophomore year, hopefully not yet a wizened old lady! But she surely had tales to tell. Her family had moved from Illinois to St. Paul in 1853, arriving just a day after a battle between bands of Sioux and Chippewa. They moved down to Mankato the same year. At that time, only two houses in Mankato had roofs. Grandma Pitcher lived the rest of her long life in Mankato. She and her husband, O.O. Pitcher, had three children: Grace (mother of "Tom Slade"), Plummer (who lived with his wife for decades on Center Street), and Fanny (who was the music teacher at the high school, described in *Betsy and Joe*).

Grace Pitcher married George Fox, who moved his young family to Wisconsin in 1889, where he ran a lumber business. George injured his foot severely and died of the ensuing infection.

Coll. of Tom Hagan

Schiller Hall

Schiller Hall, where the high school dances were held, was on the third floor of the Odd Fellows Building on Jackson Street at Second. Many memorable Betsy-Tacy moments were set here.

1895 Atlas

Post Office and Pitcher Home
Second Street near Jackson

The Hart and Fox families really entertained each other on alternating Thanksgivings. Grace Fox and her sons lived with her parents, Mr. and Mrs. O.O. Pitcher, whose home was just south of the Post Office (see right side of photo). Maud wrote: "*I used to love to go there for supper and hear* [Grandma Pitcher's] *tales of the Sioux war.*" (I.V. 8-23-66)

Stan's House
123 Center Street

Herman Hayward's family lived in this house, two blocks down the hill from the Kenneys.

Al's House
133 Clark Street (East Pleasant)

Al was based on Henry Lee, who lived in this house, in the Center Street neighborhood.

Irma's House
405 Pleasant circa 1915

"Irma lived in a large substantial house, with porches and bay windows..." (BWJ p. 45)

Irma's House
405 Pleasant circa 1990

"... set in a large lawn which had diamond-shaped flowerbeds on either side of the walk." (BWJ p. 45)

After the death of her husband, Grace and her three boys, Milo, George, and Tom, lived with her mother, Grandma Pitcher, at 417 South Second in Mankato. When Grandma Pitcher died in 1926, she had been living in this house for sixty-four continuous years. The house once stood on the south side of the post office.

Grandma Slade's sour cream cake is mentioned only once in the Betsy-Tacy books, on page 223 of *Betsy in Spite of Herself.* Tom tells Betsy that "Grandma's making sour cream cake. The kind with cinnamon in it, and she said I could bring you back to supper." Betsy cries, "Wonderful!" Maud later remembered, "*We were frequent visitors and, just as in the stories, I used to love to go there for supper with Tom when Grandma Pitcher was making sour cream cake. It wasn't just the sour cream cake which delighted me. I loved* [her] *stories. She and her husband, whom I never knew, had been pioneers in our part of Minnesota. They had lived there when the land was being cleared, and at the time of the Indian massacres. I have always thought that her stories pushed me a little into the interest in Minnesota history which led me later to write some novels with that background.*"[468]

On Friday, December 20, the last day of school before Christmas vacation, Betsy, Julia, and Tacy sing a trio in the school Christmas program. A concert was given at the high school on December 20, 1907, and it included a trio by Maud, Kathleen, and Bick. The concert was not a high school Christmas program but was given to raise money for Union School.

This Christmas will be like no other, for Betsy has received an invitation to spend the holiday in Milwaukee with the Mullers, and Mr. Ray says she may go. Betsy leaves Deep Valley for Milwaukee on Saturday, December 21. Of course, December 21 did indeed fall on a Saturday in 1907. And this was the date of Maud's departure from Mankato. However, her train didn't travel through Winona and across to Milwaukee. She left at 9:55 a.m. on the train for St. Paul and visited with Connie (Bonnie) and her family until Monday morning, when she left for Milwaukee on the 8:00 a.m. train. She arrived at 9:25 p.m.

The "journal" quotation on page 106 probably came from one of Maud's marble-backed diaries, down to the last exclamation point. "'Heaven preserve us!!!' Betsy wrote in her journal [shortly before her trip to Milwaukee]. 'The boys are coming down to see me off and bring mistletoe to kiss me good-by. Horror of horrors!!!'"

Tib is waiting for her in Milwaukee "in a purple coat."[469] As with dark Tony and his red tie, and Betsy who consciously identifies herself with green, we come to associate blond Tib with purple. When she surprises the Rays at Murmuring Lake at the beginning of their junior year, Tib is wearing a "lilac-sprigged dress."[470] She wore a lilac silk skirt on her first day at Deep Valley High in *Betsy Was a Junior.* She chose lavender for the 1910 Junior-Senior Banquet in *Betsy and Joe.* "She was very fond of purple in all shades. There were touches of purple, lavender and lilac on almost all the dresses which hung neatly on hangers in her closet, smelling of lavender water."[471] Whether or not Midge Gerlach had a penchant for purple is almost immaterial. It is fascinating that Maud used this "color association" device in her books, and so effectively that one hardly notices falling under its influence.

After a look at downtown Milwaukee, Betsy and the Mullers "rode for a long time" to get to the Mullers' duplex, which was "a square red brick house."[472] The Gerlachs lived in north Milwaukee, moving from 2371 N. Fifth (no longer standing) to 2308 N. Booth sometime between 1907 and 1908.

Betsy meets all four Muller and Hornik grandparents, none of whom speak English. Just as Mrs. Muller said in *Over the Big Hill*: "Both of Tib's grandmothers came from the other side."[473] They did, and so did both grandfathers.

Tib and Betsy walk from the Muller duplex to the Horniks'.[474] This was entirely possible. Midge's family and her maternal grandparents lived fewer than eight or ten blocks apart. "To reach the tailor shop they walked toward the central part of the city ... the tailor shop was in a two-story brick building. A sign in gold letters read Alois Hornik, Schneider."[475] This brick corner building where Midge's grandparents lived, upstairs, stands at 2050 N. Third in Milwaukee. (It is closer to the central part of the city than Midge's family's duplex.) Alois was really a tailor and ran a business with his two brothers.

The Horniks were based on Midge's maternal grandparents, Alois and Katherine Irasek (who visited Mankato occasionally).

Tib tells Betsy that her grandfather Hornik was a "Forty-Eighter" (a participant in the revolution that swept Central Europe in 1848), that his mother was Viennese, and that her name was Catherine Wilhelmina. Actually, Alois Irasek was not a Forty-Eighter. His mother was Viennese - however, "Katherine" was the name of Alois' wife, and "Wilhelmina" was Midge's mother's name.

Maud's messages about the character Alois Hornik are somewhat inconsistent. On page 145, we hear that "Grosspapa was only a little boy when he came to Milwaukee, but he hates the emperor." However, on page 148, Betsy wonders why Grosspapa Hornik doesn't speak better English. After all, "he was born here." In reality, Alois Irasek was born in Austria in 1836 and married Katherine Novac (Grossmama Hornik) in Vienna in 1860.

So obviously, the real Grossmama Hornik did not come to America with her parents when she was twenty-five, as per the fictional account, but came later with her husband. Like Grossmama Hornik, however, Katherine embroidered fine linens for the Imperial House of Franz Joseph, Emperor of Austria. And like her counterpart, she was permitted to use a five-pointed crown on her work. Katherine was best known for her exquisite monograms.

Alois and Katherine Irasek's first three children arrived in Vienna, the eldest of whom was Wilhelmina (Midge's mother), born in 1862. Alois set off for America in 1865, and after a year, with his tailoring business established, he sent for his wife and children. Six more children were born to the Iraseks in Milwaukee. The youngest two appear in *Betsy in Spite of Herself*: Jack, who would have been twenty-nine at the time of Maud's visit, and Dell, who would have been twenty-six. These are, of course, Uncle Rudy and Aunt Dolly.

Uncle Rudy "was tall and slim in impeccably tailored clothes. He had a yellow pompadour, and yellow mustaches, waxed and twisted upward. Betsy promptly fell in love with Uncle Rudy. She was madly in love, for at least a week."[476] We remember Tib's uncle from *Downtown*, in which Tib gives Winona a "Schlitz beer calendar, sent by her uncle in Milwaukee."[477] Jack Irasek was really a traveling salesman for Schlitz beer. He married but had no children.

Uncle Rudy introduces Betsy to the "Merry Widow Waltz," which later weaves itself through her romance with Phil. The "Merry Widow Waltz" was in fact brand-new at Christmas in 1907. A December 1907 *Mankato Free Press* advertised a New Year's Eve performance from "The Merry Widow," the first appearance of the waltz in Mankato, given by the Twentieth Century Band, "*which shows that the band is up to date in its music.*"[478]

Aunt Dell Irasek was already married at the time of Maud's visit to Milwaukee. She married William Prescott (presumably the Ferdy of *Betsy in Spite of Herself,* "a dapper, pleasant-faced young man"[479]) in 1905. Dell had no children. Maud fairly unobtrusively imparts information from which we may deduce that Aunt Dolly was a rather shallow and vain woman. (Maud never makes this judgment herself - she leaves it to us.) Dolly dismisses the girls with a casual chilliness in *Betsy-Tacy and Tib*: "'Thank you for the flowers, children,' she said in a tone which showed that she was ready for them to go."[480] Dolly has brought clothes far too grand for Deep Valley. She is still a clotheshorse in *Betsy in Spite of Herself*. In addition, "There were mirrors everywhere. Wherever Aunt Dolly looked she was sure to see her own exquisite reflection."[481] She is a lovely but cold character.

Tib's paternal grandparents were also based on those of Midge. Midge's grandfather was Heinrich Maximilian Gerlach. Unlike the fictional Grosspapa Gerhard Muller, Grosspapa Gerlach did not manufacture beer kegs. "Max," as he was called, served as clerk of court for the city of Milwaukee. He came to Milwaukee from Burk, Germany, in 1844 and never learned to speak English. Maud never met Max Gerlach, since he died in 1899, at the age of eighty-one. Grossmama Gerlach, however, lived until 1911. She was born Marie Meyer in Friedrichstadt, Schleswig-Holstein. She came to America with her parents about 1840. Marie married Max Gerlach in 1849. Of her sixteen children, eight died at birth or in early childhood. Midge's father, Henry, was the second-born.

"Grosspapa Muller's house sat on a corner. It was a large gray stone house with wrought iron balconies. There was a carriage house in back."[482] Tib's family crossed the river to get to Grosspapa Muller's. But the Gerlach house was not really located

Coll. of Bev Schindler

Max and Marie Gerlach
(Grosspapa and Grossmama Muller)

"Grossmama Muller was small and timid. Her graying hair, which had once been fair, was drawn back into a tight bun." (BSH p. 139) Grossmama Gerlach does not look timid.

Coll. of Lynne Kleinman

Milwaukee Downer College Buildings
(Tib's Browner Seminary)

At Browner "the red brick walls were clothed warmly with ivy. There were towers and friendly bow windows, and roguish gargoyles peering down." (BSH p. 158)

MHL Archive

Kathleen and Stella in California

As the Rays discuss the prospect of sending Betsy to Milwaukee, Mr. Ray remarks that it's Betsy's turn to take a trip. Julia had been to California with Mrs. Ray. Stella and Kathleen Hart really did go to California to visit Grandma Austin in about 1903.

Home of the Iraseks
(Grosspapa and Grossmama Hornik)

The Iraseks lived at 2050 N. Third in Milwaukee. The neighborhood is not what it was in 1907.

near Lake Michigan. It did, however, stand on a corner. Max Gerlach's house probably matched the fictional description, though his widow was not living in it when Maud visited Milwaukee. No doubt Midge took Maud to see the old family home, where eight of Max and Marie's children were born, and where the family remained for many years. This house, which has been demolished, stood at Ninth and Highland.

Betsy meets Tib's tall cousin Heinrich. There was a goodly handful of Gerlach cousins in Milwaukee whom Maud surely met on her Christmas visit. Perhaps Heinrich was Midge's cousin Fritz Gerlach, two years Maud's junior. There were even twins, about Hobbie's age, like those described. One was called "Maxine," after her grosspapa. There was also an Irasek cousin whom Maud may have met on this visit - Ralph, the son of Aunt Eda. Born in 1893, Ralph was the male cousin closest in age to Maud and Midge. He was most likely to have been the inspiration for cousin Heinrich (despite the fact that Heinrich was from the Muller side and Ralph was from the Irasek side).

Maud drew the beautiful Christmas Tree scene at Grosspapa Muller's from a fascinatingly unexpected source. This gathering was based on that of a real German family - even more German than the Mullers - but far from Milwaukee. The scene was taken from Kathleen Hart's letters written home from Germany, describing the 1909 holiday with her hosts, the Hilgers.

In *Betsy in Spite of Herself* is as follows: "The double doors leading to the library were closed. The children kept trying to look through the cracks and were pulled away by their elders. At last a bell was heard. 'There's the *Christkindel's* bell,' Tib whispered to Betsy. But the company was not yet ready to answer the summons. One of the young lady cousins went to the piano, and it developed that the pig-tailed twins had prepared a surprise for their Grosspapa. They played a Mozart duet, somewhat shakily, with violin and flute and Grosspapa was pleased. After that everybody sang Christmas songs. But in the library the bell became imperative. The great doors slid back, and Betsy saw a Christmas tree so tall and majestic that it seemed to fill the large, high-ceilinged room. It was twinkling with lighted candles, sparkling with ornaments, and it threw off a delicious fragrance.

After a long-drawn breath the company joined hands and marched around the tree singing ... but in German ... 'O, Christmas tree, O, Christmas tree, How lovely are thy branches...' All around the room were tables covered with sheets. The smiling servant girl hurried about taking off the sheets, and there were tables for everyone ... the servant girl, the cook who came in from the kitchen, and old Johann, wrinkled and nut-like. There was even a table for Betsy laden with boxes of candy and cakes, hair ribbons, pin cushions, pen wipers, and sachet bags."[483]

From Kathleen Hart's letter from Europe, written to her family in December 1909: "*The Christmas tree ... is locked up in the salon, a great big room which it almost fills. The children peep through the key-hole, and can see fascinating glimpses of green and tinsel, golden balls and candles, but are not permitted into the room.*"[484] And "*The kids were so excited they could hardly see, when a bell (supposed to be rung by the Christ Kind - Christ Child, their Santa Claus), was heard, and we trooped into the room with the grand piano in it. Mrs. H., all of a flutter, came bustling up to me, and asked me to play the Christmas folk songs. Then Eugenia and Erna had prepared a surprise for their mother -- they played a nice little duet of Christmas melodies for violin and piano, much to everyone's delight. Then we sang folk songs, the Christ Child becoming more and more imperative with his bell from the next room. At last, as we finished, the curtains were drawn back, and the most beautiful tree you can imagine, filled the huge salon. We held our breaths for a moment, and then joined hands and marched about the tree singing, 'Oh Hemlock tree, how beautiful are thy branches.' All around the room were tables covered with sheets; after this, Peter took the sheets off and we all went to our places. Oh, my dears, if you could have seen my table! An umbrella, a pair of ice-skates, two pairs of gloves, a purse, stationery with envelopes, a leather brush and comb case, two dozen handkerchiefs with K.H. in the corner, three little fancy handkerchiefs, two German books from Mrs. H., two boxes of candy, a big box of Christmas cookies, a new dress, two pairs of stockings, a new blue woolen blouse, with collar and jabot, another jabot, a beautiful silver collar and belt buckle, a couple of dear little old-fashioned porcelain children from Eugenia. Well, I guess that is all, but I'm not sure -- no, a new nightgown besides. Dear me, did you ever hear of so much?*"[485] And later, "*we ate Kuchen until we were about sick.*"[486]

The Old World charm of Milwaukee has not changed Tib. When the girls emerge from Sunday morning service, Betsy is still "uplifted" by the music. She looks around at the snow, new-fallen since they arrived at the church, and says: "It seems like a miracle!" Tib's response: "We should have worn overshoes."[487]

Tib takes Betsy to visit her school, Browner Seminary, which was based on "Milwaukee Downer College." There is no official record of Midge's attendance there. When she transferred to Mankato High, it was from Milwaukee High School. It is certainly possible, however, that Midge spent some time at Downer.

Downer's buildings (now part of the University of Wisconsin, Milwaukee) are, like Browner's, really of red brick. The gymnasium which Tib showed Betsy would have been in the west wing of Holton Hall. It had no balcony, as per the fictional account, but a running track was suspended above the gym, and spectators may have observed basketball games from the track. "They looked in at the chapel, the library, the dining room. They peeked into the Dorm."[488] The chapel, library, and classrooms were located in Merrill Hall. The dining room and dormitory rooms were in Holton. Johnston and McLaren Halls had been built by 1903 as additional residence buildings.[489]

After the New Year's Eve festivities, Tib and Betsy stay up all night, make resolutions, and plan new personalities for themselves. This really happened on Maud's trip to Milwaukee. Maud recalled *"her impressions of a Christmas visit to 'Tib' in Milwaukee, where the two girls stayed up all night and decided to change their personalities. 'I was going to be tall, dark, and mysterious.'"*[490]

Betsy is also inspired with the idea of adding an 'e' to her name: "B-e-t-s-y-e." In fact, Maud started spelling her name "Maude" when she was a freshman, or even earlier. And, unlike "Betsye," "Maude" lasted beyond the end of sophomore year. Almost 150 years before *Betsy in Spite of Herself*, Jane Austen wrote in *Northanger Abbey* of *"Sally, or rather Sarah (for what young lady of common gentility will reach the age of sixteen without altering her name as far as she can?)"*[491]

The heroine of one of Maud's short stories constructed a list of things she must do to transform herself. Betsy might have written it. The list included: "*Call yourself Claire instead of Clara. Make your hair a 'crowning glory.' Be dainty. Acquire a low laugh. Shroud your past in mystery. Keep your hands exquisitely manicured. Learn some French phrases. Exploit your femininity. Persist."*[492]

Soon after her return from Milwaukee, Betsy decides to inaugurate her new personality by bagging Phil Brandish. Her enterprise is delayed by an attack of la grippe (the flu). In reality, Maud was quite ill in the late winter of 1907 (freshman year) with appendicitis - and she originally intended to use this episode in *Betsy in Spite of Herself*. An early draft of the manuscript shows the following: *"'Just try keeping soul and body together on soup,' she murmured weakly to Tacy. 'It's awful. They are STARVING me.' The next day the doctor forbade company, except for a very heavy icebag. Even whispered consultations, which she overheard quite well, as to whether or not they should operate, could not compensate for the pangs of hunger. At last, however, the pains went away and there followed a period during which Betsy could sit up in her best dressing sacque and eat all the good things with which Anna plied her. Yet her convalescence was not happy. Usually Betsy, who loved to read and loved even better to write, rather enjoyed being kept in bed now and then. But this time, although she had the new book Carney had brought and a pile of notebooks and sharp pencils, she did not have a good time at all. She had been running away from some thoughts from which now she could run no further. She was caught in bed and could not escape. The humiliating truth was that she had not succeeded in changing herself."*

Previously, Betsy and Tacy had invented words about Phil, to the tune of "Dreaming." One of the lines from this invented version appears in a tantalizing note in Maud's High School Scrapbook. On the outside, Maud has written: *"in a walnut shell."* Inside, Bick Kenney has written:

*"What is this I see. A lonely hut! A young girl of twenty sitting on a bench without. Beside her is a light haired Dutchman. Nearby is a bright red auto (Jackson). The girl is bitterly accusing the man. The man bears it all in silence then as she finished chewing the rag he pointed to the car and in terrible tones cried '**Love will not change while the auto remains**.' It is you. I see the results of a youthful flirtation."*[493]

The "(Jackson)" above is cryptic. It might refer to Jackson Street, the location of Schiller Hall (where Betsy and Phil began their romance). It is fair to assume that Maud had a friendship

Merry Widows!

Duplicated in several sources

Maud Hart

Coll. of Robert Cahill

Mildred Oleson

Duplicated in several collections

Bick Kenney at left
Pat Ahlers at right

Coll. of Louise King

Connie Davis

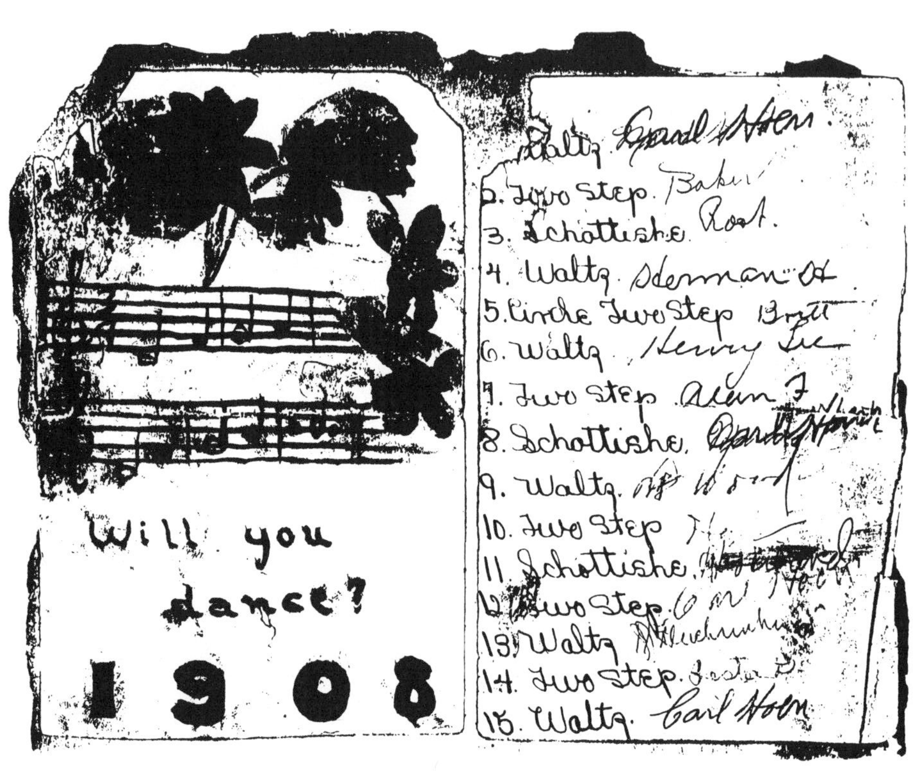

BECHS

Leap Year Dance Program

"Tacy and Alice are making the programs. They're terribly cute, with a bar from the 'Merry Widow Waltz' painted on the cover. But fifteen dances, Julia! Cab will ask me for one, of course, and Tony, and Dennie, and Pin, and Al, probably, and Squirrelly, and Harry, but that's only seven. I've fifteen to fill." (BSH p. 193) with a young man in possession of a red auto. And that the song Betsy and Tacy made up on the hill was also sung by Maud and Bick. So who is Phil Brandish? Maud furnishes the following data:

Tacy tells Betsy that she oughtn't waste her time on Phil Brandish because he goes with a senior crowd: "He's older than we are."[494] Phil lived "across the slough."[495] In *Betsy Was a Junior*, we learn that he was a grandchild of "the rich Home Brandish, who lived in a mansion on the west side of Deep Valley."[496]

"He was tall, and a lock of his thick light-brown hair hung over his forehead. His skin was a clear olive tint. His eyes were heavily lashed."[497] After over eighty years, it would be hard to prove that Phil had a historical parallel with appropriately thick eyelashes, but there are a few things we <u>can</u> ascertain.

The Leap Year Dance, to which Betsy invites Phil, was planned for the last Friday in February (in 1908, February 28). The dance programs were "terribly cute, with a bar from the 'Merry Widow Waltz' painted on the cover."[498] This program is in Maud's Scrapbook. It has violets on the cover with a bar from the "Merry Widow Waltz." It is the only homemade dance program in the Scrapbook, the others having been printed professionally. This makes sense, if the dance had been given by the economically minded sophomore class.

Julia explains to Betsy: "Your escort always writes his name down for the first dance and the last one, and usually one in the middle. If he really likes you, he asks for four."[499]

The real "Merry Widow" dance program thus supplies vital clues about the identity of Phil. There were fifteen dances, and familiar friends on Maud's dance card included "Baker" (E. Lloyd Harrington), "Herman Hayward" (Stan), "Henry Lee" (Al), "D. Wood" (Fred - Julia's boyfriend). The first, last, eighth, and twelfth dances were taken by Maud's escort, a boy named Carl Hoerr.

Carl Hoerr did not live across the slough in a big house. His father dealt in livestock, probably quite profitably, and they lived at 416 N. Broad. Carl worked as a repairman for D. D. Cummins & Co. in 1908. Cummins dealt in nothing less than "*automobiles, storage and repairing*"[500] at 515-517 S. Front. Carl was crazy about autos, but according to his children, he does not appear to have owned one as a young man. He did drive an auto for a doctor in Mankato, and since the doctor didn't drive, Carl may well have had the use of it in his off-duty hours.

Bick's note depicts the red-auto boy as a fair-haired Dutchman. In all probability, Bick meant a person of German descent. ("Deutsch" was corrupted to "Dutch," as in "Pennsylvania Dutch".) Carl Hoerr was German. So surely Carl was Phil? Not exactly.

According to Maud, "*A small and amusing complication is that while some of the characters are absolutely based on one person -- for example Tacy, Tib, Cab, Carney -- others were merely suggested by some person and some characters are combinations of two real persons.*"[501]

Phil is one of the "loose" characterizations. The fictional Phil appears to have been inspired by two or even three boys (none of them twins, as Phil was). When Maud described the boy who invited her to the Leap Year Dance, she was probably describing Carl Hoerr. But Maud and Carl didn't last through the end of the school year, as did Betsy and Phil. Carl didn't belong to the Crowd, as did Phil (escorting Irma throughout *Betsy Was a Junior*). Carl was not a member of the Omega Deltas, as was Phil. Carl didn't graduate from Mankato High School, since he moved with his family to Oregon.

Perhaps Maud set her cap for a second boy that winter of 1908. This may have been Clayton Burmeister of the class of 1909. Clayton didn't live in a big house across the slough either, though he lived a lot closer to it than Carl. Clayton Burmeister's parents were both from Denmark. He was one year older than Maud, like Phil. Clayton was definitely an Omega Delta, like Phil. His middle initial was J, like Phil's.[502] Clayton had a brother, Clarence, who was in the class of 1910 with Maud. The name Clayton appears more than a dozen times in the Scrapbook, and Clarence not at all.

Some aspects of the character Phil are reflected in Malcolm Morehart, who graduated in 1911. In October of 1907, Maud confessed in her diary to having "*a fearful crush on Malcolm who has been going to a boys' school in St. Paul and has manners to kill.*"[503] A month later, he asked her to a dance.

It appears that Maud was inspired by the beautiful home overlooking the slough (and Little Syria as well) that was owned by the Brandrup family (note the similarity to "Brandish"). The Brandrups had boys, but none were close in age to Maud (the closest was son Holley, who was the same age as Helen Hart).

The puzzlement over identifying Phil is reminiscent of Freddie's reaction to Betsy's Mirror Palace game in *Betsy-Tacy and Tib*. "He knew how to play that someone was another person, but he hadn't ever played that someone was two other persons. He thought he had better change the subject."[504]

The Leap Year Dance was held in Schiller Hall. "It's just at the foot of our hill."[505] Julia describes the hall to Betsy. "You go up three flights of stairs."[506] In *Betsy and Joe,* Schiller Hall is on the fourth floor.[507] The real Schiller Hall (name unchanged) was actually located on the third floor of the Odd Fellows building, so one would have had to ascend only two flights of stairs. The Odd Fellows building stood on the south side Jackson at Second Street. Therefore, it was at the foot of the Harts' hill (foot of Cherry) but one block over (foot of Jackson).

This is Betsy's first dance and the first time we meet Mamie Dodd. "Mamie was a senior but she never danced at high school parties. She earned money playing the piano for them."[508] In *Betsy Was a Junior*, we learn that Mamie, like Joe, had no father to look after her.[509] This girl's real name was Mamie Skuse, and her name appeared frequently in the newspapers of the time as the provider of musical accompaniment at a variety of school and community functions. (Mamie later played the pipe organ at the Sandon Theater in Mankato.) She graduated from Mankato High School in 1909, so at the time of the Leap Year Dance, Mamie was a junior rather than a senior. Her father, Frank, was alive and well at this time. They lived on the north side of town at 722 N. Fifth. Intriguingly, not long before Maud began work on *Betsy in Spite of Herself*, Delos had finished writing his biography of Ike Eisenhower. In it, he describes Ike's marriage to a pretty girl named Mamie Doud. Might the name have stuck in Maud's head, to emerge as "Mamie Dodd" here?

The heroine in Maud's pre-Betsy-Tacy short story, "I Am Curly," is escorted to her first dance by a jerk named "Phil Downer." She wears a daisy dress with a daisy wreath in her hair. They dance to the "Merry Widow Waltz," and Phil is sulky.

However, this Phil is a rejected beau of Curly's older sister, and he ungallantly abandons Curly at the dance.

In Betsy's sophomore year, the school forms a Girls' Debating Club. "Carney was excited about it and anxious for Betsy to join." Betsy, thinking Phil wouldn't like it, didn't initially sign up. But Maud joined when the Girls' Debating Club was formed on October 17, 1907. The program of debates in Maud's Scrapbook is for the winter and spring of 1908. (See Chapter 8 herein for debating details.)

Betsy is unwilling for Phil to witness her Cat Duet with Tacy, so she declines to perform it. He doesn't like the idea of the Essay Contest either. In fact, Phil dislikes those things about Betsy which are most Betsyish. This is not a problem as long as she is willing to pretend that she is someone else, but it is obvious that the relationship with Phil is doomed. When the break-up comes, there is a minor time-reference error. Betsy had known before "last night when everything toppled"[510] that her relationship with Phil was going to end. She says this on Sunday afternoon, but everything toppled on Friday night, the night before the essay contest, not on Saturday night. It was a very upsetting time - no wonder she was confused.

We know that Betsy's birthday comes at the end of April, but the exact date is never given. In *Betsy in Spite of Herself*, Betsy's birthday is on a Thursday. Maud's own birthday, April 25th, did not fall on a Thursday in 1908.

For her birthday, Betsy receives "A gold linked bracelet, the first really fine piece Betsy ever had owned."[511] This choice of phrasing rings bells loudly - surely Maud received a gift like this for her sixteenth birthday. (Since the preceding paragraph was written, an MHL letter, written in 1956, has come to light, containing the sentence "*The bracelet Julia gave to Betsy in Betsy in Spite of Herself is on my wrist.*")[512]

Julia and Mrs. Ray bring the bracelet back from St. Paul, where they have been attending Grand Opera, thanks to the thoughtfulness of Mr. Ray. They actually made this trip in the spring of 1907, rather than 1908 - so Maud apparently received the bracelet for her fifteenth (not sixteenth) birthday.

Mr. Ray had made reservations at the Frederick Hotel (sic) for his wife and daughter. Mrs. Poppy was staying there, too. In 1904, Mrs. Nettie Snyder and her husband built the Hotel Frederic at 45 E. Fifth Street in St. Paul, which was named after Mr. Snyder and patterned after Mankato's Saulpaugh Hotel. (The Frederic Hotel burned down in 1961.)

Mrs. Snyder not only attended Grand Opera, as Mrs. Poppy did, but she became the St. Paul manager of the Chicago Grand Opera Company. She hobnobbed with Geraldine Farrar and Enrico Caruso, the opera stars mentioned in *Betsy in Spite of Herself*. The *Mankato Free Press* reported that Mrs. Snyder had lunched with Farrar in Chicago before an opera performance. Mrs. Snyder told the paper that "*Caruso, the great tenor singer, must have his grapefruit and must have it cold. In Chicago yesterday he told his waiter at the Congress Hotel that he'd give him $5 if he would take away one which had been served and bring back one well frosted.*"[513]

Julia coerces Tacy into singing a solo for rhetoricals. Tacy's musical talent is suggested for the first time in *Heaven to Betsy* when Betsy brings her a mouth organ as a souvenir from her trip to the Taggarts' farm.[514] (Remember too that Mr. Kelly played the violin.) We later learn that "Tacy's voice was true and sweet. It was like an Irish harp .... And Tacy loved to sing."[515] Bick Kenney did have an excellent singing voice, and she sang at many high school functions. Tess (Katie) Kenney sang too, which is perhaps even more surprising than Bick having the nerve to get on stage, given how much Katie hated reciting the Gettysburg Address in *Over the Big Hill*. Kathleen really gave Bick singing lessons, after the removal of the two families to Minneapolis, if not also before. Programs of concerts given by Kathleen's students in Minneapolis include Bick's name. Bick herself later gave voice lessons, following in Kathleen's footsteps at the MacPhail School of Music (now part of the University of Minnesota) in Minneapolis.

At the end of *Betsy in Spite of Herself*, Betsy puts on "an old blue sailor suit" for the picnic at Page Park.[516] Is it the same one she wore on the first day of high school, a year and a half earlier, then new, now old? It would be typical of Maud to insert such a detail.

The Zetamathians win the athletics cup and the Philomathians take the debating cup. Though Betsy loses, the Zets also win the

BECHS

Sibley Park
(Page Park)

Page Park was a favorite picnic spot for the Crowd.

Coll. of SSW

Front Street

This view was taken from the corner of Main Street, looking south. A sign for the Corner Cafe can be seen on a post on the left side of the photo. (Anna's beau was a bartender down at the Corner Cafe.) The Saulpaugh Hotel is on the right. Maud never mentions the trolleys in town. The track was laid in 1907.

essay cup. This is exactly the way the cups were really divided in 1908.

Maud does not provide any fictional grades for this year. The actual grades for Maud's sophomore year were geometry, 77; Caesar, 82; modern history, 89; English, 89.

Kathleen didn't exactly graduate on a "sweet June night,"[517] since Commencement exercises were held on May 29, 1908. "*The stage was tastefully decorated by the class of 1910 with the senior colors, green and white. Evergreens, snowballs and palms were used for this and a large green background on which '08 was worked with snowballs, hung above the graduates.*"[518] According to page 263 of *Betsy in Spite of Herself*, "The chorus was singing 'Damascus.'" And according to the newspaper, the opening prayer was followed "*by a selection by the chorus. This song, 'Damascus,' from Naaman, was one of the best of the evening, and well received.*"[519] Kathleen sang two solos.

"*This event closes the school year and the high school days of the class of 1908.*"[520]

[428] *Minneapolis Tribune*, 11-9-52.

[429] MHL to L. Demp, 11-2-56.

[430] M. Hart, "I Am Curly," p. 1.

[431] *Betsy and Joe,* p. 234.

[432] KPH letters, p. 125.

[433] MHL to J. Tessari, 8-11-73.

[434] *Heaven to Betsy,* p. 237.

[435] Lovelace Interview, University of Michigan.

[436] *Betsy in Spite of Herself,* p. 63.

[437] Ibid.

[438] *Mankato Free Press*, 9-4-41.

[439] 1910-1911 Mankato Directory, p. 226.

[440] *Betsy in Spite of Herself,* p. 65.

[441] Ibid., p. 51.

[442] *Mankato Free Press,* 9-7-07.

[443] D.O., p. 4.

[444] *Betsy in Spite of Herself,* p. 52.

[445] Ibid., p. 54.

[446] *Heaven to Betsy,* p. 236.

[447] *Betsy in Spite of Herself,* p. 75.

[448] *Betsy Was a Junior,* p. 44.

[449] High School Scrapbook.

[450] *Betsy Was a Junior,* p. 44.

[451] Ibid., p. 176.

[452] *Betsy and Joe,* p. 33.

[453] *Betsy in Spite of Herself,* p. 34.

[454] *Mankato Free Press*, 4-25-08.

[455] Ibid.

[456] *Betsy in Spite of Herself,* p. 79.

[457] *Emily of Deep Valley,* p. 220.

[458] *Betsy in Spite of Herself,* p. 81.

[459] Ibid.

[460] Ibid., p. 39.

[461] Ibid., p. 85.

[462] Ibid., p. 89.

[463] Ibid., p. 88.

[464] Ibid., p. 89.

[465] Ibid., p. 94.

[466] *Mankato Free Press*, 9-4-08.

[467] *Betsy in Spite of Herself,* p. 97.
[468] MHL to J. Ellen, 9-10-67.
[469] *Betsy in Spite of Herself,* p. 119.
[470] *Betsy Was a Junior,* p. 16
[471] Ibid., p. 30.
[472] *Betsy in Spite of Herself,* pp. 121-122.
[473] *Over the Big Hill,* p. 75.
[474] *Betsy in Spite of Herself,* p. 144.
[475] Ibid., pp. 144-146.
[476] Ibid., p. 131.
[477] *Downtown,* p. 30.
[478] *Mankato Free Press,* 12-26-07.
[479] *Betsy in Spite of Herself,* p. 150.
[480] *Betsy-Tacy and Tib,* p. 126.
[481] *Betsy in Spite of Herself,* p. 152.
[482] Ibid., p. 138.
[483] Ibid., pp. 139-141.
[484] KPH letters, p. 140.
[485] Ibid., pp. 143-144.
[486] Ibid., p. 145.
[487] *Betsy in Spite of Herself,* p. 128.
[488] Ibid., p. 158.
[489] *Milwaukee Sentinel*, 5-4-1899.
[490] *Minneapolis Tribune*, 11-9-52.
[491] Jane Austen, *Northanger Abbey* (Oxford: Oxford University Press edition, 1980), Volume I, Chapter II, p. 6.
[492] M.H. Lovelace "Love's Daily Dozen," *Delineator*, August 1925, p. 6.
[493] High School Scrapbook.
[494] *Betsy in Spite of Herself,* p. 17.
[495] Ibid., p. 3.
[496] *Betsy Was a Junior,* p. 5.
[497] *Betsy in Spite of Herself,* p. 198.
[498] Ibid., p. 193.
[499] Ibid.
[500] Mankato City Directory, 1908.
[501] MHL to A. Wiecking, 9-22-61.
[502] *Betsy in Spite of Herself,* p. 194.
[503] D.O., p. 160.
[504] *Betsy-Tacy and Tib,* p. 75.

[505] *Betsy in Spite of Herself,* p. 191.

[506] Ibid., p. 193.

[507] *Betsy and Joe*, p. 96.

[508] *Betsy in Spite of Herself,* p. 199.

[509] *Betsy Was a Junior,* p. 243.

[510] *Betsy in Spite of Herself,* p. 257.

[511] Ibid., p. 240.

[512] MHL to L. Demp, 11-2-56.

[513] *Mankato Free Press,* 4-14-10.

[514] *Heaven to Betsy,* p. 22.

[515] *Betsy in Spite of Herself*, p. 88.

[516] Ibid., p. 249.

[517] Ibid., p. 270.

[518] *Mankato Free Press,* 5-30-08.

[519] Ibid.

[520] Ibid.

CHAPTER EIGHT
On *Betsy Was a Junior*
August 1908 to June 1909

Betsy Was a Junior opens among the water lilies on Babcock's Bay at Murmuring Lake, where Betsy is daydreaming in a rowboat. *Betsy Was a Junior* provides our first of two good looks at Ray family life at the lake (the other is at the beginning of *Betsy and Joe*). We know that the summer before Betsy's sophomore year was also spent at the lake but only in flashback; by the first page of *Betsy in Spite of Herself*, the family has returned home to High Street after two months away. Betsy tells Tacy that she would "row over to the bay where the water lilies are, take along a notebook and pencil, and write."[521] Babcock's Bay is therefore not entirely new to us, though this is the first time we hear it called by name. The fictional name was inspired by the sister of "Irma," Loretta Oleson Babcock. In 1920, she and her husband bought a cottage on Madison Lake, directly across from Point Pleasant.

In *Betsy and Joe*, we hear that the cottage occupied by the Rays "was one of half a dozen."[522] (There were actually ten cottages around the Inn.) In *Betsy in Spite of Herself*, Maud describes "the cottage which stood with its feet in the water,"[523] but in *Betsy Was a Junior*, the cottages are up on the high bank above the lake. The latter description is accurate. Cabins still trail the Inn like chicks, but they are several generations new, having burnt to the ground more than once. We are told that a view of Mrs. Ray's girlhood home can be had from the Ray cottage on the point. This is true - the former Austin Park is clearly visible across the lake.

Murmuring Lake Inn was based on Point Pleasant Hotel (or Inn) of Madison Lake. Still called Point Pleasant, the "Inn" is sprawling and white-painted, and it has served a chicken buffet on Sundays even in modern times. The dining room feels authentic - it is easy to imagine the Rays eating there to contentment and beyond - but unfortunately, the current Inn is not the one from Maud's day, though it stands on the same spot.

Courtly Mr. Van Blarcum and busy Mrs. Van Blarcum, first introduced in *Betsy Was a Junior*, were based on Jesse M. and Lucetta Barclay. The Barclays built Point Pleasant Hotel and the surrounding cottages in the 1880s. As Maud described in the books, Point Pleasant attracted vacationers from surrounding states.

Old Pete, the keeper of the boathouse, mentioned on page 11, was probably based on Guy Moore, who had charge of the launch at Point Pleasant.

Two new members of the Crowd, Dave Hunt and E. Lloyd Harrington, are first encountered at Murmuring Lake.

Dave Hunt "was over six feet tall and very thin, with a stern, spare face."[524] The girls in the Crowd talk Dave over on page 67, bemoaning the fact that he has so little to say and would therefore not be much of an escort. Winona demurs, "Oh, I don't know. You could look at him." Mr. Ray refers to him as "Silent Dave."[525] This was Robert W. Hughes, called "Bob."

Bob Hughes' father was William F. Hughes, an attorney and judge of probate court in Blue Earth County. The family lived in a home at 120 E. Liberty (now gone). Before coming to Mankato, Judge Hughes practiced law in Fair Haven, Washington, where Bob was born. The family moved to Mankato in 1893. William and his wife Susie had four children: Burton, Everett, Lillian, and Robert. Although Maud would have known of Lillian Hughes (they were just three years apart in school), only Bob appears in the Betsy-Tacy books.

E. Lloyd Harrington was James Henry Baker. He was the son of General J.H. Baker, a Civil War veteran (see Chapter 10). Jim was born when his father was sixty years old and his mother was thirty-eight. (Jim's mother, Zulu, had an interesting background. She was the great-granddaughter of a signer of the Declaration of Independence.)

"Lloyd Harrington wasn't on the (football) team," being of the artistic type.[526] Jim Baker's children confirm that their father did not play football in high school. (Like Lloyd, Jim was one of the Omega Deltas.) His family spent at least three weeks of every summer at Point Pleasant. Jim and Mildred Oleson (Irma) went together for some time during high school.

Another addition to the Crowd appears at Murmuring Lake, but she is not new to us. As a dramatic surprise, Tib comes out with Mr. Ray in time for dinner at the Inn - and she is back from Milwaukee to stay! In fact, the Gerlach family returned to Mankato in April 1908. They did not return to the chocolate-colored house, however, because they had sold 503 Byron on

Coll. of Point Pleasant

Point Pleasant Inn
Madison (Murmuring) Lake

The main building of Murmuring Lake Inn "was old. It had received so many additions at different periods that it had quite lost its original shape and sprawled in strange directions, unified only by white paint and a narrow open porch across the front." (BWJ p. 13)

Stairs Down the Point

Betsy "ran up a steep flight of stairs, which spanned the high bank through a tangled growth of bushes and trees." (BWJ p. 12)

MHL Archive

Kathleen (Julia)
at the lake

"She was shorter than Betsy, but made the most of every inch of height longing to be tall because of her operatic ambitions." (BWJ p. 13)

Coll. of Point Pleasant

Point Pleasant Inn
Dining Room

Betsy and Tib "reached the supper table late, but by this time they had quieted down enough to remember that they were sixteen, and they walked demurely across the dining room. Mrs. Van Blarcum had put a chair for Tib at the Ray family table." (BWJ p. 17)

Coll. of Point Pleasant

Point Pleasant Inn
South Side Cottages

Cottages "ranged in an uneven semicircle among old apple trees. The Rays had the cottage on the end of the point. It consisted only of two bedrooms with a porch in front." (BWJ p. 13)

MHL Archive

Helen, Kathleen, Tom, and Stella Hart

The Ray cottage "smelled freshly of the lake which could be seen in a rippling silver sheet through the foliage outside the windows." (BWJ p. 13)

MHL Archive

Maud and Midge (Betsy and Tib)

Tib makes a dramatic return to the series at the beginning of *Betsy Was a Junior*. In real life, her family returned from Milwaukee the previous spring (1908). Maud and Midge made a good twosome, just as Betsy and Tib did.

Coll. of Louise King

The Crowd at the Lake

From left to right: Tess Kenney (Katie), Mil Oleson (Irma), Bick Kenney (Tacy), Marion Willard (Carney), Maud Hart (Betsy), and Eleanor Johnson (Winona II).

Coll. of Robert Cahill

Jim Baker
(E. Lloyd Harrington)

"E. Lloyd Harrington was highly social. He, too, was tall, but fragile. He had beautiful manners and loved to dance. He usually wore glasses." (BWJ p. 14)

1910 Annual

Bob Hughes
(Dave Hunt)

"Dave Hunt seldom ... smiled. But when a smile flickered over his stern, clean-cut face, it changed him from a deacon into a daredevil." (BWJ p. 62)

E. Lloyd's House
104 Parsons

Jim Baker lived just across the street from the Andrews (Humphreys) boys.

Coll. of Minnesota Valley Regional Library

Maud and her Christmas Furs

Mr. Ray wrote Betsy a note which read "Hunt" (and led Betsy to her Christmas furs, hidden in the vegetable bin). Did Mr. Hart write Maud a note advising her to take up the "Hugh and cry"?

February 3, 1906, upon their departure for Milwaukee. After returning to Mankato, the Gerlachs lived for a month at 128 South Broad before leasing the former Longini home at Byron and State in May 1908.

Though not late in the summer, the Gerlach family did return in time for the beginning of Maud's junior year. It was, however, Midge's sophomore year. Perhaps the move to Milwaukee interfered with her academic year in some way and she was put back. Or perhaps her parents held her back at some stage, since she was so small for her age. In any case, Midge Gerlach graduated with the class of 1911, though she was a month older than Maud, who was in the class of 1910. Midge wasn't the only "elderly" member of the class of 1911 - there was also Ruth Williams (Alice), who was born in October 1891, five months ahead of Midge.

In addition to time at the lake, Maud spent a week of July 1908 with the Dossett family of Madelia. (A small town called "Medelia" appears fleetingly in *Carney's House Party*.) Mr. Dossett was cashier of the Madelia State Bank.

"Betsy could swim only a little, but she had fun with water wings and floated a long time."[527] She sounds more confident in *Betsy and Joe*: "Betsy swam with a joyfully vigorous breast stroke."[528] Maud wrote to a fan, "*Tib was a good swimmer and Betsy a fair one. Tacy wouldn't go out above her ankles. She had fun though.*"[529] Elsewhere, Maud remarked of Bick, "*in swimming, she has gone out as far as her ankles, and the shock has almost killed her.*"[530] Maud's first cousin, Bill Gerretson, remembered visits by Maud and Delos to his family's Minnesota lake home and said that both Lovelaces were good swimmers. According to a 1934 newspaper report about Maud: "*Although she says she has no real hobby she does enjoy swimming in the salt-waters of Long Island Sound.*"[531]

On the other hand, Maud was hardly an athlete. In 1929, she was quoted as commenting: "*I don't care much for sports.*"[532] She also wrote: "*I'm no more athletic than Betsy was!*"[533] (Then could Betsy have rowed two watery miles, each way, across Murmuring Lake?[534] That's a long haul by rowboat.) Suffice it that Maud Hart Lovelace could swim (and perhaps row), but she was not on the whole particularly athletic. Nor did she enjoy sports as a spectator: "*Delos used to say when he took her to a ball game, she always asked for a hot dog when Babe Ruth was hitting a home run.*"[535]

The Harts must have been particularly glad they were at Madison Lake rather than at home in the summer of 1908. In late June 1908, a typhoid epidemic broke out in Mankato. The city well at Washington and Broad was not properly connected to the mains and became contaminated by surface water. Bacteria was spread through the water supply until the cause was discovered. Residents were then warned to boil their water. The head of the public works board, J. E. Porter, resigned and the city engineer, M.B. Haynes, was removed from office, accused of various derelictions of duty.

Madison Lake was far enough away to be relatively safe. Ads for Point Pleasant in the Mankato newspaper boast of the safety and pure water at the lake: "*This is a splendid time to come to Madison Lake and catch fish. Here you can find the purest water and the sanitary conditions are perfect. The Point is supplied with water from a well that is 130 feet deep, pure and as refreshing as the breezes that unfold over this beauty spot. Trains leave Mankato in the morning and afternoon each day.*"[536]

The Betsy-Tacy books contain no direct reference to the tragedies of the summer of 1908. In fact, Betsy has just the kind of summer a girl ought to have when she is sixteen. But Maud's inspiration for the fictional demise of Cab's father at the end of *Betsy Was a Junior* was almost certainly related to the deaths of the typhoid epidemic.

Jab Lloyd (Cab) did not lose his father at the end of his junior year. Peter Lloyd, Jab's father, was a teacher for several years, having graduated from the Normal in 1877. He held county and city offices, and was a city alderman at the same time Tom Hart was county treasurer. (Peter Lloyd was county treasurer himself from 1888 to 1896.) Mr. Lloyd lived to the ripe age of eighty years, passing away in 1931. While this may be comforting to admirers of Cab, the story of the death of a parent is true; in fact, several of Maud's friends lost their fathers about this time.

Paul Ford (the character Dennie) lost his father, Julius D. Ford, in July 1910. Paul's mother had been dead since he was six. Andrew Burmeister, father of Maud's friend Clayton, died of typhoid at Immanuel Hospital in September 1909. (Clayton and his brother both graduated from high school on schedule.) Typhoid struck in the homes of other Crowd members, with varying degrees of severity. Some of the sick included Irma and her parents, Tacy's father, and Carney's father, all of whom fortunately survived the illness.

When word came of the death of Cab's father, "The Rays grew suddenly sober, as people in a happy home do when death strikes in another happy home."[537] Tom Fox (Tom Slade) had lost his father when he was three years old. His mother, Grace Pitcher Fox, died of typhoid fever at her mother's home on July 25, 1908, at the age of forty-six. Grace's death was obviously a severe blow to the Fox family, and it hit the Harts hard. Maud wrote, "*It was a great grief to us when she* [Grace Fox] *died in the summer of ... 1908 ... when Mankato had a typhoid epidemic. We Harts were all out at Madison Lake (Murmuring Lake) where, you will remember from the high school books, we often spent vacations. It was very hard on George, Milo and Tom to lose such a wonderful mother. But they were fortunate in that they all had been living with their Grandmother Pitcher and their mother's sister, Aunty Fanny, so they still had a home base.*"[538]

The Hart and Fox families celebrated Thanksgiving dinners together, probably at the instigation of Tom Hart. Joe tells Betsy that Mr. Ray is "always thinking about doing something for somebody else ... for some widow across the slough."[539] Mrs. Fox wasn't the widow Joe was speaking of, but Tom Hart, known for his kind heart, must have felt particular concern for the fatherless Fox family, since they were old friends from Center Street days.

Maud used the sad story of a parent's death to reinforce the "moral" of *Betsy Was a Junior*. Betsy and her friends are all brought up short by the death of Cab's father. The frivolity of their junior year is brought into perspective, and their fun seems suddenly childish. "I wouldn't want another year this foolish," Betsy says. "We're getting a little old for this sort of thing," Tib responds severely.[540]

Another high school friend who experienced family tragedy was Mike Parker, the real-life model for Tony. Maud seemed always to protect him from the scrutiny of her curious readers. For the most part, she answered fans' inquiries cheerfully - told them about her high school life, her clothes, her home, her family, and her friends. Maud identified most characters, if asked. But she never identified Tony. She had the following to say about him: "*I did use a neighbor boy for that character. He had Tony's looks and personality and talent for singing. He died in Minneapolis* [sic] *before he was thirty. I try not to identify him, so this is between you and me.*"[541] But even here, Maud hasn't identified Tony! Sadly, Mike did die young, of Bright's disease (a kidney ailment) in Mankato.

Mike had a sad start in life, too. He was born on May 24, 1890, in Howard Lake, Minnesota. His father, Jesse Lindon Parker, had died of tuberculosis some five months earlier. Emma Willcutts Parker, her new baby, and her four older children lived in Howard Lake until 1906. At this time the family moved to Mankato so daughters Minnie and Caroline could attend the teachers' college. (They were beloved Mankato teachers for decades.) Mike's siblings do not appear in the Betsy-Tacy books. Tony's mother is the only relative mentioned.

Tony "was, in fact, almost like a brother to the Ray girls. Betsy was very fond of him.... Tony was nothing if not lovable. But she worried about him, too. She didn't always like the company he kept."[542] It may be because Mike was so dear and also rather a "bad" sort of boy, that Maud shielded him from readers' questions, just as Betsy loyally concealed her concerns about Tony from Joe in *Betsy and Joe.*

Tony was dear to all the Rays. After the family returned from the lake in *Betsy Was a Junior*, "Tony lounged in first. He tried to act nonchalant about their return but the affection he felt for them all shone in his big black eyes. He sat down on the couch and Betsy and Julia sat on either side of him, with Margaret cross-legged on the floor in front. 'Hi!' he called to Mrs. Ray, 'Call off your daughters, can't you?' 'But we're glad to see you, Tony,' the girls protested."[543]

Tony understood Margaret's lack of ambition, as well as the forces driving Julia (music) and Betsy (writing). "He could listen.... Betsy talked more about herself with Tony than with any boy she knew."[544] Perhaps Mike even had a nickname for Maud as Tony had "Ray of Sunshine" for Betsy. "Hart of my Heart?" "Queen of Harts?"

When Julia returns from Europe at the end of *Betsy and Joe*, the first friend she asks about is Tony, and indeed, Kathleen's letters from Europe attest to Mike Parker's intimacy with the family. Kathleen mentions him numerous times. She doesn't ask about any other Crowd friends, except Tess (Katie). At one point she writes, "*Give everybody my love -- Mike and all the girls.*"[545] Kathleen also reports getting "*a letter from Mike, the dear.*"[546] Elsewhere she mentions writing a separate letter to him - which she never has time to do for any other friends or relatives, she says.

Mr. Ray tells Tony that he doesn't approve of trips to Minneapolis for baseball games: "You might lose a leg some day, hopping a freight."[547] (Twice in *Betsy and Joe,* on pages 61 and 226, Betsy reminds Tony of Mr. Ray's advice.) A similar accident befell Mike's brother, Edgar. Edgar lost his leg under a freight car, but he wasn't hopping a train. He had taken a summer position with the Great Northern Railroad, and the accident occurred while he was on the job. This abruptly ended Edgar's academic career at the University of Minnesota, where he had been studying civil engineering. Edgar Parker was twenty-one years old when the typhoid epidemic hit Mankato. He was its first casualty, dying July 20, 1908, after battling the disease for ten days. Caroline Parker also contracted typhoid but survived.

One other death related to the series occurred in 1908. This would not have affected Maud as personally as Mike's brother and Tom's mother. But since her father was a pallbearer at the funeral, Maud may well have attended it. The death was that of James Ray Tinkcom (Mr. Meecham from *Over the Big Hill*), who died on November 14, 1908.

The summer of 1908 may have been a gay one for Betsy, but it couldn't have been for Maud. By autumn, the epidemic was over, and life in Mankato could return to normal. Perhaps the hilarity of the school year, as described in *Betsy Was a Junior*, was a reaction to the fear and sorrow of the past summer.

The first day of school is a Tuesday (it would have been September 8, 1908). Betsy wore a navy and red sailor suit. (She'd worn a pale blue one freshman year but a new blouse {waist} and skirt sophomore year. As a senior, she chose a pink chambray dress.)

This year Tib and Betsy attempt to tease Tacy into wearing a pompadour. Tacy refuses: "I want to go down in history as the only female of my generation who didn't wear a pompadour."[548] She remains firm even when, as a senior, she sings solos and finally graduates. Maud wrote to a fan: "*Tacy and her husband were visiting when your letter came. I read her the question about her pompadour and she said that she tried one, one time, for just a few days but went back to her coronet braids.*"[549]

On the first day back at school, Betsy "observed that there were several new teachers. Some of the old ones were gone, and she was thankful that Miss Bangeter was not among the missing."[550] We know that this was the autumn in which the real Miss Bangeter <u>was</u> among the missing. Though Miss Fullerton was principal for only two of Maud's high school years, she obviously made a significant impact. Upon leaving Mankato, Miss Fullerton went to Stillwater High School for a year, then to China to work as a missionary for the Episcopal Church. The Mr. Norby who succeeded Miss Fullerton as principal of Mankato High School appears to have been perfectly competent, but he apparently didn't have a "presence," as Miss Fullerton did. (He is not mentioned in the Betsy-Tacy books.) "I feel sorry for high schools that haven't Miss Bangeter for principal," Betsy thought.[551]

We are not surprised to learn that Mr. Gaston has been switched from English to science, for Julia has scornfully observed that Mr. Gaston couldn't appreciate Betsy's writing, having come to town to teach science. "He's a science teacher, really."[552]

Miss Gwendolyn Fowler is the new English teacher. Her real name was Gwendolyn Evelyn Fischer, but she was called "Evelyn." Like Miss Fowler, Miss Fischer was a Bostonian. She and her sister Edna arrived in Mankato from Boston on September 6, 1908, to take positions as teachers. Maud wrote that she "*received great inspiration from an English teacher, Evelyn Fisher* [sic]."[553]

A young Swedish pill named Miss Erickson came to teach Latin at Deep Valley High. This must have been Miss Helen Cooper, who was indeed just out of college (as Miss Bangeter points out, in excuse of Miss Erickson's villainy, on page 100). It was Carleton College, and Miss Cooper had taught one year at St. James High School before coming to Mankato.

Coll. of SSW

Miss Caroline Bangeter
(Miss Caroline Fullerton)

"There was something noble about this high school principal. She was commandingly tall. A knot of black hair topped a dark hawklike face which was usually grave, but knew how to flash into humor." (BWJ p. 34)

1910 Annual

Miss Gwendolyn Evelyn Fischer
(Miss Gwendolyn Fowler)

Betsy was drawn to Miss Fowler, who "had come from Miss Bangeter's Boston and looked not unlike her, having heavy black hair and white teeth." (BWJ p. 34)

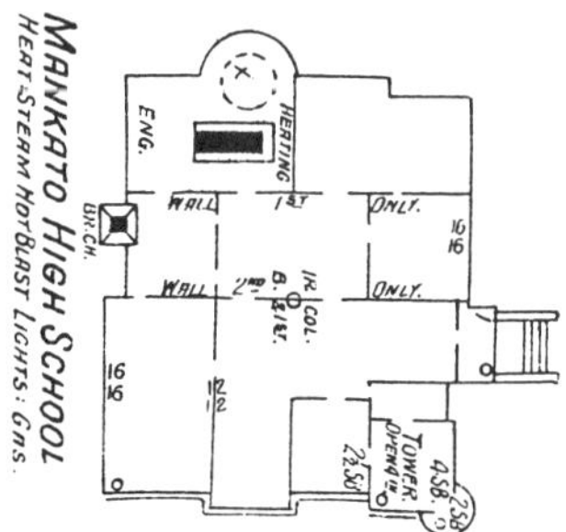

Mankato High School

A 1908 insurance map provides the layout of the high school building.

Miss Erickson
(Miss Cooper)

Blond Miss Erickson had "tried to teach" Betsy Latin, and she was Betsy's German teacher senior year.

1912 Otaknam

Interior of High School
Domestic Science Room

"One great advantage to being a junior girl was that you were eligible to take Domestic Science.... The Domestic Science room was a fascinating place, provided with rows of little stoves, small shining pots and pans." (BWJ p. 38) Betsy and Tacy took Dom. Sci., but Tib did not. In real life, Maud took Domestic Science, Bick did not, and Midge did - as a senior.

1912 Otaknam

Interior of High School
Principal's Office

Perhaps Maud was really sent to the principal's office in disgrace, as Betsy was, when Okto Delta got her into trouble.

The expression "old pill" was actually in use by the Crowd about this time, as evidenced by a note in Maud's High School Scrapbook, part of a parody written by one of her friends: *"Oh dear, I'll be so mad at Lester Door, the old pill, if he doesn't ask me."*[554] (Lester Door was a peripheral member of the Crowd but does not appear fictionally.)

Gentle Miss Benbow was the domestic science teacher, who didn't get annoyed even when Betsy thought she needed a needle and thread to baste a chicken. This was Myrtle Francis. At the end of the year, Miss Francis resigned her position, and the girls in the domestic science class presented her with a gold watch fob.

Joe is no longer working at the Creamery this year. (As an aside, John Kenney, Bick's older brother, worked at the Creamery.) Joe is now working at the *Deep Valley Sun*. "Irrationally, for she could take no credit, she felt proud of his new job."[555] Betsy feels proud of him, because her feelings are flowing from the pen of Joe's wife. None of the boys in Maud's Crowd worked at the *Mankato Free Press*, though Clay Burmeister worked at the *Review*.

The character Phyllis Brandish (Phil's twin sister) was introduced for the purpose of being Joe's girl. Maud may have been picturing Mildred Robertson, a visitor to Mankato for whom Marney gave a party in September 1908. According to Maud's diary, Mildred was *"a terribly flossy girl, been abroad twice, goes to a swell boarding school in Washington."*[556] Fortunately, whoever Phyllis was, she never got her paws on the real Joe!

The party Irma gave for Phyllis sounds elegant: "They wore light summer dresses, held parasols, and all of them, except Betsy, carried little silk sewing bags on their wrists."[557] There were flowers throughout Irma's house, and at the dining-room table were "more flowers, pink candles, little pink baskets filled with candy and nuts."[558]

This party sounds, in some ways, very much like one given by a Mankato girl named Mabel Moore on Saturday, September 7, 1907. The party was described by the *Mankato Free Press: "The guests came arrayed in dainty summer gowns and provided with needlework. The parlors and dining room were decorated with flowers, the color that predominated being pink. The affair was entirely lacking in formality. After an elaborate supper had been served, through the assistance of Misses Maude Hart and Marion Willard, most unique and fun favors were given out, which helped to make it a jolly afternoon.*"[559] Were Maud and Marion inspired to wear their fathers' dress suits again? Dress suits or no, Mabel's party sounds far less stuffy than the one given for Phyllis!

After the party for Phyllis, Betsy and Carney go downtown to buy a jabot which Betsy will embroider for Carney. (Maud really embroidered one for Marion.) Betsy and Carney purchase the jabot at the Lion Department Store. This store was also mentioned in *Betsy in Spite of Herself*, when Betsy shopped for pink lace stockings to match her daisy dress.[560] (Emily of Deep Valley buys at the Lion, too.) The department store in Mankato at this time was Brett's at 327-329 S. Front, which remained in business until 1992. Maud spoke in a letter of "*Brett's where our family used to shop.*"[561]

But there were other department stores in town. Kruse's (pronounced "crew-zies") was one block down from Brett's, at 417-419 S. Front. Nyquist's, at 210-212 S. Front, no doubt inspired the fictional Alquist's, which supplied the senior class with "skull caps made up in the class colors of violet and gray" in *Betsy and Joe*.[562] (The colors of the class of 1910 were indeed lavender and gray.) Other notable department stores included Lappin's at 109 S. Front, Silber & Steiner at 413 N. Front, and Richards' at 402-406 S. Front. A golden lion once stood before Richards' Dry Goods. Our only fictional look at the decorative lion occurs in *Downtown*, in which the store is first mentioned. "In front of the Lion Department Store a bronze lion stood guard over a drinking trough."[563] Though Richards' golden lion obviously inspired Maud's choice of the fictional name, she may well have been picturing Brett's when she described visits to the department store.

Before Julia departs for the "U," she and Betsy take a farewell drive through town. The description of their route yields a concise directory of public places in Deep Valley.

"They would drive down High Street past the high school and court house to the end, turn and drive up Broad past the library, the Catholic, Presbyterian, Baptist and Episcopal churches, and Carney's house. At Lincoln Park they would turn and angle down

Coll. of Gamma Phi Beta Sorority

Kathleen with the Gamma Phis

At the end of her freshman year, Julia received a bid from the Epsilon Iota sorority. Kathleen joined Gamma Phi Beta. This photograph was probably taken in Kathleen's first year at the University of Minnesota (1908-1909).

Coll. of Gamma Phi Beta Sorority

Kathleen Again

Julia said of the Epsilon Iotas, "They're just my kind. I'm going to be an Epsilon Iota. And if I am, Bettina, you will be too, and so will Margaret. Sisters always join their sister's sorority." (BWJ p. 76) Maud and Helen did join Gamma Phi.

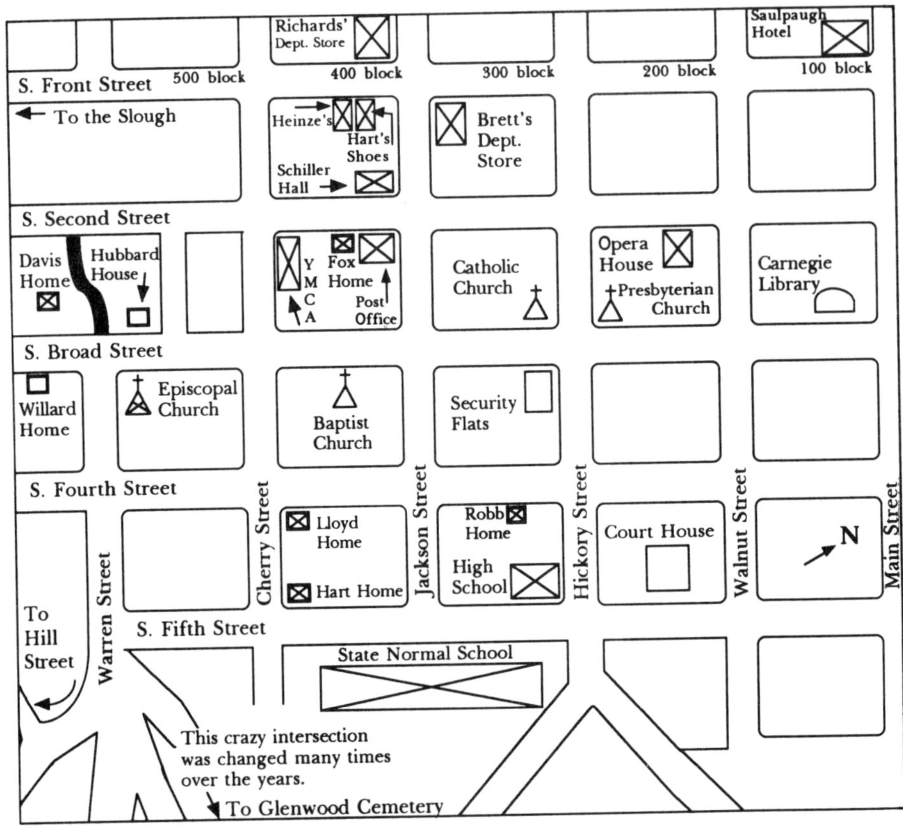

Map of Mankato/Deep Valley Streets Circa 1910
Note: some streets have been rerouted, notably Warren Street.
Buildings which no longer stand are marked with an X.

"To find the Deep Valley of the Betsy-Tacy stories in this bustling, modern Mankato is not easy. You must wipe out the changes time has brought and bring back the horse and buggy days." (Maud Hart Lovelace, MFP 10-9-61)

Second where there were more homes and more churches, livery stables, the post office, the fire house, the Opera House. Then, turning again, they would drive up Front past the Big Mill and the Melborn Hotel and Mr. Ray's shoe store. Sometimes they stopped for ice cream."[564] When Maud says they drove up High Street to the end, she meant the end of South Fifth. At Main Street, it became "North" Fifth. The town stopped at Main, in the eyes of some Mankato residents.

Betsy began taking piano lessons in her junior year. In fact, Maud began piano lessons in the fall of her sophomore year. Maud remembered: "*Some of us went downtown to take piano lessons.... I studied first with the heroic Kate Robb.*"[565] (In her junior year, Maud took lessons with May Brett Taylor.)

Kate Robb appears in the Betsy-Tacy books as the fictional Jessie Cobb. "Everyone in Deep Valley began piano study with Miss Cobb, a large, mild, blonde woman who was a Deep Valley institution, and one of its most widely admired heroines.... Years before, on the death of a sister, she ... had taken the sister's four children to raise. The little girl had followed her mother and the youngest boy had followed his sister. One of the two remaining boys was delicate."[566] In *Emily of Deep Valley*, we learn that the ailment was tuberculosis.[567]

As a young woman, Kate Robb left her hometown in Ohio to study music in Leipzig, Germany. (Miss Cobb had studied abroad, too.[568]) Upon completion of her studies in about 1873, Miss Robb returned to America to live at the home of her uncle, the Reverend J.B. Little, in Mankato. While there, she must have grown close to her cousin Alice, for in 1881, Miss Robb joined the household of her cousin (now Mrs. T.H. Williams). Mrs. Williams died in 1891, and Miss Robb committed herself to raising her cousin's four children. Whether Miss Robb also broke an engagement to marry, as per the fictional account, is possible but doubtful.

The eldest boy and girl died young. The third child, Walter Williams, is fictionally represented by Miss Cobb's delicate nephew, Leonard, who is fifteen in 1908. (Walter would actually have been twenty-two that year!) Bobby is the robust youngster. In *Emily of Deep Valley*, we learn that in 1912, Bobby is in fifth grade, so he would have been a first-grader during *Betsy Was a Junior.* Bobby was Robb (after his cousin Kate) Williams, who was really four years older than Maud and graduated from high school two years ahead of her.

Leonard and Bobby are "Cobbs," but if they were the children of Miss Cobb's sister, their last name would not have been "Cobb." And in reality, they were of course the children of Kate Robb's cousin, rather than her sister. Miss Robb did have a sister, but she was unmarried and lived in Chicago.

At the end of *Betsy Was a Junior,* Leonard is sent to Colorado, in hope that the change might offer a cure. Kate Robb accompanied Walter to Denver, departing August 18, 1908 (which was after Maud's sophomore, rather than junior, year). They joined Miss Robb's mother, who was living in Denver. Leonard died there in the spring of 1910, per *Betsy and Joe.* The real Leonard also died of tuberculosis in Denver, on April 1, 1910, at age twenty-four.

When Betsy goes to the Cobb house for piano lessons, it is on a "steep hillside below the high school."[569] In 1902, when Kathleen took lessons with her, Miss Robb lived in a large duplex at 508 S. Fourth. In 1904, she moved to 313 S. Fourth, which was on the hill below the high school. Maud says there was "a long flight of wooden steps" leading to Miss Cobb's cottage. This is likely, since the house, now gone, was on a fairly steep hill (the west side of the street). Upon her return to Mankato (from Colorado) in the spring of 1910, Miss Robb reopened her music studio, at 411 Cherry Street.

Piano lessons are one of Betsy's few serious interests this year. There are many exciting distractions. For instance, Carney sews a pennant for Dave, though he won't say why he wants it. The girls find out on their way to school on page 65. Dave had climbed to the top of the "cupola which rose high above the main building." And the pennant was now "floating from the top of the peaked cap of roof."[570] George Scherer, who graduated from Mankato High School in 1911, recalled: "*One year either a Philo or a Zet put their flag on the high school flagpole. The other one tried to take it down and in the brawl the iron railing around the roof was broken. That was a night to remember.*"[571]

Gene Skrupijis

Artist's Rendering of
Oktw Delta Pin

A local jewelry store did indeed engrave "eight gold pins with the mystic Okto Delta symbols." (BWJ p. 106) By spring, "the pins were lost, or dropped into jewel cases and forgotten, or given away to boys who forgot to return them." (BWJ p. 210) At least one pin (which once belonged to Ruth Williams) has survived.

Coll. of Louise King

Rear View

Tib's "clothes were fragile, lace-trimmed, and beribboned." (B&J p. 28)

Coll. of Louise King

Shoebox Lunch

From left: Midge Gerlach, Mil Oleson, and Bick Kenney. Midge looks the way we picture Tib, who is "slender and swaying." (B&J p. 28)

Coll. of Louise King

Shutterbug

Many of the photographs used in this book were snapped by Ruth Williams (Alice) shown here holding her camera. She shared prints with her friends. From left: Harriet Ahlers, Eleanor Johnson, Mil Oleson, Midge Gerlach, Ruth, and Marion Willard.

Duplicated in several collections

In the Willard (Sibley) Reo

Midge Gerlach is at the wheel with Eleanor Johnson beside her. Bick Kenney is at the left side of the photo in the back seat. Beside her is Margaret Wilcox (N/C).

This year Chauncey Olcott comes to town in *Ragged Robin. Ragged Robin* was indeed performed in Mankato on Tuesday, September 15, 1908. The songs from the play mentioned in *Betsy Was a Junior* are "Don't You Love the Eyes That Come from Ireland?" and "Sweet Girl of My Dreams."[572] Other songs from *Ragged Robin* were "If You'll Remember Me," "A Laugh with a Tear in It," and "I Used to Believe in Fairies."[573] Warwick's Bookstore on Front Street sold sheet music for these songs for twenty-five cents each.

Another exciting event of the autumn is the arrival of the Sibleys' auto. The reader has long been aware that the Sibley family was planning to purchase one. In *Heaven to Betsy*, Carney says: "Papa's threatening to get an automobile."[574] Two years later, the Crowd has indeed got itself an automobile, thanks to Mr. Sibley. On page 26, we learn that it's a Buick. The Willard family did buy a car about this time (actually a year earlier), and it was a Buick. W.D. Willard, Marion's father, wrote, "*We bought our first automobile June 14, 1907 - a two-cylinder Buick, two seater, engine under the floor, right side steering, shift outside, acetylene lamps (which were very uncertain) - $1,178.95. The alley back of our house had just been filled in and the barn razed. It was very difficult to get in and out, so we kept the car in Dick Rose's barn across the street.*"[575]

The Crowd has piled into the Willard Reo (like the one Gladys drove in *Emily of Deep Valley*[576]) in the photograph on page 238. 237W.D. explains: "*In 1909, Alba Lewis* [of the hardware store] *persuaded me to trade in the Buick for a Reo.*" But by 1911, the Sibleys are driving a Maxwell.[577] W.D. explains again: the new Reo "*was a mistake as the four-cylinder cars were coming into use. So, the next year, 1910, I traded with Harry Perrin for a Maxwell '4.*'"[578]

When Maud began work on the later Betsy-Tacy books, she wrote to high school friends to ask for their memories. She must have asked Marion to send a history of the Willard automobiles. It is amazing that Maud went to this trouble, since she had no idea that we would one day be following her research trail with such lovingly relentless interest.

Julia's departure for the "U" is very sad for the Rays, but none of them cry at the station. "The Rays didn't believe in crying at trains."[579] According to *Betsy Was a Junior*, Julia departed on a

Tuesday.[580] Kathleen's train left Mankato on Monday, September 14, 1908, for Minneapolis and the "U." (Out-of-staters are charmed to learn that the University of Minnesota is still known as the "U.")

Julia's friend Roger Tate may have been based on University of Minnesota student Hanford Cox, a friend of Kathleen's, who visited the Harts in Mankato a number of times. (Maud gave the name "Harley Cox" to the hero of a short story she wrote in 1915.)

Like Julia, Kathleen returned home for a weekend after a short time at the U. She may not have awakened her family with a rendition of "Howdy Cy," but Kathleen came home on September 18 and stayed until Tuesday morning, the 22nd. The "Julia" character in "I Am Curly" also surprises her family with a midnight serenade, in this case "The Maple Leaf Rag."[581]

Julia has been able to surprise her sleeping family because "nobody locked doors in Deep Valley."[582] The Harts probably started locking their doors about a year later, after an attempted break-in, described in the *Mankato Free Press*: "*An effort was made to enter the residence of County Treasurer T.W. Hart, at the corner of Fifth and Cherry streets, but for some reason the burglar gave up the job, possibly frightened by someone approaching on the walk. This morning Mr. Hart found a dining room chair from some other house and a homemade ladder ten feet long on the south side of his house. The chair was under one of the dining room windows, and the legs were sunk an inch into the lawn, showing that the burglar was a full grown man. The burglar had evidently attempted to get the window screen off, but was unable to reach the screw or button at the top.... The window inside the screen was open, and had he succeeded in getting the screen off he would have gotten right in. Mr. Hart had very little money in the house, and the burglar would not have been well rewarded.*"[583]

Julia has returned from the "U" telling magical tales of sororities. Betsy decides to begin a Deep Valley High sorority, consisting of the girls from the Crowd. This is exactly what Maud did. A page from her Scrapbook is titled: "*And in my junior year, we invented Oktwa Delta for our amusement and edification.*" Maud and her friends generally used the spelling Oktw Delta. Therefore, when referring herein to the actual group, "Oktw Delta" is used, and when referring to the fictional group, "Okto Delta." The

Morning Cy!
Barn
Dance
THE UNIVERSALLY ACCEPTED TUNE FOR THE FAMOUS BARN DANCE
5

Howdy Cy

9
TRIO.
It was "Morning, Cy! Howdy, Cy! Gosh darn, Cy-rus, but you're look-ing spry.
Right in line, all the time, Jimmin - y crickets, but you're look-ing fine.
Morn-ing, Cy! How-dy, Cy!" Ev - 'ry rube a-round the town would cry.
"How-dy do, Same to you," And when they saw him com-ing, it was "Morn-ing, Cy!"

Howdy Cy

"Oktw" or "Oktwa" in the Vera Neville illustration on page 105 is a mystery. Perhaps it indicates that the spelling Maud originally used in the manuscript for *Betsy Was a Junior* was "Oktw" or "Oktwa," and an editor at Crowell decided "Okto" was preferable.

Betsy, Tacy, and Tib establish Okto Delta on October 5, 1908. The initiation is at Betsy's house on October 10. The girls inducted are the real Oktw Deltas: Maud, Bick, Tess, Midge, Marion, El, Mil, and Ruth. These are the same friends to whom *Betsy Was a Junior* is dedicated, except for two: Connie (Bonnie) and Pat (N/C = not a character).

Bonnie/Connie was not in Okto/Oktw Delta, of course, since she was no longer living in Mankato. Connie is no doubt included in the dedication because in real life, she was still an important member of the Crowd, even after she had moved away. Unlike the fictional Bonnie in *Heaven to Betsy*, Connie hadn't gone back to Paris. She'd moved no farther away than St. Paul, and she often came to Mankato to attend Crowd festivities. One instance is chronicled in Maud's Scrapbook: Connie came down for an Oktw Delta "blue jay" sleighing party. Pat, meanwhile, was Harriet Ahlers, who graduated in the class of 1910. Maud may have regretted that Harriet was excluded from the sorority (as Betsy regretted the exclusion of Hazel Smith) and therefore included her in the dedication of *Betsy Was a Junior*.

The Okto Deltas have a wonderful time at the St. John game. "The St. John game was always the climax of the football season in Deep Valley."[584] Maud surely had St. Peter, Minnesota, in mind here. Only about ten miles apart, the towns were predictable football rivals.

Betsy is in the Girls Debating Club again this year. They "argued in November [1908] that 'Immigration should be further restricted.' She and Hazel Smith were given the affirmative side."[585] A program from the "*Girl's* [sic] *Debating Club*" in Maud's Scrapbook lists the first debate, December 12, 1907, featuring "Maude" Hart, who argued (affirmative), that "*Immigration should be further restricted*."[586] Her partner was Gladys Benner. Could this be Hazel Smith? Probably not. There was a "Hazel" in the Club, who was, in fact, president. This was Hazel Schoelkopf. She and her sister Mabel graduated from Mankato High School in 1909.

Perhaps Hazel Schoelkopf partly inspired Hazel Smith. For yet another theory, see Chapter 11 herein.

Other significant debaters on the actual program included Marion Willard (Carney) and Tessie Kenney (Katie) who argued (negative), "*That Trade Unions do not operate to the advantage of the labor classes*." Eleanor Johnson (Winona II) argued (affirmative), "*That the United States should hold the Phillipine Islands permanently*." Francis (sic) Kenney (Tacy) and Ruth Williams (Alice) argued (negative), "*That the canteen should be reestablished in the U.S. Army*." Frances Kenney and "Maude" Hart argued (negative) against Ruth Williams (Alice) and Ella Markham (N/C), "*That street railways should be owned and operated by municipalities*."

The Philos win the Debating Cup on page 153. They did, indeed, in January 1909.

The boys form Omega Delta to keep up with the girls. The fictional eight would have been Lloyd, Al, Cab, Dennie, Dave, Phil, Pin, and Squirrelly. A program in Maud's Scrapbook reveals that eight Mankato High School boys gave a party for the Oktw Deltas. Seven of the fictional Omega Deltas are listed: *James Baker* (Lloyd), *Henry Lee* (Al), *Paul Ford* (Dennie), *Robert Hughes* (Dave), *C. Burmeister* (Phil Brandish-ish), *Earnest* (sic) *Jones* (Pin), *Earl King* (Squirrelly). Jab Lloyd (Cab) is not on the list. Instead, Everett Dodds appears. Everett was the son of Robert (a veterinary surgeon) and Sophia Dodds. They lived at 823 S. Front. Everett did not graduate with the Crowd, having moved to Decoria, Minnesota.

Betsy resumes the reforming campaign she had begun in sophomore year, gathering a pipe from Dave, a sack of tobacco and cigarette papers from Dennie, and a cigar from Cab (which was only his father's, after all). One of the pages in Maud's Scrapbook contains the inscription: "*When I was a 'reformer'*." Pasted onto the page is a bag which once contained "*Plaza Cube Cut Pipe Tobacco*" and some papers from "*Blackwell's Durham Smoking Tobacco (5 cents)*."[587]

Maud went with Bob Hughes during her junior year, just as Betsy went with Dave Hunt. Bob Hughes squired Maud to high school dances in the fall of their junior year, including the Thanksgiving Dance on November 25, 1908. Maud does not

Duplicated in several collections

The Oktw [sic] Deltas

From left: Midge Gerlach (Tib), Mil Oleson (Irma), Bick Kenney (Tacy), Maud Hart (Betsy), Eleanor Johnson (Winona II), Marion Willard (Carney), Ruth Williams (Alice), and Tess Kenney (Katie).

Coll. of Robert Cahill

More Oktw [sic] Deltas

Back row, from left: Bick Kenney (Tacy), Maud Hart (Betsy), Eleanor Johnson (Winona II), and Mil Oleson (Irma). Front row, from left: Midge Gerlach (Tib), Tess Kenney (Katie), Marion Willard (Carney), Ruth Williams (Alice).

Duplicated in several collections

The Oktw Deltas in Costume

From left: Tess Kenney (Katie), Maud Hart (Betsy), Ruth Williams (Alice), Midge Gerlach (Tib), Mil Oleson (Irma), Bick Kenney (Tacy), Marion Willard (Carney), Eleanor Johnson (Winona II). The kilt Eleanor Johnson is wearing in the above photo appears on her fictional self in *Carney's House Party*. Winona "always wore the same Scottish kilt to masquerades." (CHP p. 79)

Duplicated in several collections

More Oktw Deltas in Costume

From left: Eleanor Johnson (Winona II), Marion Willard (Carney), partially hidden - Tess Kenney (Katie), Midge Gerlach (Tib), Ruth Williams (Alice), Maud Hart (Betsy), Mil Oleson (Irma), Bick Kenney (Tacy).

MHL Archive

Winona, Betsy, and Dave

Eleanor Johnson, Maud, and Bob Hughes are enjoying a visit to Minneopa Falls. Bob's height, like Dave's, was an impressive six foot three.

BECHS

Maud in her Princesse Dress

Betsy had a coveted new princesse dress in red. This cartoon shows Maud in a similar dress. The name on the dance program she is holding is "Bob." Tib draws a place card with a cartoon of Betsy in her new red princesse dress.

BECHS

A second cartoon of Maud is labeled "*Miss M.R.P. Hart in her senior year, her hair as curly as ever, still the object of devotion of all the H.S. boys.*" Both cartoons were pasted into Maud's High School Scrapbook.

Duplicated in several collections

1907 Mankato High School Football Team

Members of Maud's Crowd who are pictured: back row, second from left, Pin Jones (Pin). Front row, third from left, Henry Lee (Al). Front row, second from right, Herman Hayward (Stan).

Duplicated in several collections

1908 Mankato High School Football Team

Crowd members pictured include back row, second from left, Bob Hughes (Dave); third from left, Henry Lee (Al); fifth from left, Pin Jones (Pin). Middle row, second from right, Paul Ford (Dennie). Front row, second from left, Herman Hayward (Stan); third from left, Jab Lloyd (Cab).

mention a Thanksgiving Dance in *Betsy Was a Junior.* The holiday dance to which Dave Hunt takes Betsy is a Christmas Dance. Dave wrote his name three times on Betsy's program. "She two-stepped happily with Cab.... Tony had asked her for the barn dance.... She and Dennie sang [while they danced]." Phil and Betsy had a schottische together.[588]

According to the actual program, Bob Hughes did take the first dance, as her escort, as well as three additional dances. Maud two-stepped with Pin and Mike. She had two schottisches with Bob. She had a waltz with Mike and a barn dance with Everett Dodds. She danced a half-step with Clayton Burmeister. The fifth extra she danced with Paul Ford.

Betsy burns her hair while curling it in preparation for this dance. (We also saw her heating the curling tongs in the kitchen in preparation for a dance with Phil on page 197 of *Betsy in Spite of Herself.*) The day before Christmas vacation, joke presents are given out at school. Betsy is summoned to the platform as: "Miss Betsy Warrington Ray Humphreys Markham Edwards Brandish Hunt and so forth." The card reads, "This is to curl the bang now growing on your lily-white intellectual brow."[589]

There is a card in Maud's Scrapbook which reads: "*Miss Maude Rosemond Palmer Hart Jones Gifford Hodson Wells Hoerr Morehart Ford Hughes Weed & etc. We would like to see you curl that new crop of whiskers now flourishing on your lily-white intellectual brow and with this end in view we present you with this valuable and priceless instrument.*" It is signed "*Class '09.*" Maud has written above the card: "*Accompanying a curling iron.*"[590]

The real names on the card break down thusly: *Jones, Pin '09* (Pin); *Gifford, Frank Ambrose '08* (N/C); *Hodson, Herbert '09* (N/C); *Wells, Zelora '10* (N/C); *Hoerr, Carl G. - didn't graduate MHS,* (partly Phil); *Morehart, Malcolm '11* (also Phil-like); *Ford, Paul '11* (Dennie); *Hughes, Robert '10* (Dave); *Weed, John '09* (Hank Weed).

Every Christmas the Rays put joke presents in one another's stockings. Mr. Ray was given an old boot or shoe from Helmus Hanson who ran the rival shoe store.[591] There were quite a few shoe stores in town. Those on South Front included Draver's at 407, across the street from Hart's; Louis Janda's at 309 S. Front; Johnson's at 418 S. Front; and Spicer's at 222 S. Front.

The Okto Delta progressive dinner sounds like great fun. Maud filled a page in her Scrapbook with place cards from the "*Oktw Delta Progressive Dinner*."[592] The December 30, 1908, *Mankato Free Press* described the event: "*The young ladies of the Octra* [sic] *Delta club gave a progressive dinner party last night in honor of Miss Constance Davis, who is the guest of Miss Willard. The club is composed of eight girls and the dinner was a most unique affair, one course being served at the home of each member.*"[593]

Maud commented in later years: "*During the Christmas holiday season our crowd of girls used to give progressive dinners, a different course in each house. We would go gaily through the wintry night, singing ... to the Willards', Johnsons', Olesons', Kenneys', Gerlachs', Williams's, our house, and still others in various years.*"[594]

Okto Delta went out with the school year, we hear on page 210 of *Betsy Was a Junior*. The Oktw Delta organization, however, appears to have outlived its fictional counterpart. At any rate, the eight girls held reunions for several years. According to a December 1910 article in the *Mankato Free Press*: "*The Oktw Delta club gave its annual progressive dinner last evening.... On Monday evening, the club gave its annual Christmas tree.*"[595]

A young man named Charles Holden came to Mankato about this time to attend the teachers' college. He boarded at 324 Clark (East Pleasant), across the street from Eleanor Johnson's home. (Many homes near the Harts boarded students. The proliferation of college students in Mankato homes is one thing that hasn't changed.) Perhaps it was through neighbor Eleanor that Charlie Holden met Tess Kenney (Katie). By December 1909, Maud was referring to him as "*Tessie's man*" in her diary.[596] Charlie and Tess were married in Minneapolis on October 28, 1913. In the Betsy-Tacy books, Katie marries Leo. Leo attended Deep Valley High School and is first mentioned in *Heaven to Betsy*.

January brought mid-term exams. "Betsy's grades weren't what she had planned on Murmuring Lake: Botany, 83; Domestic Science, 84; Cicero, 87; U.S. History, 90; Foundations of English Literature, 93."[597] Maud's academic record for the first semester of junior year: *Domestic Science, 84; Cicero, 87; American History, 80; English, 95*. Maud took Botany (one semester only) in her senior year, rather than in her junior year. Miss Comstock taught one

Coll. of Louise King

414 N. Fourth Street
about 1911

Midge (Tib) is seen emerging from her home. She appears to be wearing a boudoir cap (B&J p. 148). Paul Ford (Dennie) is waiting on the walk.

414 N. Fourth Street
about 1990

The Gerlach family lived in this house at the time Midge graduated from high school.

Coll. of Louise King

Tacy is Camera Shy?

Bick Kenney, third from left, appears loathe to be photographed. Midge (Tib), Ruth (Alice), and Pat Ahlers attempt to encourage her. The background, right, reveals how little developed (and unpaved) North Fourth Street was in 1911.

1910 Annual

Harriet Ahlers

Harriet, whose nickname was Pat, inspired, in part, the character Hazel Smith. Harriet Ahlers was not an Oktw Delta.

Mankato Free Press

Combing Jacket

For Christmas, Julia and Betsy both receive combing jackets, which were the latest fad. "Lacy and beribboned, they hung on one's bedpost when not in use." (BWJ p. 142)

Coll. of Louise King

Picnic Time

Harriet (center of photo) is shown picnicking with (from left) Eleanor Johnson (Winona II), Mil Oleson (Irma), and Bick Kenney (Tacy).

MHL Archive

Chums

Clayton Burmeister on a picnic with Eleanor Johnson (left side of photo) and Maud Hart (right side).

semester of American History. The second semester of history was "Civics."

"The new term brought basketball contests with all the neighboring towns."[598] Betsy went to games with Tib and her escort, since Dave was on the basketball team. The spectators roared adoringly, "What's the matter with Hunt? He's all right!"[599] The same cheer is repeated elsewhere. In *Betsy and Joe*, it's "What's the matter with Maddox?"[600] The cheer also appears in Jean Webster's *Daddy-Long-Legs*, a book Betsy remembered in *Betsy and the Great World*. *"What's the matter with Judy Abbott? She's all right. Who's all right? Judy AB-BOTT!"*[601]

An intriguing basketball reference appears in Wanda Gag's *Growing Pains*. On Saturday, February 5, 1910, Gag's entry reads: *"I got another ticket for the basket ball game.... Our girls and boys won tonight. Did we cheer? I just think we did! Oh but those girls were pretty. Especially one who wore a red sweater and had light, fluffy hair. She looked for all the world like a Harrison Fisher girl. And Cute! I wish I could have sketched her. She was a perfect picture. I had visions - just as I was dropping off to sleep - of basket balls and basket ball players. I remember distinctly the New Ulm H.S. players at the very tip top of a sort of tree, and the Mankato players being trampled on unmercifully as our players were ascending to victory."*[602] It seems unlikely that Wanda would have taken sudden notice of a girl from her own high school. The pretty blonde must have been from Mankato. Could it have been Midge?

With basketball games, rhetoricals, and Okto Delta parties, the winter passed gaily for Betsy. And she was delighted when little Margaret confided her own desire for a party. It was to be a party for Margaret's dog and cat, to celebrate their February birthdays. The grey and white cat, presented by Fred in *Heaven to Betsy*, was named Washington. The cat's real name was General Baker (after Jim Baker's father!).

"I don't want to invite a lot of children," Margaret said.[603] The party for the pets was to be on Thursday, February 18. (February 18th <u>was</u> a Thursday in 1909.) Betsy forgot about Margaret's party, distracted by peach pecan sundaes with Tib, Dennie, and Cab. Betsy's wrenching guilt is perhaps even more painful for the sympathetic reader than Margaret's disappointment.

Margaret was not only disappointed by Betsy's non-appearance, but she had a dangerous run-in with an exploding stove (which curled her eyelashes). Helen did burn her eyelashes, but it had nothing to do with a party ... or with Maud. Helen recalled the incident in a 1946 letter to Maud: "*One time, Mother was gone and Daddy and I were going to be alone for lunch. He was at the court house then. I don't remember what food I had planned to give him (I thought it was fried eggs), but I had to light the oven for it. Anyway, when I lit it, it exploded, scared me, and burned my eyelashes. About that time, Daddy came home and got the lunch. I was quite disappointed as I had planned on being a big girl and getting my father's lunch. Anyway, for several days, I had lovely, curly eyelashes. I liked them so well, I might have repeated the exploding stove experiment again to make the curled eyelashes a more permanent thing.*"[604]

It is soothing to note that Helen had a very successful February party. The *Mankato Free Press* reported that "*Miss Helen Hart entertained fourteen of her young girl friends at her home on South Fifth Street from four to seven o'clock last evening at a valentine party. The decorations were hearts and other seasonable emblems. The party played games, and afterwards partook of a delightful supper. The young hostess received many compliments on her party. She is a daughter of County Treasurer and Mrs. T.W. Hart.*"[605]

Julia arrives home for Easter with an Epsilon Iota pledge pin on her shirtwaist. She tells the thrilling story of Pledge Day at the U, and later, Mr. Ray announces that she may have to make a choice, since he is willing to send her to Germany next year. Julia says there is no choice. "The girls are swell; it was nice of them to ask me. But I don't know what choice you mean."[606] Julia will give her life to music. This is no surprise to us. She has been talking about opera as far back as *Betsy-Tacy and Tib*. On a picnic with Katie, "They were talking about what they would be when they grew up. Julia thought she would be an opera singer."[607] And in *Downtown*, Julia tells Jerry that although she enjoyed *Robin Hood* at the Opera House, she is sure she'll "like grand opera better."[608]

Kathleen did spend a year studying music abroad. She did not, however, give up joining a sorority in order to go to Germany. Kathleen had pledged Gamma Phi Beta and lived at the house before the end of her freshman year at the U.

Julia was the star of *The Mikado* during her first year at the U. *The Mikado* was performed by the students at the U while Kathleen was on campus, but she does not appear to have taken part. Maud attended this May 1909 performance in Minneapolis. Fictionally, Mrs. Ray is the only member of the family to attend. On an earlier visit to Julia at the U, Mrs. Ray bought a corset for Betsy. According to her diary, Maud did get a new corset this year, a Nemo, "*so tight I can hardly wiggle.*"[609]

Julia left in June for a tour of Europe with the Rev. Mr. Lewis' group from the Episcopal church. The tour group was really led by the Rev. Dr. Willisford of the Baptist church. The Mankato paper reported: "*Miss Kathleen Hart, daughter of Mr. and Mrs. T.W. Hart of this city, left this morning for Boston, Mass., from which city she will sail on Saturday for Europe. She will join a party going to Europe under the guidance of Rev. Willisford of this city. Miss Hart will make a three months' tour of that country* [sic] *and then go to Berlin, Germany, where she will receive instructions in vocal music for a year.*"

End-of-the-year activities and festivities descend upon the Crowd. The track meet comes on page 210, and the Philos win. (Normally Maud refers to this as the Athletics Cup, but it was limited to field work at a single track meet.) The Philos did not actually win in 1908 - the Zets did. This is the first time Maud's description differs from historically factual cup winnings.

The Junior-Senior Banquet was "the outstanding social event of the spring."[610] We might postulate that Maud and her friends received no banquet committee appointments due to the unpopularity their sorority engendered. However, Maud wrote in her Scrapbook: "*I was chairman of the entertainment committee. How I worked! The whole affair was a howling success.*"[611] Betsy served on the decorating committee under Hazel Smith, and her idea of creating a park setting was carried out. The *Mankato Free Press* reveals that this was exactly the theme of the decorations on May 7, 1909. "*The upper hall was most attractively decorated to carry out the idea of a park, and was an especially artistic feature, with its fish-pond, trees, swings, lovers' lane, fortune-telling camp, and many other out-of-door and nature suggestions that had taken much time in its preparations, but for which the students felt amply repaid, at the appreciation and approval expressed by everyone present.*"[612]

As they finish decorating for the banquet, Betsy remarks: "It's going to make history, Stan. The banquet given by the class of 1910 will never be forgotten."[613] Truly the affairs of the class of 1910 will not be forgotten, since the Betsy-Tacy books will (hopefully) live forever on library shelves and in home "shrines."

The menu which appears on page 226 of *Betsy Was a Junior* was taken almost word for word from the program of the banquet given by the class of 1910 for the class of 1909. The only differences: rather than "Shakespeare" after the first quotation, the program reads "*Macbeth*." And two quotations, instead of one, appear before "Fruit Cocktail." The second (which does not appear in *Betsy Was a Junior*) is "*Things which in hungry mortals' eyes find favor,*" from *Don Juan*. And rather than simply "Coffee," the program reads, "*Half Cups of Coffee.*"[614]

The second page of the program contains the toasts. Mr. J.M. McConnell (superintendent of schools) spoke on "*The Event.*" Herman Hayward (Stan), president of the junior class, spoke on "*The Sunny Side of Life.*" The principal, Mr. Norby, addressed the seniors. Phil Comstock (brother of the real-life Miss Clarke) gave a toast "*To Everybody,*" and George Scherer Sr. (a Mankato businessman) toasted "*The Coming Millennium.*"

Maud's banquet dance program included waltzes with Bob Hughes (Dave), Jay Lloyd (Cab), Walter Sanborn (N/C), Tom Fox (Tom Slade), Ellsworth Boynton (N/C), and Pin Jones (Pin); two-steps with Earl King (Squirrelly), Henry Lee (Al Larson), Johnnie Weed (Hank Weed), and George Pond (N/C); and a schottische with Lester Door (N/C).

Just as in *Betsy Was a Junior*, Dave (Bob Hughes) had taken the first dance. Mike Parker (Tony), however, did not dance with Maud, because he didn't attend the Junior-Senior Banquet. Herman Hayward (signing Maud's program with his unlikely nickname, "Pinkey") danced one of the extras with her. The eleventh dance was not scratched, but was taken by George Pond (N/C).

The Essay Contest is swept by the Philos this year, three cups out of three. In fact, the <u>Zets</u> won the Essay cup in 1909, but Maud made good dramatic sense by allowing the Philos to win so resoundingly. The excitement is riding high on the evening the essay cup will be awarded, since the Philos had already won the debating and athletics cups. The Philos win the freshman and sophomore essay points, so when Joe wins the junior points, the crowd goes wild: "No matter where the senior points went, the Philos had won now, and they almost went mad with joy." Even the reader (who has purely Zetamathian loyalties, of course) exults in Joe's "moment of splendid triumph." Holding three cups out of three gives the Philos an "almost unprecedented honor."[615]

It was an unprecedented honor. Neither society took all three cups during Maud's high school years. In both 1905 (the year the societies were established) and 1906, the Zets took two of three. In 1907, the Zets got only one; and in 1908 they racked up two. In 1909, the Zets took one and tied one; and in 1910, they obtained only one.

At the end of *Betsy Was a Junior*, when the girls and Cab are walking to school to get their report cards, Tacy cries: "What's that crowd doing in front of the high school? Is it on fire?"[616] Other references to the school burning down appear in *Betsy in Spite of Herself* (page 244) and *Betsy Was a Junior* (pages 65 and 152). Mankato High School finally did burn down on July 19, 1941. Fortunately, there were no injuries.

Betsy's final report card results for junior year: English, 95; History, 93; Latin, 90; Botany, 75.[617] Maud's grades for the second semester of junior year: *English, 87; History, 83; Latin, 87; Domestic Science, 87.* When she took Botany in the second semester of her senior year, Maud scored an 86.

The 1909 Commencement ceremony is described on page 238. The two songs really performed by the chorus that evening were "The Pilgrim's Chorus" from *Tannhauser* and "Estudiantina." The newspaper account of the event describes "*a very pretty sight that greeted the very large audience as the curtain rose bringing to view the graduating class seated on the stage.*"[618] Mamie Skuse (Mamie Dodd) presided at the piano.

Like Carney, Marney presented a Commencement speech. Maud doesn't specify the subject of Carney's fictional recitation, but the speech given by Marion Willard was on "Norwegian Music." She spoke about the composer Grieg, an appropriate subject for piano-playing Carney.

Lora Lulsdorff, who later studied music in Berlin along with Kathleen Hart, sang a solo called "Flowers Awake." Henry Lee (Al Larson) was class valedictorian. He spoke on "The Conservation of Natural Resources" (which was the essay contest topic in *Betsy and Joe*!).

Other details on Commencement Week for the class of 1909 are found in Chapter 11 herein on *Emily of Deep Valley*. This is because the real Emily was one year older than Maud, rather than two years younger. Emily therefore graduated in 1909, rather than 1912.

It was during Commencement Week that "PHILOMATHIAN" was painted on the school roof, and from Maud's description of this incident, we can estimate the population of Deep Valley High. Miss Bangeter asks all the Philo boys in the school to march past her desk (to examine their shoes for telltale signs of tar or orange paint) and 100 boys get to their feet. This would mean that there were approximately 400 students, assuming roughly equal numbers of Zets/Philos and boys/girls. Actually, there were considerably fewer high school students in Maud's day. When Maud was a freshman, there were 257 students attending the high school. By the time she was a senior, there were nearly 300 - however, only about 50 members of each class graduated.

Painting "PHILOMATHIAN" on the high school roof was not the only skullduggery in which the high school boys indulged. Their most notorious prank was pulled off in the summer of 1909. We never hear a fictional account of this very dramatic event, which the town remembered for many years, even though the boys in Maud's Crowd were responsible.

On the Fourth of July, 1909, a group of boys set off the old Civil War cannon, an eight-inch mortar gun, in Lincoln Park. The *Mankato Review* reported that "*the explosion seemed to shake the earth to its very bowels, caused houses to tremble on their foundations and the noise it created reverberated back and forth between the bluffs on either side of the river.*"

The boys had packed the cannon with gun powder, a five-foot fuse, "*grass, paper, an old flour sack, and an old umbrella.*" (The next day, the umbrella was found inside out on a church roof!) The gun weighed 3,000 pounds and was mounted on a stone foundation, but "*the recoil of the explosion lifted the gun and carriage bodily from where it sat and deposited it upon the grass seventeen feet in the rear of its former position, ploughing a deep furrow where it struck the ground.*"[619] Windows were broken in numerous nearby houses, but no injuries resulted. There was a near miss at the home of the Rev. F.B. Cowgill, though, where a young boy was sleeping on a screened porch. His cot was pushed up next to a large plate-glass window which was shattered by the blast. Fortunately, the little boy was covered with a blanket which the glass fragments did not penetrate. He didn't even wake up!

The newspaper does not identify the perpetrators. "*There has been no attempt or desire upon the part of any of these young men to conceal their identity or deny their responsibility for this affair, most reprehensible as it is. And the fact that their names are purposely withheld by the Review is no indication that their offense is in any way condoned or apologized for. They are all sons of prominent citizens and young men who bear the most excellent characters. Their act was not inspired by any malicious motive, but was conceived rather in that ardor with which all young Americans are imbued in the celebrations of Independence Day.*"[620]

Pin Jones (Pin) and Jab Lloyd (Cab) were two of the seven boys involved. In 1952, a columnist in the *Mankato Free Press* requested that someone involved in the cannon firing come forward and "tell all." Merle Harter (Mankato High School class of 1910) wrote a letter from Minneapolis identifying himself as one of the seven. He names two others: Robert Hughes (Dave Hunt) and Malcolm Morehart (Phil-like). Merle (N/C) says that "*the seven of us were members of the 'Poopy Cat Club.' What a name - and where or who conceived the name I do not know. But anyway that was the name and we had our clubroom over Malcolm Morehart's dad's garage. As I remember it was a pretty good-sized garage and the room upstairs was the same.*" (This sounds like the Omega Delta clubhouse-over-garage proposed by E. Lloyd Harrington.) "*We played cards most of the time. It was here at one of our meetings that we conceived the idea of firing off the cannon.*" The fuse hole of the cannon had been leaded closed, and it took the boys three nights to open it with a hand drill. They were all ready on the night of July third to light the fuse at midnight. "*What a thrilling sight it was in the dark - one I*

Crowd Shots

Duplicated in several collections

From left: Midge Gerlach (Tib), Marion Willard (Carney), Maud Hart (Betsy), Mil Oleson (Irma), Margaret Wilcox (N/C), and Eleanor Johnson (Winona II). At one point, Tacy reminds Betsy that she has the "smallest waist of any girl in the Crowd." (HTB p. 109) And of course, Tib can fasten her father's collar around her waist (he had a very thick neck).

Duplicated in several collections

From left: Midge Gerlach (Tib), Marion Willard (Carney), Mil Oleson (Irma), Maud Hart (Betsy), Margaret Wilcox (N/C), and Eleanor Johnson (Winona II). It looks as though Midge has dressed Maud's hair in puffs.

BECHS

The Mankato Y

After their big victory over St. John, the Deep Valley football team "went into the Y.M.C.A. for showers and rub downs but the hullabaloo continued in the street outside." (BWJ p. 115) The Y once stood at the corner of Second Street and Cherry.

BECHS

1909 Graduate

Carney was "the only girl Betsy had ever seen who looked prettier in glasses than she could possibly have looked without them. They were eye glasses and suited her demure, piquant face." (HTB p. 66) Marney Willard is wearing her *pince-nez* eyeglasses in her graduation photo.

Coll. of Paul Ford

Cannon Ride

Paul Ford (Dennie) sits astride the Lincoln Park cannon which he helped to set off on July 4, 1909.

Eleanor Johnson's House
325 Clark (East Pleasant)

The girls go to Winona's house for the appetizer on the Okto Delta progressive dinner.

Coll. of Robert Cahill

Minnesota Slims?

Senior year, when the progressive dinner is repeated, Betsy notes: "That Winona is a scream. She had fixed up their dining room to look like a beer garden. And we drank grape juice and smoked cubebs. They're just for asthma, of course, but the boys who were looking in the windows thought they were real cigarettes." (B&J p. 150) Perhaps in an effort to shock the boys, the girls brought cubebs along on a Sibley Park picnic. From left: Harriet Ahlers, Mildred Oleson, Midge Gerlach, and Eleanor Johnson! (See the box from their deck of cards on the bench beside El.)

never will forget. After the explosion I remember I was scared to death and hit for home as fast as I could run.... The next day we kept to the alleys, too scared to be seen anywhere.... As time went on we got more scared and finally we got together and told Bob Hughes' dad about it and confessed and agreed to pay all of the damage that was done." (Bob's father, remember, was the judge!)

Glenn Allyn, a contemporary of Maud's, identified another of the culprits as Everett Dodds (an Omega Delta). The seventh prankster may have been Herman Hayward or Henry Lee.

The Milton quotation on the frontispiece of *Betsy Was a Junior* was certainly apt: "*Haste thee nymph, and bring with thee Jest and Youthful Jollity.*" They had a rollicking junior year!

[521] *Betsy in Spite of Herself,* p. 14.

[522] *Betsy and Joe,* p. 13.

[523] *Betsy in Spite of Herself,* p. 143.

[524] *Betsy Was a Junior,* p. 14.

[525] Ibid., p. 147.

[526] Ibid., p. 112.

[527] Ibid., p. 15.

[528] *Betsy and Joe,* p. 19.

[529] MHL to A. Lebeck, summer 1946.

[530] MH to MW, summer 1912.

[531] *Minneapolis Tribune,* 9-28-34.

[532] *Minneapolis Journal,* 9-26-29.

[533] MHL to L. Demp, 11-2-56.

[534] *Betsy Was a Junior,* p. 1.

[535] MLK to SSW, 11-15-91.

[536] *Mankato Free Press,* 7-17-08.

[537] *Betsy Was a Junior,* p. 241.

[538] MHL to J. Ellen, 9-10-67.

[539] *Betsy and Joe,* p. 126.

[540] *Betsy Was a Junior,* p. 220.

[541] MHL to J. Tessari, 8-11-73.

[542] *Betsy and Joe,* p. 7.

[543] *Betsy Was a Junior,* p. 24.

[544] *Betsy and Joe,* p. 20.

[545] KPH letters, p. 26.

[546] Ibid., p. 86.

[547] *Betsy and Joe,* p. 19.

[548] *Betsy Was a Junior,* p. 30.

[549] MHL to R. Green, 8-14-48.

[550] *Betsy Was a Junior,* p. 33-34.

[551] *Betsy in Spite of Herself,* p. 56.

[552] Ibid., p. 25.

[553] *Mankato Free Press,* 4-10-52.

[554] High School Scrapbook, p. G.

[555] *Betsy Was a Junior,* p. 46.

[556] D.O., p. 7.

[557] *Betsy Was a Junior,* p. 44.

[558] Ibid., p. 49.

[559] *Mankato Free Press,* 9-9-07.

[560] *Betsy in Spite of Herself*, p. 196.
[561] MHL to A. Wiecking, 9-22-61.
[562] *Betsy and Joe,* p. 72.
[563] *Downtown*, p. 14.
[564] *Betsy Was a Junior,* p. 52-53.
[565] *Mankato Free Press,* 4-10-52.
[566] *Betsy Was a Junior,* p. 54-55.
[567] *Emily of Deep Valley,* p. 114.
[568] *Betsy Was a Junior,* p. 69.
[569] *Betsy and Joe,* p. 68.
[570] *Betsy Was a Junior,* p. 65.
[571] *West Side Story*, May 1989, p. 2.
[572] *Betsy Was a Junior,* p. 68.
[573] *Mankato Free Press,* 9-16-08.
[574] *Heaven to Betsy*, p. 75.
[575] W.D. Willard, unpublished memoirs, p. 37.
[576] *Emily of Deep Valley*, p. 49.
[577] *Carney's House Party*, p. 38.
[578] W.D. Willard, memoirs, p. 38.
[579] *Betsy Was a Junior,* p. 59.
[580] Ibid., p. 52.
[581] M. Hart, "I Am Curly," p. 7.
[582] *Betsy Was a Junior,* p. 71.
[583] *Mankato Free Press,* 9-8-09.
[584] *Betsy Was a Junior,* p. 109.
[585] Ibid., p. 124.
[586] High School Scrapbook, p. D'.
[587] Ibid., p. C.
[588] *Betsy Was a Junior,* p. 136-7.
[589] Ibid., p. 139.
[590] High School Scrapbook, p. F'.
[591] *Betsy Was a Junior,* p. 141.
[592] High School Scrapbook, p. F.
[593] *Mankato Free Press,* 12-30-08.
[594] Ibid., 4-10-52.
[595] Ibid., 12-28-10.
[596] D.O., p. 13.
[597] *Betsy Was a Junior,* p. 152.
[598] Ibid., p. 154.

[599] Ibid.

[600] *Betsy and Joe*, p. 94.

[601] Jean Webster, *Daddy-Long-Legs* (New York: Bantam edition, 1986, first published 1912), p. 76.

[602] Wanda Gag, *Growing Pains,* p. 63-64.

[603] *Betsy Was a Junior,* p. 163.

[604] HHF to MHL, 8-21-46.

[605] *Mankato Free Press*, 2-15-10.

[606] *Betsy Was a Junior,* p. 202.

[607] *Betsy-Tacy and Tib*, p. 116.

[608] *Downtown,* p. 9.

[609] D.O., p. 8.

[610] *Betsy Was a Junior,* p. 175.

[611] High School Scrapbook, p. H'.

[612] *Mankato Free Press*, 5-8-09.

[613] *Betsy Was a Junior,* p. 225.

[614] High School Scrapbook, p. H', innards 1.

[615] *Betsy Was a Junior,* p. 234.

[616] Ibid., p. 235.

[617] Ibid., p. 237.

[618] *Mankato Free Press*, 6-5-09.

[619] *Mankato Review*, 7-6-09.

[620] Ibid.

CHAPTER NINE
On *Betsy and Joe*
July 1909 to June 1910

Little more than a month has passed since the end of *Betsy Was a Junior*, but already Betsy seems different: she has the aura of a senior. Driving out to Murmuring Lake, Betsy gives Old Mag a rest at the top of Agency Hill and looks out over her town. Through Betsy's panoramic gaze, Maud reminds us of our fictional surroundings. She provides the compass points of Deep Valley (with a corresponding overview of Betsy's childhood) and fills us in on what has been happening since the beginning of June, before bringing us back to Betsy in July 1909.

Betsy had been "in town because Carney Sibley was entertaining a house guest whose visit had brought on an unexpected summer crop of parties."[621] Did Maud introduce this house guest simply to give Betsy an excuse for being at the top of Agency Hill that July day? Probably yes, since no reference to the house guest is made before or after. On the other hand, we know that Marney Willard did have several house parties at about this time: "*Miss Maud Hart gave a most enjoyable one o'clock luncheon yesterday afternoon at her home, 428 South Fifth Street, in honor of a house party who are guests this week of Miss Marion Willard. The luncheon was served in six courses, and was a rose luncheon, the decoration being pink and white roses. The afternoon was spent in playing '500.'*"[622]

The only member of this house party with whom the reader would be familiar was Connie Davis (Bonnie). The other girls were from Duluth, St. Paul, and Madelia. Connie and her mother spent most of July 1909 as guests of the Willards. Maud spent part of the summer working for her father at the court house, to earn some spending money for the big year ahead.

Senior-year Betsy, "as she grew older liked increasingly to be alone." Junior-year frivolity has been left behind. Betsy's maturity is also marked in physical terms: "She did not look like the Betsy Ray who had entered high school four years before. At thirteen, grown suddenly tall and thin, she had been plainly in the awkward age. Now she enjoyed being tall and slender."[623]

The phases of maturity through which we pass with Betsy heighten our perception of her as a real person. This effect is not found in other girls' series books, such as Nancy Drew, in which Nancy, though charming, is always eighteen and blond. Betsy evolves, with gradual and convincing progress. And the fact that Betsy has evolved through her high school years, both physically and mentally, is a tribute to Lovelace as an introspective person, and as a writer too honest (and too adroit) to insult her readers' intelligence with a hollow heroine.

Betsy's writing, and her attitude towards it, has been developing along with the rest of her. As a freshman, she hid her scribbles away and prepared for the Essay Contest so offhandedly that she lost. Sophomore year, Betsy actually considered turning down the Essay Contest for fear of Phil's disapproval. The flighty frivolity of her junior year cost Betsy the chance at the Essay Contest, but even Okto Delta couldn't keep her from working hard on essays for Miss Fowler's Foundations of English Literature. Betsy has also begun a novel, and she read "an original poem for rhetoricals. It was named 'Those Eyes' and sounded a little like Poe."[624] On December 17 of her senior year, "Maude" Hart wrote a poem for a "Zetamathean" program. The poem was read by Marjorie Gerlach. (The title of the poem was not given by the newspaper report of the program.)

By senior year, Betsy has begun to submit her short stories to magazine editors. The stories are continually returned, but she stubbornly sends them out again and again. (In *Betsy and the Great World*, we hear that one story brought in sixty-one rejection slips!)

Maud began sending her work to magazines much earlier than Betsy (apart from the never-heard-from story on pink stationery, sent to the *Ladies' Home Journal* in *Downtown*). One of the first publications Maud barraged was *St. Nicholas*. At the turn of the century, *St. Nicholas* featured a club with thousands of young members. The *Minneapolis Tribune* also had a young people's page (like the *Minneapolis Journal*'s "Journal Juniors"). Maud was on the members' roster of the *Tribune*'s "Little Mother's Club" in 1904. Before long she was sending items to prominent publications. Charles Dwyer, editor of the *Delineator* (with offices in London, Paris, and New York!), wrote a gentle rejection letter to "Maudie Hart" on December 12, 1905. He tells her: "*If you will cultivate the faculty of expression in verse making and study carefully the works of the best poets, you will, in time, have your verses accepted by the magazines.*"

Maud must have taken his advice, for she strongly recommended poetry reading for young writers when she became a successful writer herself.

One of her college professors described the early phase of Maud's writing career: "*She was a very charming, feminine person, and very persistent. When she wrote a story, she kept sending it out until she marketed it. It is that same persistence which has made her successful at the type of work which she has done -- historical research.*"

Maud no doubt did a good deal of writing during those high school summers at the lake. At the end of *Betsy Was a Junior*, the Rays are busy packing for the lake. Actually, two days after Kathleen departed for Europe, Maud set out for a three-week visit to Willmar, Minnesota, to visit cousins. The Harts were at Madison Lake for several weeks at the end of the summer.

The Kelly family never vacations at the lake in the Betsy-Tacy books, but in real life, the Kenneys spent time at Madison Lake in August 1909.[625]

As already explained, Midge Gerlach was no longer living in the big house at the corner of Bradley and Byron. The family apparently had financial reverses as the result of a serious accident which befell Henry Gerlach. Shortly before or after the move to Milwaukee, he inadvertently swallowed some lye. How this accident occurred is not known. (One might imagine that the lye was in an unmarked bottle on the top shelf in the kitchen, and he took a dose of it in the middle of one night, thinking it was the Milk of Magnesia.) Mr. Gerlach was treated by a St. Paul specialist in the years that followed, but he never entirely recovered. In 1924 the *Mankato Free Press* reported that Henry Gerlach died "*after a lingering illness of throat and stomach trouble.*"[626]

During Maud's senior year (Midge's junior year), the Gerlach family moved to the Security Flats at the corner of Broad and Hickory. The name of this apartment building sounds somehow unsavory, but it was in no way disreputable. Flossie Macbeth, the daughter of Mankato meat-packing baron Charles Macbeth, lived in the Security block, too. Interestingly, the Security Flats were built of steel used in the buildings at the Chicago World's Fair in 1893 (which was attended by Tom, Stella, and little Kathleen Hart, while one-year-old Maud stayed with friends on a farm near

Mankato). The Gerlachs left the Flats and bought a house at 414 N. 4th Street. The fictional Mullers, of course, were still living in the chocolate-colored house right up through *Betsy's Wedding*.

Julia departed for Europe a month before the opening scene of *Betsy and Joe*. Her letters home were a regular feature of the Rays' summer, as well as the fall, winter, and spring that followed. Kathleen Hart left Mankato on Wednesday, June 30, 1909, to spend the summer on a European tour conducted by the Rev. Edwin Willisford. He was referred to as "Dr. Willisford," and Kathleen called him "Doctor." The group sailed from Boston on the S.S. *Romanic* July 3, 1909. At the end of the summer, Kathleen went to Berlin to begin voice training with Fraulein Schoen-Rene, who was fictionally Fraulein Hertha von Blatz.

The ritual reading and rereading of Kathleen's letters was such a fixture of their days that the Harts posed for a portrait listening to Maud as she read one. Grandma Newton never visits the Rays in the series. We see from this photo that the real-life Grandma Austin certainly did! Kathleen refers to Albertine Austin's visit in a letter home: "*I suppose Grandma will be there before long.*"[627]

Grandma Austin arrived in September and stayed in Minnesota, with the Harts and with other relatives, until March 19, 1910. (Her second husband, Chauncey Austin - Grandpa Newton - had passed away in 1908.) She no doubt came in order to attend the wedding of her husband's granddaughter in Mankato, which took place in October 1909. (The top of the Harts' silver coffee pot was somehow melted at the reception for this wedding.)

Grandma Austin enjoyed hearing Kathleen's letters read aloud every evening, along with the rest of the family. "They were long letters. And if ever one person took four others through Europe by means of pen and paper, it was Julia."[628] The first two letters, Julia says, were written on board the *Romanic,* en route to Naples. This is exactly the case. The actual letters are dated July 6, 1909, and July 11, 1909, both written on board the *Romanic*, a ship of the White Star Line. As per *Betsy and Joe*, the ship embarked from Boston for Naples.

Shipboard life was not as perfectly idyllic as Julia's letters suggest. In a letter home, Kathleen related, "*I hopped up into my little berth. It is very comfortable, though very narrow, and I expected a*

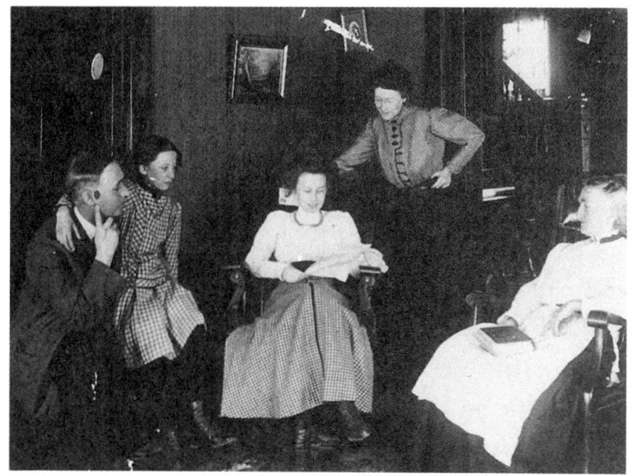

Coll. of Minnesota Valley Regional Library

The Hart Family

Maud (wearing her Venetian beads) is reading aloud from one of Kathleen's letters from Europe. Stella peers over her shoulder. Stella's mother (the fictional Grandma Newton) is seated at right. In *Betsy and Joe*, "Mr. Ray usually took Margaret on his knee to listen." (B&J p. 70)

Duplicated in several collections

Roughing It

Some of the boys in Betsy's Crowd took a canoe trip up the Minnesota River. Here are Bob Hughes (Dave) and Herman Hayward (Stan) on their canoe trip. The boys camped along the river and visited friends after reaching Minneapolis.

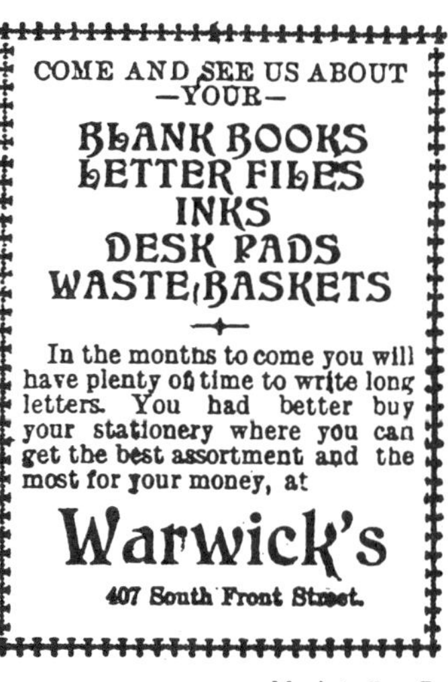

Mankato Free Press

School Supplies

After the first day of school, Betsy and her friends usually went to Cook's to buy supplies. Maud may have been picturing Warwick's.

lovely night's sleep, when lo! I saw a rat at the foot of the bed up on the railing. I screamed, and I rang for the steward, a Welsh man who was highly amused at my fright. He said it was a good luck sign to have rats on board, but that they seldom happened in the staterooms. You can imagine how much sleep I got that night. I made up my bed on the couch that seemed safer some way and dreamed of rats all night. Next day, the people who have the other staterooms near ours said they had seen it too so I guess they set traps for it. It was a good, big rat, and I tremble every night when I go to bed, even though I haven't seen it since."[629]

Almost every time Maud quotes from Julia's letters, she is quoting from Kathleen's letters. For instance, on page 14, we hear, "Oh, I'm so happy! I can't believe it is I, Julia Ray, who is traveling in Europe having all her cherished dreams fulfilled." On Wednesday, July 7, 1909, Maud's sister wrote, "*Oh, I'm having the most delightful trip. I can't really believe it is I, Kathleen Hart, who is travelling* [sic] *in Europe, having all her cherished dreams fulfilled.*"[630]

Meanwhile, there are exciting events taking place in Deep Valley. Joe Willard has returned from work on the *Courier News* in Wells, North Dakota. Joe and Betsy are finally going to go together! He appears at her front door, straight from the train, on page 45, "his hair looking the color of silver above his tanned face." Joe Willard has had a lot of tans. On page 8, Maud writes: "he was a stalwart light-haired boy with blue eyes and a strong tanned face." But how long is anyone tanned in Minnesota? Forever, in the mind's eye, if one likes the picture. In Maud's novel *Early Candlelight*, the character Jasper Page managed to stay tanned through January (without leaving Minnesota)!

When Joe's good looks are mentioned, so is his tan, or at least the fact that he is blond. In *Betsy in Spite of Herself*, "His summer tan made his blond pompadour look even blonder."[631] In *Betsy Was a Junior*, "The summer in the harvest fields had hardened his muscles and had tanned him so deeply that his smooth pompadour and heavy eyebrows looked almost white."[632] Tilda, of *Betsy and the Great World*, "admired Joe's picture, for even a snapshot showed how blond and muscular he was."[633] In *Betsy's Wedding*, Joe "looked so wonderful in his olive drab," because "he was tanned from drilling in the sun, and above his brown cheeks his hair looked almost silvery."[634]

Maud's predilection for blond, blue-eyed men also appears in her adult fiction. Richard, in *Gentlemen from England*, runs his hands across his "*flaxen*" hair just as Joe often does.[635] When blond Felicien returns from Mexico in *Petticoat Court*, his eyes "*were very blue in his brown face*."[636] Don, a short story hero, walks the streets of London (not a city known for its warm sun or tanned populace) "*so tanned that his light hair stood off like a cap.*"[637] Even before she had met Delos, Maud observed, "*A big man with abundant blond hair tans most attractively.*"[638]

Most of the good-looking males in the Betsy-Tacy series are blond and tanned. Even in *Downtown*, the Greek God, Chauncey, had "blond hair and blue eyes and tanned rosy cheeks."[639] Herbert Humphreys, of course, was blond. And in *Heaven to Betsy*: "in vacation tan, blonder, bigger, and brawnier than ever, he was outstandingly good looking."[640] Of the two officers who ogle Betsy in *Great World*, the good-looking one is blond and the dark one is positively "ugly."[641] Well yes, both Tony Markham and Marco Regali, though very dark, are devilishly handsome ... but neither one gets the girl!

Betsy sits with her handsome blond friend on her porch steps in the crisp twilight. The air was "filled with the smell of burning leaves."[642] But surely there were not enough leaves to burn as early as this (barely September)? Maud just wanted to give the flavor of autumn. And the reader is not going to quarrel. Betsy and Joe are finally together - "How completely and utterly satisfactory!"[643]

Delos Lovelace, on whom Joe was based, did work his way north with the harvest, to North Dakota. He did work on a newspaper there but not as early as 1909. Delos began work for the Fargo *Courier* in 1913, coming from high school in Detroit, Michigan. He began as proofreader and progressed to general assignments, including sports writing.

As Joe and Betsy become better acquainted, he tells her that his father was "a lumberman, yanked down trees in the north woods. I've always been strong as a horse, and I guess it's because of him."[644] Delos' father was indeed a lumberjack.[645]

Joe soon begins to feel at home at the Ray house. He enjoys listening to Betsy's father's stories, told out in the kitchen during the ceremonial sandwich making. As mentioned in the previous chapter, Joe admires Mr. Ray's compassion for others. Mr. Ray is always thinking about doing something for "the shoemaker who works for him or some poor widow across the slough with a house full of kids."[646] The shoemaker who had worked for Maud's father passed away in 1910, leaving behind a widow on North Front Street with a houseful of ten children. Fred Kronfeldt had been making shoes in Mankato for twenty-five years when he died. By this time, Tom Hart was no longer in the shoe business, but he was no doubt dismayed by the death of his old friend and made efforts to assist the shoemaker's family.

During one of their evenings by the Ray fireside, Joe tells Betsy that he once attempted to read through all the books in the library: "I was about fourteen. I started with the A's, progressed to the B's, and read straight along the shelves. I bogged down about the time I reached the M's."[647] (He was stopped by George Barr McCutcheon, who wrote *Beverly of Graustark,* a novel that was made into an operetta to which Joe takes Betsy.) Maud revealed: *"My husband tells me that at an early age he made a secret resolution to read through the entire book collection of the Detroit Public Library. He began with the A's and proceeded systematically along the alphabet until the vastness of his project dawned and he abandoned it at last."*[648]

At the start of her senior year, Betsy registers for German, because of Julia's "constant references to the need of modern languages out in the Great World."[649] Kathleen did indeed recommend modern languages, in her letter of January 20, 1910. *"I want to say something to the girls, if there is any possibility of their studying German or French, or both, in the next two or three years, they really should do it. I think every educated person should speak at least three languages. It is absolutely necessary for artistic work in any line of writing, singing, professional work, and for business or traveling it is indispensable. I would give a great deal if I had learned French or German, or both, as a child. In high society in Europe, the people all converse in French or English or German as easily as breathing -- business men here must do it, and it makes one so infinitely broader to be able to read the masters of all literature in the original. I suppose Maude can't this year, but she can next, and at the Normal Helen can surely get languages soon."*[650] Julia made her recommendation in time for

Betsy to sign up for German in her senior year (which made possible some great exchanges at the Beidwinkles' farm at the end of *Betsy and Joe*). But Maud did not take German in high school. (The real Miss Erickson, Helen Cooper, didn't teach German anyway!)

At the U, Maud took French, as reported in *Betsy and the Great World.* She also took German, but like Betsy, she didn't learn much until she lived in Germany in 1914. Despite her lofty recommendations, Kathleen did not speak French, and her German, after five months in Germany and no lessons, hadn't progressed much beyond "*Ach, sehr schoen.*" She certainly had read no great books in the original by this time, and she probably never did. Nevertheless, her assertions certainly sound impressive - which was part of Kathleen's charm!

It is fortunate that the reader is busy celebrating the fact that Betsy and Joe are finally together, for otherwise the loss of Carney might be more keenly felt. Marion Willard did attend Vassar but first spent a year at Carleton College (in Northfield, Minnesota). She departed Mankato for Carleton on September 13, 1909. It was obviously simpler (and more exciting) for Maud's fictional purposes, to send Carney to Vassar in the fall of 1909, without the one-year detour to Carleton.

In *Betsy and Joe*, Carney went off to Vassar wearing "a tweed suit with a brown velvet collar and a brown velvet tricorn Gage hat." Carney's other new clothes included "a store-bought party dress! It's pale pink with elbow sleeves and a square neck."[651] Seeking descriptions of Marney's college wardrobe for use in *Carney's House Party,* Maud wrote to Marion Willard Everett: "*I'll send you a copy of Betsy and Joe as soon as I can get my hands on one, or a set of galleys. For in that book Carney goes off to college, Vassar, in the clothes you described for me. Since I used them for fall of 1909, the clothes which actually came a year later ... the brown suit and the store bought party dress ... you'll have to tell me about some more clothes.*"[652] In other words, Marion did go off to Vassar with the clothes described in *Betsy and Joe* - but the real time was autumn 1910 rather than autumn 1909.

Tom Slade has returned to Cox, with plans to attend West Point next year.[653] Tom Fox, however, wasn't a senior in the fall of 1909. He had graduated from Mankato High School in June 1909. Tom received his cadetship to West Point in December 1910.

Squirrelly and Al were off to the U at the beginning of *Betsy and Joe*. Earl King does not appear to have attended the U, but Henry Lee did, matriculating in 1909, like his fictional self, Al. Henry received his B.A. in economics in June 1913.

Autumn 1909 was a happy time for Betsy. "She had never, she thought, been so happy in her life."[654] These words have that "certain" ring. Surely Maud had a wonderful senior-year autumn. Just as surely (and based on the same intangible ring), Maud, like Betsy, had a miserable senior-year spring. Was there a man in Maud's life? We know it couldn't have been the real Joe, as she didn't meet Delos for another seven years. If she had a special beau in her senior year, who was he?

One possibility is Jab Lloyd. Though it has been said that Jab did Maud's math homework while she wrote his essays, Jab (unlike Cab) did have a literary flair. Maybe Maud and Jab (who was a Philomathian) even competed in the 1908 essay contest. Did Maud have a wonderful autumn in 1909 because, after years of being friends, she and Jab were finally going to go together? Perhaps they broke up around Christmas, accounting for that heart-wrenching New Year's Eve Ball and her miserable spring. One thing is certain: Jab must have had some importance in Maud's senior year, because he was her escort to their Junior-Senior Banquet in 1910. Maud wrote in her high school diary, "*Jab is absolutely the cutest thing I ever saw.*"[655]

There is no question that the personality of Joe Willard was based entirely on that of Delos Lovelace; but just maybe the fictional name was inspired by Maud's real senior-year beau, "Jab" or "Jay" (as Jab was sometimes called in high school). Is it a coincidence that "Jab" and "Joe" are both three-letter names beginning with J? Why didn't she convert "Delos" to something like "Daniel" or "David" (two-syllable D names)? Of course, Maud may very well have been inspired by Delos' mother's name, "Josephine." Yet again, she may have selected the name because of Joe Stein, whom she also dated in her senior year.

Perhaps Merian Lovelace Kirchner should have the last word

on this very speculative discussion: "*I have no trouble accepting the plot of Betsy and Joe as pure fiction. I'd almost rather it was, and here I think I am letting personal bias get in the way of objectivity. Because it's a story Maud made up about how she and Delos might have met, it's especially precious.*"[656]

Shakespeare's *As You Like It* plays a part in Betsy and Joe's romance. In fact, *As You Like It* was performed at the Opera House on September 17, 1909, at the beginning of Maud's senior year. Perhaps she was taken to see this play, and it functioned in an actual senior-year romance. The Shakespeare quotations used on page 72, "Dearest Chuck" and "Sweet My Coz," also appear in Maud's High School Scrapbook.

No Chauncey Olcott play sweetens the autumn in Deep Valley this year. Olcott appears not to have visited Mankato in September 1909, though he was back in the fall of 1910, and for many years thereafter. The peak of his success was still ahead. Olcott didn't write the lyrics for "When Irish Eyes Are Smiling" until 1912. And one of his most successful musicals, *The Heart of Patty Whack*, was produced five years after the Harts left Mankato. (There is a movie of Olcott's life - *My Wild Irish Rose*, starring Dennis Morgan, which is apparently not particularly accurate.)

There really was an "interloper" named Fiske O'Hara who played in shows at the Opera House. Old-time Mankatoan Frank Manning worked at the Opera House from 1913 to 1917. He recalled that Fiske O'Hara came to Mankato in an Irish musical every year. Fiske turned his nose up at the dressing rooms in the basement of the Opera House. (Maud describes these dressing rooms in *Betsy and Joe.*) The temperamental singer insisted that a tent be set up backstage for his personal use. If a baby in the audience cried, Fiske would stop singing until the mother took her child out. "'The copycat!' muttered Anna, rolling out cookies as though she had Fiske O'Hara under the rolling pin."[657]

Before Halloween, "*Beverly of Graustark* came to the Opera House, and Joe took Betsy to see it."[658] We don't know who invited Maud, but *Beverly*, based on *Beverly of Graustark,* came to the Mankato Theatre (the Opera House) on Thursday, November 11, 1909. (In *Growing Pains,* Wanda Gag was trying to scrape together 50¢ on November 13, 1909, to go to *Beverly of Graustark* in nearby

New Ulm.) Later in the autumn, Joe goes down to the roller rink to cover a skating exhibition. There was a skating rink in Mankato, at 225 S. Second.

There were two other "shows" in Mankato at this time which are not mentioned in *Betsy and Joe*. These were the celestial events of a total eclipse and Halley's comet. Some of the young people in town had "comet parties."

On Halloween, Betsy, Joe, Tib, and Dennie crash a dance that is "strictly for juniors."[659] They are tossed out to the strains of "Tonight Will Never Come Again" and hope that it won't, as they limp away. The juniors did hold a Halloween Dance in 1909. *"The junior class of the high school held a pretty Hallowe'en dancing party last night at Schiller hall. Miss Mamie Skuse* [Mamie Dodd] *furnished the music and Miss Fischer* [Miss Fowler], *of the high school faculty, chaperoned the party. The hall was decorated in jack-o-lanterns and corn husks."*[660]

Once again, Betsy's autumn is punctuated with weekly football games. Mr. Stewart is the coach of the football team and is "familiarly known as Stewie."[661] There appear to have been several football coaches during the time Maud was in high school. Perhaps the one she had in mind was W. T. Crawford (Crawfie??).

No marching band is mentioned until *Betsy and Joe*, and not in any detail until *Emily of Deep Valley*. The high school band was not organized until November 1909, which may explain why it wasn't a fixture in the Betsy-Tacy books.

We hear much of the Deep Valley rooters' enthusiasm for football games. After *Betsy in Spite of Herself*, the Crowd begins taking the train to away games as well as attending those on the home field. The Deep Valley High game against Faribault was the last home game of Betsy's senior year. "It had been preceded by elaborate goings on. There was a big rooters' meeting, and the school marched to the field in a body with the band at the head of the procession. But all to no avail! The score was forty to nothing."[662]

A newspaper description of the fervor raging before Mankato High's game against Faribault in 1909 sounds hauntingly familiar. *"Tomorrow's contest between the local high school and that of Faribault promises to be the biggest event of the season. Excitement among the student body has reached its highest pitch, and preparations for the contest are nearly completed. Big mass meetings of the students were held yesterday and today."* The game had a start time of 1:30 p.m. on Saturday, and "*all loyal townspeople are expected to bolt lunch and join the bunch on the sidelines. All the students are to assemble at the high school at 12:30 from whence they will go down Hickory street to Front and along Front street to the fair grounds. Join the parade and make a noise!*"[663] Unfortunately, Faribault won that game 9-0.

The football field was located at the Mankato fairgrounds (on First Avenue), nearly two miles from the downtown business district. In *Heaven to Betsy*, the girls "drove in the Sibleys' surrey to the football field at the far end of town."[664] In *Betsy in Spite of Herself*, they took the Sibleys' auto down Front Street "on to the football field at the edge of town."[665]

The Deep Valley High School football team lost its first game of the season to Red Feather. The team "played Wells, it played Faribault, it played Blue Earth, and the scores didn't get better."[666] Mankato High School's football team, like Deep Valley's, had a very unfortunate 1909 season. They lost to Wells and Faribault, but they didn't play Blue Earth or Red Wing (Red Feather) that fall. They lost to St. James, tied scoreless with Austin, and won only one game, the first of the season, against Lake Crystal.

On more than one occasion, Betsy is looking at the scenery instead of concentrating on the team. "She stole these glances guiltily, aware that she should be thinking only of the game. She knew that her interest in football would always be pretended, not real and burning like Joe's or Winona's. She wanted to win, and she liked the excitement, but she liked the flying landscape more."[667]

When Maud wrote of Betsy's inattention to the proceedings on the field, she was describing her own lack of interest in sports. And up until now, Maud's plots hadn't required sports by-play. The real action had been on the sidelines: Betsy watching Joe with Phyllis, the reaction of Hazel and others to Okto Delta, etc. But in *Betsy and Joe*, the action on the field became important. Tib had told Maddox that she wouldn't go with him ever again if the winless Deep Valley team didn't beat undefeated St. John - so the game itself was now the focus. Maud needed help putting the scene together, and she evidently turned to the man of the house. (The Lovelaces divided up their historical writing in a similar way: "*She writes the parts appealing to women; and he, those in which the masculine viewpoint is needed.*"[668])

The football commentary on pages 87 and 107-114 has Delos Lovelace's name all over it. Maud would never have chosen phrases like "magnificent broken field runner," "drove through tackle," "sliced left," and most of all, "nice interference." Maud never even used the expression "first down" until this fourth of the high school books. As Tib said, "Betsy still doesn't know a touchdown from a field goal."[669] (Those who do know touchdowns from field goals might be interested to know that at this time, a first down consisted of only eight yards.) In addition to the specifics of the game, Delos included some un-Maudlike, but effective, gory descriptions!

Delos probably supplied Betsy's knowing remark about "those rough Spaulding [sic] rules" for basketball in *Betsy Was a Junior.*[670] He also wrote the pep rally scene in *Betsy and Joe,* as well as the sports-related remarks in *Carney's House Party,* the account of the wrestling match in *Emily of Deep Valley,* and the paragraph in *Betsy in Spite of Herself* which states: "It was the custom for spectators to watch the games from the sidelines ... they saw it as it is never seen from grandstands."[671]

Delos also wrote: "The score, according to the point system used in those days, was 8 to 0."[672] This is the only reference to "those days" in the Betsy-Tacy books. As far as Maud is concerned, when she is writing about 1909, it <u>is</u> 1909. As Kathleen Chamberlain has written in an article about the Betsy-Tacy books, "*Another reason that the books seem oddly modern is that Lovelace never dwells on or explains the period detail. It is just there, part of the milieu, the way things are. Lovelace does not comment on such things as hitching posts, wood stoves, or calling cards any more than a writer today would think of explaining stop signs or airports or freeways.*" In contrast, "*Laura Ingalls Wilder was obviously conscious that she was writing for an audience that would find her past distant.*"[673]

The fact that there is telltale evidence of Delos' handiwork may be significant on a personal level. It may tell us something about Maud and Delos' relationship and why, perhaps, it was so successful. At least when it came to Delos, Maud was neither judgmental nor territorial. It probably wouldn't even have occurred to her to say, "Let's tone down the sports writing, honey. This just isn't my style." It's not that she was nonconfrontational - for she wasn't a shrinking violet - she simply thought everything Delos did was wonderful (and he thought the same of her). Maybe this is the secret to a relationship in which she claimed they NEVER quarreled (a statement some married couples have found hard to swallow). Maud's admiration for Delos may help to explain the "somebody has to have the final say" attitude in *Betsy's Wedding*. This independent-minded woman might not have let her husband have the final word if she hadn't admired the man so unequivocally.

As autumn makes way for winter in *Betsy and Joe*, we find Margaret singing Christmas carols in the seventh grade chorus. But we know that Helen Hart (and Margaret, too, in *Betsy's Wedding*) graduated from high school in 1917, so in 1909 she would have been eleven years old and in the fifth grade (not the seventh). Margaret's grade level in *Carney's House Party* (entering high school in the fall of 1911) remains consistent with that established in *Betsy and Joe*. If Margaret began high school in 1911, she would have graduated in June 1915. But according to *Betsy's Wedding*, Margaret is only just starting her senior year in the fall of 1916. In the end, Helen and her counterpart graduate in the same year, 1917.)

"Margaret showed talent for the piano, and she was a better student in school than either of her sisters had been. But she had none of the ambition which burned in their breasts."[674] Helen very likely was a better student. She was the only one of the three Hart girls to graduate from the University of Minnesota (in 1921). Helen was proficient on the violin. In 1926, the *Mankato Free Press* called Helen Hart Fowler a "*violinist of merit.*"

When December arrives, Betsy finds that the current issue of "the *Ladies' Home Journal* had an impressive page entitled 'Twenty Christmas Cookies from One Batter.' Betsy showed it to Anna who sniffed. 'Ja, and I'll bet they all taste alike.'"[675] Maud either had kept among her memorabilia an issue of the December 1909 *Ladies' Home Journal* or had looked through one at a library while doing background work for *Betsy and Joe*. There is, in that particular issue, an article by Anna Barrows entitled "Twenty Christmas Cakes from One Batter." The change from cakes to cookies was logical, since cookies were a Crowd staple, and what Anna Barrows called "cakes" or "cakelets" were actually cookies anyway! "*When we wish to make a variety of cakes from one batter we should measure or weigh half a cupful, or a quarter of a pound of butter, one cupful or nearly half a pound of sugar, two small eggs, a quarter of a cupful of milk, and one pint of flour into which one teaspoonful of baking powder has been sifted. To give flavor and variety we also should provide extracts and spices, a lemon, an ounce of chocolate, whole and chopped walnuts, shelled peanuts, chopped raisins, citron, candied cherries, some of the macaroni alphabets and some sugared caraway seeds.... With the great variety of flavors available it would be possible to have each 'cakelet' differ from every other in flavor and form.... Let the mixing bowl stand in warm water for a few moments, then wipe dry and the butter may be creamed more easily. Gradually add the sugar, break one egg, and blend the yolk with the butter and sugar; then add the other egg and beat all thoroughly; then work in the flour, adding the milk gradually and alternately with the flour. If the dough is too soft now more flour may be added, or it may be chilled for an hour or two and then it will stiffen so that it may be rolled thin and cut in fancy shapes.*"[676]

Gifts at the Crowd Christmas tree "caused laughter, for everyone received at least one boudoir cap. The coquettish little mobcaps, trimmed with lace, flowers, or bows of ribbon, were the rage."[677] Regarding exhibit items for Betsy-Tacy Day in 1961, Maud wrote: "*We should add a boudoir cap to the Suggested List. Do you remember the ridiculous things? How our fathers hated them!*"[678]

The girls in the Crowd repeat the progressive dinner of the year before. The first course was grapefruit at Irma's, where "the table was in red." Bouillon was served at Hazel's. The third course was fish at the Rays', with the table in pink. The meat course was at Carney's - "it was, however, chicken, and there was cranberry ice." At Tib's they had "delectable salad"; at the Kellys', mince pies; and at Alice's, after-dinner coffee, "and her decorations were in the holiday colors." They ended with grape juice at Winona's, where the dining room was fixed up "to look like a beer garden."[679]

Compare the above to the following account from the January 4, 1910, *Mankato Free Press*: "*The Oktw Delta girls enjoyed one of their unique and pleasurable progressive dinner parties last night. The first course, the appetizer, was served at the home of Mildred Oleson, where the decorations were a pretty arrangement of red candles with shades of the same color. The second course, of bouillon, was partaken of at Eleanor Johnson's, where the table and rooms were decorated with the season's colorings of red and green. The third course was served at the home of Maude Hart. There the party enjoyed a fish course where the decorations were especially artistic and were of pink, with dainty pink dishes at each place for salted nuts. The dinner course, the fourth in order, was enjoyed at the home of Marion Willard, where the Christmas and holiday decorations made the dining room a cheery scene. The salad course was served at the home of Marjorie Gerlach, where the Oktw Delta colors of orange and black were prettily combined for decoration. At the home of Frances and Tessie Kenny* [sic], *where the sixth course, that of the dessert was served, the decorations were of Japanese effect, and at the last event, which was the after-dinner course at the home of Ruth Williams, tiny Christmas trees were at each place with ribbons extending to a larger one in the center of the table.*"

Tib made her own dress for the New Year's Eve Ball. In fact, Tib made many of her own clothes. "'I was so fussy that Mamma told me I'd better make them myself, and I told her all right I would,' said Tib, running daring scissors through a length of pink silk spread out on the bed."[680] Maud wrote of Midge: "*Her clothes were eye-catching; she early took over from her mother and started making them herself. There was one blue voile party dress, high-waisted in the directoir* [sic] *style with pink roses at the belt, and she covered her white slippers with more of the voile.*"[681]

The New Year's Eve Ball was held at the Melborn Hotel. Here we have our first look at Lamm's Orchestra. (It plays again in *Emily of Deep Valley*.) There really was a Lamm's Orchestra. The leader was Edward L. Lamm, who lived at 230 N. Front and owned Lamm's Drug Store at 307 S. Front.

Harry Kerr is introduced on page 166 as "a fine looking young man, very well groomed. He was moderately tall, with broad shoulders and a frank open face, lively blue eyes, fresh color, strong white teeth. He looked very good-humored, but something in the set of his jaw showed the determination Mr. Ray had described. He looked predominately likable." Harry was a "gray-beard" of twenty-seven or twenty-eight, a good ten years older than Tacy. (By the end of the series, however, Harry simply "topped the rest by a few years.")[682]

Charley Kirch, the real-life Harry, was only two years older than Bick Kenney. Charley and Bick met in Minneapolis, ten years after the fictional meeting of Harry and Tacy. Charley would have been a gray-beard of thirty by that time! See Chapter 13 on *Betsy's Wedding* for particulars regarding the real Harry Kerr.

Deep Valley High School's winter doldrums are forestalled by the arrival of Mr. Maxwell, Mrs. Poppy's brother, with diamond stickpin gleaming. Up and Down Broadway, sponsored by the Elks' Club, was in fact performed while Maud was a high school senior, but it was in November rather than in February (as per *Betsy and Joe*). The director was one Donald MacDonald, no relation to Mrs. Saulpaugh. He was, however, the brother of a Mankato lady, Mrs. Munson Burton (whose husband ran the Mankato Mills Company).

According to the *Mankato Free Press*, Mr. MacDonald was *"one of the foremost dramatic coaches of the country."*[683] It sounds as though Mr. MacDonald may have been as dictatorial as his counterpart, Mr. Maxwell: the paper reported that *"rehearsals will be prosecuted with great vigor."*[684] Mr. MacDonald staged *Up and Down Broadway* in numerous towns. After Mankato, he went to Detroit, where the *Detroit Free Press* called him "*the Belasco of the amateurs.*" The cast of *Up and Down Broadway* did consist of community talent, along with several professionals who traveled with MacDonald. Sixty young Mankatoans were included in the cast.

According to *Betsy and Joe*, the high school girls opened the show with the "Glow Worm" song: "The stage was dark at first and the girls carried phosphorescent wands. Then the lights went on and the girls in their black and orange costumes were themselves the glow worms. The audience stamped and whistled."[685] It didn't actually open the show, but "The Glow Worm" was one of the numbers in *Up and Down Broadway*. It was led by a local talent, Cornelia Mansfield. "*One of the prettiest numbers is the 'Glow Worm,' ... the chorus carrying electric lanterns, the effect of which is stunning.*"[686]

Coll. of A. Eldridge

Mike Parker (Tony)

Tony in one of his rare serious moments.

Coll. of A. Eldridge

Mike

Tony posed for a photo of the group with which he sang. They traveled only around southern Minnesota.

Coll. of A. Eldridge

The Parker Girls

Mike Parker had three sisters: Minnie, Jessie, and Caroline. The sisters do not appear in the Betsy-Tacy books.

MANKATO DAILY FREE PRESS
Wednesday, November 17, 1909
SCENE IN "UP AND DOWN BROADWAY," MANKATO THEATRE, NOVEMBER 23 AND 24—BENEFIT OF ELKS.

Mankato Free Press

The Chorus of *Up and Down Broadway*

Somewhere in this sea of faces is that of Maud Hart.

Mankato Free Press

The Red Mill

The Red Mill came to Deep Valley, and this time Tony invited Betsy before Joe did. *The Red Mill* did come to the Mankato Theater on October 12, 1909.

In an earlier Deep Valley theatrical, *Wonderland*, described in *Betsy in Spite of Herself*, "Betsy's crowd of girls was in the chorus. They were to dance a Scarf Dance. Through November the entries in Betsy's journal were all about [it]."[687] The Scarf Dance was actually presented in November 1909, rather than November 1907, as part of *Up and Down Broadway*, and was described by the Mankato paper as "*an exquisite song entitled, 'Starland' in which Mrs. Bartle is assisted by sixteen young ladies, who dance charmingly with long silken scarfs, on which the calcium lights play with beautiful effect.*"[688] (Mrs. Bartle was one of the out-of-town professionals who traveled with the show.)

Apparently, neither Bick Kenney (Tacy) nor Mike Parker (Tony) appeared in the real production of *Up and Down Broadway*. But like Tib, Midge Gerlach danced in *Up and Down Broadway*: "*One of the snappiest numbers on the program is 'I Can't Do That Sum,' in which Miss Marjory* [sic] *Gerlach and Mr. MacDonald appear, dressed as little school kids, and assisted by a chorus of ten young misses who sit on a wall.*"[689] Midge was said to be "*a bewitching little personage in her part, and her dancing brought forth a round of applause, which was well deserved. Meanwhile the little 'kiddies,' perched high on a big board fence, looked very cute with their dollies, slates and teddy bears.*"[690] It is curious that both times Tib appears on the stage of the Opera House (in *Downtown*'s *Rip Van Winkle* and in *Betsy and Joe*'s *Up and Down Broadway*), she is in the garb of a Dutch girl.

As Maud mentioned in *Betsy and Joe*, Easter came early in 1910, on March 27. Julia's letter arrives with the news that she is to spend Easter at the Von Hetternichs' castle in Poland. The aristocratic family with whom Kathleen actually lived was that of Herr Gemeinrat Begrat Hilger. The Hilgers did have a castle about forty miles northwest of Krakow in what was then German Poland, near the city of Katowice.[691] In February 1910, Kathleen wrote home: "*There are only about one hundred rooms - the rest of the castle is old and locked up.*"[692] In *Betsy and Joe*, Julia wrote home: "Only a hundred rooms are open," underlining the "only."[693]

Easter week was no doubt as fun-filled for Maud as it was for Betsy - and as exhausting. Maud left Mankato on April 3, 1910, for a week at the "Heidwinkles" farm near Mankato. Maud's visit there was probably very much like Betsy's at the Beidwinkles.

Joe gives Betsy red roses for her eighteenth birthday in April. (When Phil Brandish sent roses for her sixteenth birthday, they were pink.) "Tacy and Tib came for supper-with-birthday-cake."[694] Maud spent her eighteenth birthday similarly. "*Miss Maude Hart entertained eight of her girl friends at a six o'clock dinner party at her home on South Fifth Street last evening in honor of her eighteenth birthday. After an elegant repast had been discussed* [sic], *the remainder of the evening was spent in playing 500.*"[695] Just as Mr. Ray did, Mr. Hart gave a jade and silver ring to his middle daughter for her eighteenth birthday. He had given Kathleen an emerald and pearl ring on her eighteenth.

At the end of their senior year, Betsy and Tacy sing their Cat Duet on stage for the last time. "They had sung it every year since they were in the fifth grade and the audience now joined in the caterwauls."[696] But on page 216 of *Betsy in Spite of Herself*, Maud stated that the girls had sung it since sixth grade. Meanwhile, on page 141 of *Heaven to Betsy*, Maud said it has been since "Fourth Grade"! A look at *Over the Big Hill* (page 65) shows that Betsy and Tacy first sang the Cat Duet in fourth grade! That first performance was a big hit. Miss Dooley, their teacher, said, "'Betsy and Tacy will have to sing the Cat Duet again for us next year.' And so they did. In fact they sang it every year until they graduated from high school."[697] The Cat Duet is even mentioned in *Betsy's Wedding*, when newly-returned-from-Europe Betsy and usually-graceful-but-now-cumbersomely-pregnant Tacy sing a few bars. Eleanor Wood reported in 1946 that "*Betsy and Tacy still sing the 'Cat Duet' when they get together.*"[698]

There is a precursor of this tradition in one of Maud's adult novels: "*Did she remember the funny Cat Duett* [sic] *that the Praeger family had sung in Cloudman? Well, Aunt Jenny Lind had taught it to Violetta and Norma. They meowed just like cats and pinned paper tails to their dresses.*"[699] (Cloudman was based on Mankato.)

The full title of the comedic piece is "Duetto Buffo di Due Gatti," or "Comic Duet for Two Cats." Written for two voices and piano, the "Duet for Two Cats" has been attributed to Rossini, but Phillip Gossett, a Rossini scholar at the University of Chicago, contends that Rossini was not its composer.[700] Rather, the duet was put together in Vienna in the 1820s, the first part composed by a Dane named Weyse, and the second part being a parody of the Rossini opera *Otello*. Gossett is backed up by the journal *Bollettino Del Centro Rossiniano Di Studi* of Pesaro, Italy, in which Edward J. Crats writes: "*Not only is it filled with infectious humor, but the vocal parts (identified only as First Cat and Second Cat) lend themselves well to performance by almost any combination of male or female voices. Highlighted by celebrated recordings of such diverse teams as Christa Ludwig/Walter Berry and Elisabeth Schwarzkopf/Victoria de los Angeles, the duet's current vogue dates back to 1955, when it received its first 20th-century publication in the collected works of Rossini. Stylistically, the 'Duetto buffo' is exactly the sort of thing in which Rossini revelled. However, without additional evidence, a positive identification would be impossible.... Considering the complex origins of the music, the fairest and most accurate description of the piece might be: 'a potpourri based on the works of C.E.F. Weyse and G. Rossini, arranged by G. Berthold.' In any case, the charming musical whimsy of the 'Duetto buffo' has obviously won a secure place in the affections of cat fanciers and concertgoers alike.*"[701] It was certainly well received at Deep Valley High School!

End-of-the-year events follow closely on the heels of each other. The Zets win the Inter-Society Track Meet. But "the Philos had already won the athletics cup."[702] This can't be. The track meet and the athletics meet were one and the same. The missing cup was the debate cup, which Maud must have intended the Philos to have already won. In reality, the Philos won the debate cup and also the athletics (track) cup in 1910. The Zets took the essay cup.

Betsy <u>finally</u> prevails over Joe in the Essay Contest this year. Unfortunately, Maud did not win the 1910 Essay Contest in real life. Kathleen wrote home: "*Hurrah, for our side, that Maude got second place in the essay contest! How I pity the poor creatures who do not bear Hart for their last name, and what a fool I will be if I ever change it.*"[703]

Maud's chief rival in the Essay Contest, far from being Joe, was another girl. In a 1932 interview, Maud described "*a letter which arrived after the publication of her first book from a former classmate, who during their school days always won all the first prizes in writing contests, 'while I came in second.' This schoolmate now writes the author frequently and only recently sent a picture of her eleventh baby.*"[704] This was Alice Alworth, who graduated with Maud in the class of 1910. Alice wrote an article in the November 1932 edition of the *Minnesota Journal of Education* in which she reported that Maud "*thinks that raising children is a marvelous career for any woman - which is balm to many of us.*"[705]

Maud's high school transcript shows credit for the Essay Contest in twelfth grade but for no other year. Perhaps the school began to award academic credit only in her senior year, since Maud also competed (and lost to Alice) as a junior. These were the only two essay contests.

The subject and contestants were selected and announced each October and the essays written on the Saturday before the close of school for Christmas vacation (rather than the fictional Saturday in May). The essays were written on a subtopic of the subject, revealed on the morning of the contest. The actual subject of the essay contest in 1910 was "James J. Hill and the Great Northern Railway: Its Influence on the Development of the Northwest." This is the subject of the fictional 1908 contest, given in *Betsy in Spite of Herself*. The fictional topic in 1910 was "Conservation of Our Natural Resources."

Contestants were selected by the two societies, as Maud describes, but they were not selected evenly from each high school class - they tended to be mostly seniors. And in 1910, each society selected thirteen contestants, so twenty-six students competed, rather than the fictional eight.

When Maud's essay was awarded second place in 1910, she scored more points than all but one of the other contestants. The only person to outscore her was, of course, Alice Alworth, who was also a Zetamathian. The papers were graded on a percentage basis, and the names of the top ten scorers were announced in February, with the first-place writer winning the silver loving cup for his/her society.

Betsy has her class pictures taken at Mr. Snow's Photographic Studio. (Maud's were taken by A.J. Smith's studio in Mankato.) She posed for two: a dreamy one in her Class Day dress, the batiste Julia had sent, and a "Betsyish" one in shirtwaist with class pin. Kathleen really brought Maud's Class Day dress home from Europe. "*Lucerne, in fact all Switzerland, is the best place in the world*

1912 Otaknam

Fanny Pitcher

Fanny Pitcher (the aunt of Tom Fox) was represented fictionally - albeit loosely - by the character Miss Raymond.

Duplicated in several collections

Maud Hart
Graduation Photo

Maud is wearing the necklace of Venetian beads from Kathleen. JoAnne Ray describes this photo aptly: "*a young woman with an upswept hairdo ... smiling somewhat wistfully, perhaps because of a conflict between a desire to smile broadly and a wish to conceal the gap between her two front teeth.*" (Women of MN p. 164)

BECHS

Interior of Carnegie Library

Maud studied here for the Essay Contest. "There was a good feeling of respect at that table, and a pleasant mingling of camaraderie and rivalry." (BSH p. 222) *for embroidery dresses.* [Kathleen bought Maud] *a lovely pale blue batiste for five dollars, just heavy with lovely embroidery - a scalloped edge for the bottom of the skirt, and such a dainty rose pattern. I do hope she'll like it. ... And then* [in Paris] *I got a pale blue plume for Maude's* [sic] *graduating hat - double, you know, and very well made, but not unusually large, for $3.55.*"[706]

The Junior-Senior Banquet menu is again "full of literary allusions.... And the dinner was marvelous, beginning with fruit punch, and ending with demitasse and 1910 mints. In between were prime rib roast of beef, asparagus, fruit salad, and other good things."[707]

The program for the event, held May 6, 1910, is in Maud's High School Scrapbook. The same quotation from *Macbeth* is at the top of both the real and fictional menus: "...sit down; at first and last, the hearty welcome."[708]

The actual courses (shown in Maud's Scrapbook[709]) consisted of:

Fruit Punch Wafers
Prime Rib Roast of Beef
Potatoes on Half Shell Asparagus on Toast
Rolls Olives
Mint Jelly
Fruit Salad
Wafers Cream Dressing
Neapolitan Ice Cream Nabisco Sticks
1910 Mints
Demi-tasse Saratoga Flakes
Cheese

Toasts were given by the president of the junior class, Fred Mott, and the president of the seniors, Herman Hayward (Stan).

Midge (a junior) was in charge of the decorating committee. "*In the double doors to the assembly room was arranged the senior flower garden, and each senior was invited to pick a flower, and each flower contained a takeoff that was amusing. Palms, pillows, rugs, etc., were used in the decorations. The decorations largely reflected the originality of Miss Marjory* [sic] *Gerlach.*"[710] In *Betsy and Joe,* the motif chosen by the decorating committee is a street fair, featuring paper-tissue frankfurters with fortunes inside. The fortune frankfurters were actually provided at the Junior-Senior Banquet in 1907 (the year Maud was a freshman).

Julia, coming home from Germany to see Betsy graduate, surprises the family on a rainy Memorial Day, May 30, arriving from the depot in Mr. Thumbler's hack. Monday, May 30, 1910, was Memorial Day, and Kathleen (coming home from Germany to see Maud graduate) arrived in Mankato by train at noon that day. She had traveled on the steamer *America*.

It is clear from her letters that Kathleen's trip home at this time was not a surprise - she had always intended to return for Maud's graduation. She wrote on August 6, 1909, that she would be home in fewer than eleven months. In September 1909, Kathleen wrote: "*But June comes soon, and then we can be together again.*"[711] At one point she said that she hoped to remain in Germany until the fall of 1910, but changed her mind when she found that Fraulein (her teacher) was going to Minneapolis for the summer of 1910 (so there was no use staying in Berlin).

Kathleen had been offered a position at the Hamburg Opera but decided to pursue her career at home. She did not return to Germany. Upon her arrival in Mankato, the newspaper reported: "*Miss Hart is looking well.*"[712] It does not specify that she has put on a few pounds and is now, as Mrs. Ray described her, "fat as a roll of butter."[713]

One of the first friends whom Julia asks about upon her arrival home is Tony. By this time, Mike was long gone from Mankato High School. At the beginning of *Betsy and Joe*, Tony already thought that he "probably wouldn't graduate."[714] Mike spent only one year at the high school. According to his transcript, the reason he dropped out on May 2, 1907, was his "*unwillingness to work.*" He had done well in mechanical drawing and shop, but he obviously disliked academics. Even forbearing Miss Comstock, the history teacher, gave him a semester grade of 30! According to *Heaven to Betsy*, Tony had to retake most of freshman year, since his family's move to Deep Valley had interrupted it the first time. Julia's remark to Tony in *Heaven to Betsy* was accurate: "We all know you're taking sophomore history."[715] Mike did indeed take sophomore history and English, along with freshman mathematics, and he dodged Latin altogether.

Mike never graduated, but he did not give up high school for a musical career. And though he left high school, he did not leave town. By profession Mike was a plumber, though he did have a beautiful voice and sang in a group called the "Grand Male Quartet." They traveled around a bit but never left southern Minnesota.

When Betsy goes to Miss Clarke to ask about Tony's disappearance, Miss Clarke takes off her glasses and polishes them "nervously."[716] Miss Clarke has polished those glasses in each of the high school books. In *Betsy Was a Junior*, an editor at Crowell appears to have interfered with this ritual. "'Betsy,' said Miss Clarke, taking off her glasses and wiping her eyes...."[717] Maud probably wrote, "taking off her glasses and wiping them," and an editor thought Maud meant Miss Clarke's eyes rather than her glasses and so made the change. But Miss Clarke was not crying, as we can surmise from a description two paragraphs later: "Miss Clarke, who had just replaced her glasses took them off and started rubbing them again."[718] If she is doing it "again," then she must have been wiping her glasses, not her eyes, on the previous page. In *Betsy in Spite of Herself*, "She took off her glasses and polished them until she almost wore them out."[719] Miss Clarke first displayed this nervous habit on page 220 of *Heaven to Betsy*: "She had taken off her eyeglasses and polished them and put them on again." And she did it once more on page 228, for good measure. This repeated ritual makes Miss Clarke endearing, if predictable.

Singing in the school chorus is an important part of Betsy's high school days, but it isn't until senior year that the chorus director gets a name. "Miss Raymond" (more a literary device than a character) represents Mankato's Fanny Pitcher (the aunt of Tom Fox {fictionally, Tom Slade}). Said Maud of Fanny: "*She taught art and music in the Mankato Public Schools and was in charge of the High School Chorus you have heard about in the books. She was a handsome black-haired woman with a great enthusiasm for her work and not afraid to teach us good music, great music sometimes. And although we doubtless did not do it justice, we learned it and loved to sing it and never forgot it.... The Chorus is mentioned repeatedly and the references to what we were practising* [sic] *and singing came out of my own diaries as well as my memories. I have heard many of my old high school friends speak gratefully of Miss Fanny Pitcher. (Fan Pitcher, she was usually called.) My dear friend who is 'Tacy' in the books and who herself taught public school music in later life, and I have often spoken of the good music Miss Pitcher 'pounded' into us, leaving us loving it and eager for more.*"[720]

Maud does not supply a fictional report card for Betsy's senior year. We know that she has taken Shakespeare, German, Physics, Civics. Maud actually took the following courses, with the following final grades: English, 91; English Grammar (first semester only), 95; Botany (second semester only), 86; Physical Geography (first semester only), 89; Physics, 79.

"The Honor Roll was announced," and Betsy's name was included! "She would give an oration at Commencement and Tacy would be singing a solo. Tib had the leading role in the class play."[721] The play is *A Fatal Message*. This was really a class play, but it was given on Junior Entertainment night in 1909, and Midge Gerlach wasn't in it, because she was in the class of 1911. The lead was played by Fern Hoag, a peripheral friend of Maud's Crowd. "Maude" played Mrs. Edward Bradley, and Charles Bishman (N/C) played her husband. "Jay" Lloyd was also in the cast. An operetta called *Bobby Shaftoe* followed the play. Paul Ford played the lead, while Frances Kenney played "Betty Lobsterpot - the belle of the village." Maud played one of the girls in the chorus, along with Harriet Ahlers and Ruth Williams.[722]

At the end of their senior year, the play given by the class of 1910 was a comedy called *Bachelor Hall*. The only Crowd member in the cast was Jab Lloyd. The play was performed on Class Day, which was June 1, 1910 (as reported in *Betsy and Joe*). The words to the Class Song were written by Frances Kenney.

Commencement came on "that never-to-be-forgotten third of June."[723] Naturally, the Mankato High School class of 1910 did graduate on June third!

"This was the first appearance of the graduation dress. It was a fine white voile trimmed with yards of lace and insertion, ankle-length, with elbow sleeves."[724] In April 1910, Maud noted in her diary that "*Miss Roush* [sic] *is here making my commencement clothes*."[725]

Commencement began with "Morning, Noon and Night in Vienna" by the high school orchestra. According to the

Commencement program in Maud's Scrapbook, this overture (by Suppe) was played - but by Lamm's Orchestra (since there was no school orchestra at this time). The chorus next sang "Hark! Hark! the Lark" by Schubert, just as described in *Betsy and Joe.* In the actual program, the chorus is also listed as performing "The Owl" by Hotchkiss and "In the Dawn" by Capua. Several orations followed. "The Farmer of the Twentieth Century" was given by Philip Comstock. This topic is the closest to Joe's "Bread Basket of the World." But Maud mentions "The Farmer of the Twentieth Century" as a separate oration in *Betsy and Joe.*[726]

Hazel, the star debater, preceded Betsy at the podium. The oration before Maud's was "The Value of Play" by Ethel Korsell. The chorus then sang "Old Ironsides," before Maud delivered her oration, really on "The Heroines of Shakespeare." (On this program, as on the 1910 banquet program, she is "Maud" rather than "Maude.") Maud spoke chiefly about Juliet, Rosalind, Ophelia, Lady Macbeth, and Imogene.

The other commencement speech topics Maud mentions in *Betsy and Joe* were "For Pearls We Dive" and "Factory Life for Women." The former does not appear on the actual program, although the latter does, given by classmate Alice Alworth (the valedictorian). Harriet Ahlers spoke on "Oberammergau and the Passion Play."

Frances Kenney sang a solo, "The Evening Wind" from *Samson and Delilah* by Saint-Saens. Her encore was "Sylvia," which is the song Tacy sang at commencement in *Betsy and Joe*. (Bick had first sung "Sylvia" at a rhetorical on March 18, 1910.) The newspaper reported, "*She possesses a very sweet soprano voice*."[727]

The president of the school board, Dr. J. S. Holbrook (a physician in town), spoke at the ceremony, but his topic was not "After Commencement Day, What?" He really said: "*This day is the one you have long looked forward to. ...Chances are all about you, and all you have to do is reach out and take them. Every day is a fresh beginning, every sunrise is but a new birth for you and the rest of us -- the beginning of a new existence and a great chance to put to new and higher uses the knowledge you have gained.... The board of education congratulate you, the class of 1910, on your success in fulfilling the requirements for graduation, and extend their hearty wishes for continued success in your life work, whatever it may be, and I have the honor to present to you for this board your well earned diplomas. I hope you will hang them where you will see them daily, so that they will be constant reminders of your determination to make each day a new beginning of a newer, brighter, and truer life for yourselves and those about you.*"[728] Maud and her friends may not have wiped away pretend tears, but they must have thought this speech a bit silly.

Hints about a post-high-school future appear throughout the book and, of course, especially at the end. On page 125, Betsy had pointed out that the girls were on what might well have been their last Christmas shopping trip together: "Well, next year I'll be at the U. You'll be going to Browner College in Milwaukee, probably ... or maybe on the stage; it wouldn't surprise me ... and Tacy will be going to the College on the hill studying Public School Music." On page 254, Betsy tells Joe that she is indeed going to the U in the fall: "A writer needs a lot of education."

We also have had a small hint of an eventual connection between Winona and Dennie: "Clutching mistletoe, Dennie pursued Winona over the tops of the desks."[729] (In *Winona's Pony Cart*, published several years after *Betsy and Joe*, eight-year-old Winona and Dennie like each other.) The two later marry, in both fiction and real life!

Even Mr. Ray is thinking ahead: "We'll be having grandchildren around in a few years, don't forget."[730] Unfortunately, we never get a look at the Ray grandchildren. The first Hart grandchild, Kathleen's son, didn't arrive for twelve more years.

Betsy was very nostalgic throughout her senior year. She would probably have loved looking over these old family photos!

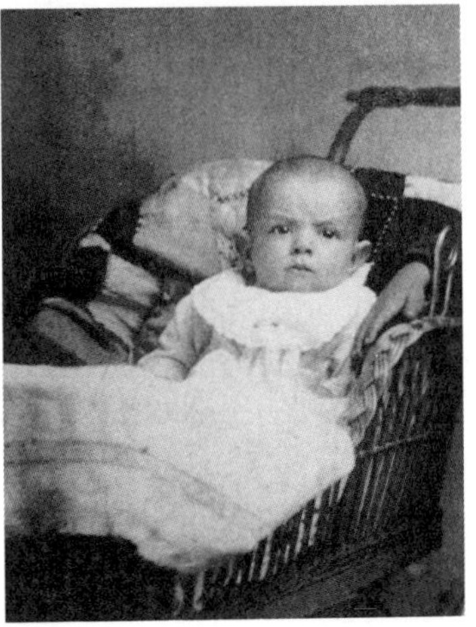

Coll. of A. Eldridge

Mike Parker
(Baby Tony)

Coll. of A. Eldridge

Emma Parker
(Tony's Mom)

Coll. of A. Eldridge

Jesse Parker
(Tony's Dad)

Coll. of Pat Kresin

Helmus and Rupe Andrews
(Little Herbert and Larry)

The Andrews boys are shown (standing) in an orange grove on a visit to California.

Maud's Godparents

Mankato, Its First Fifty Years

Charles N. Andrews
(Herbert and Larry's Dad)

Coll. of Pat Kresin

Mary Andrews
(Herbert and Larry's Mom)

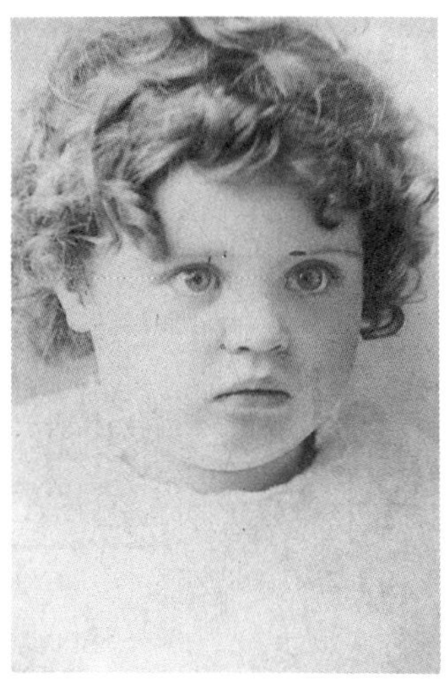

Coll. of Paul Ford

Paul Ford
(Baby Dennie)

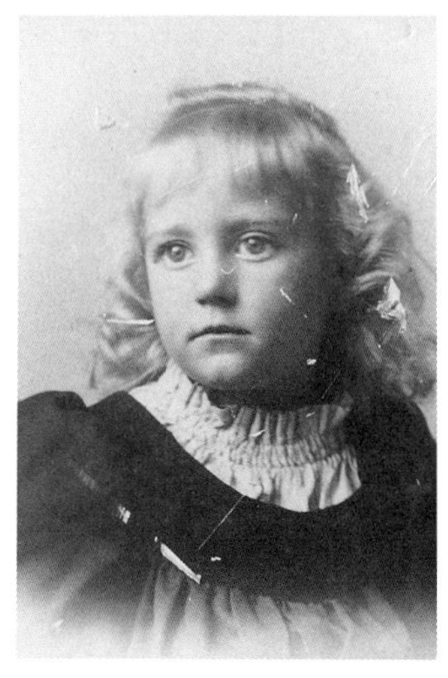

Coll. of Paul Ford

Eleanor Johnson
(Baby Winona II)

History of Blue Earth County

Frank Hunt
(Father of Winona I)

Coll. of Ruth Hudgens

Patrick Kenney
(Father of Tacy)

The little girl in the photo is the daughter of Tess Kenney (Katie Kelly).

1895 Atlas

Peter Lloyd
(Father of Cab)

Mankato, Its First Fifty Years

Rev. George W. Davis
(Father of Bonnie)

1895 Atlas

Judge William F. Hughes
(Father of Dave Hunt)

Coll. of Louise King

Marion Willard
(Baby Carney)

Coll. of Louise King

Mr. and Mrs. W.D. Willard
(Carney's Parents)

Mrs. Sibley "had sparkling dark eyes, and her small, heart-shaped face was framed in abundant dark curly hair." (CHP p. 40) Mr. Sibley was Carney's "tall, handsome father with his smiling eyes and trim, close-clipped moustache." (CHP p. 37)

[621] *Betsy and Joe*, p. 3.
[622] High School Scrapbook, p. B'.
[623] *Betsy and Joe*, p. 4.
[624] *Betsy Was a Junior*, p. 156.
[625] *Mankato Daily Review*, 8-6-09.
[626] *Mankato Free Press*, 6-20-24.
[627] KPH letters, p. 25.
[628] *Betsy and Joe*, p. 13.
[629] KPH letters, pp. 10-11.
[630] Ibid., p. 29.
[631] *Betsy in Spite of Herself*, p. 29.
[632] *Betsy Was a Junior*, p. 35.
[633] *Betsy and the Great World*, p. 176.
[634] *Betsy's Wedding*, p. 236.
[635] *Gentlemen from England*, p. 56.
[636] M.H. Lovelace, *Petticoat Court* (New York: John Day Co., 1930), p. 305.
[637] M.H. Lovelace, "Carcassonne Flyer," *Sunset*, April 1925.
[638] M.P. Hart, "The Episodes of Epsie," *Ainslee's*, March 1916.
[639] *Downtown*, p. 112.
[640] *Heaven to Betsy*, p. 59.
[641] *Betsy and the Great World*, p. 161.
[642] *Betsy and Joe*, p. 47.
[643] Ibid., p. 51.
[644] Ibid., p. 214.
[645] *Nassau Daily Review-Star*, 9-25-41.
[646] *Betsy and Joe*, p. 126.
[647] Ibid., p. 91.
[648] Lovelace, "A Child's Reading."
[649] *Betsy and Joe*, p. 56.
[650] KPH letters, p. 151.
[651] *Betsy and Joe*, p. 37.
[652] MHL to M. Everett, 5-17-48.
[653] *Betsy and Joe*, p. 133.
[654] Ibid., p. 71.
[655] D.O., p. 9.
[656] MLK to SSW, 11-15-91.
[657] *Betsy and Joe*, p. 74.
[658] Ibid., p. 91.
[659] Ibid., p. 95

[660] *Mankato Free Press*, 10-29-09.

[661] *Betsy and Joe*, p. 84.

[662] Ibid., p. 98.

[663] *Mankato Free Press*, 11-05-09.

[664] *Heaven to Betsy*, p. 97.

[665] *Betsy in Spite of Herself*, p. 111.

[666] *Betsy and Joe*, p. 93.

[667] Ibid., p. 106.

[668] Nelson et al., eds.,*Minnesota Writes*.

[669] *Betsy and Joe*, p. 94.

[670] *Betsy Was a Junior*, p. 154.

[671] *Betsy in Spite of Herself*, p. 69.

[672] *Betsy and Joe*, p. 108.

[673] "A Few More Thoughts on the Betsy-Tacy Books," *The Whispered Watchword*, August, 1992.

[674] *Betsy and Joe*, p. 77.

[675] Ibid., p. 127.

[676] *Ladies' Home Journal*, December 1909, p. 46.

[677] *Betsy and Joe*, p. 148.

[678] MHL to A. Wiecking, 9-4-61.

[679] *Betsy and Joe*, pp. 149-150.

[680] Ibid., p. 120.

[681] *Mankato Free Press*, 2-4-65.

[682] *Betsy's Wedding*, p. 121.

[683] *Mankato Free Press*, 11-05-09.

[684] Ibid.

[685] *Betsy and Joe*, p. 180.

[686] *Mankato Free Press*, 11-13-09.

[687] *Betsy in Spite of Herself*, p. 88.

[688] *Mankato Free Press*, 11-16-09.

[689] Ibid.

[690] *Mankato Free Press*, 11-24-09.

[691] Ed. note: "Kattowitz" is now "Katowice."

[692] KPH letters, p. 158.

[693] *Betsy and Joe*, p. 191.

[694] Ibid., p. 222.

[695] *Mankato Free Press*, 4-26-10.

[696] *Betsy and Joe*, p. 222.

[697] *Over the Big Hill*, p. 68.

[698] Lippert memoirs, p. 11.
[699] *The Black Angels*, p. 111.
[700] Interview with P. Gossett, 5-31-91.
[701] *Bollettino Del Centro Rossiniano Di Studi,* #3, 1977.
[702] *Betsy and Joe*, p. 224.
[703] KPH letters, p. 169.
[704] *Minneapolis T.*, 4-20-32.
[705] *Minnesota Journal of Education*, Vol. XIII, No. 3, November 1932, p. 87.
[706] KPH letters, p. 85-93.
[707] *Betsy and Joe*, pp. 233-234.
[708] Ibid., p. 233.
[709] High School Scrapbook, p. J' innards.
[710] *Mankato Free Press*, 5-7-10.
[711] KPH letters, p. 129.
[712] *Mankato Free Press*, 5-30-10.
[713] *Betsy and Joe*, p. 237.
[714] Ibid., p. 61.
[715] *Heaven to Betsy*, p. 199.
[716] *Betsy and Joe,* p. 228.
[717] *Betsy Was a Junior*, p. 182.
[718] Ibid., p. 183.
[719] *Betsy in Spite of Herself*, p. 93.
[720] MHL to J. Ellen, 9-10-67.
[721] *Betsy and Joe*, p. 190.
[722] High School Scrapbook, p. G'.
[723] *Betsy and Joe*, p. 244.
[724] Ibid., p. 245.
[725] D.O., p. 15.
[726] *Betsy and Joe*, p. 248.
[727] *Mankato Free Press*, 6-4-10.
[728] Ibid.
[729] *Betsy and Joe*, p. 130.
[730] Ibid., p. 144.

CHAPTER TEN
On *Carney's House Party*
June 1911 to September 1911

Though *Carney's House Party* and *Emily of Deep Valley* are not part of the "main-line" Betsy-Tacy series, accounts of these books appear here between chapters on *Betsy and Joe* and *Betsy and the Great World*, because both *Carney* and *Emily* contain details which create an important bridge between the two Betsy-Tacy books. Without these two satellite books, the gulf between Betsy in Deep Valley and Betsy on the *Columbic* is extraordinarily wide (though, of course, navigable). It is through Carney's eyes that the reader gets her first look at post-high-school Betsy and is thereby prepared for the changes in store.

June of 1911, the setting upon which *Carney's House Party* opens, is the end of Carney's sophomore year at Vassar, but it would have been the end of freshman year there for Marion Willard. After graduating from high school, Marion studied at Carleton College for a year (1909-1910) before being admitted to Vassar as a freshman. She graduated from Vassar in 1914.

Vassar friends portrayed in *Carney's House Party* include Win and Winkie, "tennis stars, roommates and great friends."[731] Winkie was based on Marion's friend Annie Green. Win was most likely based on another Vassar girl, Adeline DeSale. A third fictional friend, Sue, was probably Sybil May. Maud originally intended to use the name "Susie" for this character.[732]

Isobel Porteous, Carney's roommate, was lovely. "Her golden brown hair was slightly disordered, breaking at every twist into airy curls."[733] Isobel was based on Marion's roommate, Dorothy C. Brinsmaid. Unlike Isobel, Dorothy does not appear to have visited Marion in Minnesota. A Vassar friend named Ruth Rilling came to visit Marion during their college years, but apparently not during the same summer that Rupe (Larry) came back.

Isobel is faintly reminiscent of Aunt Dolly - as two of the least likeable characters in the series, they're both as vain as they are lovely. At any rate, Isobel was a good roommate - and she wasn't too sophisticated to enter into the fun of the North Tower.

Also sharing a room with Carney at Vassar was a dear friend of very long standing - her china doll. "Suzanne, her beloved baby since childhood, was now the mascot of the North Tower."[734] Maud wrote to Marney while writing *Carney's House Party* to ask

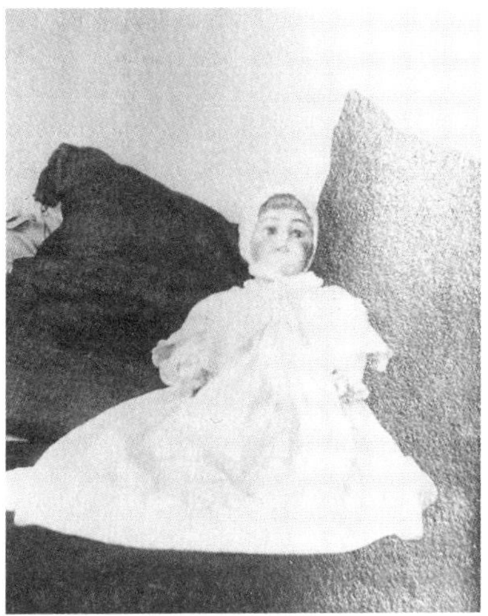

Coll. of Louise King

Suzanne

Marion Willard's childhood doll was really the mascot of her friends at the dormitory.

Coll. of Louise King

Marion Willard (Carney Sibley)

This photograph was taken during the time Marion was a student at Vassar.

Coll. of Louise King

Vassar Daisy Chain

This photograph, taken in 1912, is reminiscent of the Vera Neville illustration on page 24 of *Carney's House Party*. "The shoulders were padded with tiny pillows, for the daisy chain was heavy." (CHP p. 32) As stated in the book, the chain was made by Saltford's, a Poughkeepsie florist. Saltford's made the chain for fifty years, until it was taken over by Boch's, also a Poughkeepsie florist.

Coll. of Louise King

Marion and Dorothy
(Carney and Isobel)

Marion's Vassar roommate was Dorothy Brinsmaid.

Coll. of Louise King

Annie Green
(Winkie)

"Winkie was short, with thick braids of light hair bound about her head, and deceptively grave eyes." (CHP p. 13) Annie Green, like Winkie, was a tennis player.

Coll. of Louise King

Dorothy
(Isobel)

"Her lips were mobile and were often curved in a faintly mysterious smile." (CHP p. 28)

Coll. of Louise King

Dorothy's Wedding
(Isobel as a Bride)

By the end of *Carney's House Party*, we learn that Isobel is engaged to Howard Sedgwick of Harvard. His real name was Arthur Jackson.

Coll. of Louise King

Marion Willard

Tom Fox sent Marion flowers when she graduated from Vassar in 1914.

Coll. of Tom Fox

Tom Fox
(Tom Slade)

This photo was taken when Tom was in his final year at West Point.

about the real doll (really the Tower mascot). Maud said that she planned to use the name "Nancy Jane" but asked Marney for the real name. Marion responded: "*I would never thought of calling her that for Nancy was the name of one of Dad's first horses and Jane was that of a queer woman in church. She was first called 'Ethel' (horrible) but in college she was Suzanne.*"[735]

Miss Chittenden was "Vassar's piano teacher."[736] Kate S. Chittenden was head of the "pianoforte" department of Vassar College for almost twenty years. She was also director of the American Institute of Applied Music in New York. Miss Salmon was Carney's history professor. Carney admired her clear, orderly thinking. Lucy Maynard Salmon taught history at Vassar from 1887 to 1926.

The twenty-four sophomore girls who carried the daisy chain, "selected for their pulchritude, were dressed in long white gowns."[737] Carney likes the daisy-chain tradition. "I hope they will still have it when my daughter comes to college."[738] Her daughter and granddaughter did follow Marion to Vassar.

"Carney went down the Hudson to attend a dance at West Point with her old friend Tom Slade."[739] Marion did just this. Tom Fox and Marion Willard both graduated from high school in 1909. Like Marion, Tom had remained in the Midwest for his first year of college, studying mechanical engineering at the University of Illinois at Urbana, before enrolling at West Point.

In *Betsy and Joe*, we learn that Carney was the first Deep Valley girl to go east to college.[740] In fact, Kate Hubbard (daughter of the owner of the "Big Mill") had gone to Smith three years before Marion left for Vassar - and Kate was probably not the first.

It isn't until *Carney's House Party* that we learn much about Carney's family. On page 37, we finally learn the fictional names of Carney's brothers: Hunter, Gerald (or Jerry), and Bobbie.

Grant Robbins Willard (the real Hunter) was only eighteen months younger than Marion, graduating from high school two years behind her, in 1911. In *Carney's House Party*, Hunter was also eighteen months younger than his sister Carney, so he too should have graduated in 1911, rather than 1912 (as fictionally depicted). If Grant were really less than two years younger than Marion, wouldn't he have been part of the Crowd? Katie Kelly

Coll. of SSW

Marion Willard

This is the way "Carney" looked in 1914 when she graduated from college. In real life, she had not yet met "Sam."

Coll. of Louise King

W.D. Willard Family

Standing, left to right: Grant and Harold. Seated: Louise, W.D., Marion, and John.

Coll. of Louise King

John Willard
(Bobbie Sibley)

John really sent away for a baseball suit one summer. "The shirt and bloomers were gray, with narrow red stripes. There were two big red letter B's." (CHP p. 136)

Willard Sleeping Porch

W.D. Willard and his sons really built a sleeping porch on the rear of their home at 609 S. Broad Street. "Sleeping porches were new and very popular." (CHP p. 38) was included - though two years older than Tacy. A number of Crowd members (Midge, Ruth, and Paul) were actually in the class of 1911 (rather than 1909 or 1910) - so being a little younger should not have excluded Grant Willard from the Crowd's activities. In fact, it didn't.

Grant's name appears in Maud's High School Scrapbook, since he danced with Maud on more than one occasion. But Grant probably also had a crowd of his own, since Maud writes that it wasn't until Carney was in college that Hunter "had passed some invisible sign post and entered her world. The eighteen months' difference in their ages which had been so important in the past was important no longer. Now, although he was only just entering his senior year in high school, even a college girl would look at him with interest."[741] Grant was actually preparing to begin college in 1911. We learn in *Emily of Deep Valley* that Hunter Sibley enrolled at Carleton College. Grant Willard, and later his brother John (Bobbie), did attend Carleton, in Northfield, Minnesota (as did Grant's sons after him).

Hunter's girlfriend is "Ellen" in *Carney's House Party*. (Hunter and Ellen are still together in *Emily of Deep Valley*.) Grant did not meet his future wife, Dorothy, in high school. She was a Vassar girl, but surprisingly, they did not meet through Marion. Grant and Dorothy met at a party on Lake Minnetonka, where Dorothy (from Pennsylvania) was a house guest of her college roommate. Grant and Dorothy were married just a month after Marion. Three of their four children were born in Mankato, where Grant was a banker and financial advisor.

Jerry Sibley was Harold Willard, whose nickname was, curiously, Tib. "Tib Willard" - and confusion reigns! This family's surname certainly inspired Joe's surname, and Harold Willard's nickname in all likelihood gave rise to Marjorie Gerlach's fictional nickname. "Tib" was the result of the little boy's attempt to pronounce his middle name, "Sibley." His brothers and sister called him "Tibley" and later, "Tib." He went by this nickname all his life. Like Jerry, Tib Willard was really bookish. Fictionally, Jerry Sibley was one year behind Emily Webster, so he would have graduated from high school in 1913. Sure enough, Tib Willard did graduate from Mankato High School in 1913. He later obtained a Ph.D. in animal husbandry and became a professor. Tib and his wife Grace had three children.

The youngest brother, Bobbie (consistently spelled "Bobby" in *Betsy and Joe* and *Emily of Deep Valley*), was Marion's youngest brother, John Harrington Willard. Born in 1901, John would have been ten in 1911, rather than nine, as stated in *Carney's House Party*. After a year at Carleton College, John went east to Pennsylvania, where he completed his education in medicine. Dr. John Willard and his wife had no children.

Mrs. Sibley, Maud tells us, had once been the prettiest girl in Chester, Vermont. She had come west to visit an uncle (whose real name was Zina Harrington) and "Hunter Sibley, college-bred son of a wealthy pioneer family, would not let her go home without a large three-diamond ring."[742] There is a minor boo-boo here, since later in the book, Carney's father is "Will" Sibley.[743] Giving the fictional name of "Hunter" to Carney's oldest brother was logical, since it is the maiden name of Carney's mother (Carney's mother's mother being "Grandmother Hunter"). It would not have made sense (or at any rate, it would have been an unlikely coincidence) for Carney's <u>father</u> to be Hunter Sibley. "Will," however, was the perfect fictional name, since it was not only Marion's father's real first name but is reminiscent of his real surname, Willard.

W.D. Willard did not give Louise Robbins (of Chester, Vermont) a three-diamond ring. A "flashy" ring was not the Willard style. But it <u>was</u> the Everett style. Marion Willard married Bill Everett. Bill's grandfather, William Everett, gave Bill's grandmother, "Madame" Everett, a three-diamond ring. Marion probably mentioned this family heirloom in a letter to Maud, and Maud transferred it to Mrs. Sibley for use in *Carney's House Party*.

As a young wife, Mrs. Sibley "had painted china with a teacher three mornings a week."[744] Louise Willard did paint china. W. D. Willard described their 1890 honeymoon trip: "*I had taken my Botany with me so we analyzed many flowers and Louise sketched them in her notebook and later used the sketches in decorating china - cups, saucers, plates, etc.*"[745]

One of the most popular dishes served on those lovely Willard plates may well have been Welsh rarebit. It was Mr. Sibley's specialty, as onion sandwiches were Mr. Ray's. Maud's Scrapbook contains a handwritten supper menu for the "*Palace Family Hotel (M. Willard, Prop.)*" dated November 8, 1906. The second course was "*Welsh Rarebit.*"[746]

In Carney's bedroom, "The furniture was of heavy bird's-eye maple -- a high-backed bed, a bureau, a dressing table with a nest of drawers beside the mirror, a slender desk, a rocker and straight chair. Photographs of relatives adorned the walls which were papered with yellow poppies."[747] By request, Marion (in 1948) sent Maud a description of her girlhood bedroom furnishings. "*Heavy bird's eye maple, bed, high back board and foot half as high. Dresser, slender bird's eye desk, rocker and straight chair. Always had millions of photos around, especially of all my old relatives. Wall-paper with yellow poppies - rug blue. Door between my room and boys'.*"[748]

The first thing Carney does after walking through the door is to take off her traveling suit and put on "a faded blue dress she found in her closet. It was a pleasure to wear something she had not had at school."[749] This is such a genuine sensation, yet perhaps not one that is likely to have been remembered by Maud forty years after her college days. And after all, Maud was never away at college for a year at a time, or even half a year. She had only to cross the river in Minneapolis to go home (as she no doubt did very often) to retrieve or deposit things in her bedroom closet. Moreover, she lived at home during much of her time at the U. Maud may have based elements of Carney's return home on comments that daughter Merian made on coming home from college for vacation. (Merian had entered Smith in 1948.)

"There would be an extra good dinner, Carney thought contentedly, because she had come home. Boiled custard, probably. That was her favorite dessert."[750] Maud had written to Marney to ask, "*Did you have any favorite dish which your mother prepared when you came home?*" Marion responded, "*Boiled custard!*"[751]

Mrs. Sibley tells Carney: "Your Crowd isn't the same since the Rays and the Kellys went away."[752] This is, of course, the first we hear of it. "Both families had moved to Minneapolis, a happy coincidence since Betsy Ray and Tacy Kelly were inseparable friends. But Betsy had gone farther. During her freshman year at the University, she had had an appendicitis operation. About that time her step-grandfather had died in California and Betsy had gone to San Diego to stay with her grandmother."[753] She sees the Humphreys boys there. Maud did go to California after her attack of appendicitis (see Chapter 12 on *Betsy and the Great World*), and Maud did see the Andrews boys in San Diego. "*On my trips to California, I always saw them.*"[754]

The Willards really built the sleeping porch but possibly a little earlier than 1911. Carney's house party was based on "*the houseparty* [Marney] *really did give some years earlier, and on the houseparty* [Maud] *gave at Lake Crystal. It was a very housepartyish period ... probably due to the Little Colonel.*"[755] Marion's earlier house party was given in June 1908. The house party Maud gave at Lake Crystal began on July 22, 1907. The guests were Bick, Tess, Marion, Mildred Oleson, and Eleanor Johnson. Marion had a number of house parties during her college summers, usually consisting of friends from St. Paul and Duluth.

In the summer of 1912, Marion invited Connie, Bick, and Maud for a visit. Maud and Bick came from Mahtomedi, Minnesota, where the Harts were staying for the summer. Maud's lengthy letter of acceptance to Marion's invitation reads:

"*After dispatching the final chapter of 'She Loved But Left Him,'* [the full title of a drama presented at an Okto Delta meeting in *Betsy Was a Junior* was Woman versus Woman, or She Loved But Killed Him[756]] *and dismissing the editor of 'Diamond Dick,' who had been begging her in a most touching interview to furnish him a serial, the harassed young authoress sat down at the typewriter in her awfully attractive looking den, and dashed off a note of acceptance. In the adjoining chamber, the most popular debutante of the season was in the hands of her maid, and thru the door came her cheerful whistle - whistling 'Paddy dear, and did you hear.' (She was of Irish extraction, and her unconscious manner of whistling at all times, and crossing her knees in public, and whiffing her cigarette added to her naive charm. She too was intending to sit down and dictate a note of acceptance to her secretary, as soon as she could snatch a few moments from the gallants who surrounded her.) Their prospective hostess was a higher educated girl who combined with her air of academic distinction, a coy manner most attractive to the opposite sex, and their fellow guest had a drooping manner, much piety and domesticity. Therefore all concerned were looking forward to the congenial party which would combine soulful genious* [sic], *giddy frivolity, grave learning, and sweet girlishness.*

"Perhaps it is just as well that you see your guests at this crucial moment thru their own descriptions and not with the eye of the flesh. For the authoress has a slightly worried expression due to her pet story having been rejected four times, her hair is suffering from one of her periodical resolutions not to curl it, and her morning gown could not honestly be called immaculate or crisp. While the debutante is attired in the negliest sort of negligee, and her actions would better fit a chorus girl trying out for a job on the front row than a society queen whose ancestors came over in the steerage of the Mayflower. But never you fear, we will remedy all this when we come to Mankato. I will see that Bick is properly clothed and in her right mind, and I will try and put the stamp of the city upon her, tho she takes more naturally to the stamp of the rural districts. (In a sudden fit of reckless daring, Maud let Bick read this questionable epistle, and in return Bick gave Maud a flying journey into the lake at the toe of her bedroom slipper. But since Maud was an eel in the water, she readily swam homeward, with all the grace of her sex, not in the least perturbed, but smiling the smile of a siren, and the female who planned and perpetrated the ghastly deed now looks out thru the bars with gloomy eyes. But she will be pardoned out before the fatal 19th [of July].

"Yes, my dear, we would both be perfectly delighted to come. We have both set our maids to replenishing our ward-robes, and our secretaries are busy breaking all the engagements, which we had inadvertantly [sic] *contracted for the week in question.*

"I think it's very nice that you like Rupe so well. I was sure you would. I thought he was perfectly charming. It makes me just sick for old times, to hear about the larks you have been having. Kath and I so often think how much fun it would be to get the old bunch together for an old fashioned sing around our fireplace, but how impossible it would be! Everything is different now just because we have to go and get grown up. I don't think it's half so nice for one man to ask to come and call, and then come, and sit and talk properly for an evening, as it is for a whole bunch of crazy kids to come tearing in and raid the pantry.

"It is awfully dear of you and your mother to want us, and we will try and not be any trouble at all. "With many thanks for the invitation, and love to all, I must draw this young novel to a reluctant close. As ever, Maud."

Crowd members who make an appearance in *Carney's House Party* include Tom, Lloyd, Dennie, Cab, Winona, Alice and, of course, Bonnie and Betsy. Alice is enjoying Teachers' College, which would have been the Mankato Normal. "It doesn't take four years, and I'm anxious to get out into the world," Alice said.[757] (It took only two years.) Winona liked it because it was near Dennie. "Winona and Dennie were going together."[758] Their counterparts, Eleanor and Paul, really did get married.

Tacy, meanwhile, "is engaged to that Harry Kerr."[759] Later Betsy says that Tacy's "going to get married. But she'll never tat, and neither will I."[760] Bick may or may not have tatted, but she didn't marry until 1920.

Bonnie is finally back in Minnesota. "The Andrews are back from Paris as you have probably heard. They are living in St. Paul, and I've invited Bonnie for July."[761] As already explained, the Davis family moved to St. Paul, rather than Paris, when they left Mankato in 1907. Connie would certainly have been in St. Paul in 1911. But she would not have been preparing for her freshman year, as she was in the story; she would already have finished a year at the University of Minnesota.

Twice the girls advise Bonnie to marry a clergyman: "Bonnie ought to marry a minister."[762] "Your Minister is waiting somewhere!" they remind her.[763] But her future husband, Arthur Houlihan, was not a minister. His family owned a brick-manufacturing company.

Betsy says that Howard Sedgwick's sprawling script "isn't so handsome as Joe's."[764] Delos and Maud actually had strikingly similar handwriting. Betsy and Joe's romance is running smoothly this summer. As we know, Maud did not yet know her future husband during this period. But there was romance in her life. She became engaged several times ... to the same man. She had a recurring engagement to Russell McCord. (See Chapter 12 herein on *Betsy and the Great World.*)

Betsy adores Kosmeo. Kathleen Hart used it, too. *"It had been so hot all day that most people's faces were one big blister, but, thanks to Kosmeo, I didn't have anything but blistered feet."*[765]

"My mind is working. Maybe I'm making up a story.... This is an awfully romantic situation, Larry coming back."[766] Maud has

1913 Gopher

Connie Davis
(Bonnie Andrews)

"Of course, like the rest of them Bonnie was four years older. But she was still short and cozily round. Her blond hair was as smooth as always, her blue eyes as mirthful and as calm." (CHP p. 67)

Coll. of Billie Andrews

Helmus Andrews
(Herbert Humphreys)

Maud saw Helmus while visiting her grandmother in California in 1911. This is how he looked about that time.

Duplicated in several collections

Marion and Rupe
(Carney and Larry)

The Crowd went out to Madison Lake while Rupe was visiting. It's too bad Maud didn't write about the anecdote which must be captured in this photo. The photo was taken by Ruth Williams. Larry "had thick hair and a crooked, somewhat quizzical smile. Betsy Ray had said he always seemed to be laughing at you." (CHP p. 30)

Coll. of Louise King

Rupe Andrews
(Larry Humphreys)

Marion kept a photo of Larry in his track suit on her dresser at college.

Duplicated in several collections

Grant and Rupe
(Hunter and Larry)

The Willard auto has suffered a flat tire on a drive to Madison Lake. Grant is taking a break from the air pump while Rupe prepares to repair a hole. This photo was taken by Ruth Williams.

Coll. of Billie Andrews

Three Generations of Andrews Men

Rupert and Helmus Andrews with their father and their grandfather, outside the family home in San Diego. "Carney saw only a tall, strapping, broad-shouldered young man in a handsome light-colored suit, wearing a bow tie." (CHP p. 130) been building up to this romantic situation for four years. She wrote to Marion Willard Everett in 1948 to tell her about *Carney's House Party* *"I want to use the affair with Larry (Rupe) which I've kept alive through all four books."*[767] Maud intended to write about it all along, though she seems not to have considered making Carney the main character until the spring of 1948. Maud never lets us forget the long-distance relationship between Carney and Larry.

In *Betsy in Spite of Herself*: "Everyone in the Crowd missed the Humphreys but not as Carney did. The letters which passed steadily between Deep Valley and San Diego did not fill Larry's place. Neither did any of the many boys who were attentive to her."[768] Carney remarks to Betsy, "Larry has been gone for a whole year now, and I like him as much as I ever did."[769]

In *Betsy Was a Junior:* "'I wish I could see Larry,'" she said. 'I'm afraid that until I see him again, no one else is going to interest me....' 'He'll come back to see you sometime,' Betsy prophesied."[770]

In *Betsy and Joe*: "'I want to see Larry,' she said firmly. 'I have to find out whether I still like him. Maybe he's changed. I feel as though I couldn't ever ... get married to anyone else until I know.' 'Have you told him that?' asked Betsy. 'No, I haven't. But I should think he'd feel the same way ... about seeing me.'"[771]

Rupe came back in the summer of 1912, before Marion's junior year at Vassar. (Larry, of course, comes back in the summer of 1911.) Early in *Carney's House Party*, Carney ruminates over a letter she received from Betsy in California the previous winter. "I've done gone seen him! And he's most attractive. I don't think you'll be a bit disappointed in him, Carney. Maybe you'll be a little afraid of him. I was. He always seems to be laughing at me, and he has a sort of ... touch me not, I'm already spoken for ... air. Now who has spoken for him, Miss Caroline Sibley?"[772] When Betsy arrives in Deep Valley, she and Carney have a late-night confab, and Betsy tells more about Larry. "He was cautious even with me. He acted as though we had just been introduced, talked about the climate and his school and things like that. I didn't have a marriage license in my pocket, but he wasn't taking any chances. ...I had quite a heart-to-heart talk with Mrs. Humphreys. She gave a party for me when the boys were home for spring vacation, so I met their crowd. And the general impression - both with Mrs.

Humphreys and the crowd - seems to be that you and Larry have been as true as steel and that you're both pining for the day when your hearts can be reunited. ... Larry scorned every girl in San Diego High School, and he's doing the same at Leland Stanford, and they all lay the blame on your shoulders."[773] Later, Betsy tells Carney about her life in California. "I always went at my writing. I certainly led a lively bunch of heroines to the altar."[774]

Maud wrote almost the same words to Marion in a February 7, 1911, letter. "*Dear Marion Elizabeth,- Eh bien, ma cherie, I done gone seen him. He is most attractive, and I don't think you'll be a bit disappointed in him. Maybe you'll be a little afraid of him, I was. He's fearfully reserved, I thought, and has sort of a - touch me not, I'm already spoken for - sort of an air, which rather irritated me. For tho' I had no desire to hustle the dear man off to the nearest Justice of the Peace, I would have liked to have acted a little more as if we hadn't just been introduced and didn't have white gloves on. You can see at once why I couldn't deliver your message. He didn't give me a shadow of a chance. We talked mostly about the climate, his school, and everyday affairs. Now don't let this worry you, because I know he won't act at all that way with you. I just must have looked as if I had a marriage license in my pocket and I had designs upon him. Do you know, when I left Mankato I had the impression that you and Rupe had sort of a lukewarm interest in each other, which would probably cool off entirely, before you ever saw each other, but since I've been out here, I've had that idea jolted out of my head. I had quite a heart to heart talk with Mrs. A. and then I've met many members of the boys' crowd. And the general impression seems to be that you and Rupe have been as true as steel and are pining for the day when your severed hearts can be united. At any rate, Rupe has scorned every girl in San Diego and is doing the same at college, and all the injured and slighted ones lay the blame on your shoulders. Rupe is planning to go East in 1912, as you probably know, and he's coming like Young Lockinvar out of the west. I would like to be sticking around when you two meet. ...I am enjoying my winter here immensely. I do nothing but write all day long, and I'm leading a lively bunch of heroines to the altar.*"[775] (In *Carney's House Party*, Sam is credited with drawing the analogy to Lockinvar.)

When he comes to Deep Valley, Larry stays with Tom in *Carney's House Party*. Rupe actually stayed with Jim Baker (Lloyd

Harrington). (Rupe's sister Alice had come back from California to see friends and relatives at Christmas of 1907, and she stayed with the Baker family, too.)

A dinner dance at Point Pleasant, hosted by Marion, was written up in the *Mankato Review*. The guests were Frances Strader, Louise Van Sandt of Goucher College in Baltimore, and Esther Coffin of Duluth. Rupe was the guest of honor. Dancing came after a five-course dinner. The company included some familiar names: Eleanor Johnson, Paul Ford, Mildred Oleson, Henry Lee, Grant Willard, James Baker, and C.J. Burmeister.

Larry is a great athlete, pitching a mean game of baseball at Two Falls Park. Maud once suggested that a Betsy-Tacy fan "*drive out to Minneopa Falls ... that masquerades under another name in Carney's House Party*."[776] Minneopa State Park is located five miles west of Mankato. There are two falls at Minneopa. "First the creek took a downward jump of about the height of a man. Then, as though it had gained courage, it took a truly heroic leap, fifty feet or more, through a wild gorge."[777] There are actually several smaller falls, followed by the big one Maud describes. According to tourist information from 1912, "*The creek leaps sixty feet over the ledge of rock into a deep pool, and then runs for over a mile through a picturesque gorge to the river. The state has put in an artesian well, steps, bridges, shelters and other conveniences for picnic parties, but without disturbing the natural beauty of the spot.*"[778]

Delos' writing style peeks out again in the description of the baseball game at Two Falls ("popped a feeble little fly"[779]). It is almost as though, after reading Delos' enthusiastic descriptions and trying to understand, Maud marveled: "How endlessly men could talk about sports ... as they passed from a discussion of football and baseball teams to wrestlers and championship matches."[780]

Larry is particularly interested in the Orono dam because he is "studying to be an engineer."[781] He was. Rupert Andrews graduated from Stanford in 1914 with a degree in electrical engineering and later became head of the Sierra Nevada Power Station. The dam at Orono was the Rapidan Dam. Construction on it began when Maud was a senior in high school. "*During the year 1911 the Consumers Power company completed the Rapidan dam and power-house, at a cost of $500,000. It is located on the Blue Earth* *river, nine miles southwest of Mankato. The total capacity of the station is about 3,500 horsepower.*"[782] These were the sort of details about which Larry was asking the engineer, while Carney sweltered in the heat. ("Did they use the reaction-type turbines? How much power did the plant generate? What was the hydraulic head?")[783]

When they go to Orono, Larry rents "the best Phillips' Livery Stable had to offer."[784] There really was a G.G. Phillips' Livery Stable at 119-125 E. Walnut. Less accurate was the fictional fact that Carney's birthday was on a Wednesday in 1911.[785] Marion's birthday (June 24) fell on a Saturday that year.

As the house-party girls rummage in the attic, preparing for Carney's costume party, they learn about a Sibley family legend. They find a parasol which "belonged to Aunt Lily, who was stolen by the Indians during the Sioux Rebellion.... She saw her parents killed before her eyes. She hid in a cornfield but the Indians found her and held her captive for months. She came back and married Uncle George."[786] Again this is a piece of Everett family lore which has been transferred to the Willard family. Lillie Everett Curtis was the child of William Everett (Bill's grandfather) and his first wife. Lillie's mother, sisters, and brothers were killed in the Indian uprising of 1862. Lillie, aged nine, was held hostage for some time. She was finally rescued by the Army in Montana.

Grandmother Sibley was Anna Willard, wife of John A. In 1864, Anna was the first woman to head the Mankato Post Office. Her real maiden name was Sibley - no doubt the inspiration for the Willards' fictional surname.

Grandma Hunter (whose fictional maiden name was Laurenza Parke) was based on Marion's maternal grandmother, Abbey Baldwin Robbins. (Abbey's mother's name was Laurenza.) Abbey and her husband, George Robbins, of Chester, Vermont, followed their only daughter to Mankato in 1893, after she had married W.D. Willard. Both of Marion's grandmothers passed away in 1917 (Anne at age seventy-five, Abbey at age seventy-four).

Marion's granddaughter, Caroline King, has a sampler that has been passed down from mother to daughter five times. It begins with Laurenza Williams (m. Baldwin), to Abbey Baldwin (m. Robbins), to Louise Robbins (m. Willard), to Marion Willard (m. Everett), to Louise Everett (m. King), to Caroline King (m.

Nicholas). Each young girl embroidered her name and a verse on the sampler. It will be passed next to Caroline's daughter.

Herbert comments to Larry in *Heaven to Betsy* that it won't take his brother long to say good night to Carney. Larry responds, "It never does. But that isn't my fault." And Carney flashes a dimple.[787] Larry never does kiss her (though of course, they are apart for better than half of their seven-year courtship). "None of her beaus had ever kissed her."[788] Appropriately, Sam administers her first kiss - and Carney appears to feel a lot of physical attraction for Sam.

Bill Everett and Marion first met after she had graduated from Vassar. Bill spotted Marion in Waseca, Minnesota, where she had taken a teaching job. The first time Bill's fictional self, Sam Hutchinson, lays eyes on Carney, she is taking her grandmothers to the circus, wearing "a crisp pink linen dress."[789] The dress is significant, because the first time Bill Everett saw Marion, she was wearing pink. To reinforce the romantic pink association, Maud has Carney wear it again on the day Isobel maneuvers to visit the Hutchinson place. Sam says to Carney: "Don't spoil your pretty pink dress. I like pink. It's my favorite color."[790] (Marion really took her grandmothers to the circus at some point: "*Could you tell me a little more about the time you took your grandmothers to the circus?*" Maud asked Marion.[791])

Maud had invited Marion to choose a fictional name for her husband. "Sam Hutchinson" seemed to fit. (Hutchinson was the surname of a family of Marion's cousins.) Maud wrote to Marion: "*I would like to make Bill recognizably Bill, and you could help me a lot, if you would, by telling me when and where you met and giving a few incidents of your courtship.*"[792]

The Everett home was very much as described in *Carney's House Party*. However, the house was not located on Madison Lake, nor on any lake. It was in Waseca. A beautiful house built by Bill's father in the 1890s ... it no longer stands.

Sam has a little sister, Genevieve. Bill's little sister was named Constance, and as in *Carney's House Party*, she was substantially (eleven years) his junior. Marion and her friends would not have known Sam's "semi-invalid"[793] mother, since Antoinette Miller Everett had passed away in 1909.

Sam tells Carney: "You always look so clean ... as though you'd just come from the Spotless Town in the Sapolio ads."[794] It is apparently coincidental that Kathleen Hart used a similar analogy in a letter home in 1909. She was describing a town on the Azores Island of St. Michael's. *"The quaintest little town you ever saw. It must have been the original 'Spotless Town' of Sapolio fame, for all the houses were white, pink or brown cement."*[795]

Sam imagines Carney's first child: "He had decided that her oldest child was a boy -- and musical. Carney could almost see him. He had thick dark hair and a crooked smile."[796] (But of course, Carney's son wouldn't look like Larry - he'd be Sam's boy!) Later, in *Betsy's Wedding,* Maud gives Carney a firstborn girl. Marion's firstborn was a son. Perhaps Maud simply gave Carney a little Judy because of the sad memory of Marion's son Ted, who had been killed during the Second World War.

Fascinatingly, a letter courtship had begun between Marion's son Ted and Ruth's (Alice's) daughter Fallie. If Ted had not been killed, we might have had our first second-generation Crowd marriage.

The reader, of course, knows that Carney is in love with Sam long before she knows it herself. On page 144, Carney "knew instinctively" that Sam disliked Larry. But she only "suspected" Larry's dislike for Sam. And of course we know why she is annoyed by the thought that Sam might be falling for Isobel, even though she herself doesn't realize that she is jealous. Maud teases us with numerous clues. The smell of the roses Sam sends Carney permeates the house. "It was turning very warm, and the heat seemed to make the fragrance all the sweeter.... Carney kept inhaling deep intoxicating breaths."[797] The "dizzily sweet"[798] pervading scent, together with the "queer"[799] way Carney felt when Sam "encircled her shoulder with his big arm" are as close as the series gets to sensuousness. A Lovelace short story from 1925 contains a similar vein. When the heroine brushed against her beau's old army sweater, "a frightened delicious faintness ran down her body."[800]

Of course, this is hardly torrid; and we are not forgetting that the Betsy-Tacy books were written for children!

Coll. of Louise King

Marion and William Everett

This photograph was taken on their wedding day, August 27, 1919.

Coll. of Louise King

Bill Everett
(Sam Hutchinson)

"He was really remarkably good-looking. And not even very fat, she thought, marveling. In proper clothes, he was just stocky and strong." (CHP p. 90)

Coll. of Louise King

The Everett Home

"A wide driveway curved upward through a green tree-shaded lawn to a big white clapboard house. It was almost concealed by foliage, but they could see a tower and many porches." (CHP p. 56) The child in the foreground is Bill Everett.

Coll. of Louise King

Marion in her Grandmother's Dress

Grandma Hunter's wedding dress was a "dress of changeable green taffeta" worn with "a black lace shawl, and the cameo brooch and earrings." (CHP p. 77)

[731] *Carney's House Party*, p. 13.

[732] *Carney's House Party*, draft p. 17.

[733] *Carney's House Party*, p. 15.

[734] Ibid., p. 17.

[735] MHL to M. Everett, 7-29-48.

[736] *Carney's House Party*, p. 7.

[737] Ibid., p. 32.

[738] Ibid., p. 33.

[739] Ibid., p. 7.

[740] *Betsy and Joe*, p. 59.

[741] Ibid., p. 37.

[742] Ibid., p. 41.

[743] Ibid., p. 152.

[744] Ibid., p. 41.

[745] W.D. Willard memoirs, p. 24.

[746] High School Scrapbook, p. A'.

[747] *Carney's House Party*, p. 39.

[748] M. Everett to MHL, 7-29-48.

[749] *Carney's House Party*, p. 39.

[750] Ibid., p. 42.

[751] MHL to M. Everett, 7-29-48.

[752] *Carney's House Party*, p. 41.

[753] Ibid., pp. 41-42.

[754] MHL to J. Tessari, 8-11-73.

[755] MHL to M. Everett, 4-14-48.

[756] *Betsy Was a Junior*, p. 107.

[757] *Carney's House Party*, p. 117.

[758] Ibid.

[759] Ibid., p. 69.

[760] Ibid., p. 141.

[761] Ibid., p. 8.

[762] Ibid., p. 153.

[763] Ibid., p. 200.

[764] Ibid., p. 114.

[765] KPH letters, p. 21.

[766] *Carney's House Party*, p. 141.

[767] MHL to M. Everett, 4-14-48.

[768] *Betsy in Spite of Herself*, p. 47.

[769] Ibid., p. 262.

[770] *Betsy Was a Junior*, p. 50.

[771] *Betsy and Joe,* p. 39.

[772] *Carney's House Party*, p. 8.

[773] Ibid., pp. 83-84.

[774] Ibid., p. 119.

[775] MPH to MW, 2-7-11.

[776] MHL to L. Demp, 7-23-58.

[777] *Carney's House Party,* p. 139.

[778] *Mankato, The City with a Future* (Mankato: Commercial Club, 1912).

[779] *Carney's House Party,* p. 143.

[780] Ibid., p. 144.

[781] Ibid., p. 179.

[782] *Mankato, The City with a Future*.

[783] *Carney's House Party,* p. 179.

[784] Ibid., p. 178.

[785] Ibid., p. 159.

[786] Ibid., p. 76.

[787] *Heaven to Betsy*, p. 163.

[788] *Carney's House Party,* p. 197.

[789] Ibid., p. 45.

[790] Ibid., p. 59.

[791] MHL to M. Everett, 5-17-48.

[792] Ibid., 4-14-48.

[793] *Carney's House Party*, p. 92.

[794] Ibid., p. 88.

[795] KPH letters, p.18.

[796] *Carney's House Party,* p. 108.

[797] Ibid., p. 168.

[798] Ibid.

[799] Ibid., p. 169.

[800] M.H. Lovelace, "Love's Daily Dozen," *Delineator*, August 1925.

CHAPTER ELEVEN
On *Emily of Deep Valley*
May 1912 to May 1913

Emily Webster's story is, of course, even farther from "Betsy-Tacy-book" status than *Carney's House Party*, since the main characters are completely new to us. *Carney's House Party* is very Betsy-Tacyish (despite the fact that we're looking through Carney's eyes, rather than Betsy's), because Carney was a part of Betsy's Crowd, and her Deep Valley friends were all Betsy's friends, too. Most of Emily's friends (Annette, Don, Gladys, Nell, etc.) are strangers, though Hunter and Scid are the younger brothers of Crowd members. But the real Emily, Marguerite Marsh, was part of Maud's Crowd, at least to some extent. In other words, Marguerite was a closer friend to Maud than Emily was to Betsy.

Since Maud wanted to use Marguerite after, rather than during, the Betsy-Tacy high school books, she moved her counterpart, Emily, forward in time (to the class of 1912). Marguerite was actually almost two years older than Maud, graduating in 1909 with Carney, Pin, Al, etc.

Maud describes Emily as "a wistful, lonely figure."[801] The idea of Marguerite, living with her old grandfather on the other side of the slough, was probably an appealing one to romantic young Maud, and it was this appeal that led her, many years later, to tell Marguerite's story. Maud was pleased with the resulting book, *Emily of Deep Valley*. She commented: "*My publishers say it is the best one yet.*"[802] *Emily of Deep Valley* is an extremely well-crafted book.

Grandpa Webster is certainly John Quincy Adams Marsh. Born in Chesterfield, Vermont, John moved "West" (to Mankato), following his brother George, in 1854. John and George opened the first general store in Mankato. The two brothers also carried the mail between Mankato and St. Paul. For every twenty miles of the route, they earned one section of land. Both brothers thereby acquired substantial land holdings and sold their store in 1858. John was one of the original investors in the Creamery Packaging Manufacturing Company on Van Brunt Street in Mankato. He was elected county treasurer in 1855. On December 29, 1859, John married Sarah Hanna, a member of one of the first families to arrive in Mankato in 1853. Like Emily's grandmother, Sarah had taught the first Mankato school in the summer of 1853. She taught twenty-three students in a warehouse on Walnut Street.

Coll. of Minnesota Valley Regional Library

Marguerite Marsh
(Emily Webster)

Emily "was shy and quiet, although her blue eyes, set in a thicket of lashes under heavy brows, often glinted with fun." (EDV p. 4)

Mankato, Its First Fifty Years

John Q.A. Marsh
(Grandpa Webster)

Emily lived with her Grandpa, who had a "round mild face with arching heavy brows." (EDVp. 19)

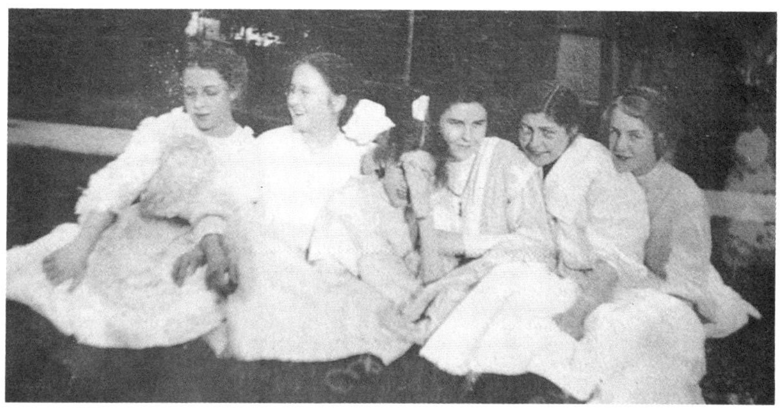

Duplicated in several collections

Marguerite with the Crowd

Proof of Marguerite's friendship with Maud's Crowd comes in the form of this 1907 photograph. In 1910, the girls included a stop at Marguerite's on their annual progressive dinner. Perhaps she served frog legs! From left: Ruth Williams (Alice), Marion Willard (Carney), Maud Hart (Betsy), Marguerite (Emily), Mil Oleson (Irma), and El Johnson (Winona II).

John and Sarah had two children, Charles and Mary. Mary died at the age of twenty. Charles, father of Marguerite, married a girl named Alice when both were twenty-three years old, in 1886. Their first child was born in July 1887. The little boy died. Three years later, on the 4th of July (appropriate for patriotic Emily), Marguerite Elizabeth was born.

The dates on Emily's family's tombstones are close to the actual years of birth and death for Marguerite's parents and grandparents. Emily's grandmother was Emily Clarke Webster, born 1835, died 1904. Sarah Hanna Marsh did die in 1904, but she was born in 1833. Fred Webster (1868 - 1896) was Emily's father. In actuality, Charles Marsh was born in 1863 and died after 1904. Charlotte Benton Webster (1873 - 1894) was Emily's mother. Marguerite's mother, Alice Marsh, was born in 1863. She may have been a teacher, but she was not from Binghamton, New York, as was Emily's mother. Alice was from Pennsylvania. She died when Marguerite was a baby. Grandpa (John Q.A.) Marsh was from New England, not Ohio like Grandpa Webster.[803] He died on the day after Christmas in 1915.

Emily of Deep Valley is naturally not as fact-based as the other series books, since Maud was not writing about her own life. Moreover, by the time this book was written, Marguerite had been dead for many years. Maud had no one to send long lists of questions to, as she had with her other books.

Annette, Emily's cousin, has no obvious counterpart. Annette's father was Emily's father's cousin. If John's brother, George Marsh, had had a granddaughter, she would have been to Marguerite what Annette was to Emily. It may be that Maud intentionally made the genealogical relationship seem vague because Annette was a fictional figure, with no counterpart in Marguerite's extended family.

Perhaps it is a coincidence that of the many sororities at the University of Minnesota, Annette joins the Epsilon Iotas, like Betsy. Perhaps it is a coincidence that Annette's trademark color is green, like Betsy's. Perhaps it is a coincidence that Annette was brunette, popular, and dressed by Miss Mix, like Betsy. Or perhaps Maud had the same sort of feelings about Marguerite that Annette had - liking her, but not including her in activities as a full member of the Crowd. Though not a "lemon," Marguerite may have been awkward to have around, the way Emily was. Maybe Maud disguised a part of herself as Annette because she felt a bit ashamed of the way she had treated Marguerite, as Betsy regrets the way Hazel Smith was excluded in *Betsy Was a Junior*.

Emily of Deep Valley gave Maud a chance to explore some feelings she never really had the opportunity to express in the Betsy books. She did so through Emily as well as through Annette. Some of Emily's pain was certainly Maud's, who felt as Emily did about leaving high school (and soon after, Mankato). The Hart family's move to Minneapolis must have been hard on her, feeling the way she did about home and high school.

We get our first taste of this plaintive sensibility in *Carney's House Party*, in which Carney feels strangely out of place when she returns from Vassar: "It was wonderful to be home, and yet Deep Valley was different in a melancholy way, because she was out of high school. The pattern of life she had lived there for eighteen years had been broken.... The boys still belonged to Deep Valley and Deep Valley to them, but Carney felt herself cut off."[804] Practical Carney was not likely to have felt this way. Not only was Carney unsentimental, but this was the end of her second year away from home, not her first. The pattern was broken long ago, and Carney would not have been still sighing, if she had ever sighed. It was Maud who had felt displaced, and she took her first opportunity of expressing these powerful memories through the arriving-home character Carney.

Emily thinks that high school is "closed like the covers of a book that could never be read again no matter how much one might wish to do so."[805] (If she'd been born fifty years later, she could simply have opened a Betsy-Tacy high school book!) "She had known this strange feeling that something was ending which you had never really expected to end."[806] When Emily returns to visit the high school in the fall, she finds "the familiar smell of chalk dust and healthy perspiration. The stairs were crowded, but the students seemed younger than they had seemed last year. They seemed to belong to a different world."[807]

During her own last year of high school, Maud may have built herself up for a fall. "About everything she did, she kept thinking whether or not she would do it again.... Betsy kept thinking how different everything would be next year. A pattern was breaking, never to be re-established."[808] After the excitement of graduation subsided, Maud must have felt the wrench very unpleasantly. Post-graduation is anticlimactic for everyone, but Maud particularly disliked change. "Betsy had clung to every phase of childhood as it passed. She always wanted to keep life from going forward too fast. ... You grow older in spite of yourself, Betsy thought resentfully."[809]

After graduation, Emily "worked on her High School Memory Book. She lingered over every page - the program of Philomathian rhetoricals, the announcements of debates, the place cards of parties with the girls."[810] This is a description of Maud's High School Scrapbook. Maud noted on the first page of her Scrapbook that it had been "*Compiled after graduating from High School. Being an incomplete record of the 'larks' enjoyed in that worthy institution.*" One can easily picture Maud poring over her high school memorabilia, just as Emily did. Of course, Maud (unlike Emily) had things to look forward to. But it would have been easy for Maud to dwell on the past, since she was convalescing from appendicitis the summer after high school (rather than during her first year at the U, as reported in *Betsy and the Great World*). And her subsequent unhappiness at the U that fall would not have helped to ease the transition.

We know that Betsy experienced negative emotions as powerfully as happier ones. In *Heaven to Betsy*, she feels (to put it mildly) "wretchedly, desperately, nightmarishly" homesick.[811] Almost a year after this difficult visit to the Taggarts', Betsy had a "sudden, smothering" memory of her homesickness.[812] Much later, in *Betsy and Joe*, we are told that she had suffered so much homesickness at the Taggarts', that "for months the mere memory of it had filled her with desolation."[813] Losing Tony to Bonnie was an even more difficult experience. Betsy felt "completely wretched" and "sunk into a well of grief."[814] Thinking of Bonnie and Tony "made the winter twilight deepen, made her feel homesick on the very steps of home."[815] (Interesting that Maud chooses homesickness to compare to the painful loss of Tony!) These intense feelings are not just adolescent pangs. Betsy feels similarly wretched, again with homesickness, in *Betsy and the Great World*. "A hateful sensation which Betsy had almost forgotten began to creep back into her body. It was that feeling of forlornness, of not belonging."[816] In Munich, she felt "desolate."[817]

These are rather weighty psychological states for Betsy. The only other character who struggles with depression is Emily. Maud uses the same simile to describe their gloom. In *Heaven to Betsy*, depression invades Betsy's room "like a sudden fog."[818] Meanwhile, in *Emily of Deep Valley*, "depression settled down upon her, and although she tried to brush it away it thickened like a fog." Emily says: "A mood like this has to be fought. It's like an enemy with a gun."[819] Betsy fights her misery over Tony in *Heaven to Betsy* by adhering to her New Year's resolutions "as though they were laws laid down,"[820] and she fights her unhappiness in Munich by adhering to her schedule of activities "rigidly."[821] In *Betsy and Joe*, she feels "blue" and "cross" for months after breaking up with Joe, and "sadness weighed Betsy down."[822] But again she fights her depression: "She was surprised at how much it helped unhappiness not to give in to it."[823] These feelings and the way Betsy (and Emily) contended with them may give us some insight into the mind of their creator.

This is not to say the feelings didn't also truly belong to Marguerite - it is precisely because they were fitting feelings that Maud was able to express herself through Emily. Maud seems to have gotten this out of her system in *Emily of Deep Valley*, for she never particularly attributes these troubles to Betsy herself. Of course, the reader never actually gets a look at Betsy in the first year after high school. Maud wrote of this period in her life, "*I should have been happy but much of the time during those years I was not happy at all. I lost for a time my usual cheerfulness, friendliness, and zest for life. Of my characteristic traits, I retained only my stubbornness.*"[824] And of the short stories Maud wrote during this difficult time, she later commented, "*It looks as though the author resented moving away from a small town and also growing up.*"[825]

The road Emily followed home across the slough was West Front Street, later called "Park Lane," and finally "Riverfront Drive." "The Deep Valley slough (pronounced 'sloo') was the marshy inlet of a river."[826] The Mankato slough was once fairly extensive, covering the area on which West High School was built. Randall's Food, city garages, and a Burger King restaurant were also built on slough land. "*Centuries ago both the Le Sueur and Blue Earth Rivers converged on the Minnesota River at Mankato, at different but nearby locations. The fickle Le Sueur River, however, subsequently changed its course, selecting to join the Blue Earth River miles southwest of Mankato, the two streams then combining in the Minnesota. Vestiges of the Le Sueur River stream nevertheless continue to migrate through urban Mankato, as if by habit or gravity.*"[827]

Though patches of the marshy slough remain, there are no marigolds or thunderpumps in the area where Emily's house once stood. John Q.A. Marsh built his home at 115 West Front, on the southwest side of the street. This location was later occupied by the beautiful Schmidt house, which was demolished to make way for the YMCA (the address of which is 1401 S. Riverfront Drive).

Emily enjoyed their big lawn. "From the front gate at the north and the slough on the east it rose in a tree-lined slope."[828] The front gate was on the north and the slough on the east. Emily's bedroom looked east, "over the slough, which extended back into the sheltered valley that the town called Little Syria. From her windows she could see the humble rooftops of the Syrians. She could see the sun rise over the marsh and the pond."[829] John Marsh's house faced north, so Marguerite's room must have been at the back of the house on the east side. The house was surrounded with a white picket fence.

Grandpa Cyrus Webster had served with the First Minnesota at Gettysburg.[830] In fact, John Marsh was not a Civil War veteran. Maud appears to have based Grandpa Webster's experiences on those of Captain Clark Keysor (fictionally called Cap' Klein). Judge Hodges, meanwhile, was probably based on General J.H. Baker. "Judge Hodges used to tell them about Nashville, and old Cap' Klein about fighting the Sioux."[831]

Captain Clark Keysor, from New York state, arrived in Mankato with his wife, Amy, in 1858. In August 1862, he enlisted in the Ninth Minnesota Volunteers. He was made a captain in 1865. He saw active duty in the Civil War but was not with the First Minnesota at Gettysburg.

Judge Hodges was a veteran of the Fifth Minnesota. General

Baker had actually been in the Tenth Minnesota Volunteers and, like Cap' Keysor, had served under General Sibley (no relation to Carney/Marney) in suppressing the Sioux in 1862. (General Baker was the father of Maud's friend Jim, on whom she based the character E. Lloyd Harrington.) *"Old Cap Keysor and General Baker used to visit the various grades on Decoration Day to tell us about the Civil War."*[832] In *Emily of Deep Valley*, the town's "old soldiers always visited the schools on Decoration Day morning."[833]

Bick Kenney's brother led the Decoration Day parade in 1901, the year he returned from the Spanish American War. *"Slim in his two-toned blue, he rode the Kenney's frisky black colt. We children nearly burst with pride as he came down Front Street on dancing Mae with the pipe and drum corps behind."*[834]

Decoration Day is a unique opening setting for a Deep Valley book. Graduation usually occurs at the end of the story, rather than at the beginning. Emily "stopped at the shop of Windmiller, the florist, to order flowers for herself for [graduation]."[835] Windmiller's Florist Shop also delivered a long box of flowers for Julia in *Betsy and Joe*.[836] Max and Pauline Windmiller operated a florist shop at 101 Rhine in Mankato. The Windmillers also sold fresh flowers in Lamm's Drug Store on Front Street.

The Class Day play was *One Night Only* when Emily graduated in 1912. And the class play was really *One Night Only*, given on June 1, when Marguerite graduated in 1909. The cast, however, was very different from the one described in *Emily of Deep Valley*.

The cast actually consisted of members of Maud's Crowd. Earl King (the fictional Squirrelly) played the lead. Jim Baker (the fictional E. Lloyd Harrington) also had a role. In *Emily of Deep Valley*, we hear about "Jim Baxter's difficulties with the monocle he wore as Lord Mulberry - or Hunter on his knees to Nell Hennesy, his wife - or Scid's exaggerated courtship of the maid, Annette."[837] The characters from *One Night Only* were taken from the program for the play, which Maud had pasted in her Scrapbook. In reality, Lord Mulberry was played by George Pond (N/C), and the man and wife were Clayton Roblee (N/C) and Birdie Tompkins (N/C). The maid was played by Hazel Schoelkopf, a debater and friend of Maud. The real sister of the character Dennie, Nellie Ford, also had a part. In fact, *Emily of Deep Valley*'s "Nell" was originally to be cast as a Farisy - Dennie's sister - rather than a Hennesy.[838] In later years, Nellie Ford assisted Maud in verifying Mankato facts for use in the Betsy-Tacy books.

The name "Scid" was fitting for Cab's younger brother. Scid was really the nickname of Clayton Burmeister. And it was Clayton whose father died at the beginning of Maud's senior year (as Cab's father died just after junior year). Clayton was called "Scid" or "Scidover." In *Emily of Deep Valley*, Maud explains the origin of the nickname this way: "He was ... called Scid because he had said in class one day that Columbus 'scidovered' America."[839]

"Emily was on the star debating team which had won the Southern Minnesota Championship for two years running."[840] On the 1908 Girl's (sic) Debating Club program in Maud's Scrapbook, Marguerite Marsh is listed as arguing negative, "*That the United States senate should be elected by direct vote of the people.*"[841] The program also reveals that Marguerite was vice-president of the Debating Club. Jerry Sibley calls her fictional self a "star debater."[842] In the fall of 1908, three students were chosen to represent Mankato High School in debating contests with other schools. They were James Baker (Lloyd Harrington), Marguerite Marsh, and George Pass (N/C).

In both *Betsy Was a Junior* and *Betsy and Joe,* we are told that Hazel Smith was "the best girl debater in the state." Is it possible that Emily and Hazel were both based on Marguerite Marsh? Possibly - particularly considering that both Emily and Hazel are kept on the periphery, looking in at the Crowd from the outside. But Hazel Schoelkopf, also of the class of 1909, has too much in common with Hazel Smith to be dismissed as a real-life inspiration for the character. The "Hazel S." similarity is obvious. And Hazel Schoelkopf was nearly as prominent a debater as Marguerite. Hazel Schoelkopf was president of the Girls' Debating Club in 1908. Perhaps to the extent that Emily was a debater, she was a composite of Marguerite Marsh and Hazel Schoelkopf.

At Emily's 1912 commencement, "The graduates were seated on the stage against a resplendent back-drop of red, white and blue bunting. Suspended above them were the numerals 1912."[843] This sounds just like the commencement of the class of 1909. "*The graduating class was seated on the stage completely surrounded with stars*

Coll. of Gail Palmer

Windmiller's

Emily "approached Mrs. Windmiller with friendly dignity. 'Will you send me a dozen pink roses Friday afternoon? They're for my graduation.'" (EDV p. 33)

Coll. of Gail Palmer

Brett's Department Store
(Lion Department Store)

This is the ladies' apparel section where Emily "found a rose-colored wool trimmed with brown velvet, buttoned up one side with a long row of brown velvet buttons. (Side fastenings and up and down rows of buttons were the newest thing.)" (EDV p. 118)

Cornell College

Myron Wilcox
(Jed Wakeman)

Jed had "friendly observant brown eyes." (EDV p. 98)

1913 Otaknam

Marguerite
(Emily)

With her hair up, Emily had a "winning air of maturity." (EDV p. 102)

Mankato, Its First Fifty Years

Cap' Keysor

"There were ... old Cap' Klein's chin whiskers." (EDV p. 47)

Mankato, Its First Fifty Years

General Baker
(Judge Hodges)

Judge Hodges was "tall, gaunt, bearded." Judge Baker was the father of Maud's friend Jim.

and stripes as a background and canopy, while above suspended was the class year in green and red, the senior colors."[844] (Note: Eleanor Johnson {Winona II} wrote the words to the 1909 class song.)

Don Walker spoke on "The Need of an Artistic Life in America." Don "decried America's dearth of art galleries, museums and symphony orchestras."[845] There was just such an oration given at the commencement of Marguerite's class on June 4, 1909. It was presented by a girl named Elna Malzahn. The title was "The Need of an Artistic Environment in America." The speaker drew comparisons between the Old World and America, pointing out the lack of art galleries and the importance of developing an artistic climate in this country.

In any case, Don's prototype could not have given this oration, for he was not a Minnesotan, much less a Mankatoan. And he wasn't born for another twenty years. According to Merian Kirchner, the inspiration for Don came from a classmate of her own in Garden City, New York.

There was no oration similar to Emily's on Hull House, nor did Marguerite Marsh present an oration on any subject.

Before her friends go off to college, Emily gives a party for Annette. "She was too sensitive about her home to entertain often. But the giddiness got into her blood."[846] This may have been the Oktw Delta giddiness, for among the Oktw Delta souvenirs in Maud's Scrapbook is a place card from a party given by Marguerite Marsh for the girls in the Crowd. It shows a man peering through a long telescope at the moon. Marguerite, presumably, wrote: "*To inspire a parody on 'The Maiden's Fancy.*'"[847]

As a first attempt to muster her wits, Emily marches across the slough to buy a new hat to accommodate her new hair style. (In "Emma Middleton Cuts Cross Country," the short story mentioned in *Betsy and the Great World*, the first step in the heroine's transformation is also the purchase of a new hat!) Emily stops to cool off with a soda at Roxey's drug store on page 102, where she runs into Cab. Perhaps Maud was remembering Doxey's drug store at 701 S. Front. Certainly this wasn't far from Marguerite's home. Jab Lloyd's family did not have a furniture store next to Roxey's, or anywhere else, for that matter. In later years, however, Lloyd's Lumber (founded by Jab and headed by his son Bob) was built in this area of town.

The friendship between Emily and Cab is a literary device, a bridge between Emily's Deep Valley and Betsy's. Because Cab takes Emily out, we learn that E. Lloyd Harrington had gone to the U but had dropped out. (Jim Baker did not drop out - he went on to Columbia before pursuing a distinguished career as a foreign correspondent.) Winona had finished Teachers' College. (Eleanor Johnson had finished at the Normal and was teaching in Ely, Minnesota, in 1912.) Through Emily's eyes, we are brought up to date on the characters who most interest us.

The first reference to Betsy-Tacy appears when we learn that "The Ray family had moved away; Mr. Ray's shoe store was someone else's now, but people still called it Ray's."[848] Mankato shoppers probably did call Wood & Baker's store "Hart's" for some years!

When Emily sees our class-of-1910 friends at the high school Christmas party, we find ourselves looking at the Crowd from the outside, for once. Emily "was interested to see Fred's pretty blond sister who went to school in Milwaukee, and Tacy Kelly who used to sing at rhetoricals, and Betsy Ray - especially Betsy, because she had written short stories which had been published. She was practically an author."[849] This odd detachment gives one a rather lonely feeling, but at least we're getting an update on the Crowd.

Emily visits the Sibleys to enlist Bobby in the Boys' Club, and we discover that Sam has finally saved enough to buy Carney an engagement ring. Carney "was a pretty fresh-faced girl who wore an enormous diamond on her engagement finger - the biggest diamond, Emily thought, that she had ever seen."[850] (Marion Willard Everett's first diamond solitaire from Bill was pretty but modest. After the birth of her first son, named after her husband's father, her father-in-law presented her with an enormous diamond - probably the one Maud had in mind when she described Carney's.)

At Alice's party, Emily hears Betsy complain that Tib is "wasted" in Milwaukee while Betsy goes through the U with her hair in a bun. Midge was at the Milwaukee Art Institute in 1912, so in fact Maud probably did wear her hair in a bun quite a bit!

Betsy, trying to help Emily, tells about the challenges in her own life over the last year. The reader already knows that Betsy fell behind a year in college: "I had to stop in the middle of my freshman year," she said in *Carney's House Party.* Joe, meanwhile, has gone off to Harvard.[851]

"Miss Fowler lived in a small apartment in a big private house on Broad Street."[852] Actually, Miss Fischer, the English teacher, lived in a big private house at 615 S. Second Street. Miss Fischer was not in Mankato long enough to have assisted Marguerite in working for the establishment of classes in English for foreign-speakers, as her counterpart assisted Emily. However, W.D. Willard might conceivably have been involved, as Mr. Sibley was. W.D. Willard was on the school board from 1914 to 1927. He no doubt voted "aye" when the first night school was authorized in February 1916.

Jed Wakeman was loosely based on Marguerite's husband, Myron Wilcox. He was not a Southerner but was from Iowa (which is slightly south of Minnesota!). Myron had been born in the south of China, where his parents were Methodist missionaries. As a little boy, he spoke only Chinese. In 1897, when he was five years old, Myron was sent to America with his older brothers and sisters for the sake of their education. He studied at Cornell Academy and received his B.S. from Cornell College (of Iowa) in 1914. Myron taught high school for a few years (but not in Mankato), then undertook graduate studies at the University of Iowa in 1917. Myron was a First Lieutenant in the 41st Infantry, Statistics Branch. After the war, he went to Columbia University in New York City, where he met Marguerite in 1922. For Marguerite finally did have the opportunity to attend college!

Jed Wakeman is headed for a master's in sociology at Tulane at the end of *Emily of Deep Valley.* Myron actually received his master's and later his Ph.D. (in educational psychology) from the University of Iowa in Iowa City. There is reason to believe that Maud was acquainted with Myron (see Chapter 15), so perhaps his personality is truly reflected in Jed, as Marguerite's was in Emily.

Maud had a special feeling for *Emily of Deep Valley. "In many ways, that book told a true story."*[853]

[801] *Emily of Deep Valley*, p. 92.
[802] MHL to T. Edwards, 4-12-50.
[803] *Emily of Deep Valley*, p. 26.
[804] *Carney's House Party*, p. 43.
[805] *Emily of Deep Valley*, p. 4.
[806] Ibid., p. 58.
[807] Ibid., p. 83.
[808] *Betsy and Joe*, p. 73.
[809] Ibid., p. 4.
[810] *Emily of Deep Valley*, p. 94.
[811] *Heaven to Betsy*, p. 3.
[812] Ibid., p. 266.
[813] *Betsy and Joe*, p. 205.
[814] *Heaven to Betsy*, p. 194.
[815] Ibid., p. 232.
[816] *Betsy and the Great World*, p. 101.
[817] Ibid., p. 138.
[818] *Heaven to Betsy*, p. 59.
[819] *Emily of Deep Valley*, pp. 89-90.
[820] *Heaven to Betsy*, p. 206.
[821] *Betsy and the Great World*, p. 136.
[822] *Betsy and Joe*, p. 189.
[823] Ibid., p. 161.
[824] U/Mpls. file, sec. IV, p. 2.
[825] U/Mpls. file, "The Period," p. 4.
[826] *Emily of Deep Valley*, p. 14.
[827] Ken Berg, *Mankato Free Press*, 7-10-90.
[828] *Emily of Deep Valley*, p. 64.
[829] Ibid., p. 15.
[830] Ibid., p. 19.
[831] Ibid., p. 41.
[832] *Mankato Free Press,* 4-10-52.
[833] *Emily of Deep Valley*, p. 40.
[834] LWW, p. 34.
[835] *Emily of Deep Valley*, p. 33.
[836] *Betsy and Joe*, p. 239.
[837] *Emily of Deep Valley*, p. 37.
[838] *Emily of Deep Valley*, draft p. 14.
[839] *Emily of Deep Valley*, p. 6.

[840] Ibid., p. 2.

[841] High School Scrapbook, p. D'.

[842] *Emily of Deep Valley*, p. 97.

[843] Ibid., p. 59.

[844] *Mankato Free Press*, 6-5-09.

[845] *Emily of Deep Valley*, p. 60.

[846] Ibid., p. 78.

[847] High School Scrapbook, p. I.

[848] *Emily of Deep Valley*, p. 44.

[849] Ibid., p. 152.

[850] Ibid., p. 178.

[851] Ibid., p. 182.

[852] Ibid., p. 115.

[853] MHL to J. Tessari, 8-11-73.

CHAPTER TWELVE
On *Betsy and the Great World*
January 1914 to August 1914

When the curtain rises on *Betsy and the Great World*, an unsuspecting reader finds herself far from cozy Deep Valley. Here is the wintry gangplank of a ship in Boston Harbor. We soon find that Betsy is not only far from home, but that home is no longer Deep Valley; the Rays have moved to Minneapolis.

This sudden loss of familiarity is more abrupt than the similar breach occurring between *Downtown* and *Heaven to Betsy*. We knew that Betsy would be going away to college, but we had no hint that the family would be leaving Deep Valley. *Carney's House Party* and *Emily of Deep Valley* do contribute some cushioning updates on Betsy and the Rays. But because these two satellite books are not part of the body of the Betsy-Tacy books proper, this effect, though salutary, is negligible - particularly since copies of *Carney* and *Emily* have been virtually unavailable for many years. In *Heaven to Betsy*, we are comforted by the fact that Betsy is as conscious of the change in herself as we are; and the move to High Street takes her as much by surprise as it does us. But in *Betsy and the Great World*, Betsy doesn't seem at all surprised to find herself uprooted from the only town she ever called home, nor to find that she is so hopelessly old! (As twenty-one seems on a first reading at age twelve or so.)

Yet the changes which took place in the Hart family between 1910 and 1914 were not made effortlessly. As discussed in Chapter 11, change was never pleasant for Betsy. (She didn't entirely accept the new house on High Street until the very end of *Heaven to Betsy*, when she finally realized that she was through with the Hill Street cottage "except in her memories.")[854] We know that Betsy "always liked things to go on as they had gone before."[855] Of course, Maud knew that things <u>don't</u> go on forever, as evidenced by the quotation she chose for the frontispiece of *Heaven to Betsy*: "*All things must change, to something new, to something strange.*" The time of transition itself, however, was still especially painful.

Passing over major or distressing change in the Betsy-Tacy books is something of a *modus operandi* for Maud. Given the fact that she chose this method in 1945 for *Heaven to Betsy*, it should not be surprising here. The early throes of adolescence (an awkward time) and Midge's move to Milwaukee (a painful time) were skipped over, just as were the uneasy months after graduation (an unhappy time). Maud packages the skipped interval in a flashback at the beginning of *Betsy and the Great World*, prefaced with: "Why should she be in the bowels of a ship ploughing through sullen, turbulent waters, going to a foreign continent alone? Why? Why? She turned her thoughts backward and tried to pull all the reasons together."[856]

In Maud's own words: "*I didn't adjust to college very well. I was just recovering from an appendix operation. My older sister, Kathleen, had joined a sorority before she left for Germany (in spite of what I said in Betsy Was a Junior). As her sister, I was taken in to Gamma Phi at once and went to live in the house, but when I went home for Thanksgiving my family saw that I wasn't well and they kept me at home until after Christmas when I went to California, and that was a very happy experience.*"[857]

In *Betsy and the Great World*, Maud reported that appendicitis "interrupted" Betsy's freshman year. In fact, Maud underwent an appendectomy in Mankato on Wednesday morning, June 8, 1910 (just five days after her graduation from high school), and returned home on June 17.

Maud must have felt physically recovered in time for college in the autumn, but as she said, she was not entirely well. (A portion of her university malaise was certainly homesickness.) Maud officially withdrew from the university on November 22, 1910, two days before Thanksgiving. She was home little more than a month before departing for California, and by the time she returned to Minnesota, her family had left Mankato permanently.

The Rays' removal from Deep Valley is obviously the most consequential of the changes which occurred in the interval between *Betsy and Joe* and *Betsy and the Great World*. Maud explained that her father "*was elected Treasurer of Blue Earth County in 1904, and retained this position until the end of 1911. In 1911 we moved to Minneapolis.*"[858] (Maud meant the end of 1910.)

Mankato newspapers supported Tom Hart's campaign for re-election to the office of county treasurer. On September 29, 1910, the *Mankato Post* stated: "*Mr. Hart was nominated again for county treasurer by the largest majority he ever received which would indicate that the taxpayers of the county appreciate the way he has conducted the office. Two years ago in the general election, Mr. Hart was elected by the largest vote of any man on the ticket; his majority over A.G. Johnson was 649 votes. The farmers especially seem to like Mr. Hart. Every farmer in the county now gets through the mail a tax statement and he can buy a post office order of his mail carrier for a few cents and send it in and pay his land tax without leaving the farm. This is not done in any other county in the state."*

The *Mankato Free Press* printed the following endorsement on November 5, 1910: "*The treasurer of Blue Earth county certainly has something to do. The total receipts of the treasurer's office is something over five hundred thousand dollars a year, and the handling of this vast sum requires expert bookkeeping and the best of business experience, and we do not believe that the office of county treasurer was ever run in a more satisfactory manner than it has been during the last six years. Tom Hart has certainly made good.*"

Unfortunately for Tom, 1910 was a good year for the Democrats, and old A.G. Johnson had his revenge. The Republicans really took a beating on the county ballot. Although Tom received more votes than Johnson in twenty of the thirty-one towns in the county, he lost overall. (He lost in Mankato, 50 to 157 votes.) The countywide results were 2,669 to 2,853, so Tom lost by only 184 votes on November 8, 1910.

It has been suggested that there were bad feelings in the air after Tom lost the election. This seems improbable. By all accounts, Tom wasn't the sour-grapes type. It's more likely that he was simply at loose ends. The shoe store had long since been sold. Tom was interested in returning to the shoe market but on the wholesale end. If he were to be on the road a good deal, the family would be more conveniently based in Minneapolis. Kathleen, meanwhile, was back from Europe and perhaps already had her foot in the door at the MacPhail School of Music, where she became a teacher. She, no doubt, favored a family move to Minneapolis. Maud planned to return to the university for a second crack at freshman year, so she must have voted for the move. And Helen hadn't yet started high school, so it was good timing for her, too.

The *Mankato Free Press* had this to say about the Harts' departure: "*Mr. Hart has been a resident of Mankato for twenty-eight years and Mrs. Hart for a longer period. They are highly respected and have many friends who will regret their going away. Mr. and Mrs. Hart did not want to move, but the fact that their daughter Maud is attending the university and Miss Kathleen is interested in matters musical in Minneapolis, and the further fact that Mr. Hart is on the road for Foote-Schultze & Co. determined the question of their removal.*"[859]

It must have been difficult for Maud, being away in California when her family said good-bye to Mankato on March 29, 1911. Maud convalesced in California from January to June, 1911. She left Mankato for San Diego on the night of January 2, 1911, traveling by train with a friend from Stillwater, Minnesota.

Maud's trip to California took place just as described in *Betsy and the Great World*, though she did not go out immediately following her grandfather's death in 1908. Uncle Frank (Uncle Keith) was living in California at this time, on a ranch at Hillsdale. "An uncle who grew grapes near San Diego had given her a typewriter, and she had sold her first story."[860] Maud told a fan that in 1911, her uncle "*was ranching, not far from San Diego, and came to Grandma's often, and was banging the piano and making me sing and (for he was a writer as well as an actor) helping me with my writing, brought me his typewriter, etc. I sold my first story there.*"[861]

In another letter, Maud relates: "*Uncle Frank Palmer, who lived then at El Cajon, took a great interest in my constant writing of stories and their consistent rejection by the magazines. He suggested that perhaps they failed to sell because they were hand-written. He loaned me his old Oliver typewriter ... He tried to give it to me, but I refused the gift because I knew he liked to write stories, too. On this, I pecked out 'Number Eight' and sent it to the Los Angeles Times Sunday Magazine. My visit was just ending and soon Grandma and I took the train to Los Angeles.... A newsboy came through our car and I bought a copy of the Times. I scrambled through the magazine section and there was 'Number Eight'! ... The moment I saw that story in print was one of the happiest of my very happy life.*"[862]

Maud tells this story in almost exactly the same words on page 119 of *Carney's House Party*, although "Number Eight" is not mentioned by name either there or in *Betsy and the Great World*. The story, for which Maud was paid $10, appeared in a magazine-style Sunday supplement to the *Los Angeles Times* on June 4, 1911.

Over the next several months, two more of her short stories, "A Brave Coward" and "The Mayflower Lady," were published in the *Los Angeles Times*.

Maud's train journey back to Minnesota must have been made festive by the fact that her first story had been published on the last day of her California visit - and she was no doubt still riding high when she arrived in Minneapolis.

The Hart family lived for less than a year at 2731 Fremont Avenue South in Minneapolis before purchasing 905 West 25th Street, which was the fictional 909 Hazel Street. The Harts lived at 905 until 1934.

Like Betsy, Maud joined her sister's sorority, Gamma Phi Beta. Maud joined Gamma Phi Beta as a freshman in 1910, rather than in sophomore year, as reported on page 16 of *Betsy and the Great World*. Pledge Day was not until the second Saturday in April, but sisters and daughters of members were permitted to pledge during the first week of the term. Maud joined Gamma Phi upon her arrival at the U and lived at the sorority house that fall (1910).

Despite the fact that Maud joined the sorority, she obviously had negative feelings about Greek organizations. Betsy "joined a sorority although she had never liked them. It wasn't a good thing to do."[863] Maud's disapproval is expressed more emphatically in *Betsy Was a Junior*. Sororities "weren't at all what she had thought them to be. Julia's experience made them seem shallow, and the ease with which Julia had abandoned the idea of joining one had been an eye-opener, too. Sisterhoods! That, thought Betsy, was the bunk. You couldn't make sisterhoods with rules and elections. If they meant anything, they had to grow naturally."[864]

The friendships Maud found at the U couldn't compensate for the loss of the girls in the Crowd. So it must have been a great consolation that the Kenneys (like the fictional Kellys) moved to Minneapolis in 1911. Maud must have afforded comfort to Bick, too, when her sister, Nora Kenney, died of cardiac ailments in 1911. Perhaps the family had known for years that Nora was not strong, but it must have been hard to bear when she died a few days before Thanksgiving at age twenty-five.

The Kenneys lived for a year at 3145 Clinton Avenue South when they first moved to Minneapolis. The family appears in the

Gamma Phi Beta Sorority

Maud Among the Gamma Phis

Maud followed in her sister Kathleen's footsteps and joined the Gamma Phi Beta sorority at the University of Minnesota. She is at the top left of the photo above. Connie Davis (Bonnie) was also a Gamma Phi. She is at the right side, in the second row from the bottom (with a pin on her bodice). Betsy "made a few close friends in the group, but not many." (GW p. 16)

Gamma Phi House

The Gamma Phi Beta house still stands at 311 10th Avenue SE in Minneapolis and is visible from Interstate 35W.

MHL Archive

Albertine Austin

Maud's freshman year ended when she left the university in the late autumn of 1910. At the end of December, Maud left for a long visit with her Grandma Austin in California.

MHL Archive

Maud and Russell

After her return from California, Maud became engaged to a young man from the staff of the *Minnesota Daily* named Russell McCord. Fictionally, he may be the "tall well-dressed young man named Bob Barhydt." (GW p. 15)

MHL Archive

Maud and Bick

This photo was taken on a "Betsy-Tacy" picnic along the Mississippi.

MHL Archive

Midge, Bick, and Maud.

The immortal trio posed for this photo in Minneapolis about 1916.

Minneapolis city directory in 1912, listed at 2618 Third Avenue South. (They lived there until 1915, then moved to 2640 Colfax Avenue South, where they remained until after Patrick's death in 1920. They subsequently lived for one year at 4417 Xerxes. By then marriages had begun to scatter the flock.) The Kenneys had sold their house on Center Street in Mankato on January 6, 1916.

Maud returned to the University of Minnesota in the fall of 1911 and completed that academic year. She still belonged to Gamma Phi Beta (though she lived at home) and worked on the college paper, the *Minnesota Daily,* as Society Editor/Woman's Editor. The *Daily* office was in the basement of Folwell Hall.

Well-dressed frat boy Bob Barhydt takes notice of Betsy once she joins a sorority. There was no Bob on the *Daily* staff in Maud's time. But there was a "double-B" name: Bill Brewster.

Of Bob Barhydt, Merian Lovelace Kirchner remarks: "*She got that rather odd name from a couple - John and Babbie Barhydt - who ran a wonderful inn in the Berkshires where we went for several family vacations. Bert and I went there on our honeymoon, too, and in a couple of other summers.*"[865]

Though Bill Brewster escorted Maud to the Junior Ball on February 14, 1912, he was not her sweetheart. The young man to whom Maud became engaged (several times) during this period was Russell McCord. He, too, was on the *Daily* staff. Maud took him away from one Donna McKinstry. "*Although my fiance and I were always getting engaged, we never got married. He left the University where we had met and went to work in another city. He wrote regularly, though, spent large sums on long distance phone calls and remembered with flowers or a book every monthly anniversary of the night on which we had become engaged. This was through the last engagement which I finally broke as I had the others with a sort of heart-sick relief. It should have occurred to me, and perhaps at last it did, that we were always happier apart than we were together. Not that we quarreled, but he had put me on a pedestal and it was a strain to stay there. We never, as a matter of fact, got to know each other. I have no idea what he was really like, and he certainly knew nothing whatever about me. I was charmed by his beautiful eyes and a certain arrogant lift of his lip. I played the Victorian girl, delicate, ailing, modest but full of high flown sentiments. My long sleeved chiffon blouses had lace ruffles at the wrists and I remember that he loved my white hands. It would have astounded him to see me, feet wound firmly around the legs of a walnut desk chair, pounding with inky fingers at my Oliver.*"[866]

After her trip to California (with Tom, Stella, and Helen) in 1915, Maud (again) broke her engagement with Russell McCord and left Minneapolis to spend six months in New York City with Kathleen. They stayed for a time in a boarding house at 64 W. 96th Street. Maud took a short story class with Tom Uzzell and was told that she showed the least promise of all the students in the class. She was advised to give up writing. Disgusted (but not dissuaded), Maud returned to Minneapolis in the early summer of 1916. Before beginning work with Mrs. Wakefield in the spring of 1917, she spent several months in Seattle.

The Harts liked Russell, but were relieved at the final break-up, since they didn't think he and Maud were congenial. He was certainly devoted. He wrote to Maud four and five times a week while she was in Europe. "*There was a bond between us which I do not wish to belittle, nor the tears and grief, but although later he was back in the picture, in Minneapolis and even in uniform, his fascination had vanished, for by then I had met my true love.*"[867]

The ice cream parlor at the U was called the "Elm Tree," rather than the fictional "Oak Tree." Annette sums up the Oak Tree in *Emily of Deep Valley*: "It's the Heinz's of the university."[868]

The yearbook for 1912 does not seem to show Maud "riverbanking" (that is, strolling along the banks of the Mississippi). But there are numerous unlabeled candid shots in which it is difficult to identify faces. Perhaps she is among the pictured riverbankers. Looking through an old college yearbook, Maud noted: "*Winter snapshots of campus show big hats, furs and muffs, long coats and skirts. We look fifty.*"[869]

Betsy "wrote stories which were accepted by the college magazine. One was better than the others. It was really good and Betsy didn't quite know why, for it was just a simple story laid in her Uncle Keith's vineyard. But the famous professor, Dr. Maria Sanford, had praised it. She had written Betsy a letter about it."[870]

This is exactly what happened in May 1912. "Her Story" by Maud Hart appeared in the *Minnesota Magazine*. "*I never, I am sorry to say, met Dr. Sanford, nor, so far as I am aware, even saw her.*

But while at the University I had a fictional piece, called 'Her Story,' published in the Minnesota Magazine. *To my amazed delight, I received the letter from her.... What thrilled and moved and influenced me was the actual letter, written in her own hand."*[871]

Dr. Maria Sanford was an institution at the University of Minnesota for thirty years. (Her first name was pronounced "Mariah.") Dr. Sanford was the entire English department when she arrived at the University of Minnesota in 1880. With a reputation as an educational trailblazer and her enthusiasm for good writing and speaking, she touched the lives of many Minnesota students. Dr. Sanford was seventy-three years old when she wrote her letter to Maud. She retired the same year (1912) but remained involved in the academic community until her death in 1920. In 1958, Dr. Sanford's contribution to university education was recognized nationally when a bronze statue of her was unveiled in the Rotunda of the U.S. Capitol building. The statue stands in the hall connecting the Senate Chamber with the Rotunda. Those present at the statue's unveiling included Hubert H. Humphrey and Eugene McCarthy.

"Her Story" got a good review in the college newspaper, too. *"'Her Story' by Maud Palmer Hart is the strongest piece of fiction in the number and is unusual in college work. In simplicity, in directness, emotional power and skill in the structure, it is superior to the average story found in our best magazines."*[872]

Maud enjoyed English courses with Dr. Burton and Miss Whitney, and she earned high grades: Excellent in Composition and Rhetoric, Excellent in French I, and Good in Botany. Maud avoided mathematics in 1911-1912, but Higher Algebra was on the schedule for 1912-1913. She left college for good on December 14, 1912.

In 1973, Maud recalled her time at the University of Minnesota: "*My greatest interest was the Daily where I became woman's editor and around which my social life gravitated. Though I did enjoy many Gamma Phi girls. Of course, Delos was not in Minnesota yet. And we knew nothing of each other."*[873]

Delos left Detroit in 1913, after high school, and began work on the *Courier-News* in Fargo, North Dakota. He became a reporter for the *Daily News* in Minneapolis in 1914. Delos wrote that he *"was fired for telling the very good city editor to Gotohell and caught on with the Minneapolis Tribune, perhaps because the city editor was a good friend of mine."*[874] In 1915, Delos began work for his good friend, Harry B. Wakefield (see Chapter 13 herein), at the *Minneapolis Tribune*. Delos continued on the *Tribune* in 1917 but was also freelancing for the Wakefield Publicity Bureau (see Chapter 13). He was living near the university at the time, at 301 SE Fifth Street, a building which no longer stands. Delos' roommate was writer (and later, filmmaker) Merian C. Cooper (co-creator of *King Kong*), for whom the Lovelaces later named their daughter.

The changes which have occurred since we last saw Betsy extend far beyond the family's move to Minneapolis; we learn during Betsy's shipboard flashback in *Betsy and the Great World* that Julia and Tacy had "faithlessly" married! (Maud obviously knew how her young readers would take this news.) However, Tacy did not really marry Harry Kerr in June 1912. She hadn't met him yet. Moreover, he was to marry someone else in 1916. Charley Kirch married Lillian Maurer on September 26, 1916, at St. Stephen's Church in Minneapolis. (This is the same church in which Katie and Leo {Tess Kenney and Charlie Holden} were married on October 28, 1913.) Two months after the Kirchs' first anniversary, Lillian was dead of tuberculosis. Charley apparently knew that she was sick when he married her. Charley's niece, Margaret Fahey Thuente, remembers being taken by her mother to see Lillian during her illness. Margaret was given a beautiful doll which Lillian had had since childhood. Lillian Maurer Kirch is buried at Crystal Lake Cemetery in Minneapolis.

Since the Kenneys were attending St. Stephen's as early as 1913, perhaps Bick and Charley met at a church function. Perhaps Bick had seen or known Lillian.

Bick and Charley may have met as late as 1919. Like Harry Kerr, Charley Kirch was a salesman for a knitwear company. It was previously the Northwest Knitting Company, then became Munsingwear Corporation. One of the companies Tom Hart represented was Strutwear Knitting Company. Perhaps Tom and Charley met through business contacts, and Tom brought Charley home for Sunday Night Lunch, where he met Maud's pretty redheaded friend.

Coll. of Margaret Thuente

Charley Kirch

His first son, Robert, is standing at the feet of Charley Kirch. Charley's twin sister is standing behind him, on the left side of the photo.

MHL Archive

Bick Kenney Kirch

This photo was taken shortly after Bick and Charley's move to Buffalo, New York, in the late 1920s.

St. Thomas Church

Bick and Charley Kirch were married in this Minneapolis parish in September 1920.

1912 Gopher

Eugene Bibb

Kathleen Hart's first husband, a lawyer, was a graduate of the University of Minnesota.

Duplicated in several collections

Frohman Foster

The character Paige was based on Kathleen's second husband, Frohman Foster. Paige "was a very attractive young man, tall, light haired, and ethereal looking." (GW p. 24)

Hennepin History Museum

The Bibb House

Kathleen was a great favorite with the whole Bibb family and a frequent visitor to their home at 2208 Girard Avenue South in Minneapolis.

MHL Archive

Kathleen Hart

This photo (in which the resemblance between Kathleen and Maud is particularly evident) was taken about the time of her first marriage in 1913.

Tacy and Harry "had planned a festive wedding with her sister Katie as maid of honor and Betsy and Tib as bridesmaids. But early that spring Tacy's father died. Everyone agreed Tacy's marriage should not be postponed, but it was celebrated quietly with only Katie and Harry's brother present."[875] Festive wedding plans were really changed when Patrick Kenney died on June 4, 1920. Bick and Charley were married quietly on September 18, 1920, at St. Thomas Church. The witnesses were Tess Holden (Katie) and Charley's brother-in-law, Edward Fahey.

Julia too has fallen in love. "She had met Paige in New York, where she was singing in the opera. Like Julia, he had attended the University before studying the flute in the East."[876] Paige was based on Frohman Foster, whom Kathleen met during one of her four seasons with the William Wade Hinshaw Mozart opera company. He played flute in the orchestra. Frohman had studied at Carnegie Tech in Pittsburgh, after college in Indiana. His close friend, Paige Cavanaugh, inspired Maud's choice of a fictional name for Frohman. Maud and Delos, after their move to California, enjoyed many years of friendship with Paige and his wife, Edna.[877]

"Julia wanted to be married at Christmas time. ...Margaret... carried ribbons down the aisle of the Episcopal Church. Betsy, wearing green chiffon over pink, was maid of honor. Julia, in trailing bridal white, looked gravely lovely. An Indiana friend of Paige came to be best man, and afterward there was a merry supper at the Ray house."[878]

Maud has neatly untangled an untidy reality with a scenario that fits perfectly into *Betsy and the Great World*. In fact, Kathleen Hart was married at Christmas time in 1913. The details of the wedding were just as described. But this wasn't Kathleen's marriage to Paige's real-life counterpart. The real Paige, Frohman Foster, was her second husband. Kathleen's first marriage, in 1913, was to Eugene Sharp Bibb, whom she had known at the University of Minnesota before her trip to Europe.

While in college, Kathleen had grown close to the Bibb family. She was very congenial, though not romantic, with fellow student Frank Bibb, who had a flair for university theatricals. But his younger brother, Eugene, fell in love with Kathleen, and she married him perhaps more because of her affection for his family than for himself. He was a law graduate of the University of Minnesota. Alice Dunnell, inspiration for the character Louisa in *Betsy's Wedding,* said that "*Eugene Bibb was to my mind a pompous little rooster*."[879] The marriage ended in divorce about 1927.

Kathleen married Eugene Bibb on December 3, 1913. Julia's wedding was "candle lit and flower scented."[880] Kathleen's was too. The candles were needed since she was married at eight o'clock in the evening. But the wedding was not at the Episcopal church - rather it was at the Bibbs' Trinity Baptist Church (at the corner of Lincoln Avenue and Bryant Avenue South in Minneapolis). Kathleen and Eugene were married by Dr. Lathan A. Crandall, who later married Maud and Delos. As per *Betsy's Wedding*: "'I'll take Joe to call on Dr. Atherton,' said Paige. Dr. Atherton was the Episcopal clergyman who had married him and Julia."[881] The name and denomination were changed, but Maud and Kathleen <u>were</u> married by the same clergyman!

Unlike Julia's fictional ceremony, Kathleen's wedding was not "small." There were several hundred guests. The church was decorated with white chrysanthemums, smilax (a vine), and white satin ribbons. The processional was "Bridal March" by DuBois. (The recessional was Mendelssohn's march.) Helen and cousin Edith Hart, wearing white lace over blue, "stretched" the ribbons. There were three bridesmaids, all Minneapolis friends (not mentioned in the Betsy-Tacy books). "*They wore minaret gowns of white charmeuse, the triple tunics being of crepe chiffon and the bodices of shadow lace, the rainbow shades were carried out in the gowns. Miss Allen was in pink, Miss Sullivan in lavender and Miss Ennis in yellow. They held arm bouquets of chrysanthemums to match their gowns. Miss Maud Hart was her sister's maid of honor. Her gown was of pale green messaline with a lampshade tunic of shadow lace and trimmings of pearls. She held an arm bouquet of pink roses.*"[882] According to *Betsy and the Great World*, "It was a beautiful dress -- filmy green chiffon over pink, with roses sewn into the bodice. The sleeves were short...."[883] Betsy wore it to the Captain's Ball on the *Columbic,* with "the jade and silver pendant Julia had given her for a maid-of-honor gift."[884]

Kathleen wore bridal white, of chantilly lace over crepe de Chine and a charmeuse train. She wore the tulle veil with orange blossoms mentioned in *Betsy's Wedding*. Her bouquet was white orchids, bride roses, and lilies of the valley.

Stella Hart wore a golden brown messaline with an overdress of pale blue appliqued with gold decorations. Her flowers were roses and, appropriately, violets.

The reception that followed at the Hart home was for relatives and close friends only. Frances Kenney was one of those assisting in the dining room. The house was decorated in poinsettias, pink roses, ferns, and hyacinths. Kathleen's going-away suit was dark blue camel hair over a dark blue charmeuse blouse with chantilly lace and brocaded chiffon trim. She wore a black velvet hat with martin fur and an aigrette. Maud does not subject the reader to this level of detail in her description of Julia's wedding, but since Betsy-Tacy fans generally seem to enjoy wedding particulars, they are provided here.

Mr. Hart was inspired with the idea of sending Maud to Europe much the way Mr. Ray was. "*My father* [decided] *I would be helped in my writing by a year abroad, which was quite true....*"[885] Mr. Ray says that Betsy is entitled to a trip to Europe, just as Julia was. "Maybe when Margaret goes, Mamma and I will go along."[886] They did. The lovely formal dinner dress which Stella took on this voyage is in the collection of the Blue Earth County Historical Society in Mankato.

Six weeks after Kathleen's wedding, Maud set off for Europe. She sailed on Saturday, January 31, 1914, from Boston on the S.S. *Canopic* (similar to the fictional name, *Columbic*). Maud wrote home, "*If I lived in Boston I believe I would come to wearing red, white and blue costumes and eagle head dresses,*"[887] which is almost exactly what Betsy says on page 26 of *Betsy and the Great World*.

The sighting of the newly mustachioed Joe Willard was obviously fictional - since, as already explained, Maud hadn't met him yet. (Furthermore, Delos Lovelace never worked on the *Boston Transcript*.) Maud did some research on Harvard, circa 1914, intending to describe a little of Joe's life there. She abandoned this idea. Delos really grew a mustache - but not until 1917, when Maud requested him to do so. He wrote to her from camp, "*I am doing my best in the matter of a mustache but she must not build too many hopes. Two weeks is a very short time to comply even with a direct order.*" And a few days later, "*Gol darn it! I can no more raise a mustache in two weeks than you could raise a beard.*"[888]

Betsy is presented with a map of Europe with "a picture of the newest steamship of the line, a monster of 46,000 tons."[889] This truly would have been a monster. The *Canopic* was only 12,268 tons. The new monster must have been a triple-screw such as the *Olympic* or the *Titanic.*

The *Canopic,* a ship of the White Star Line, was 578 feet long and was capable of a speed of 16 knots per hour. She was a twin-screw with two masts and one funnel. The ship was built in 1900 at Belfast, Ireland, for the Dominion Line and was originally known as the *Commonwealth.* In 1903, she was purchased by White Star and renamed *Canopic.* The *Canopic* began U.S./Mediterranean service in 1904. The ship was finally sold in 1925 and scrapped at Briton Ferry. The White Star Line was a British company - hence the accents of the stewards and stewardesses on Betsy's voyage.

The Wilsons, Betsy's traveling companions, were unlikely to have been based on friends of Maud's father's brother, as reported. (Tom Hart's brother Steve was a graduate of Northwestern University (1902), though he was not a professor.) Judging from Maud's letters home, the Wilsons seem to have been based on a Dr. and Mrs. Craig.

When Betsy boards the *Columbic,* she has an umbrella in hand. Maud didn't take an umbrella abroad - but she bought one in Munich. She wrote home to her family, "*I loathe umbrellas, but everyone was so horrified when they learned that I was travelling* [sic] *without one, that I weakly yielded and bought one. It doesn't pay to bow down to convention. The old thing broke the first time I opened it. So I only paid for learning the useful lesson that to yield to the imbecilic demands of a degenerate society is moral cowardice and is properly punished by providence. (Accent the p's. The effect is charming.)*"[890]

As Maud said, "*I wrote that book* [*Betsy and the Great World*] *from my letters home, of which mother had saved every one.*"[891] When Maud quotes one of Betsy's letters home, she is quoting one of her own letters or - more surprisingly - one of Kathleen's! An inventory of quotations from *Betsy and the Great World* which were taken from Kathleen Hart's 1909 letters from Europe appears in the separate *Companion* appendix.

Coll. of SSW

S.S. *Canopic*

Maud sailed from Boston on the *Canopic* in February 1914.

Coll. of SSW

Canopic Letterhead

When Maud (like Betsy) sat in the ship library scribbling notes for the pilot to take back, she used stationery with the letterhead shown above.

MHL Archive

Maud on the *Canopic*

Betsy "roamed over the ship with [her] square box camera." (GW p. 43)

Coll. of SSW

Minnehaha Falls circa 1910

Betsy's new friends on the *Columbic* are fascinated to learn that she lives near the Minnehaha Falls. "Have you actually seen the Minnehaha Falls?" she is asked. (GW p. 34)

The two ladies' maids, Taylor and Rosa, who so interested Betsy were actually named "*Williams and Rosa*."[892] In *Betsy and the Great World,* we hear (for the first time) about Celeste and Hortense, the maids Betsy and Tacy had christened for themselves.[893] But we had a sneak preview of these imaginary maids in *Betsy in Spite of Herself* when Betsy said jokingly to Tacy: "Celeste, my smelling salts, please!"[894] (Celeste is also the name of the heroine's maid in "The Episodes of Epsie.") Maud mentioned the two maids in a letter written home from Munich. "*Every day when I come from getting my mail, Celeste asks my pardon and says could she be so bold as to inquire have I heard from Mademoiselle Kenney and did she parlez vous as to how was her chere Hortense. The poor girl is* desolated. *Really. Tell Bick so.*"[895] This is echoed by the character Maida (Betsy's shipboard friend), who claims that "Gabrielle is desolated" when she leaves the Columbic at Madeira.[896] When she was told about Celeste and Hortense, Maida had cried that she wanted a French maid, too. So do the rest of us!

Betsy finally gets a devoted maid in Munich, in the person of Hanni. This is not the first beloved German maid named "Hanni" in Lovelace's fiction. Lady Meta's maid was Hanni in *Gentlemen from England*.[897] "Hannie" was really the name of the maid Maud liked in Munich. Maud remarked, "*Hannie is certainly good to me. Celeste is quite peevish. But her disposition was never of the best as you doubtless will remember.*"[898]

One of the first friends Betsy makes on the boat is Mr. O'Farrell. "'He's a charmer!' Betsy thought. Looking after the trim erect figure in nautical blue, she decided to go down for a nap and put her hair in curlers."[899] Mr. O'Farrell was based on William James O'Hagan, who, according to ship's logs at the Public Record Office at Kew in England, became purser of the S.S. *Canopic* on February 23, 1912.[900]

Maud told her family about her friendship with the purser in much the same way Betsy did. '*This letter, and I guess all my letters so far, have a decidedly O'Haganish flavor. Don't be worried. I haven't lost my young heart. But my young wits are certainly being sharpened. He is thirty-seven years old, is terribly handsome, has traveled to every corner of the globe, served in South Africa with distinction, and tells about his adventures with a flood of eloquence that takes you off your feet.*

He has read absolutely everything and he has a perfectly inexhaustible knowledge of history. He speaks French like English, wears evening clothes just right, and knows how to speak to waiters. I guess you know what kind of a person he is. Absolutely cosmopolitan. And one of the first little lessons I've learned on my travels is due to him. This is it, said Maud with the air of imparting wisdom. He likes me heaps and I certainly like him. No one could help it. He is perfectly winning. We've talked perfect volumes and are the best of pals, and what do you think, he's never told me he's married. To be sure, he's never told me he wasn't - but then he never had told me he was. He doesn't think I know it, but Mr. Hollis mentioned 'O'Hagan and his wife' just as casually, one day. The last day out I'm going to tell him that I knew. I guess the lesson is obvious. I've learned that all married men aren't middle aged and fatherly."[901] Maud told Mr. O'Hagan just as Betsy did - by quoting the last line of her letter home.

Maud was not the only writer to be charmed by a purser. In a book describing a slightly earlier period, British author M.V. Hughes writes of her transatlantic voyage: "*At some time each day the purser sat down for a chat. He was a charming fellow, full of droll anecdotes, and I began to suspect that pursers were chosen simply for their ability to make the voyage agreeable for passengers.*"[902] Mr. O'Farrell is certainly agreeable, until Betsy finds that he is married!

Until then, she attempts to charm him. "Like most girls she had worked out a technique for fascination. With Betsy it was thoroughly curled hair, perfume, bracelets, the color green, immaculate daintiness, and a languid enigmatic pose."[903] Betsy's technique isn't new to us. She first forged the concept with Tib in *Betsy in Spite of Herself*, despite the fact that (according to Tib) blue has always been her best color.[904] (And in *Heaven to Betsy*, Julia remarks that Betsy looks "divine" in blue.[905]) Betsy's technique is now far more refined than in those early days, and the reader enjoys seeing how she has changed and improved it.

Maud really purchased a pair of jade and silver bracelets at Gibraltar for sixty cents. "*I wear them both on one arm and with my green and lace dress, or my blue poplin with the green bows, or in fact almost any of my clothes, so much does green predominate in them.*"[906]

The Captain's Ball, described on pages 83 - 89 of *Betsy and the Great World* is very like a dance Maud attended on the *Canopic*.

"The deck was hung with the flags of all nations and red and green electric lights strung all along it. The floor was waxed and the orchestra stationed in a corner. There were rows of chairs at one end for the lookers and lots of little corners for fussers. It looked so pretty. The sea was like glass and a full moon. I wore my green and lace dress with my jade pendant, ring and bracelets - some outfit. I felt just like dancing and had a glorious time. I learned "The Marjory Step" and a new "Hesitation" from a man who is a friend of the Castles [Mr. and Mrs. Vernon]. *I* [was] *told that I had a tropical beauty. Fancy! He was a mustached Englishman and thought he was complimenting me when he told me that he would never believed me an American. He said I had tropical beauty and the charm of an European. I told him that a tropical beauty from Minneapolis was a joke - and I didn't dance with him again though he asked me twice. Oh it was all such fun. And chocolate ice cream and lemonade and sandwiches served in the intermissions."*[907] Maud no doubt danced with Mr. Hollis, upon whom the character Mr. Chandler was based.

Betsy's dinner table companions on the *Columbic* discuss one of her favorite books - *The Beloved Vagabond* by William J. Locke. This book was first published in 1906. The English lady didn't like it when Paragot put his hairbrush in the butter[908], but in fact, it had simply fallen into the butter.[909]

Names of historical figures heard at the dinner table "brought back a red Morocco set of *Stoddard's Travel Lectures* in the bookcase at home."[910] Elsewhere Maud wrote about the books she grew up with. "*I can still see and feel the books in that breakfront desk* [in her home].... *Enthralling to me were the travel lectures of John L. Stoddard. I read them through, from one red marbled cover to the other, all ten volumes. I have the old set now, and in the changed world geography of 1952, I found it very useful when writing Betsy and the Great World, which dealt with travels in 1914."*[911] There were quite a few editions of the Stoddard Lectures. The set in Maud's home was most likely the 1899-1901 edition. The last edition consisted of fifteen volumes and was published in 1924.

On St. Michael's, Betsy sees "orange trees with shiny green leaves, white blossoms, and golden fruit."[912] It doesn't seem biologically possible for a tree to have both flowers and mature fruit at the same time. Perhaps anything's possible in the Azores.

Betsy leaves the *Columbic* in Genoa and travels by train to Munich. She really received a box of candy from Mr. Burton, whose real name was Mr. Richmond. But the guardian angel on the Zurich train who helped Maud get dinner during a fifteen-minute stopover, who got her a berth on the train to Munich, and who waited for two hours at the station to see her safely on that train was not Mr. Brown. It was a big bearded German gentleman named Carl Meincke. He invited Maud to visit with him and his wife at their home in Lincoln (England).

Maud arrived in Munich on the morning of February 16, a Monday. She stayed for one week at the luxurious Pension Washeim where Miss Surprise (really Miss Siboni, an artist) was staying. Maud then moved a few blocks away to the more affordable Pension Schweiz at 78 Schellingstrasse.

Betsy's room at the Geiger is delineated in such painstaking detail[913] that one suspects Maud must have been consulting a sketch when she wrote the description in *Betsy and the Great World*. She no doubt made a sketch of the room to send home to her family in 1914. (The picture Maud put on her nightstand was of Russell!) Her room really contained a desk big enough for a congressman, over which she pinned the map from Mr. O'Hagan. And across the street was "*an old building the walls of which are all frescoed in colors with kings and shepherdesses and apostles and any number of things. In the daytime I look out on a regular fairy story.*"[914]

Life at the Pension Schweiz was very similar to that at the fictional Pension Geiger. "*Off to the right of me, some future Melba began to warble grand opera and not only warble but to rant and rave whole scenes over which her dramatic teacher had evidently been struggling with her. While she was in the midst of the Butterfly aria, an aspiring baritone on my left began a similar performance, and I sat down on my trunk and howled, it tickled me so. Especially when I thought of my friend the artist painting madly across the hall.*"[915]

After her arrival in Munich, Maud devised a list of daily doings. "*You know living on a schedule is the delight of my life.*"[916] Betsy felt the same way. "Lists were always her comfort."[917] We remember from *Betsy Was a Junior*: "She thought about those lists she had made in her programs for self-improvement. She hadn't followed them out by any means, but they had revealed her ideals."[918]

MHL Archive

Storybook House

Maud's pension in Munich was really on Schellingstrasse, and across the street was really a house with walls "frescoed in lovely faded colors with kings and shepherdesses and cherubs." (GW p. 119)

MHL Archive

Else
(Tilda)

"The girl with the crimped hair began to smile. She had a monkeyish, cute little face." (GW p. 142)

MHL Archive

Hertha
(Helena)

"She was tall but delicately built, with black hair and eyes and a pale soft skin. She wore a gray suit, a white blouse, and a crisp black straw hat." (GW p. 136)

MHL Archive

Maud's New Hat

"One end touched her shoulder, the other shot off toward the sky, and under the skyward edge, next to her hair, was a luscious pink rose." (GW p. 182)

HarperCollins

Betsy's New Hat

In both real-life and Betsy-life, the hat was purchased with part of the earnings from a short story called "Emma Middleton Cuts Cross Country."

Coll. of *Bayerische Staatsgemaldesammlungen, Schack-Galerie*

Franz Von Lenbach's *Shepherd Boy*

"A barefoot boy had thrown himself down on a hilltop. The sky was intensely blue, the grass was starred with flowers, and the boy was happily relaxed, one arm over his eyes. He reminded Betsy of herself and Tacy and Tib on the Big Hill back in Deep Valley." (GW p. 140) The *Shepherd Boy* was painted in 1860.

In *Betsy's Wedding,* we hear: "Betsy was always making lists. She had done it for years, resolving at various times to brush her hair faithfully, or to manicure her nails, or to study French, or to read through the Bible."[919] In *Betsy and the Great World*, Maud gives us a similar list of her lists: "For years she had made lists of books she must read, good habits she must acquire, things she must do to make herself prettier - like brushing her hair a hundred strokes a night, and manicuring her fingernails, and doing calisthenics before an open window in the morning. (That one hadn't lasted long.)"[920]

We never actually see Betsy doing the calisthenics, but it isn't hard to imagine her doing them (particularly in her freshman year). "Perhaps people who liked to write always made lists! Just for the fun of it."[921] Perhaps the kind of person who becomes a lifelong Betsy-Tacy reader is likely to be of a word-loving turn (since Betsy is telling and writing stories from the first book), for most of us seem to enjoy lists, too. And sharing this curious enjoyment with Betsy from book to book makes us love her more and brings us close to the real person beneath the thin veneer of the character.

One of the items on Betsy's daily schedule was a bath. The story of how she eventually achieves her one and only bath in Munich forms one of the book's classic chapters. Maud tells the same story in a letter home. "*Some time ago, I was unreasonable enough to feel a desire for a bath, and I communicated it one night to black-armed Mildred* [Hannie]. *She grew visibly agitated and retired but when I saw her again she made no reference to it, and indeed she assumed the magnanimous attitude of one who had decided to forgive and forget. Being, however, as you know, of a persistent disposition, I was not going to relinquish my fell purpose so easily. I rang for the other maid and announced my will in the matter. She also grew deeply agitated and attempted to remonstrate with me but I told her my mind was made up and she could call me when my bath was ready. All this did, however, was to bring a bevy of people into my room and from their combined chatterings I finally gathered the truth. That the one bathroom in the house was in the suite of a couple of officers who objected to having others use it and as they were at home this evening I could not very well get access to the bathroom. I told them all to be on the lookout for a chance to get me a bath and they promised and with that I was obliged to be content. But oh, those officers seem to be of most domestic habits! Night after night they stayed at home with watchful eyes upon the bathroom. They guarded their treasure with dog-like fidelity, but I was biding my time. In the meantime, rumors of my presumptuous desire were spread abroad. The poet contributed the comforting information that when he took his last bath, he emerged from the bathroom to find an enraged officer lying in wait for him. Well, this morning, black-armed Mildred burst into my room to tell me that at last the coast was clear. I leaped into a kimono, collected soap and towels, and followed where she led. Outside the door, we were joined by a bodyguard of servants. On we went, into the sacred precincts of the officers, at last into the very bathroom itself and there they left me. It was cluttered with huge boots and swords. It recalled the rights of the officers so visibly that I fairly trembled while I bathed. I knew my faithful sentinel guarded me from without, but even so fear oppressed me. When I emerged at last, my hair bewitchingly braided, and myself arrayed in my small pox dress, in order to quell with my charms the wrath of any officer who might confront me, I found the servants ready to hustle me back into neutral ground. And thus I went safely thru the horrible ordeal."*[922] Maud's "small pox" (polka dot) dress was a great favorite on her trip to Europe - the counterpart to Betsy's comforting cherry-red bathrobe.

Her writing was, of course, the most important part of Betsy's day. Maud really produced stories called "The Disappearing Dancer" and "Meet Miss So and So." She told her family that she spent one morning engaged in "*the brain bursting occupation of finding synonyms for 'he said' and 'she said.'*"[923]

In Munich, Betsy (and Maud) learned that "Emma Middleton Cuts Cross Country" had been accepted by *Ainslee's* magazine. Maud was paid $75 for the story, which was published in June 1915. "It's about a little dressmaker, like the one who made my Junior Ball dress. She gets disgusted with everything and walks out and makes a new start."[924] Exulting over the sale, Betsy quotes from the immortal manuscript. "Added hours had but heightened the wonder of the day," does indeed appear on p. 141 of *Ainslee's* for June 1915. But "his gray gaze was inscrutable" is actually an altered version of a line on page 143 about the hero's eyeglasses "*rendering his eyes inscrutable.*" (This hero was based on a family friend named Jack Sickle - the same man upon whom Mr. Bagshaw in *Betsy's Wedding* was based.)

Trying to keep loneliness at bay, Betsy explores Munich's museums. The National Museum, near the English Gardens (still there) is as described, with "life-sized models of armored men on horseback."[925] The Shack Gallery is nearby. There "she found one painting she really liked. A barefoot boy had thrown himself down on a hilltop. The sky was intensely blue, the grass was starred with flowers, and the boy was happily relaxed, one arm thrown over his eyes. He reminded Betsy of herself and Tacy and Tib on the Big Hill back in Deep Valley. She could remember the warmth of the sunshine, the smell of hot grass, the hum of insects. She bought a print of the Shepherd Boy -- by Lenbach, her guidebook said -- and put it up in her room."[926] Later Betsy and Joe hang the *Shepherd Boy* over the old walnut table in their first apartment.[927] Maud also mentioned the painting in a 1916 short story called "In Butterfly Lane."

Betsy found a friend at the Geiger - a little Swiss, Tilda, who was a singer. Tilda was based on Else, who really invented a fictional American fiance to discourage a suitor in Munich! Maud wrote of Else, who was from St. Gallen: *"She is small and not at all pretty but she's exceedingly graceful and has a very sweet manner. It's queer how even a difference in language can't keep two congenial spirits apart. I never get tired of her and she never gets tired of me."*[928] Maud and Else enjoyed many "bats" and "prowls" around Munich. Else also made the pension seem more like home. *"Friday evening Else was up in my room and we talked until it was late and we were ravenously hungry. Then she suggested that we go down to her room and try and scrape up a lunch, and being a true Hart, I acquiesced with enthusiasm. It was anyway midnight and we were in kimonos, but we made tea on her alcohol lamp and ate rolls and sausage and kuchen. It was much fun."*[929] Else had trouble pronouncing "Maud" so gave her the nickname "Tilda." (Maud's choice of fictional names in the Betsy-Tacy series was rarely arbitrary.)

Betsy's other friend in Munich, Helena von Wandersee, was based on a young baroness named Hertha von Einem. Hertha's mother was English. Her father was a German baron, whom Maud suspected of being a "dope fiend." Hertha studied piano in

Munich. She and Maud attended a concert given by the pianist Gabrilowitz on Sunday, March 1, 1914. Hertha "*loathes being reduced tho' she is resigned. She takes it out on the other pensionares by snubbing their heads off. Why under the sun she approves so of me, I don't know. I take delight in telling her how common and ordinary I am. And I make her do all kinds of things that she isn't used to doing and take her into places that she never before put her titled nose into.*"[930]

Maud is said to have received from Hertha, "a tall china cup, striped in pink and gold and blue."[931] The stripes of the cup run vertically, and it sits on a matching saucer. The poet Goethe was said to have sipped from it.

With Helena or with Tilda, Betsy explores Munich. "Once they looked through an iron fence into a small enclosure with a shrine and two rows of graves. It had been a cemetery for some monks, Tilda said. Late sunlight lay on the plain black crosses, and green shoots of crocuses were pushing up from the graves. It was strange, thought Betsy, the stillness in there, when the world was so giddy with spring."[932]

Maud described this same scene to her family. "*We looked thru an iron fence into a little oblong enclosure. At the far end was a shrine, and there were two rows of graves with a plain black cross at the head of every one. It was the cemetery of the monks. That little glimpse I had of it, made me feel, I can't tell you the way it made me feel! But I am positive that as long as I live I can close my eyes at any time and see it. The sunlight of late afternoon slanting thru the bars upon those plain black crosses, and the pale green shoots of early crocuses coming up upon the graves! It was so still in there, and the world was just giddy with spring.*"[933] Not only did Maud remember this all her life, but she passed on the lovely image to generations of Betsy-Tacy fans.

Not long after her trip to Europe, Maud wrote a short story called "The Vagabond." It contains numerous elements which were later used in *Betsy and the Great World*. The heroine (called only "the Vagabond") cherishes a map "*given to her by a purser who looked like Chauncey Olcott.*"[934] The description of early evening in a student pension is essentially that of Betsy's first evening at the Geiger on page 126 of *Betsy and the Great World*, except that the style of the earlier version would have been far more irritating to Mr. Gaston, had he ever seen it. "*In a student pension, the hour preceding* abendessen *is the noisiest hour of the day. A pianist in the room above now broke in upon her pensive reverie with a gleaming cataract of scales. 'Scales!' muttered the Vagabond in exasperation. 'Scales - and such a twilight! That girl has no temperament.' As in the early morning one bird is awakened by another into happy song, so was a violinist in the room beneath inspired by the pianist in the room above, so was a cornetist off at the right somewhere impelled to emulate the violinist, and a lusty tenor off at the left emboldened to lift his voice. Then the din was pierced by a clear soprano note. There followed a fragment of song in the same voice, a bit of brief but fervent dialogue, a shriek, a fit of sobbing triumphing over the heartless discord of cornet, violin and piano, ignoring the persistent pleading of the tenor, the aspiring prima donna continued to warble and trill, to threaten and beseech, to stamp and bang, and to go off in gales of maudlin laughter.*"[935]

Before leaving Munich, Betsy buys herself a new hat. So did Maud. "*It was a very extravagant hat, I'm afraid, but I have a weak chin when it comes to buying new gear. It was so adorable that I couldn't any more resist it than I could fly. It's a little extreme but my taste always was extreme and that it is good looking and becoming no one could deny. It's large and of black straw and so one sided that one end touches my shoulder while the other shoots off toward the sky. Under the edge that shoots off toward the sky, next to my hair, is a luscious pink rose, and some black ribbon comes on up over the edge of the part and down to the end that touches my shoulder where there is a second pink rose, as delicious a one as the first. Can you see it?*"[936] The same hat is described somewhat more concisely on page 182 of *Betsy and the Great World*. After making her purchases, Maud had dinner at an expensive restaurant, "*with that inexplicable feeling that one always has, that when one has spent too much money one might as well spend some more.*"[937]

From Munich, Betsy goes to Sonneberg to see the "doll-making center of the world." Sonneberg is situated in central Germany at the foot of the Thuringian Mountains, and it is still a center for toy-manufacturing. Previously part of East Germany, in the Suhl district, Sonneberg is thirty-six miles southeast of the closest town, Meiningen, and its population is about 30,000.

In her room at Krug's Hotel in Sonneberg, Betsy sits down to read Tacy's letter (after thinking about her all day) and learns that

Tacy is going to have a baby. Bick (Tacy) didn't have her first child until October 1921. The baby whose advent Maud probably heard about while she was in Europe in 1914 was the child of Bick's sister Tess. Krug's Hotel, at Fernsprecher No. 2, really had the running water and electricity which so delighted Betsy. Maud said that breakfast at Krug's "*was served to me in state by a modest little waiter who blushed every time he looked at my corset which I had inadvertently left in a conspicuous position.*"[938]

From Sonneberg, Maud traveled to Bayreuth and Nuremberg, then returned to Munich. A week later, Maud and Else left together for Oberammergau.

Oberammergau has no doubt changed a great deal since April 1914, but the Passion Play is still given every ten years, and the same family names still appear on the playbills. In 1980, the Christus was Rudolf Zwink. According to *Betsy and the Great World,* Ottile (sic) Zwink played the Virgin Mary in "the last Passion Play."[939] (Ottilie Zwink last played Mary in 1890, not 1910.) Maud met her while visiting Oberammergau.

Maud and Else stayed at the Pension Schweizerhaus, which was the home of "Tante Rosa" and "Fraulein Alice" Wilkoszevska. In *Betsy and the Great World*, Betsy and Tilda stay with Else and Max Baumgarten. Their servant girl is Hedwig. Her name was really Theresa (but a maid at Maud's Munich pension was Hedwig!). Maud's third-floor room really had a balcony.

Anton Lang (pronounced "Laang") was the Christus of the Passion Play. He played the role for three seasons, beginning in 1900. Lang was really a potter, and he gave Maud (and Betsy) a pottery angel - two, in fact. They were ceramic cherub heads, about three inches high. The Harts hung them on the face of their fireplace at 905 W. 25th. According to a family friend, "*they were exquisite! The most beautiful things in the whole house. Have you ever seen a Dresden doll? The china material, the expressions on the cherubs' faces were so gorgeous. The hair was flaxen. The eyes were blue. The wings were gold tipped.*"[940]

After leaving Oberammergau, Maud visited the castle at Linderhof and the city of Innsbruck. Of the alpine scenery, she wrote: "*lofty snow crowned mountains block every vista.*"[941] Spoken like a true Midwesterner!

Passion Play of Oberammergau

Anton Lang

On her visit to Oberammergau in 1914, Maud met Anton Lang, Christus of the Passion Play. "He had flowing light brown hair and beard, and a strong face with keen, humorous, light-blue eyes." (GW p. 211)

MHL Archive

Oberammergau *Hauschen*

In Oberammergau, Maud, like Betsy, stayed in a house on which "a balcony ran around the second story, and a smaller one stretched across the front, up under the eaves." (GW p. 208)

MHL Archive

Sonneberg in 1914

Maud visited the little town of Sonneberg, then an important doll-making center. "Sonneberg was a little like Deep Valley," Betsy discovered. (GW p. 193)

Sonneberg Tourist Information

Sonneberg Toy Museum

The Toy Museum Maud visited in Sonneberg is located on Beethovenstrasse. It really has a model of Gulliver covered with Lilliputians.

Duplicated in several collections

Maud on Fusina

This photo was taken on the trip Maud and Paul made to Fusina. It was just like Betsy and Marco's - down to the heartache.

MHL Archive

Paul Conte
(Marco)

Marco Regali "was very good-looking, with thick black hair, just slightly wavy, and expressive dark eyes that seemed darker and brighter because of heavy brows and lashes." (GW p. 220)

MHL Archive

Paul Conte

"He was olive skinned, clean shaven; white teeth shone when he smiled." (GW p. 220) This photo was taken in the garden of the Conte's home in Venice.

MHL Archive

Maud at St. Mark's

Marco took photos of Betsy feeding the pigeons. "They bought a paper bag full of corn, and the pigeons perched on her shoulders, her arms, her fingers! 'I know it's a touristy trick, but I don't care,' Betsy said." (GW p. 233)

Betsy bids farewell to Germany and heads south to Italy. Maud's itinerary had not been specifically planned beyond the stay in Munich. Her decision to see Venice was a surprise to her family. Writing to tell them about it, she said: "*Paragot has nothing on me. I'm going to Venice. 'Venice!' gasped father, turning to mother. 'Venice!' shrieked mother, clutching Kathleen. 'Venice!' choked Kathleen, clinging to Gene. 'Venice!' sputtered Gene, glaring at Helen. 'It would seem,' observed Helen, 'that she's going to Venice.*'"[942] (The family really called Helen "the Persian Princess.")

"Emerging from the station, Betsy gasped. Of course she had known that Venice had streets of water. Yet it was a shock."[943] This is exactly what the traveler to Venice still experiences when walking out of the station, expecting for a moment to see a street at the bottom of the steps. A Betsy-Tacy reader arriving in Venice may have this same sensation of surprise, then a second sensation of *deja vu*, followed by a third sensation of warmth and pleasure, realizing that this is just what happened to Betsy - which is why it is familiar!

In Venice, Betsy lives at the House of the Yellow Roses. Maud stayed at the pension of the Conte family at San Gregorio, 234. The proprietors had spent many years in Boston where Mr. Conte, a Methodist minister, worked with a society for the protection of Italian immigrants. Their pension was very popular with Americans. The Contes had two daughters, Adelaide and Nita, as well as a handsome son, Paolo - Paul, who met Maud's train at the station. On her first day in Venice, Paul rescued her from a pushy Englishman, whom they promptly ran into at a church - to which they had gone for the sake of the view from the tower. (Just as described in *Betsy and the Great World.*) Maud wrote to her family, "*And out in Venice by daylight I could see better how nice-looking he was, or rather, I didn't mean to say that. I could see the vivid color of the sky and water and the picturesque shabbiness of the buildings.*"[944]

Maud and Paul became good friends ... just like Betsy and Marco. "*Of course, I rather like him or I wouldn't have started curling my hair again. You've heard about emotions coming in waves!*"[945] Maud wrote. Betsy writes almost the same thing to her family on page 230 of *Betsy and the Great World.* Betsy liked Marco very much, but she didn't love him.

Refusing Paul's proposal was very difficult for tender-hearted Maud. She marked a letter to her family "Personal" - meaning that it was not to be routed to friends and family, as her other letters were. It describes almost exactly Betsy's experience with Marco in chapter 18 of *Betsy and the Great World.*

"*I know you are reading between the lines about Paolo Conte, so I will tell you that when I had just been here a week he told me that he was in love with me, and now he tells me every day in three different languages, so I guess there is no doubt about it. Of course, I am not in love with him, but I am dreadfully sorry for him. He is a dear and for all he is 24 and an Italian, it is really his first* [love] *as he has always been wrapped up in his music and indifferent to women. He says, 'Oh you Americans! You can't feel. You are like ice.' But I do feel like a murderer, just the same.... I am not at all in love with him, so don't think that. Russell ... is an old dear and I think lots of him, but I'm not going to marry anybody for years and years and I'm planning on 1917* [for a family trip to Europe] *as much as you are.*" Several days later she wrote: "*I am just about sick today, because everything came to a head yesterday. You will read in my home letter about our wonderful day at Fusina* [which was May 29, 1914]. *Well it was late afternoon when we were sitting down in the grass by the water that he told me he must have a definite answer. He said he knew I could not tell him I loved him and that I would marry him when we had only known each other three weeks and he had not met you folks or anything but that he must know if he had a chance or not, for he would never get over it if he let himself go much farther. He has told me since that the minute he saw me he said to himself, 'There is the girl I can lose my head about' and as he helped me with my bags and into the gondola he kept praying, 'Oh, I hope she will be stupid. Oh I hope she will be stupid,' for he didn't want to fall in love, but I wasn't, and so! I'll tell you, we are both artists and are <u>absolutely</u> congenial. I never get tired of him. I don't care how I look, if I am sick or tired or quiet, and neither does he. He loves me like Bick does, and the family. (I just happened to think I hadn't told you I refused him and you might be worrying. I did. So don't.) He is the most affectionate disposition I ever knew and adores his mother and sisters and they him and they are too sweet together for anything. He will be just the same with his wife, too. I don't know. I have a feeling that if I married Russell and my own family wasn't always by me to back me up, I would* *be desolate and get sick and die. But Mr. Conte would love me and pet me and take care of me and baby me. You see the kind of a man he is? ... He was very quiet and I could see how bad he was feeling and then I'm such an idiot and not used to refusing people I guess and I cried and kind of went to pieces in my usual way and he was a dear and went and got me some wine and said, 'Don't feel so sorry for me. I am very happy. You have been so sincere in saying no that I will be sure you are sincere when you say yes and next time you will say yes.' But I won't. We came home and right after dinner I came upstairs and undressed and went to bed and presently a couple of dozen of roses and carnations came up in a shower thru my open window. And I didn't speak to him but in an hour or so I looked out and saw him and when I went to sleep he was still there standing just as quiet down in the garden in the moonlight. You see an American man couldn't do those things. But with him they are as natural as breathing. Italians are never awkward, never self-conscious, but always graceful and at ease. ... It has been so nice to tell you all about it. I feel as if I had been in bed with you and now I could kiss you goodnight and go to sleep. You see you and Papa are doomed to have an old maid daughter on your hands and Kath will have to resign herself to my unchanging spinsterhood. You know, mamma, I am very well. And thru all this I have eaten like a perfect gourmand. I'll bet I weigh 120.*"[946]

It is perhaps surprising that Maud didn't fall in love with such a romantic man in such a romantic setting.... It is also puzzling that Maud persisted in her relationship with Russell, while believing that marriage to him would be so desperately unhappy.

We hear little of the month following Betsy's departure from Italy - just that she was homesick in Switzerland (and grieving over Marco). It appears, however, that Maud had a happier visit to Switzerland. "*I loved a little pension in Gersau ... which in my day was a village ... maybe still is. It's on Lake Lucerne, is very quaint, and oh the air and the food! I took the boat at Fluelen to get there. And took a boat to Vitznau and from there climbed the Rigi (chiefly by r.r.). Also from Gersau made the William Tell pilgrimage.*"[947]

At the Tuileries, Betsy remembered "the Empress Eugenie, who Betsy's grandmother had once seen with her own eyes, sitting on one of these benches."[948] Maud wrote that her "*Grandma and Grandpa Austin attended the Paris Exhibition of 1889, and when I was a little girl Grandma used to tell me about Paris and how she had seen the Empress Eugenie, sitting in the Tuileries Gardens. I loved hearing about this old woman in black who once had been acclaimed the most beautiful woman in the world and so, half a lifetime later, I put her into a novel.*"[949] The novel to which Maud referred was *Petticoat Court.*

Betsy and the Wilsons stay at the Grand Hotel Pension. In fact, Maud visited Paris in the company of Dr. Donovan (a Baptist minister), his wife, and their two children. They stayed at 3 Rue de l'Odeon. Maud and Mrs. Donovan went to the Bon Marche, just as Betsy and Miss Wilson did. "*You know, really, it's a very ordinary department store. You could hardly tell it from Donaldson's.*"[950] (Donaldson's was a prominent Twin Cities department store.)

Maud enjoyed the Louvre as much as Betsy did. "*You see the Venus de Milo first, outlined against dark velvet, down a long avenue of statuary, and it is so perfectly exquisite it makes you hold your breath.*"[951]

Neither Maud nor Betsy counted Paris as a place in which she had lived. Maud's pension was "*crowded and unsatisfactory, full of American tourists. I saw* [Paris] *very well, didn't miss anything, and I've always been thankful for that, as it's been a help to me all my life. (To have seen the things and places which are so constantly mentioned in books, newspapers and conversation.) But I didn't really live there as Tib did, for example, although her stay was as short as mine.*"[952]

Shortly before the publication of *Betsy and the Great World*, Maud remarked that daughter Merian "*grew up with my meeting deadlines and reading galley proofs. She can pitch in and write a chapter beautifully. In fact, she can out-Betsy-Tacy Betsy-Tacy.*"[953] Merian does admit to pitching in and writing a chapter. It was chapter 19 of *Betsy and the Great World* (for which Maud had written an outline), describing Betsy's visit to Paris.

Maud had asked for Merian's help because - though usually efficiently ahead of deadlines - this time Maud was running late. About meeting the deadlines for her books, Maud wrote: "*With my early books I was very scrupulous and, in fact, only remember one where the publisher had to hound me, and that was Betsy and the Great World, for Merian was graduating from college and I was very tied up with personal things that year; should never have signed the contract.*"[954]

Maud and the Donovans left Paris together on July 15. A rough crossing of the English channel made Maud particularly glad to reach England. The Donovans went on to Oxford and

The Bon Marche, Paris

Betsy bought her new suit at the Bon Marche. Maud bought hers at Peter Robinson's in London. This photo of the Bon Marche was taken in 1986.

MHL Archive

Henri Quatre
1914

Like Paragot in *The Beloved Vagabond*, Betsy visits Henri Quatre on the Pont Neuf, secretly hoping that the statue will point the way back to Joe (as he pointed a way out of Paragot's troubles).

Henri Quatre
1982

Betsy wanted to take a snapshot of Henri to send to Tacy. Maud took hers (photo at left) in 1914. The one above was taken in 1982.

American Express Office, Paris

Betsy attempts to tell a Paris cab driver to take her to the American Express Office at "*Onze Rue Scribe.*" Gratifyingly, the American Express Office is still located at Eleven Rue Scribe in Paris.

American Express Office, London

The American Express Office, to which all the Americans in London throng when war is declared in 1914, is still at Six Haymarket.

Bus 88

Visitors to London can find plenty of living history, including a double-deckered bus 88. "Take bus Aighty-Aight, Miss," Betsy is advised. (GW p. 280)

University College London

Taviton Street

Externally, No. 5 Taviton Street is little changed from the days when Maud lived there. The door at the extreme left edge of the photo is No. 5. "It was one of a row of attached houses, all tall and thin with neat door plates, bells, and knockers." (GW p. 278)

MHL Archive

The Crew at Mrs. Brumwell's

Betsy very much enjoyed the company of the Crew at Mrs. Heaton's boarding house. Maud enjoyed her English friends, too. Maud is in the center row, fourth from left.

Minnesota Valley Regional Library

Maud On Board

Maud, standing on the S.S. *St. Louis,* is wearing the suit she bought in London. (Betsy bought an identical one in Paris!)

HarperCollins

Betsy On Board

This Vera Neville illustration from the cover of *Betsy and the Great World* shows Betsy on her outbound journey. The photo at left was taken during Maud's return trip.

Steamship Historical Society

The S.S. *St. Louis* at the New York Docks

The *St. Louis* brought Maud home from England in September 1914.

Chester not long after their arrival. In London, "Betsy looked down four stories into Taviton Street."[955] Taviton Street (Maud used the real name) is only one block long and is located near Euston Station (served by both British Rail and the London Underground). Betsy's boarding house overlooks a green square. Gordon Square is actually in the next block down.

The boarding house in which Maud stayed, at 5 Taviton Street, belonged to Mrs. Brumwell. Life at the boarding house was much as described in *Betsy and the Great World.* "*We have big English breakfasts, porridge, ham, etc., but I have grown used to continental breakfasts and don't like them. And luncheon at 1, and tea at 4:30, a very social time. And dinner with two kinds of meat and dessert according to English custom. 'Will you have hot or cold, Miss Hart? Hot? A slice off the joint?' And 'Dr. Donovan, would you prefer cold shape or cherry tart?' 'Joint' is roast; and 'cold shape' is jello.*"[956]

Maud felt very much at home in England. Like Betsy, she enjoyed hearing English spoken again, after months on the continent. And she was charmed by the same things which delight today's Anglophile. Maud remarked that "*the two nicest things in London are busses and Bobbies. They are rather closely associated in my mind, for I never take one except on the advice of the other.*"[957]

Though Maud was not homesick in London as she had been in Munich, she must have derived particular pleasure from the presence of friends from Mankato. "*I saw a great deal of Flossie and Mrs. Macbeth in London in 1914.*"[958] Maud and the Macbeths attended Christian Science services together in London.

Maud became friendly with the group of Britishers at her boarding house. The red-eyed actress, Jean Carver, was really Jean Etty. Dolly Cohen, the artist, was based on Caroline Soloman. (She was really working on illustrations for a new edition of *Helen's Babies.*) Leonard Reed and his brother Dick were based on a Mr. Anderson and his younger brother Claude (whose aspirations were, respectively, medical and legal).

With her English friends, Maud visited Epping Forest - "that had gone into 'The Episodes of Epsie.'"[959] ("The Episodes of Epsie" by Maud Palmer Hart was published in *Ainslee's* in March 1916.) Epping "Forrest" on page 282 is one of the few typos in the series - most of which happen to appear *Betsy and the Great World.*

Betsy's adventures in London were very much those of Maud, who wrote: "*I didn't see the British Museum (it was closed on account of the suffragettes).... I loved the galleries, Westminster, the changing of the guard at Buckingham Palace, Windsor Castle and Hampstead Heath. We went boating on the Thames. (Taking tea along.) I saw Mrs. Patrick Campbell in* Pygmalion. *Even in the movies, they serve tea!*"[960]

Betsy saw "the young, slim, handsome Prince of Wales, wearing a silk hat."[961] This would have been David, who was never crowned Edward VIII, since he abdicated to marry the notoriously American (and twice-divorced) Wallis Simpson in 1936.

The outbreak of World War I was made even more stirring for Maud by a young British cavalry officer named Harry Norris who was smitten with her. One evening, just before he was shipped out, he walked her to choir practice. Maud wrote: "*I wore my crepe dress with the green buttons and green ring and green bracelets and green shoes and stockings and the effect was so fascinating that we reached choir practice as it was just dispersing.*"[962]

Maud returned home on the S.S. *St. Louis*, which sailed from Liverpool on September 5, 1914, arriving in New York on September 12. The *St. Louis* was an American vessel (on which Mr. Brown was anxious that Betsy should travel). She was built in 1884 at Philadelphia, with a tonnage of 11,629. As a troopship during the First World War, she was known as the *Louisville* and was dismantled in 1925. The friend Maud made on board was Rose Funfsehn of Seattle (represented in *Betsy's Wedding* as the incidental "Victoria").

Betsy came home in "a dark blue suit with a wide belt of crimson satin. With a black hat and a crimson veil, it made a stunning outfit."[963] Maud bought this same suit - but in London, rather than in Paris. "*The suit is such a dark blue that it is almost black, and the skirt is one of the new styles, lots of gathers around the waist, while the jacket is about medium length and has a soft wide belt of bright colored satin. With a black hat and a veil the color of the satin it will make a stunning outfit.*"[964]

Illustrator Vera Neville obviously referred to the photograph taken of Maud on deck of the *St. Louis*, for the cover of *Betsy and the Great World* is almost identical to it.

854 *Heaven to Betsy*, p. 267.
855 *Betsy and Joe*, p. 43.
856 *Betsy and the Great World,* p. 13.
857 MHL to J. Tessari, 8-11-73.
858 MHL to A. Wiecking.
859 *Mankato Free Press*, 3-29-11.
860 *Betsy and the Great World*, p. 15.
861 MHL to J. Tessari, 8-11-73.
862 MHL to M. Freeman, 5-19-64.
863 *Betsy and the Great World*, p. 16.
864 *Betsy Was a Junior*, pp. 204-205.
865 MLK to SSW, 11-15-91.
866 LWW, IV.
867 Ibid.
868 *Emily of Deep Valley*, p. 121.
869 1912 G. Notes, p. 4.
870 *Betsy and the Great World*, p. 15.
871 MHL to E. Deike, 8-25-66.
872 *The Minnesota Daily*, 5-14-12.
873 MHL to J. Tessari, 8-11-73.
874 *Minnesota Writers*, p. 206, 1961.
875 *Betsy and the Great World*, p. 18.
876 Ibid., p. 24.
877 Interview with P. Cavanaugh, 11-4-90.
878 *Betsy and the Great World*, p. 24.
879 ADB to SSW, 2-26-91.
880 *Betsy and the Great World*, p. 24.
881 *Betsy's Wedding*, p. 47.
882 *Minneapolis Journal*, 12-4-13.
883 *Betsy and the Great World*, p. 83.
884 Ibid.
885 MHL to J. Tessari, 8-11-73.
886 *Betsy and the Great World*, p. 22.
887 MPH to Hart Family, p. 9.
888 R/N *Betsy's Wedding.*
889 *Betsy and the Great World*, p. 106.
890 MPH to Hart Family, p. 140.
891 MHL to J. Tessari, 8-11-73.
892 R/N *Betsy's Wedding.*

[893] *Betsy and the Great World*, p. 3.

[894] *Betsy in Spite of Herself*, p. 101.

[895] MPH to Hart Family, p. 45.

[896] *Betsy and the Great World*, p. 63.

[897] *Gentlemen from England*, p. 50.

[898] MPH to Hart Family, p. 44.

[899] *Betsy and the Great World*, p. 32.

[900] *Canopic* log, p. 40.

[901] MPH to Hart Family, 2-12-14.

[902] M.V. Hughes, *A London Home in the 1890s* (Oxford: Oxford University Press, 1946), p. 81.

[903] *Betsy and the Great World,* pp. 32-33.

[904] *Betsy in Spite of Herself*, p. 166.

[905] *Heaven to Betsy*, p. 176.

[906] MPH to Hart Family, 2-10-14.

[907] Ibid.

[908] *Betsy and the Great World*, p. 41.

[909] *The Beloved Vagabond*, p. 5.

[910] *Betsy and the Great World*, p. 104.

[911] Lovelace, "A Child's Reading."

[912] *Betsy and the Great World*, p. 53.

[913] Ibid., p. 125.

[914] MPH to Hart Family, 2-28-14.

[915] MPH to Hart Family, 2-23-14.

[916] MPH to Hart Family, 2-21-14.

[917] *Betsy and the Great World*, p. 132.

[918] *Betsy Was a Junior*, p. 247.

[919] *Betsy's Wedding*, p. 53.

[920] *Betsy and the Great World*, p. 133.

[921] *Betsy Was a Junior*, p. 248.

[922] MPH to Hart Family, 3-10-14.

[923] MPH to Hart Family, p. 58.

[924] *Betsy and the Great World*, p. 21.

[925] Ibid., p. 172.

[926] Ibid., pp. 140-141.

[927] *Betsy's Wedding*, p. 84.

[928] MPH to Hart Family, 4-3-14.

[929] MPH to Hart Family, 3-10-14.

[930] MPH to Hart Family, p. 90 (4-9-14).

[931] *Betsy and the Great World*, p. 188.
[932] Ibid., p. 170.
[933] MPH to Hart Family, p. 50.
[934] MPH, "The Vagabond," p. 3.
[935] Ibid., pp. 5-6.
[936] MPH to Hart Family, p. 108.
[937] Ibid.
[938] Ibid., p. 104.
[939] *Betsy and the Great World*, p. 212.
[940] ADB to SSW, 3-9-91.
[941] MPH to Hart Family, p. 162.
[942] Ibid., p. 72 (3-31-14).
[943] *Betsy and the Great World*, p. 220.
[944] MPH to Hart Family, p. 166.
[945] Ibid., p. 169.
[946] Ibid., pp. 216-223.
[947] MHL to L. Demp, 8-14-62.
[948] *Betsy and the Great World*, p. 265.
[949] MHL to M. Freeman, 5-19-64.
[950] MPH to Hart Family, p. 275.
[951] Ibid., p. 292.
[952] MHL to L. Demp, 8-14-62.
[953] *Minneapolis Sunday Tribune*, 11-9-52.
[954] MHL to L. Demp, 8-14-62.
[955] *Betsy and the Great World*, p. 278.
[956] MPH to Hart Family, p. 305.
[957] Ibid., p. 309.
[958] MHL to I. Veigel, 8-23-66.
[959] *Betsy and the Great World*, p. 282.
[960] MHL to L. Demp, 8-14-62.
[961] *Betsy and the Great World*, p. 290.
[962] MPH to Hart Family, p. 355.
[963] *Betsy and the Great World*, p. 267.
[964] MPH to Hart Family, p. 306-307.

CHAPTER THIRTEEN
On *Betsy's Wedding*
September 1914 to June 1917

A wedding reception was held at the Waldorf-Astoria Hotel in New York City on September 24, 1955. The bride and groom were literally storybook characters: Betsy Ray and Joe Willard. The reception was complete with formal invitations and wedding cake. A bride doll was made for the occasion (with a veil made by author Esther Hautzig, then working in children's book promotion for the publisher, T.Y. Crowell). Subsequently, the doll (and two smaller versions) traveled to libraries nationwide, finally ending its journey at Mankato's Blue Earth County Historical Society.

Maud Hart Lovelace fans had been holding their collective breath for months, awaiting the advent of the tenth and final volume of the Betsy-Tacy series. Whether or not a Betsy-Tacy reader experienced this original "first generation" excitement, *Betsy's Wedding* is an extremely satisfying final volume. (The working title of this book had been *Mrs. Betsy*.) The following lines, from the last pages of Betsy and the Great World, present not so much a cliffhanger as a pledge of the book to come, a book to finish the story. Maud has tied no two books in the series more closely together than these last two.

After the Germans marched into Belgium, Joe had cabled to the Agony Column: "BETSY. THE GREAT WAR IS ON BUT I HOPE OURS IS OVER, PLEASE COME HOME. JOE."

Betsy had cabled in reply: "JOE. PLEASE MEET S.S. RICHMOND ARRIVING NEW YORK SEPTEMBER 7. LOVE. BETSY."[965]

As the ship comes in view of the New York skyline, a man at the rail comments, "Why it's Lilliput! You feel you could take it up on the palm of your hand!"[966] This metaphor was taken from a description written by Delos on the Staten Island Ferry. "*You feel that you could stride to the vaulting towers and pick them all up in the palm of your hand.*"[967] Delos also mentions a slender four-masted schooner just like the one Betsy sees on page 5.

On page 9, we find Joe striding across the Customs building to Betsy as she disembarks, and he loses no time in saying, "When can we get married?" (In the first draft, Betsy responded, "*When can we have lunch?*") He asks again on page 11. On page 13, he says he can wait a week. But on page 15, Betsy says, "Joe Willard, you know very well that you haven't even proposed!" He tells her to hurry and finish her ice cream so they can get to Central Park. But he doesn't propose there, either. "There isn't time now!" Joe says. They have to hurry to get to Tiffany's before it closes. "Our engagement is announced!" he says on page 19, after buying her wedding ring. Nevertheless, he still hasn't proposed. He says some very romantic things after dinner, including, "Love me always, Betsy!" and she promises to marry him. But Joe never says "Will you marry me?" (which seems to be what Betsy is waiting for). And if all those earlier remarks didn't satisfy her, the ones at the end of page 21 shouldn't have, either (unless they were made on one knee) - but they obviously did satisfy Betsy (and her loyal readers, too)!

Though in later years she destroyed their correspondence, Maud made notes from the letters Delos wrote to her. He described her as *"frail ... like a fairy lady. A slender gracefully swaying tulip lady ... rosy hued ... satin. A mere girl, so small she is lost in my arms. Gentle voice, tremulous smile, sweet lips, soft kisses. ... the gypsy tent of your fair falling darkly, softly about my face."*[968] Some of his expressions will sound familiar to Betsy-Tacy readers: *"I love you. I could set those three words to triumphant music.... Love me always. I have given my whole heart to you.... You fit into my life as perfectly as a rose fits to its stem. You and I fit together like the pieces of a broken coin."*

Joe and Betsy have lunch at the Waldorf-Astoria. This hotel is no longer at the corner of 5th Avenue and 34th Street in New York City. The Old Waldorf has been replaced by the Empire State Building. The New Waldorf, on Park at 50th, does have its own Peacock Alley, however. (Betsy is sure she has the handsomest escort when she and Joe walk down Peacock Alley at the Waldorf.) Joe calls New York a "marvelous mad city" on page 13. This expression came from Maud's 1928 diary.

Joe talks of making crepes suzette at Chez Minette. He really was a good cook. One old friend remembered that Delos made a mean strawberry shortcake, with biscuit, not cake. Shortly after Delos' death, Maud wrote to a fan, describing her new cottage with its kitchenette, *"Delossy would have enjoyed it when he felt like making a strawberry shortcake."*[969]

Chez Minette was probably based on Maria's basement restaurant on Macdougal Street. Minette appears as Madame Grevy in "Love's Daily Dozen," in which the hero had "*relished French cooking as a doughboy.*"[970] Madame Grevy's tables, like Minette's, were covered in red, and chicken was the specialty.

After a wonderful day and evening together in New York, Joe takes Betsy to the train station. For the run from Chicago to Minneapolis on the Pioneer Limited, Maud intended to have Betsy meet Dan Healey on his famous dining car - he was to have given her a box of candy. This never made it to the final manuscript.

Betsy treasures the thought of her engagement on the journey to Minnesota. It is an emotional return. "*Minnesota, hail to thee*!" Betsy whispers, staring out as the train crosses the Mississippi River. We are as glad to find the Ray family waiting for her on the platform as she is, but we are not familiar with the house to which they take her. On first reading, it seems strange to find the Rays at home in a house that is unknown to us.

The fictional address of this gray stucco home was 909 Hazel Street. In reality, the Hart family lived at 905 W. 25th Street from 1911 until 1934. The house was torn down in 1974. It stood in the block which became Mueller Park. The Hart family used to joke about a large house on the northwest corner of Bryant and 25th. "*Daddy used to call it 'the Kaiser's' because it belonged to a rich German whom Daddy thought was pro-German during the war.*"[971]

Mr. Ray points out that he has stayed home from the store to welcome Betsy. Tom Hart had no store in Minneapolis. He had returned to the wholesale end of the shoe business (at which he had been so successful before the turn of the century). Tom represented the Foot-Schultz Company and also the Strutwear Knitting Company. Floyd Smith of Minneapolis worked for Tom Hart, carting the heavy boxes of sample shoes in and out of stores. Floyd also drove for Tom, since Tom never did learn to drive.

When their new black Overland arrives, Mr. Ray coaxes Mrs. Ray into taking driving lessons. He says, "To tell you the truth ... I don't want to learn."[972] Mrs. Hart apparently took to the idea better than Mrs. Ray did, and Kathleen learned to drive, too. (Maud, however, never drove.) The Harts' first auto was really a black Overland (followed later by an Essex). Delos really drove the

MHL Archive

905 W. 25th Street about 1917
(909 Hazel Street)

The Ray home in Minneapolis was "a gray stucco bungalow, gay with striped awnings and flowers still bright in window boxes around a glassed-in porch. The porch was covered with reddening vines which her father had transplanted from their home in Deep Valley." (BW p. 25)

Minnesota Valley Regional Library

905 with Remodeled Porch

About 1919, the Harts enclosed their porch and moved the front door from its central position (see photo at top of page) to the east end of the porch. Maud wrote to a fan: "*We were a happy family in 905 West 25th Street.*" (J.T. 8-11-73)

MHL Archive

Stella in Style

Stella models a new cape on the steps of 905 W. 25th Street.

MHL Archive

Stella and Tom Hart

Coll. of Alice Brown

Alice Dunnell
(Louisa Hilton)

"... a tall exuberant girl came in." (BW p. 28) Margaret's best friend, Louisa, was based on Helen's friend Alice.

Coll. of Alice Brown

Helen and Alice
(Margaret and Louisa)

"Margaret hurried from the kitchen lugging a huge fluffy cat. 'This is Kismet.'" (BW p. 26) The Harts really had a cat named Kismet while Helen was in high school. "*They all loved that cat - no Persian - just a big alley cat - but the cat was important to everyone.*" (A.B. 3-9-91)

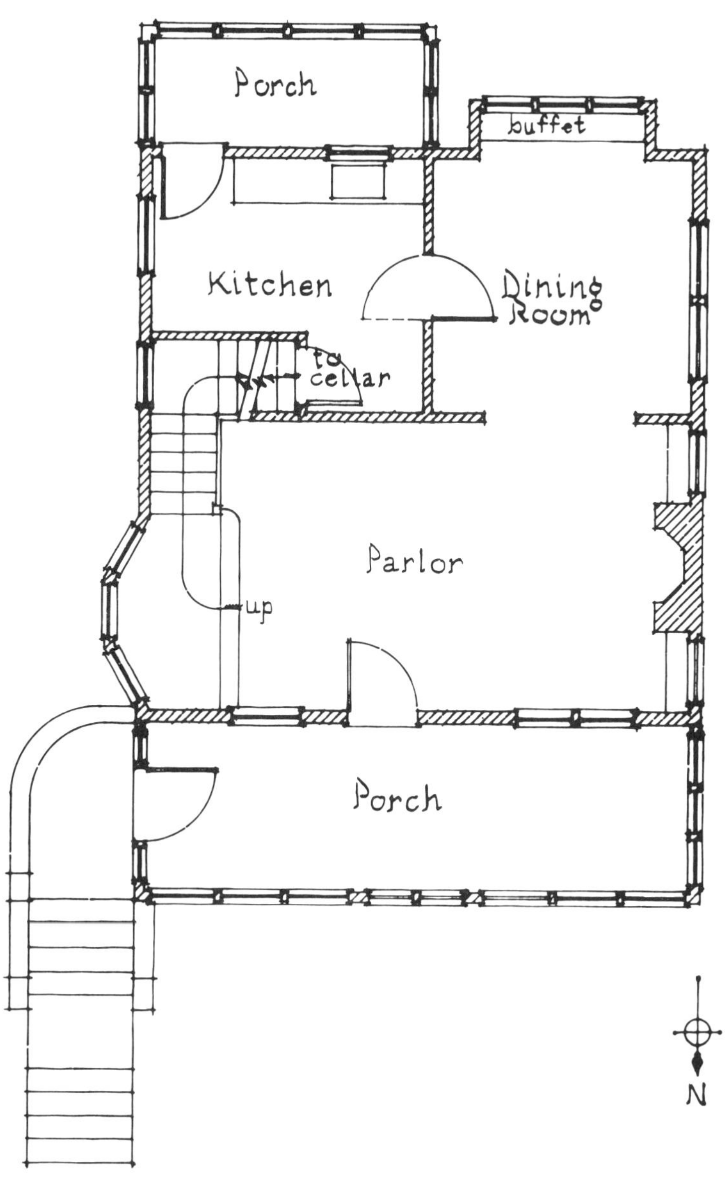

Plan by Architect Nancy Beckner Bastian

Floor Plan of 905 W. 25th Street
First Floor

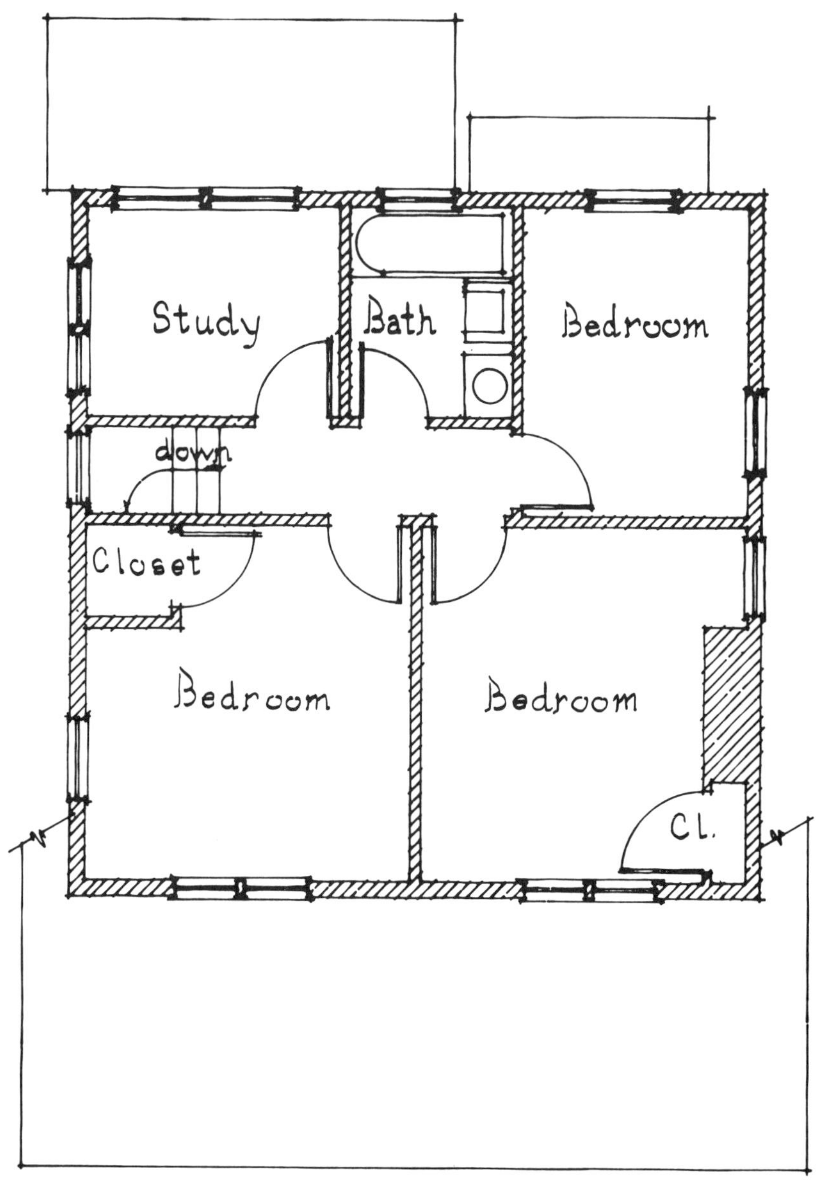

Plan by Architect Nancy Beckner Bastian

Floor Plan of 905 W. 25th Street
Second Floor

Harts around Minneapolis. The family joked about his having stripped the Overland's gears, twice. Maud once commented that *"Delos is not a good driver, but he is a fearless driver."*[973] Merian Kirchner notes that this remark must have been made in jest, since her father was in fact a good driver!

Anna is still living with the Rays. She has changed, too. "The knob of hair atop her head was gray, and her broad, kind face looked thinner."[974] But no Anna accompanied the Harts when they left Mankato. According to all family friends who can remember back to 1917, the Harts had no hired girl in Minneapolis. The house was too small.

Margaret now "looked like a young lady, in skirts to her shoetops. She wore her hair, like Tacy's, in coronet braids."[975]

Alice Dunnell appears in *Betsy's Wedding* as the character Louisa Hilton. She had "become Margaret's inseparable friend. She called Margaret Bogie and Margaret called her Boogie."[976] Alice verified that Helen's nickname was indeed "Bogie," but Alice herself had no nickname other than "Ali."

Alice remembered the Hart home with great fondness. *"I used to stay all night fairly often with Helen - and Dad Hart always brought us breakfast in bed. He had the most unusual faculty for making a person feel important - nothing he said - just the way one was treated. I loved that dear man, as everyone did."*[977]

Tom Hart wore a large, covered gold watch across his stomach. Alice recalled: *"When I first brought my baby over to Harts', Dad Hart reached for her (and she was perfectly willing to go to him). He took out his covered watch and let her suck on it. Mama Hart was horrified. He said, 'My three girls were teethed on it, so Alice's baby can.'"*[978]

When the Rays, kissing and weeping, welcome Betsy back to 905, Mr. Ray grumbles, "Darn fool girls!"[979] One of Tom Hart's favorite expressions was actually, "*Worthless girls*!" An editor apparently made the change to "darn fool."

Alice enjoyed conversations with Maud, who, like Betsy, was often back at her parents' home. *"One day Maud asked me what I wanted most in my life to do - I was in high school then. I told her I wanted a wonderful husband, a little house and children. So later, when I was married and had a husband and a home and my first baby, she said, 'Now are you happy?' I told her 'Yes!' I had everything I wanted."*[980]

Alice was married at St. Paul's Episcopal Church (the same one Maud attended) in 1921. Helen Hart was one of her bridesmaids.

Thanks to Louisa's cheerful chattering, we learn that Margaret has an admirer. "There's a tall skinny boy works in the lunch room. He's crazy about Bogie.... He just piles gravy on Bogie's roast beef sandwich. Honestly, he does! Mashed potatoes, too. The rest of us don't get a bite, hardly."[981] Helen did indeed meet her future husband, Frank Fowler, at West High School. He was the cashier in the lunch room (and perhaps also ladled out the gravy). One year younger than Helen, Frank inspired the character Clay Dawson.

Betsy met Joe at the station "in a week, less a day."[982] This would have been September 13, if you figured from September 7, the day she arrived in New York. The next day, Betsy's wedding day, would then have been September 14. But on page 22, she wakes up on the train "the second morning after leaving Joe." (She proceeds to pull her "underwear" from a hammock swinging beside her berth. An early draft showed that Maud originally intended to have Betsy pull her "girdle" from the hammock!) Betsy left Joe on the 7th, so the second morning, the day of her arrival home, would have been the 9th. Therefore a week, less a day, after her arrival home would have been the 15th - so Betsy's wedding day would have been September 16, 1914.

"They rode back down a morning-fresh Hennepin Avenue to Fourth Street where the *Tribune* and the rival *Journal* offices stood."[983] The *Tribune* did stand at 57-61 South Fourth (a subscription to the daily was 25 cents per month!), and the *Journal* was down the street at 47-49 South Fourth. Both stood between Nicollet and Marquette. There was, however, no *Courier* in Minneapolis. The only other major newspaper at this time was the *Minneapolis Daily News* on Second Avenue at Sixth (for which Delos had worked in 1915). Those of us who are not Minnesotans will perhaps be pleased to discover that Hennepin Avenue and Nicollet Avenue (Minneapolitans pronounce this "Nick-let," dropping out the middle syllable) are real Minneapolis streets.

Joe has no luck finding a job at any of the newspapers, and the cab takes them next to the Marsh Arcade. Betsy "prayed all the way up Nicollet Avenue to Tenth Street."[984] The Marsh Arcade

1917 Hesperian

Helen in Coronet Braids

Like Margaret, Helen wore her hair in coronet braids.

Minnesota Valley Regional Library

Helen Hart

This photo was probably taken in the spring of 1917, when Helen graduated from West High School in Minneapolis.

1917 Hesperian

Frank Fowler
(Clay Dawson)

"Betsy, he's a star! At everything long-legged. Basketball, track, tennis!" (BW p. 189)

Lake Place
Lake of the Isles
Lake Calhoun
Lake Harriet

James Ave.
Irving Ave. S.
Humboldt Ave. S.
Holmes Ave.
Hennepin Ave.
Girard Ave. S.
Fremont Ave. S.
Emerson Ave. S.
Dupont Ave. S.
Colfax Ave. S.
Bryant Ave. S.
Aldrich Ave. S.
Lyndale Ave. S.

24th Street
25th Street
26th Street
27th Street
28th Street
29th Street
Lake Street
31st Street
32nd Street
33rd Street
34th Street
35th Street
36th Street
37th Street
38th Street
39th Street
40th Street
41st Street
42nd Street
43rd Street
44th Street
45th Street
46th Street
47th Street
48th Street
49th Street
50th Street

1. 2400 Aldrich Ave. S. - 1st Lovelace Apt.
2. 905 W. 25th St. - Hart Home
3. 1109 W. 25th St. - Lovelace Home
4. 2900 James Ave. S. - Lovelace Apt. (1927)
5. 2533 Colfax Ave. S. - Jim Hart Family
6. 2640 Colfax Ave. S. - Kenney Family (1915-1919)
7. 2731 Fremont Ave. S. - Harts' first Mpls. residence (rented 1911)
8. 2447 Colfax Ave. S. - Fowlers (1925-1927)
9. 3532 Fremont Ave. S. - Fowlers (1928-1935)
10. 2600 Colfax Ave. S. - Bibbs (1919-1920)
11. 2530 Dupont Ave. S. - Fosters (1931-1934)
12. 4648 Dupont Ave. S. - Wakefields

"A chain of lakes ran actually through the city. Their shores were lined with homes, and even closer to the water lay the public boulevards, scattered with picnickers, fishermen, children with buckets...." (BW p. 76)

Coll. of Minnesota History Collection, Minneapolis Public Library

Meyers Arcade
(Marsh Arcade)

"The Marsh Arcade! Betsy thought to herself. Why was he going to that group of fashionable little shops? There were a few offices on the upper floors, she remembered." (BW p. 41)

Coll. of Minnesota History Collection, Minneapolis Public Library

Interior, Meyers Arcade

The Meyers Arcade led Nicollet Avenue in fashion and elegance in pre-World War I Minneapolis.

Interior, Meyers Arcade - Wakefield Publicity Bureau

This was the third-floor office of Lillian Wakefield, who was inspired with the rather brilliant idea of bringing together Maud Hart and Delos Lovelace.

Former Wakefield Office
301 Meyers Arcade

"This was the happy office of which Joe had told her so often. Mrs. Hawthorne's reddish-brown head was bent over another typewriter. At the sound of the opening door, she looked up with her queenly air." (BW p. 228)

Coll. of Lucy Crabtree

Lillian and Harry Wakefield

"Bradford Hawthorne was a small, alert man, with eyeglasses on a humorous face." (BW p. 61) was "that group of fashionable little shops. There were a few offices on the upper floors, she remembered, but could one of them hold a job for Joe?"[985]

The Meyers Arcade was at Tenth and Nicollet (920 Nicollet Avenue). It was built by former Minneapolis mayor J.E. Meyers in 1911. The building was purchased by the Nicollet Arcade Company in 1938 and renamed "the Nicollet Arcade." There was a publicity bureau in the Meyers Arcade - the Wakefield Publicity Bureau, run by Lillian Hammons Wakefield (to whom *Betsy's Wedding* is dedicated).

Lillian Wakefield first opened her publicity bureau on the third floor of the arcade in 1916 and maintained the office until 1918. During the war, she was the manager of the YMCA's publicity bureau. She reopened the Meyers Arcade office in 1919, this time on the second floor. At the end of *Betsy's Wedding*, Betsy "went up the stairs to the second floor and the Hawthorne Publicity Bureau."[986] The office would have been the third floor, 301 Meyers Arcade, when first Delos, then Maud, worked at the Wakefield Publicity Bureau.

Maud was hired to fill Delos' position when he left to join the First Officers Training Camp at Fort Snelling in the spring of 1917. Maud recalled working in Mrs. Wakefield's office. Mrs. Wakefield "*told me to look through the collection of articles and materials to see the kind of thing they were doing. I remember coming across Delos' name and saying, 'Why, what name is this? It sounds like a valentine.' Then I went on to read some of the things he had written, and I said, 'My, he certainly writes well.*'"[987] (The name sounded even more like a Valentine when Maud added a "Hart" to it!)

Lillian's husband, Harry B. Wakefield, was city editor of the *Minneapolis Tribune*. It seems likely that he would have steered Delos, and later Maud, to his wife's office. Maud and Delos had both written for the *Trib* before they met.

It was Mrs. Wakefield who brought Maud and Delos together. Maud said, "*Mrs. Wakefield was a great matchmaker, and she invited Delos, myself, and Helen to dinner at her home -- I think she invited Helen because she was young enough not to give any competition. Well, we had a lovely time. Delos and I were seated across from each other and we kept eyeing each other. I remember Helen was walked home and then*

Delos and I walked and walked, around the lakes, and talked and talked - - it was practically dawn before we reached my home."[988] This was in April 1917.

"I told Mrs. Hawthorne that I'd rather not start work until Monday. That gives us three days for a honeymoon, if we're married tomorrow...."[989] So Betsy and Joe's wedding was on a Thursday. (September 16 was a Wednesday in 1914.) Maud and Delos were actually married on Thanksgiving Day - Thursday, November 29, 1917. It was no doubt chosen because Delos could more readily obtain a military pass over the holiday, for the boss to whom Delos had to apply for a few days off was the U.S. Army! Delos had to return to Camp Dodge in Iowa on the Monday after their marriage (he had been there since September).

Anna wears a black silk dress at Betsy's wedding. She is fulfilling a promise made in *Heaven to Betsy*. Anna had just come to the Ray household, and Betsy had accompanied her to the attic bedroom to help her unpack. Anna lifted a black silk dress from her valise and remarked: "This is my best dress ... I'll wear it to your wedding, lovey."[990] Maud doesn't remind us in *Betsy's Wedding* of Anna's promise, but an attentive reader enjoys the subtle touch.

"Paige would be best man and Julia matron-of-honor."[991] In real life, Kathleen's first husband, Captain Eugene Bibb, was best man. Kathleen was matron of honor. Eugene Bibb was one of the witnesses who signed Maud's marriage certificate. (The other was Mrs. C.W. Holden, Bick's sister Tess - the fictional Katie.) While sketching the plot line for *Betsy's Wedding*, Maud considered claiming that Betsy and Joe's wedding had to be hurried so that Julia could get back to New York for the opening of *Romeo and Juliet* on September 14. Kathleen did sing with the Century Opera Company, but she was not in their cast of *Romeo and Juliet* (which did open in New York on September 14, 1914). It is perhaps surprisingly that Maud didn't feature Julia on the cover of the *New York Musical Courier* for August 1914 - as Kathleen was featured.

Mrs. Ray gets on the phone to invite "uncles, aunts, and cousins."[992] This sounds like a veritable gaggle of relatives (since references to extended family are rare in the Betsy-Tacy books).

Photos from Kathleen Hart's Operatic Portfolio

Minnesota Valley Regional Library

Duplicated in several collections

Duplicated in several collections

Duplicated in several collections

Minnesota History Collection, Minneapolis Public Library

Dining Room at Schiek's

Joe's bachelor's dinner was held at Shiek's (sic).

Coll. of Millicent Steiner

Jab Lloyd about 1917

Like Cab and Betsy, Jab was really married on the same day as Maud, November 29, 1917.

Maud is referring here to the family of Jim Hart, who lived less than a block away, at 2533 Colfax Avenue South. Jim and Maud Fowler Hart's three children were James Fowler, Edwin, and Edith. Fowler (as the eldest was known) was two years younger than Maud Palmer Hart but three years behind in school. Edwin was five years younger than Maud, and Edith was seven years younger.

The two Hart families had also been neighbors in Mankato. Jim Hart had built a house at 112 Bradley (across from Midge's), just blocks from Tom Hart's Center Street home, and he and his family later lived at 203 Clark Street. Jim moved his family to Minneapolis only a year after Tom's family left Mankato. So the two families lived in very close proximity until 1921, when the Jim Harts moved out west. Jim and his family attended Maud's wedding - Kathleen's too, in 1913. (Edith Hart was in Kathleen's bridal party, stringing ribbons with Helen.) Maud wrote: "*We lived close to each other for many years and were inseparable companions*."[993] Perhaps the reason Betsy is always so comfortable with boys in the books is that, from an early age, Maud's cousins were almost like brothers. She was no doubt prevented from representing these cousins in the series by her editors, who pressured Maud to limit the number of characters she introduced.

After Mrs. Ray invites the relatives, Betsy telephones Carney. "Sam, her husband, had been transferred to Minneapolis, and they lived with a baby daughter just a few blocks away."[994] This made for a good story, but Marion and Bill Everett didn't marry until after the war (August 27, 1919), two years after Maud and Delos were married. Their baby daughter, the fictional Judy (really named "Louise"), didn't come along until four years after the Everetts were married. Marion and Bill moved to Minneapolis in 1920, to 2949 Portland Avenue South. (More than "a few blocks" from the Harts - but only about a mile away.)

One might have imagined a group of girls from the class of 1910 to be married long before 1917. Maud was one of the first, rather than the last, of her Crowd to marry. Only Winona I (November 1914) and Irma (August 1917) were married earlier.

Cab is phoned, too, but has his own wedding to attend the next day. Jab Lloyd really married Grace Cable Reed in Jamestown,

North Dakota, on November 29, 1917 (Maud and Delos' wedding day). "It seemed beautifully fitting that she and Cab, friends of so many years, should have the same wedding day."[995]

"We'll have Bachelors' Dinner at Shiek's," Paige said.[996] Schiek's (note actual spelling) was at 45 South Third Street. This cafe was opened by Fred Schiek in 1894. It had a "family entrance" which enabled women to enter without passing the bar. There was an alley entrance through which stars from the Metropolitan Theater could enter incognito. Some of these old-time stars were mentioned in the Betsy-Tacy books; for example, De Wolf Hopper patronized Schiek's. (See *Downtown*, in which Jerry demurs when Julia asks him to sing. "I'm no De Wolf Hopper."[997]) Another connection: "*Chauncey Olcott, the Irish tenor, used to sing 'My Wild Irish Rose' to the edification of the customers when he dined at Fred Schiek's special table.*"[998] Other celebrity diners at Schiek's included "*Caruso* [mentioned in *Heaven to Betsy*[999]], *Paderewski* [mentioned in *Betsy in Spite of Herself*[1000]], *Anna Held* [mentioned in *Heaven to Betsy*[1001]], *Flo Ziegfeld* [mentioned in *Betsy and Joe*[1002]], *E. H. Sothern* [mentioned in *Betsy in Spite of Herself*[1003]], *John Drew* [mentioned in *Heaven to Betsy*[1004]], *Lillian Russell* [mentioned in *Betsy and Joe*[1005]], *and the Barrymores* [Ethel mentioned in *Heaven to Betsy*[1006]]."[1007] Scheik's was demolished in 1961 to make way for the Sheraton Hotel. The restaurant moved to 115 South 4th, the former building of the Farmers and Mechanics Savings Bank. Part of the 1904 bar from the original Schiek's was moved to the new location.

Maud was married at five p.m. on November 29, 1917. Like Betsy's, Maud's wedding was held in the evening at her parents' home. Surely Bick was present, though newspaper accounts do not mention her name. They do mention the presence of Midge Gerlach (Tib) of Mankato, and another Mankato friend, Flossie Macbeth, the opera singer.

"The sweeping white silk was frothy with tulle. It even had long tulle sleeves. And Betsy planned to wear the tulle cap and veil, edged with orange blossoms, that Julia had worn for her wedding."[1008] Maud had described her wedding dress to Vera Neville: "*I had no photograph to send her, for there were none taken at our hurried wedding and there couldn't be one taken later, because I never wore the dress after our wedding day. It was carefully preserved, just as Betsy's was. (That's how sentimental I am!) It was later lost in a fire as shall be told in a later Betsy-Tacy book, if there is a later Betsy-Tacy book.*"[1009] (There was, of course, to be no later B-T book.)

The newspaper account of the wedding describes Maud's dress as follows: "*The bride wore a gown of white taffeta and tulle. The skirt was made bouffant effect and the bodice was cut decollete and finished with long tulle sleeves.*" The dress was "*elaborated*" with silver lace. Maud also wore "*the tulle veil that Mrs. Bibb had worn at her wedding, which was caught with orange blossoms.*"[1010]

Joe asks Betsy what she would like in her wedding bouquet, and the only thing she stipulates is forget-me-nots, which, as Paige points out, will be hard to get at that time of year. Margaret brings in the box with Betsy's bouquet. "*She opened it quickly, and he had found forget-me-nots! Blue and reassuring, they were scattered among pink roses above a shower of white satin ribbons.*"[1011] The newspaper account of Maud's wedding verifies the components: "*Her bouquet was a shower of pale pink roses and forget-me-nots.*"[1012]

In research material for *Betsy's Wedding*, Maud noted that a good going-away outfit for Betsy would include a "*fur-trimmed draped velvet coat or a white chinchilla coat.*"[1013] In the book, it was a "velvet wrap."[1014] Betsy's wedding cake, meanwhile, was to have been decorated with pink, blue, and green flowers and a dove with ribbons in his mouth. The specific flower colors were not included in the final version of the book.

Julia, as matron of honor, was "dressed in pale green and carrying violets."[1015] According to the *Minneapolis Journal*, Kathleen wore "*a gown of gray chiffon with rose color beading and held pink roses and violets.*"[1016] (The *Tribune* claimed that Kathleen's gray dress was of panne velvet and the flowers were a corsage bouquet.)

The Ray fireplace "was quite concealed by fragrant greenery, and golden chrysanthemums, and lighted golden tapers."[1017] At the Hart home, "*The vows were spoken before an altar of yellow chrysanthemums and palms arranged at one end of the living room. Killarney roses were used in the dining room.*"[1018]

Portraying Delos as Joe in *Betsy's Wedding* gave Maud great pleasure. For the first time, she was writing about a period during which she had known him. Maud commented: "*It was so pleasant for me to have Delos really and honestly in the picture. I had always tried, in the earlier books, to have Joe walk and talk and behave like Delos, but as one of my friends said to me about* Betsy's Wedding, *Delos walks right off the pages*."[1019]

Betsy and Joe honeymooned at Lake Minnetonka, which is about seventeen miles west of Minneapolis. The honeymoon cottage belonged to Tacy and Harry, but Bick and Charley were not yet married in 1917, much less Minnetonka property owners. At first, Maud planned to represent the fictional cottage as Katie and Leo's (the chocolate cake left for the Willards being one of those for which Katie was famous). Maud and Delos spent part of the summer of 1921 at a house on Jennings Bay at Lake Minnetonka. The front of this green house rested on posts. Here they sat out at sunset and discussed their departure for New York.

On their honeymoon, Joe says, "It would be fun to live in a place like this." Betsy replies, "It would be perfect! Just perfect for two writers!"[1020] The Lovelaces were able to live at Lake Minnetonka by 1924, since Delos was then working freelance (writing many short stories) and would not have been required to make the journey into a Minneapolis office every day.

Though not on stilts, the lakefront house Maud and Delos bought overlooks the lake from the top of a high bank, like Betsy and Joe's honeymoon cottage. The house also has "a steep flight of steps" which go down to the lake. And "the bank here was high and wild, crowded with bronzy undergrowth and trees leaning over the water."[1021] Betsy and Joe's honeymoon cottage was probably something of a cross between the Jennings Bay house they rented in 1924 and their Casco Point cottage.

Delos described cottage as "*a shabby, rambling, delightful home on Lake Minnetonka where a rickety stairway led down to the water, asparagus tried to grow in the rear half-acre, a rustic table stood always ready for friends who usually brought half of the meal served on it, and a wide porch faced the rich Minnesota sunsets*."[1022]

The property is located at 2525 Dunwoody Avenue, on Casco Point (Maud referred to it as "Indian Point"), facing Spring Park Bay. The house was sold in 1939 to Arthur Tourangeau. Mr. Tourangeau's son, Arthur Jr., recalled that at the time his parents purchased the house, it had been winterized, but not thoroughly. The Lovelaces used it mostly for summers.

Duplicated in several collections

Maud and Delos

This photograph was taken on the porch of 905 W. 25th Street. Maud's wedding ring can be seen on her left hand, which is resting on her husband's.

Photo by Jacque Cloninger

Japanese Boathouse

"There was a boathouse with a little peaked tower.... 'We must have come to Japan on our honeymoon!' 'I never did trust that Kerr!'" (BW p. 67)

Minnesota History Collection, Minneapolis Public Library

Hillcrest Surgical Hospital

Maud and Delos' first child was born here at 501 Franklin Avenue West in Minneapolis. He died three hours after birth. Years later, Maud said she was glad to have had him ... even for such a short time.

Duplicated in several collections

Maud and Delos at Lake Minnetonka

This photo was probably taken when the Lovelaces returned to visit their lake home in 1934.

2525 Dunwoody Avenue

"In the afternoons Joe and Betsy had sat on their lofty lawn, looking out at the lake which was sometimes cloth of silver and sometimes a carpet of diamonds." (BW p. 69)

Maud explained to a fan that, though the Lovelaces bought a home at Lake Minnetonka, "*we didn't have the Japanese boat house (as planned on page 70 of Betsy's Wedding). We loved it and didn't sell it for* [some time] *after we made our change to New York*."[1023]

There are actually two oriental boathouses on the shores of Lake Minnetonka which Maud and Delos may have admired while out rowing. One is the boathouse at Noerenberg Park in Orono which has a gazebo on top. The other is near the old streetcar boat landing at Woodside, called "Wood Port."

The streetcar boats were operated by Twin City Rapid Transit Co. And they were actually painted yellow, as described. "They're yellow like the streetcars. They're fun."[1024] "*The boats which would seat between 106 and 135 passengers, were canary yellow with a light olive trim; measured about 70 feet in length and 14 feet, 10 inches at the beam, and traveled 12 to 15 miles an hour. Interiors were a cherry color.*"[1025]

Back in Minneapolis once more, Betsy and Joe are delighted with their new life together. Maud and Delos must have particularly relished setting up housekeeping, since they had been separated by the war so soon after their marriage. Maud commented that "*all the early housekeeping experiences are actual*" in *Betsy's Wedding*. The Willards budget $30.00 for monthly rent. "Not more than thirty," Betsy insisted, "if we have to sleep in the park!"[1026] Towards the end of September, with some help from Margaret and Louisa, they find one. This is probably just how the Lovelaces found their first apartment after Delos came home from eleven months overseas in 1919. Helen's best friend, Alice Dunnell, really lived in an apartment building owned by her parents, Warren (an architect) and Ida. Mrs. Dunnell was the "serene, white-haired" Mrs. Hilton.[1027] Alice let Maud and Delos know that #7 at 2400 Aldrich Avenue South was available in the late fall of 1919. Maud set the fictional monthly rent at $27.50. The actual rent of their apartment was $32.00 monthly.

Alice's parents had bought a double corner lot at the corner of 24th and Aldrich when they were married. They built a big home at 2408 and a tennis court on the corner, with an ornamental iron fence around the whole property. The family suffered a serious financial loss about 1910, and with his remaining funds, Mr.

Dunnell built an eight-apartment building where the tennis court had been. Their home at 2408 Aldrich was sold. The Dunnells and their four children moved into two apartments at 2400 Aldrich.

Betsy and Joe followed Mrs. Hilton "up a flight of carpeted stairs, to the left-hand back apartment. Betsy calculated quickly. 'It will face south and east!'"[1028] In fact, apartment number 7, the left-hand back apartment, faces south and <u>west</u>.

"They entered a small foyer, shiningly empty ... they turned left into the empty living room, and Betsy ran forward, for at the end was one of those three-winged bay windows. And it looked straight into a yellowing elm tree. Right into the branches! ... Joe turned right, into the small kitchen. He returned in a flash to the living room and turned right again, through an archway, into the bedroom. He peeked into the bathroom, and came up to Betsy who was still looking out blissfully into the elm."[1029]

"In the back side corner of the house you will see the tree I looked out at when I was writing. It's the tree nearest the last window. These were tall beautiful trees; I hope they are still there. I can still hear my husband leaping up the steps to our door when he came home at night. How happy we were there!"[1030]

"I took a snapshot of the elm outside our window which I could look at when I sat there writing -- trying to decide what to say next. Also much of the furniture I described is in my cottage right now, for I always have liked old things better than new ones."[1031] The story of Mrs. Ray's father fashioning a drop-leaf table from a black walnut tree was true. Stella kept her laundry basket on it until Maud and Delos rescued it for romantic dinners in their first apartment. In 1991, their daughter Merian wrote that the table *"is such a link with family history. I am sitting at the table as I write."*[1032]

The apartment really had two doors. When Margaret and Louisa come to call, they use the front door. The ring at the back doorbell is the grocery boy (sent by Mr. Ray). *"And of course, Daddy did send over the groceries the day we moved in."*[1033]

Joe and Betsy receive many lovely wedding presents, and it seems likely that Maud and Delos were given very similar ones. Certainly they received the set of plated silver from her parents. "There was a bird in the pattern."[1034]

MHL Archive

2400 Aldrich Avenue South in 1940
(Bow Street Apartment House)

"The apartment building was set on a large elmy lawn. It had an entrance porch with fat fluted pillars." (BW p. 81)

2400 Aldrich Avenue South in 1984

The apartment building "looked like a large, stone, private house except for sets of triple windows, bulging out." (BW p. 81)

MHL Archive

2400 Aldrich Avenue in 1940

Betsy and Joe's bay window looked out into the branches of an elm tree.

2400 Aldrich Avenue in 1984

Betsy and Joe's elm is now gone, but new trees are growing in its place.

Minnesota History Collection, Minneapolis Public Library

St. Paul's Episcopal Church

"It was a plain church." (BW p. 153) It once stood at the corner of Bryant Avenue South and Franklin Avenue East in Minneapolis.

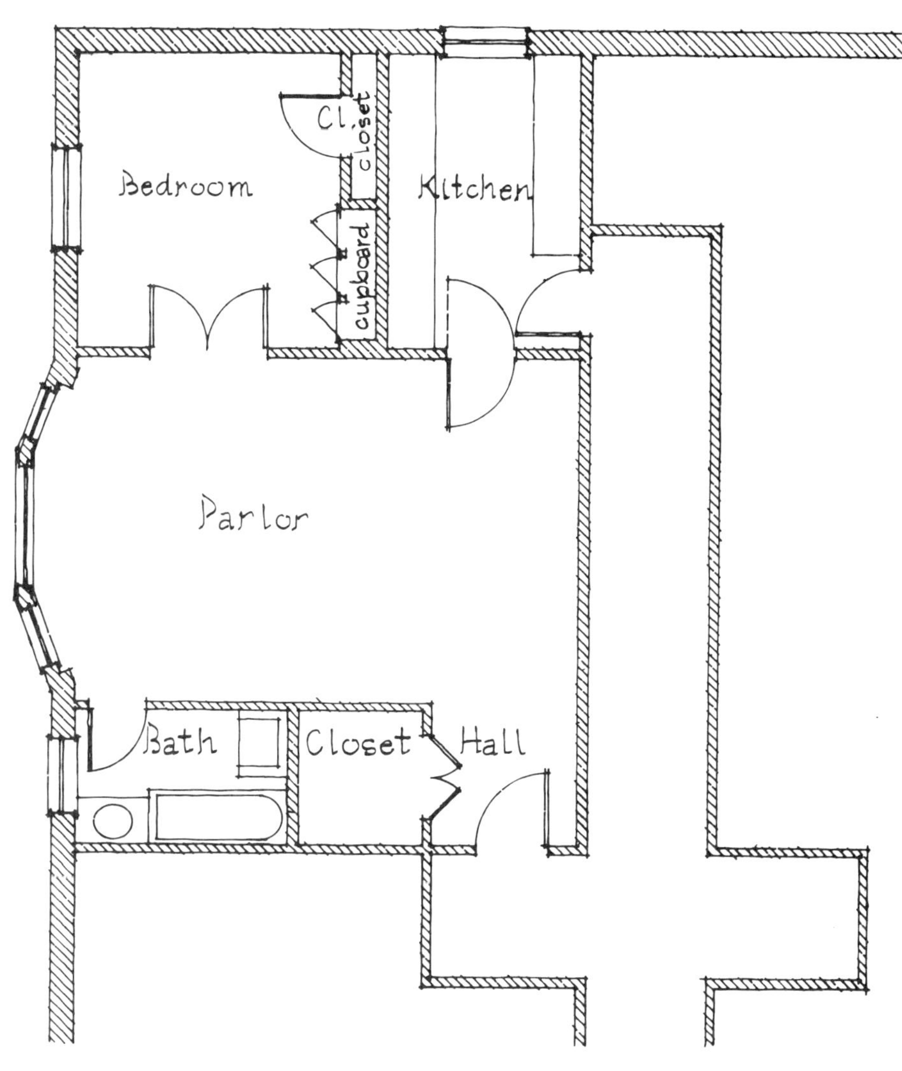

Plan by Architect Nancy Beckner Bastian

Floor Plan of 2400 Aldrich Avenue
Apartment Seven

Tacy and Harry gave them "Maxwell Parrish" pictures.[1035] *Carney's House Party* provides a second mention of "Maxwell Parrish" (whose pictures hung on Carney's dorm-room wall). The correct name, "Maxfield Parrish," appears in *Emily of Deep Valley.*[1036] (One of his prints hangs over the mantel in Annette's house.)

Betsy positions "a Japanese print of a long-legged bird in a marsh" over her desk in the new apartment. "It had always hung there. For some mysterious reason, Betsy claimed, it made her feel like writing."[1037] This is an inside joke between Maud and her readers! We all know what the mystery is. During high school summers, Betsy wrote at Murmuring Lake. The painting reminds her of the lake, which makes her feel like writing. Maud explains in *Betsy in Spite of Herself* that Betsy liked the print from Herbert because "it reminded her of the quiet bay, smelling of water lilies, and the faintly rocking boat, in which she had started her novel."[1038] Calling this piece of Betsy-Tacy history a "mystery" is done with a conspiratorial wink, and it's the sort of touch that makes readers into rereaders. In 1956, Maud wrote: "*The long-legged bird Herbert sent to Betsy, which always hung above her desk, hangs in my study now.*"[1039] Helmus Andrews sent this painting (which apparently also pictured a Japanese girl) to Maud for her birthday in 1907 (not in 1908, as per *Betsy In Spite of Herself*.)

After settling into the apartment, Betsy and Joe plan to buy groceries, for which Betsy has allowed ten dollars. "I hope ten dollars buys a lot, Mrs. Hetty Green," Joe says.[1040] Modern readers may not know that in Maud's day, Mrs. Hetty Green was considered the wealthiest woman in America, possibly in the world.

On page 105, Joe gives Betsy a cameo brooch for their first Christmas. Delos gave this brooch to Maud for Christmas in 1919. It had a white head with ringlets on onyx with crenelated borders.

"Betsy had budgeted Joe's salary of $155 a month - the budget was her department, he had said."[1041] The budget was obviously Maud's department, as confirmed by her Budget Book.[1042] The accounts begin after Delos' return from overseas, when the Lovelaces moved into the Aldrich Avenue apartment in November 1919.

The Budget Book is a window into the everyday concerns of Maud and Delos as they began married life together. Dayton's must have been Maud's favorite department store in Minneapolis. Her Budget Book reveals periodic payments (sometimes hefty ones) to Dayton's (with which most Twin Cities women can identify!). Cigarettes and tobacco are occasionally purchased. On March 30, 1920, Maud spent $1.25 for "*tea downtown*," perhaps with Bick or Midge.

Some of the grocery purchases reflect meals from *Betsy's Wedding*. In one scene, Joe "had gone back to his macaroni. It was good."[1043] On April 27, 1920, Maud purchased the following ingredients: "*cheese, milk, and macaroni*." Maud also bought coconut (17 cents), presumably for Delos' favorite cake. On December 18, 1919, she bought "*pancake flour and syrup*," no doubt for the Sunday-morning pancakes Delos, like Joe, enjoyed stirring up. Maud frequently selected pork chops (which Betsy burned on one occasion). Other meats included lamb chops, liver, "weenies," round steak, spare ribs, sausages, pot roast, beef heart, and pig heart. The most commonly appearing vegetables were potatoes, rutabagas, turnips, tomatoes, and rhubarb. Treats were purchased often: marshmallows, lady fingers, seafoam, macaroons, doughnuts, "Whip-o," ice cream, cream puffs, and chocolate.

Some of the brand names mentioned in Maud's Budget Book were: Lux (15¢), Lysol (50¢), Sapolio (8¢), Bon Ami (15¢), Mazola (38¢), Ivory Soap (9¢), and Quaker Oats (13¢). (Of course, Maud certainly never intended the items in her Budget Book to serve as product endorsements.)

The Selma mentioned in Maud's Budget Book has a fictional persona: "Betsy juggled the budget and engaged a stout Marta to come every Friday."[1044] Maud used the name Selma for the hired girl in *Winona's Pony Cart*.

The Budget Book contains a plan of attack for Maud's housekeeping. "*Monday: cleaning, icebox, breakbox, mending. Tuesday: cleaning, kitchen, white enamel, woodwork, silver. Wednesday:* [no entry]. *Thursday:* [alternately] *cleaning, kitchen floor, drawers and closets,* [or] *shampoo. Friday: cleaning, plate rail, wainscotting, shelves, white furniture,* [and] *ironing. Saturday: cleaning, bathroom floor, baking*." (What was left for Selma??) Maud obviously took her new job as seriously as Betsy did: "It's important, and very hard ... learning how to keep house."[1045]

It does not occur to Betsy that some might consider a "career" in housekeeping to be in some way demeaning. At the same time, readers are unlikely to think of Maud as a feminist. The word doesn't seem to apply because Betsy was so feminine. In fact, Betsy reveled in a hearty enjoyment of feminine trappings. In *Betsy and the Great World,* Mr. O'Farrell laughs at the idea of Betsy as a suffragette. "'You're feminine! You're pure Victorian! You don't belong to the twentieth century at all, at all.' 'Well, I can do the modern dances!' Betsy said indignantly, which made everyone laugh."[1046]

Though undeniably very feminine, Betsy invariably operated with an unconscious, matter-of-fact assumption that girls could essentially do anything boys could. She was never militant, precisely because this assumption was so deep-seated; equality was not something she felt she had to fight for - she took it for granted. Her family treated others, male or female, with respect - and Betsy chose friends who did likewise. When faced with sexist remarks like those Mr. O'Farrell made, Betsy was likely to be merely puzzled - and her response to O'Farrell was typical. She either considered his remarks to be purely for the sake of lively conversation or else she thought he was odd - but either way, it didn't matter enough to get upset about ... or to feel threatened by.

Maud's attitude on this subject is introduced way back in *Betsy-Tacy and Tib*. "'What about me, papa? Will I be an architect too?' asked Tib. '*Nein*, you will be a little housewife,' said her father. Betsy and Tacy thought that was strange, for Tib had done as much as Freddie toward building the house. But it didn't matter much, for in their hearts they were sure that Tib was going to be a dancer."[1047]

An attempt by a man to control what women can or should do "didn't matter much," since Betsy and her friends would proceed to do exactly as they pleased. When we see Tib in *Betsy's Wedding*, she is a strikingly independent young career woman. Tib ends her relationship with the irresistible Rocky because he isn't like Joe, who "thinks your work is important ... thinks <u>you</u> are important -- as a human being, not just as a girl."[1048] Tib commented: "Just because I'm small, men think I'm a clinging vine. They think I need to be protected. Imagine that! Why, I like to paddle my own canoe!"[1049] (In *Carney's House Party*, Sam asks Carney: "Do you paddle, or just sit and look beautiful?" She responds pithily, "I paddle."[1050]) Betsy was similarly independent, traveling alone through Europe. "I want to learn a way to earn my living,"[1051] she said, and we suspect that Betsy, like Maud, will successfully pursue a lifelong career as a writer. Tacy, meanwhile, wanted to get married and have babies, but it never occurred to any of them to be ashamed of this. She was doing what she wanted to do.

Since this attitude was so nonmilitant (despite being inexorable), Betsy (and Maud) saw no inconsistencies between loving creams, lotions, and curlers while being appalled by hope chests. It was not that the books were feminist "for their time." The women in the Betsy-Tacy books were like healthy women of any time: their attitudes and goals were firmly rooted in a basic self-respect.

That autumn, on the very day Betsy and Joe move into their new apartment, Tacy's son is born. It is unlikely that Maud brought Bick a doll from Germany, since Bick wasn't married when Maud was in Europe in 1914. In any case, all of Bick's three children were boys! The first, Robert Charles Kirch, was born in Minneapolis in October 1921. (According to Maud, he was really a homely, hairless baby until about age one!) Perhaps Maud received the news of his arrival in a manner similar to that described in *Betsy's Wedding*. By 1921, however, the Lovelaces had moved into the "Canoe Place" house. Maybe the phone hadn't yet been hooked up, and Charley Kirch called the Harts, who sent Helen over with the good news.

Julia tells Tacy that the more babies she has, the better she should sing. "Look at Schumann-Heink!"[1052] Ernestine Schumann-Heink was known as the world's greatest Wagnerian contralto after making her American debut in a performance of *Lohengrin* in 1898. Her career peaked in 1910 after a successful American tour. Married three times, she was the mother of eight children. Mrs. Schumann-Heink claimed that each of her eight "confinements" had added a note to her range, which explains Julia's remark to Tacy!

After three months at the publicity bureau, Joe is moved over to the *Courier*. "To discuss this change, the Willards were invited to the Hawthornes' for dinner. The Hawthorne house stood on a corner. An arc light gleamed over the snowy lawn showing tall oak trees and a tall house with so many narrow gables that it seemed to rush up into points."[1053] The Wakefield house stands at the corner of 47th Street and Dupont Avenue S. (4648 Dupont) in Minneapolis. The Wakefields built this house in 1909 and moved in right about the time of their daughter's first birthday.

Sally Day was based on Lucy Day Wakefield. She was very fond of the Harts. "*Tom Hart was one of the sweetest, gentlest men you ever met. Stella was dynamic. She was lovely looking. Beautiful red hair, not carrot red but gold red.*"[1054] Lucy remembers the sandwiches Tom made on Sunday evenings. "*He was very busy in the kitchen. They loved to entertain.*" A favorite Sunday night dessert at the Hart home was angel food cake with whipped cream and cherries.

When Lucy Day was preparing to be married, she asked Kathleen Hart to sing at the ceremony (which was held in the Wakefield house). When Kathleen asked what to sing, Lucy Day responded: "*Anything but 'By the Waters of Minnetonka.'*" On Lucy's wedding day in January 1929, Kathleen had terrible laryngitis, so she asked another singer, Mankato friend Lora Lulsdorff (who had been with Kathleen in Berlin in 1909), to take her place. The song Lora chose was "By the Waters of Minnetonka!"[1055]

Lucy Day was always accused of having interrupted Delos' proposal of marriage to Maud. One evening, after dinner at the Wakefields', Maud and Delos were sitting in the sunroom, talking in low voices. Lucy went in to see what was going on. The senior Wakefields were amused and wondered if a proposal had been afoot. Merian Kirchner notes: "*The way I heard the story, Lucy Day herself always said that she heard Delos propose to Maud! And I thought it was the very night they met. Maud used to say, when I tried to pin her down, that it might have been, but she honestly couldn't remember, she was in such a daze. Anyway, it was love at first sight.*"[1056]

Lucy Day also remembers when Delos first came to work at the publicity bureau. "*He didn't have much money. At lunch time he would go out and come back eating apples.*"[1057] Perhaps Delos really was eating an apple the first time Maud saw him, as reported in *Heaven to Betsy*.[1058] The fact that the incident is mentioned in several books makes it particularly likely to have been based on

Coll. of Lucy Crabtree

Lillian Wakefield
(Eleanor Hawthorne)

"She's tall and dark -- a vibrant sort of woman." (BW p. 43)

Coll. of Lucy Crabtree

Lucy Day
(Sally Day)

"Little Sally Day - red ringlets and a white lace dress - had the same puckish expression" as her father. (BW p. 61)

Wakefield Home

"The Hawthorne house stood on a corner. An arc light gleamed over the snowy lawn showing tall oak trees and a tall house with so many narrow gables that it seemed to rush up into points." (BW p. 101)

Courtesy of Jill Hile

Wakefield Dining Room

Maud Hart and Delos Lovelace first met at a dinner at the Wakefield house. Lillian Wakefield was something of a matchmaker. (*Betsy's Wedding* was dedicated to her.)

fact. "He was eating an apple and reading a book the first time I saw him," Betsy says in *Betsy in Spite of Herself.*[1059] "You were eating an apple and reading a book, the first time I saw you," Betsy reminds Joe in *Betsy's Wedding.*[1060]

Lucy Day's father, Harry B. Wakefield, ran a newspaper in Hutchinson, Minnesota, before the turn of the century. Lillian Hammons, a dramatic arts teacher, came to town to put on a play. Harry gave it a terrible review, and the two first met when Lillian went to his office to give him a piece of her mind. They were married on the third of May 1900. In the first eight years of their marriage, the Wakefields lost three newborn sons (two were twins). Lucy Day was born in March 1908. No doubt Maud chose the fictional name "Sally" for the sake of Lucy's daughter Sally Kee, who was born in 1933. "Day" and "Kee" were both family names.

When the Willards are invited to the Hawthornes' in *Betsy's Wedding*, "Dinner was served by a maid in cap and apron. The atmosphere, however, was anything but formal."[1061] The Wakefields' maid, Ruth Strand, wore a black uniform with white apron and cap. In addition to dinner parties, the Lovelaces often dropped in at the Wakefields' for waffles (which the Hawthornes serve on page 161).

Joe runs into a snag on his new job. The rival reporters on his courthouse beat freeze him out, keeping news sources to themselves. This is just what happened to Delos on the *Minneapolis Tribune*. Delos recalled: "*My early days on the Tribune were made nightmarish by veteran rivals on the Daily News and Journal who scooped me regularly until I began to haunt the documents room of the county courthouse. There I dug up trivial two-paragraph oddities that my rivals were too lazy to go after and these spotted the first page of the Tribune's early edition until the rivals offered to dicker. They would cut me in on their big beats if I would share the oddities, about which their City Desks were harassing them. Seemed fair. And besides, that way everyone had his afternoons free for Hearts.*"[1062] Early in 1920, Delos began working nights as head of the copy desk.

Tib has finished school in Milwaukee and has moved to Minneapolis. "Tib was now living in town; she had found a job in art-advertising with one of the department stores."[1063] Midge Gerlach was actually living with the Hart family at 2634 Portland

Avenue in 1917. (By autumn, the Harts had moved back to 905 W. 25th.) The house at 2634 Portland Avenue was a duplex. Alice Dunnell explained that the Harts had moved temporarily to the duplex because of a health situation which made upkeep of the house on West 25th difficult for Stella. They remained in the duplex (renting out their house) for just one year. Around this time, Midge dated a fellow named Daffy Dodds who was six foot four and was often kidded about bringing her to parties in his pocket. While living with the Harts in 1917, Midge was a clerk for the Northeast Furniture Company. Later (early 1930s), she did work for a Minneapolis department store (Dayton's).

Tib tells Betsy about her problems with men. "They think I'm frivolous, because I have so many pretty clothes. But you know I make most of them myself. Often I rip a dress up at night and it comes to the store a different one next day."[1064] Like Tib, Midge was an accomplished dressmaker. Midge "*loved to tear two or three dresses apart and whip them into a fourth one, brand new*."[1065]

The heroine of a Lovelace short story called "Borghild's Clothes" is very similar to Tib in *Betsy's Wedding*. Mr. Bagshaw calls Tib a "sprite," and Borghild, "*in her floating pale green draperies, was like a sprite*."[1066] Borghild's face, like Tib's, is described as "flowerlike." And one of Tib's speeches comes straight out of Borghild's mouth: "*Every man seems to have a secret notion that he is going to marry a blonde. And when he sees me, he immediately thinks I'm the one ... but I'm not at all what I seem.*"[1067] Several years before Borghild, Maud created Daphne, another short story heroine who looks helpless but isn't, complete with yellow curls and round blue eyes. "The Daring of Daphne" was published in the *Los Angeles Times* in 1921.

Tib's three romances form quite a literary substructure in *Betsy's Wedding* - the whole of which was apparently invented. (Midge lived in Minneapolis for only one year before the war. She was married in Mankato in 1918 and worked at home as a clerk at the National Citizens Bank during the war.)

Betsy and Tacy, eager to see Tib as happily married as they are, put their heads together to think of a suitable match. Their first "prospect" is dapper New Yorker Mr. Bagshaw, a friend of Harry Kerr. The Willards are invited to the Kerrs' for dinner to meet Mr. Bagshaw. Joe "hurried her along under the icy stars and into the sizzling lobby of the Kerrs' apartment building."[1068] The Kirchs never lived in an apartment building in Minneapolis. They lived in a big duplex, and its foyer might have served as the sizzling lobby. It would have been a long, cold walk from Delos and Maud's apartment! After their marriage, Bick and Charley lived at 3239 First Avenue South. They may have first lived briefly with Charley's mother, Sarah, at 4625 Stevens Avenue (no longer standing).

Mr. Bagshaw is in Minneapolis on business for a good part of 1915, but he fails to win Tib. Before his return to New York, Mr. Bagshaw invites the Crowd to "a farewell dinner dance at the Inn on Christmas Lake. This sophisticated inn, which pretended to be rustic because it was in the country, was one of his favorite places."[1069] Christmas Lake is a small lake south of Lake Minnetonka. The posh Glen Morris Inn there was located on fifty-three acres, stretching eastward from what is called "Christmas Lake Point Road" to the end of Shore Road. The Inn and its fifteen cottages were built in 1906. In 1920, the property was bought by the owners of the Minneapolis Radisson Hotel and the name was changed to Radisson Inn. It did have a "broad piazza" (240 feet long) on which the Crowd reposed.[1070] The dining room seated 250. The Inn was destroyed by fire in 1936.

"Betsy was pleased when Tib called one morning and asked her downtown for lunch. 'There's a cute new place. You telephone your order from the table.'"[1071] Minneapolitans of Maud's vintage reminisced about favorite restaurants, circa 1916. Journalist Halsey L. Hall recalled a restaurant named Smith's: "*On every table was a little telephone. You scanned the menu, picked up the phone and gave your order direct to the fountain. If you were really splurging (up to 35 cents worth or so), you ordered a banana split.*"[1072] (Smith's was a super-deluxe ice cream parlor, which means that Maud and Midge may not have found corned beef and cabbage on the menu.) Smith's was located on Nicollet at 7th Street, three blocks north of the Meyers Arcade.

Later, Tib and Rocky (match-making prospect #2) go to "that new restaurant -- you know, where a chef in a white cap makes pancakes in the window. Rocky talks, and eats stacks of

3239 First Avenue South

Bick and Charley Kirch were living in an apartment in this house when their first child was born in October 1921.

Coll. of Ruth Hudgens

Bick Kenney Kirch

Tacy herself couldn't have looked lovelier.

Excelsior Historical Society

Glen Morris Inn

Mr. Bagshaw gave a gala farewell dinner at the Inn on Christmas Lake.

MHL Archive

California Here We Come

In *Betsy's Wedding*, the Ray family takes a trip to California. This trip really took place in 1915, and Maud was a member of the traveling party. Left to right: Maud, Helen, Stella, and Tom Hart.

MHL Archive

Stella and Tom Hart

MHL Archive

Stella

Stella was forty-nine at the time of this California trip, yet she hardly looks older than her daughters.

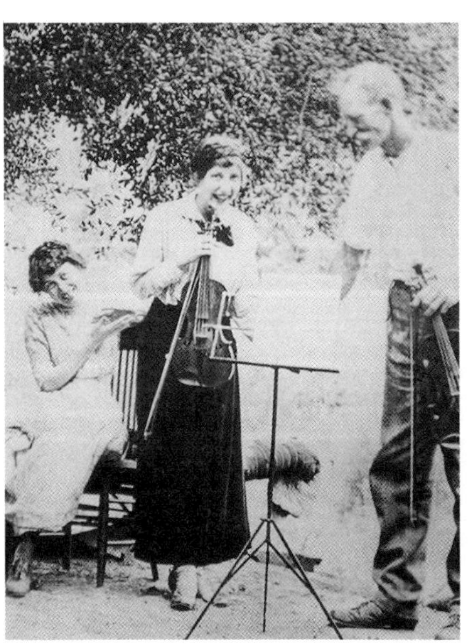

MHL Archive

Maud, Helen, and Uncle Frank

In California, Helen had a chance to play a violin duet with Uncle Frank (Uncle Keith).

MHL Archive

Maud

Maud looks very much the way we might expect Betsy to look in 1915.

pancakes."[1073] Halsey L. Hall says: "*If you wanted something substantial with the gal friend, you went to Child's, between 4th and 5th on the north side of the street* [Nicollet] ... *where the chef-hatted genius in the big window was flipping flapjacks.*"[1074] Another journalist, Bradley L. Morison, described the "*white-tiled restaurant glitter of Child's around the corner on Nicollet Avenue, where chorus girls from the Metropolitan used to snack at midnight.*"[1075]

Maud and Delos enjoyed banana splits at Circlers Drug Store at 6th and Nicollet. And "The Eat Shop" was a big favorite with the Hart family in the years after their move to Minneapolis.

Betsy enjoys dressing up to go downtown, but for the most part, her life is quiet. She is happy in their apartment during the day. "Running her carpet sweeper blithely up and down, Betsy watched a robin's nest, the eggs, the fledglings. 'I think I'll write a story about a little girl going to live with the birds!'"[1076] That's exactly what Maud did, but not until about 1936. The book, *The Tune is in the Tree*, was finally published in 1950, five years before *Betsy's Wedding. The Tune*, illustrated by Eloise Wilkin, tells the story of little Annie Jo, who, with the help of a magic hummingbird, shrinks to bird size and grows wings in order to live with the birds until her parents are able to return home. (Maud also used the name Annie Jo in a short story called "A Rendez-Vous with Fame.") Maud explained that the book was "*inspired by a song mother used to sing*."[1077] Maud never heard this song outside her family circle. One bounced a small child on one's knee while singing: "*Spring once said to the nightingale, I'm going to give you birds a ball, the birds and the birdies, great and small. Tra la la la la ...*"[1078]

The Rays come back from a trip to California, and Margaret has a new sparkle. Mrs. Ray tells Betsy it is because two boy cousins, just her age, "teased her and flirted with her and tore her dignity to tatters."[1079] These cousins would have been the children of Charles Austin Jr. There were no boys just Helen's age - however, there was a girl cousin only six months older. This was Marjorie Austin. The boy closest in age to Helen was Charles Lincoln Austin, who was three years younger. Cousin Randall Austin was Maud's age. This fictional trip may have been inspired by the Harts' California trip in the summer of 1915, on which Maud accompanied her parents and Helen.

Betsy and Joe receive a letter from Joe's Aunt Ruth. She has sold the store in Butternut Center and would like to come stay with them. Betsy first met Aunt Ruth, who was "spare, sad, and kind," in *Betsy and Joe*.[1080] Delos had two aunts. He spent some of his growing-up years in their homes. But the fictional Aunt Ruth was patterned after Delos' mother, Josephine Wheeler Lovelace (who did not die, as Joe's mother did, when he was a young boy). "She was a dressmaker ... after father died, that is. She worked hard; too hard. I can still hear that sewing machine."[1081] Josephine was a dressmaker at 148 Woodward Avenue in Detroit for some years. According to Merian Kirchner, "*Maud was very fond of her mother-in-law, and Aunt Ruth's personality is probably modeled on Josephine's, at least to some extent.*"[1082]

The prospect of Aunt Ruth's arrival seems bleak. Betsy dreads giving up their cozy privacy. She turns to church to help resolve her resentment against Aunt Ruth, whose arrival is approaching. Religion runs in a strong current through many of the Betsy-Tacy books. Maud commented: "*I like to work a little religion into these books. You'll notice that I usually manage to.*"[1083]

In *Betsy's Wedding*, Betsy becomes troubled because "she had almost stopped going to church. Joe had gone very seldom since leaving Butternut Center."[1084] Later, Betsy says, "'It's shabby the way I just go to church when I'm worried. I ought to go when I'm thankful and happy, too. I'm going to start going every Sunday.' 'I've been thinking the same thing,' said Joe."[1085] Delos, in fact, didn't become an Episcopalian until 1948, when he was baptized in Garden City, New York.

Betsy walks to St. Paul's Church. St. Paul's Episcopal Church stood at the corner of Franklin and Bryant Avenue South, close enough to their apartment for Maud to walk to services.

With Aunt Ruth on her way, the Willards need more room, and they begin looking for a house. They had planned to buy a house ... and have a baby ... since their honeymoon. "After a year or so, we'll move out of the apartment and buy a little house -- not at the lake yet....' 'And have a baby,' Betsy put in. 'A boy or a girl?' 'Both. The boy first, so he can take her to parties.'"[1086]

Maud and Delos did buy a house in Minneapolis after a few years of marriage. In that first house, Maud watched her midsection expand through the months of her first pregnancy. One Friday in February 1925, she and Delos went the handful of blocks up to Hillcrest Surgical Hospital. Hillcrest had been the scene of both joy and tragedy for Maud, who no doubt visited there on May 29, 1920, the day her sister Kathleen's first child, Eugene Sharp Bibb Junior, was stillborn. A year later, Maud must have been extremely relieved when Bick Kenney Kirch safely delivered her first son at Hillcrest, and Maud certainly visited Bick there, as Betsy visited Tacy in the hospital when Kelly was born.

As Betsy had suggested to Joe, the Lovelaces had their boy first. Born at Hillcrest on February 13, 1925, at 3:25 a.m., his lungs functioned for only three hours. The delivery was easy, and according to Maud's obstetrician, the birth was not premature. In fact, she went two weeks beyond the due date the doctor had originally given her. Maud remembered that the baby was "*still as a mouse*"[1087] during the week before his birth. No first name is given on the certificates of birth and death filed with the county, but he would have been named Thomas. He is buried in Minneapolis at Lakewood Cemetery (without a marker), not far from Kathleen's baby boy.

Alice Alworth Lynch, who attended Mankato High School with Maud, wrote an article about her in the *Minnesota Journal of Education*. After high school, "*the years went by, and at various times I heard that* [Maud] *was attending the University of Minnesota - that she was writing short stories - that she had been abroad, and that she was married. But it was not until 1925 when I lost a sister who was teaching in Minneapolis that I had any direct word from her. She had just lost her firstborn and was still far from well. We had never been intimate friends, and it had been years since I had seen her. Yet in her own grief she was thoughtful enough to send me a message of sympathy.*"[1088]

After Delos returned from overseas, the Lovelaces lived in the "Bow Street" apartment for one year. They rented 1109 W. 25th Street (the "Canoe Place" house) the next year. (Their landlords were Jean and Paul Madden, also a young couple.) The following year, the Lovelaces moved to New York City (see Chapter 14 herein). Delos became ill early in 1924, and they returned to Minneapolis, staying for a time with the Harts at 905 W. 25th. They rented a home at Lake Minnetonka in the summer of 1924, but before long, the Lovelaces were back renting the "Canoe Place" house.

When Betsy and Joe begin looking for a house, they decide that the Bow Street neighborhood is too expensive for them. But as Joe says, they feel at home in this part of town. One Sunday, instead of taking the streetcar out to distant neighborhoods, they head for the lakes. "They crossed Hennepin Avenue at a small business district and were walking toward Lake of the Isles when Betsy stopped. She waved toward a short street that cut off a pie-shaped section of more important avenues. 'I think that Canoe Place is cute,' she said, 'because it's only a block long.' Then she squealed, and Joe said, 'Well, for crying out loud!' For on a lawn halfway down Canoe Place was a For Sale sign. They started to run."[1089]

Maud wrote to a fan: "*I invented the name Canoe Place. The house we bought was on West 25th Street, but except for that, everything pertaining to the house, and our purchase of it, is exactly as it's put down in the book. Even Delossy insisting on buying it before we had been inside! ... we had dearly loved that first house*."[1090] Perhaps Delos had decided he wanted to buy 1109 W. 25th before going inside when they first saw it in 1921, but the Lovelaces had to be satisfied with renting until the Maddens were ready to sell. On May 8, 1925, they purchased the house from Jean and Paul Madden.

Betsy and Joe are told that the house sells for $4500. When they bought this house, Maud and Delos took out a mortgage for $3000 with America State Bank. They were already repaying a fairly substantial loan from Stella Hart. A $20 monthly payment to "mother" appears on the "permanent budget" page of their Budget Book. Considering that their primary expense - rent - was $32 per month, $20 was a significant payment. The Budget Book dates from the Lovelaces' year in the apartment, so Stella's loan couldn't have been for a down payment on the house.

Their new brown-and-yellow cottage has built-in bookcases, in which Betsy and Joe settle books on their first anniversary. There really was a built-in bookcase at 1109, rising all the way to the ceiling. Subsequent owners removed it to make way for a piano.

Tib and Anna both appreciate the "big, sunny" kitchen. This was poetic license. The kitchen is very small, hardly bigger than

MHL Archive

1109 W. 25th Street in 1925

"The yellow and brown cottage was set on a very small lot. ...The porch was big; it was screened." (BW pp. 155-156)

1109 W. 25th Street in 1985

"The cottage had a neat lawn, cut in two by a walk leading to the porch." (BW p. 155) The bridal wreath bushes at the side of the house in this photo were not present in Maud's day.

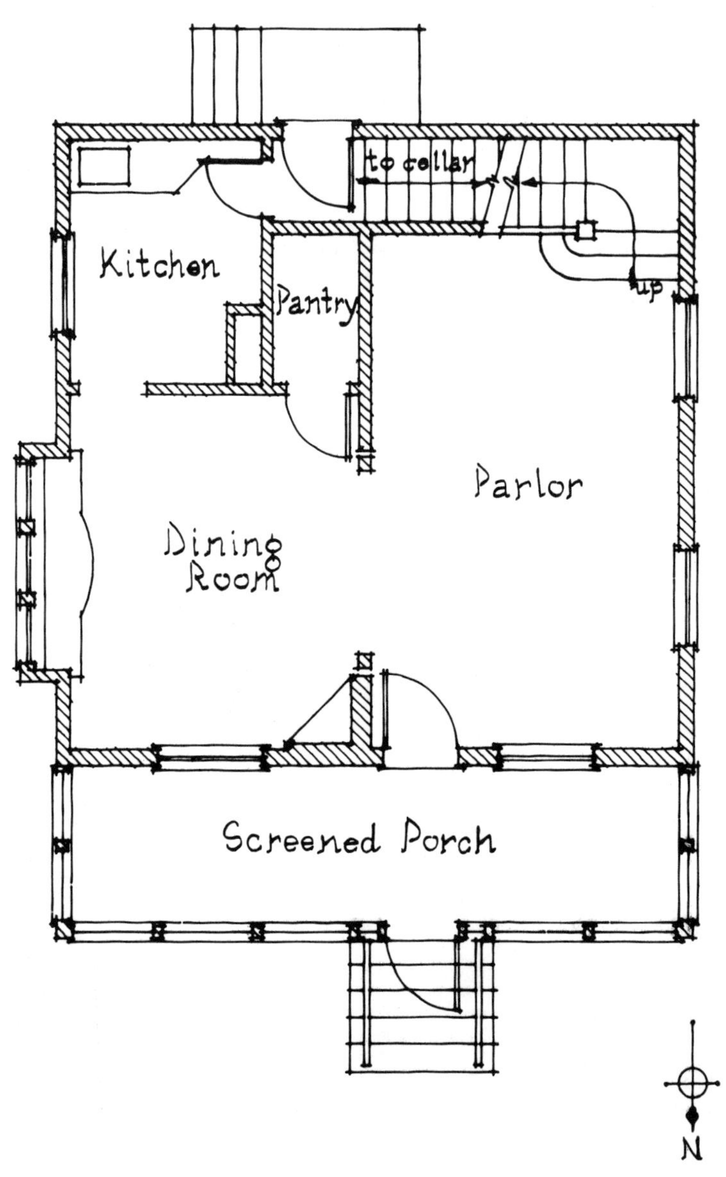

Plan by Architect Nancy Beckner Bastian

Floor Plan of 1109 W. 25th Street
First Floor

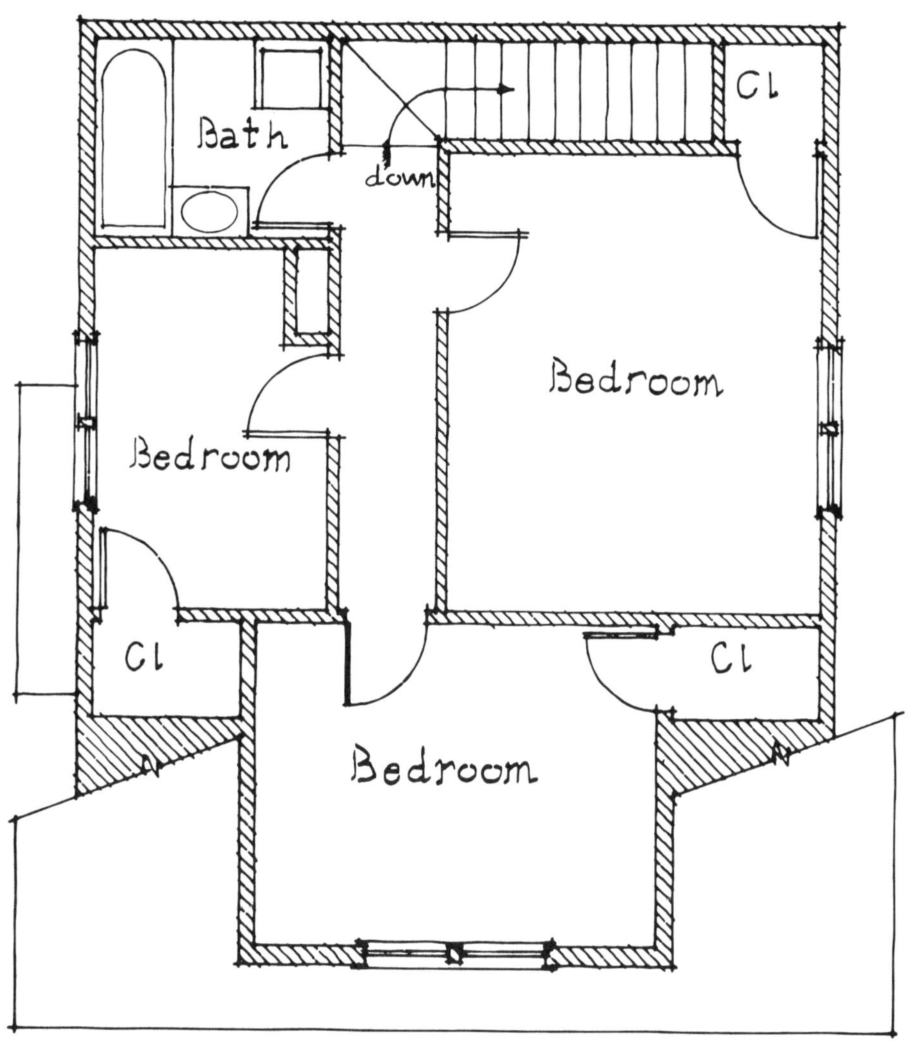

Plan by Architect Nancy Beckner Bastian

Floor Plan of 1109 W. 25th Street
Second Floor

None of the upstairs rooms looks down on the backyard, as Betsy and Joe's did. Perhaps the side bedroom belonged to Maud and Delos, and the front one, "equally large," was Josephine's.

that in the Bow Street apartment. Family and friends are all pleased about Betsy and Joe's new house. Mr. Ray plans to make a cutting of the Hill Street vine. There is no vine now on the house at 1109 West 25th, but there is a vine with an enormous "trunk" growing at the back of the property. John Daniels of Bachman's nursery and Mervin Eisel of the University of Minnesota Arboretum confirm that this Virginia creeper vine could be old enough to have been an offshoot of Tom Hart's vine.

Not long after Betsy and Joe buy their house, in the fall of 1915, Carney and Sam have their second child, a son. (In real life, their son arrived first, in March 1922, their daughter following in April 1923. Marion and Bill's third child, their younger son, was born in 1924.) Tacy is expecting her second child to arrive in the summer of 1916. (Bick's second son wasn't born until 1924.)

Tib's brother, Fred Muller, graduates from the U in 1916 - and Tib wants to "drag" Rocky to the ceremony. We have known that Freddie wanted to be an architect ever since *Betsy-Tacy and Tib*.[1091] Midge's brother, Henry Clay Gerlach, was really an architect and received his degree from the University of Minnesota on June 14, 1922. Her younger brother, William Dewey (Hobbie), also became an architect. He received his University of Minnesota degree on September 4, 1926.

On a hot July day in 1916, Joe writes "Wheat," which is accepted by *The Thursday Magazine*. Delos did write a story called "Wheat" for which the *Ladies' Home Journal* paid $600. "Wheat" was published in July 1924.

By the late fall of 1916, Joe has sold another story to *The Thursday Magazine*. Delos didn't sell a second story to the *Ladies' Home Journal* right away, but in 1925, the year after "Wheat," he began selling to the *Saturday Evening Post* (with a story called "Fiddlefoot" - not mentioned by name in *Betsy's Wedding*). Maud was probably thinking of the *Saturday Evening Post* when she named the fictional publication which published "Wheat."

Two of the short stories mentioned on page 111 of *Betsy's Wedding* were actually published under slightly different names. "Mr. Forrester Leaves for a Trip to Tibet" was signed by only Delos Lovelace and appeared in the *Los Angeles Times* in July 1921. Several months earlier, the *Los Angeles Times* had printed a Delos

MHL Archive

Maud and Midge

This photo was taken in Minneapolis in about 1917.

MHL Archive

Midge and Dolly

Midge's younger sister, seen in this 1914 photograph, was not represented fictionally in the Betsy-Tacy books.

1912 Otaknam

Henry Clay Gerlach
(Freddie)

Like Freddie, Midge's brother Henry earned an architecture degree from the U.

BEC in WWI

William Dewey Gerlach
(Hobbie)

Dewey Gerlach did enlist after graduation from Mankato High School, just as Hobbie did.

Coll. of Peg Gingerich

Mett Buell
(Marbeth Cliff)

"Modest Marbeth Cliff was the most valued critic in the club." (BW p. 175)

Coll. of Peg Gingerich

Earle Buell
(Jimmy Cliff)

"Jimmy's face, above his flowing Windsor tie, was one of the kindest she had ever seen." (BW p. 174)

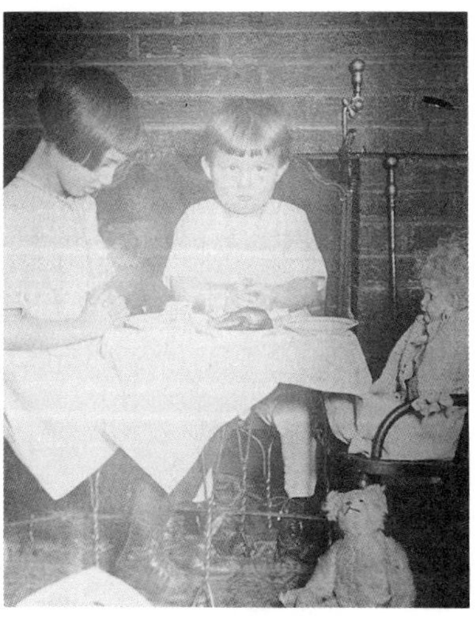

Coll. of Peg Gingerich

Jimmy Junior

The Cliff's son rode his kiddie car up and down the living room during meetings of the Violent Study Club.

Courtesy of Peg Gingerich

The Naughty Chair

When members of the Violent Study Club made a sale, they had to sit in "a chair at one side of the fireplace - a tall, straight chair, carved of dark Indian mahogany with a yellow velvet seat." (BW p. 176)

Lovelace story about the same main character. Vincent Forrester had been introduced in "The U-Boat Uppercut."

Jimmy Cliff was a fellow worker on the *Courier,* who, like Joe, carried a cane. "A reporter, he was also a poet -- hugely stout, wearing loose easy clothes, a slouch hat, and a Windsor tie."[1092] (Initially, Maud considered the name "Cliff Woods" for this character.) Jimmy was based on Earle Buell, who wrote for the *Minneapolis Tribune.* Earle truly was stout and jolly, carried a cane, and wore a Windsor tie, according to his daughter Peg. He was described similarly in *Sunlight on Your Doorstep,* a history of the *Tribune*: "*Portly Earle R. Buell, with the walking stick and the flowing bow tie, who wrote bright newspaper prose and even better verse.*"[1093]

The Violent Study Club met at the Cliffs' "to talk writing, read aloud, argue, and drink coffee while Jimmy Junior dashed up and down on his kiddy car."[1094] Marbeth Cliff was Jimmy Junior's "tall, slender mother." Marbeth was based on Marietta (Mett) Buell. Daughter Nancy says that her mother was "*known for her tact.*"[1095]

When Jimmy Junior acted up, the Cliffs deposited him in a "tall, straight chair, carved of dark Indian mahogany with a yellow velvet seat."[1096] (The modern expression for the use of a "naughty chair" is a "timeout.") Mett really designated one of her antique chairs, with carved back and upholstered seat (yellowish) as "the Naughty Chair," for the occasional use of her three children.

Mett and Earle had two daughters and a son. The son, Bud Buell, did race around on his kiddy car at Violent Study Club meetings. These meetings were hosted by the Buells at 4941 Lyndale Avenue South in Minneapolis.

One of the "regulars" at Violent Study Club meetings is the columnist "Q" - who was indeed a girl. She was Darragh Aldrich, who wrote the *Minneapolis Tribune* column "Quentin's Corner" for ten years, beginning each column with an original verse. She was born Clara Chapline Thomas on December 31, 1881, in Richmond, Indiana. She wrote: "*Quentin's Column won me a membership in the national society of Press Humorists, composed entirely of men, but - alas - after a personal appearance at their national convention in Chicago, I had to resign!*"[1097] Upon marriage to Minneapolis architect Chilson Darragh Aldrich, she immediately assumed two of his names.

Another member of the Violent Study Club is "Sigrid, the vivacious, nut-brown girl reporter" who wears a diamond on her left hand.[1098] This was Doris Edsten. Patty, the Dickens fan, was based on Ella Dickenson. Ella was also the "Effie" (Betsy's favorite sorority sister) mentioned in *Betsy and the Great World*. Maud originally intended to bring Effie into *Betsy's Wedding*. (She was to have given Betsy and Joe a wedding gift of *The Golden Treasury of Verse*.) Ella was not as appealing as Patty. Her hair was "*vaguely yellow,*" her eyes were like that of "*a startled crab,*" and her face was "*as characterless as a sheet of newspaper wadded into a ball.*" And yet, she was still "*charmingly bookish with a little tinkling laugh. Her great charm was her total indifference to the fact that where men were concerned, she hadn't any.*"[1099]

Perhaps it was at a Violent Study Club meeting that Maud met Sinclair Lewis. "*Sinclair Lewis shook his head one time and told her she couldn't write.*"[1100] How would he know?

Joe tells his wife: "Your stories don't express you, Betsy. I think you need the meadowlike space of a novel. I'm going to make you start one in 1917."[1101] Maud wrote to a cousin in 1964 about her transition from short stories to novels. "*I continued writing and selling short stories, long after my marriage to Delos W. Lovelace, and when he returned from World War I, he started to do the same. But where his were soon selling to the very best markets ... mine continued to sell mostly to the smaller magazines. I seemed to have no great gift for this field and Delos suggested that I try a novel. That turned out to be The Black Angels.*"[1102]

"A coral silk dress trimmed with silver lace was fine for going to hear Dr. Oberhoffer conduct the Minneapolis Symphony Orchestra."[1103] On one notable occasion in January 1917, Kathleen Hart Bibb sang with the Symphony Orchestra, under the direction of Dr. Emil Oberhoffer. There can be no doubt that all the Harts were there, though Maud could not have been wearing the coral silk dress - this event occurred before she had met Delos.

When Betsy goes to see Mrs. Hawthorne about getting a job, Mrs. Hawthorne tells her, "There's a big project for a social center at Fort Snelling. How would you like to be sent out there for some assignments during the summer?"[1104] Betsy moved into the job Maud really held for a time. "*Whenever possible, Mrs. Wakefield*

MHL Archive

Delos at the Hart Home

Betsy "couldn't keep her eyes away from him - from the strong, finely-modeled face." (BW p. 13)

MHL Archive

Delos Again

Coll. of Louise King

William Everett
(Sam Hutchinson)

"Sam's waxed mustaches ended in gleaming needles." (BW p. 235)

Coll. of Mary Martin

Charles Harris
(Jack Dunhill)

"The tall young man had wavy dark hair, and bright dark eyes." (BW p. 215) *would send me on assignments out to Fort Snelling, where Delos was stationed at the First Officers Training Camp,*" Maud said.[1105]

One of the stories she wrote that summer of 1917 appeared in the *Minneapolis Tribune.* Maud described the work of preparing 7,800 meals a day for the men at Fort Snelling. "*A typical bill of fare for one day contained: breakfast - bananas, farina with milk, fried steak, brown gravy, French fried potatoes, bread and butter, coffee with milk; dinner - roast prime beef, pan gravy, creamed carrots, boiled potatoes in jackets, bread pudding with custard sauce, bread and butter, buttermilk; supper - sliced peaches, assorted cold meats, combination salad with homemade dressing, hot Johnnie cake, syrup, sweet milk.*"[1106] At least Joe would have been well fed at the Fort.

Initially, Maud planned to end *Betsy's Wedding* with only a hint of the war to come - having Julia play WWI songs on the piano. But perhaps, though it left her readers wondering anxiously if Joe would ever really return, including the war setting was important to Maud, because it was truer to her own story.

The moving ending of the series begins to unfold when Tib brings a young man to the Willard house. She has just met him while skating. Tib may have met Jack Dunhill in Minneapolis, but Midge met Charles Harris in Mankato. Charles did not go to Mexico, nor did he attend the U. We are told that "Jack was an advertising man."[1107] Charles was a salesman.

The description of Tib's wedding is entirely fictional. Midge's wedding took place at eight p.m. on Valentine's Day, 1918, at her parents' home, 414 N. Fourth Street, in Mankato. She wore a gown of gray velvet and "*carried a colonial bouquet of bride's roses.*"[1108] Her matron of honor, Aunt Dell (Aunt Dolly), also wore gray velvet. Henry Gerlach (Freddie) was best man. Midge's going-away suit was navy blue.

The wedding gifts included "embroidered linens from relatives of Jack in England."[1109] Charles Harris' father had come over from England, and his niece verified that an aunt in England would have sent gifts for the wedding.[1110]

At Tib's wedding (the time of which is summer 1917), we learn that Dennie is engaged to Winona. Eleanor and Paul probably were engaged in the summer of 1917, since they were married in January 1918.

Cab and Jean are expecting a baby. As already mentioned, Jab and Grace Lloyd weren't married until 1917. They had really met in North Dakota. Like Cab, Jab was already bald at this point, having lost his hair after suffering typhoid fever at age twenty-one. He did shave the little hair that had grown back, hoping for a cure. And Jab was wearing a hat when he met Grace. Later, of course, she found out he was bald! *"But it didn't seem to bother her,"* said daughter Millicent (Mickee) Steiner.[1111] The Lloyds' first child arrived before the Kaiser gave up, as Jean was afraid might happen (per page 237 of *Betsy's Wedding*). Son Robert was born in October 1918 in North Dakota. Jab was on a base out West but was allowed to return home to see his wife and new baby.

Mildred Oleson (Irma) had a young dentist (not doctor) husband. And Aunt Dolly shouldn't have looked fortyish quite yet, since Aunt Dell was only thirty-five!

"She was in the land of dreams now, Betsy thought. The future and the past seemed to melt together. She could feel the Big Hill looking down as the Crowd danced at Tib's wedding in the chocolate-colored house."[1112]

These certainly feel like final words, and Maud was pleased with them. *"I have always felt that the last lines in Betsy's Wedding were a perfect ending for the series."*[1113]

965 *Betsy's Wedding*, p. 7.
966 Ibid., p. 4.
967 New York File.
968 *Betsy's Wedding* notes.
969 MHL to J. Schendel, 12-70.
970 M.H. Lovelace, "Love's Daily Dozen," *Delineator*, August 1925.
971 R/N *Betsy's Wedding*, summer '53.
972 *Betsy's Wedding*, p. 193.
973 Interview with P. Cavanaugh, 11-4-90.
974 *Betsy's Wedding*, p. 25.
975 Ibid., p. 24.
976 Ibid., p. 28.
977 ADB to SSW, 3-9-91.
978 ADB to SSW, 2-21-91.
979 *Betsy's Wedding*, p. 25.
980 ADB to SSW, 2-21-91.
981 *Betsy's Wedding*, p. 78.
982 Ibid., p. 35.
983 Ibid., p. 38.
984 Ibid., p. 41.
985 Ibid.
986 Ibid., p. 228.
987 JoAnne Ray, "Maud Hart Lovelace and Mankato," *Women of Minnesota* (St. Paul: Minnesota Historical Society, 1977), p. 166.
988 Ibid.
989 *Betsy's Wedding*, p. 43.
990 *Heaven to Betsy*, p. 42.
991 *Betsy's Wedding*, p. 49.
992 Ibid., p. 50.
993 MHL to R. Lee, 7-25-65.
994 *Betsy's Wedding*, p. 50.
995 Ibid., p. 51.
996 Ibid., p. 52.
997 *Downtown*, p. 10.
998 *Minneapolis Star*, 2-8-47.
999 *Heaven to Betsy*, p. 218.
1000 *Betsy in Spite of Herself*, p. 132.
1001 *Heaven to Betsy*, p. 85.

1002 *Betsy and Joe*, p. 176.
1003 *Betsy in Spite of Herself*, p. 160.
1004 *Heaven to Betsy*, p. 134.
1005 *Betsy and Joe*, p. 177.
1006 *Heaven to Betsy*, p. 33.
1007 *Minneapolis T.*, 7-10-44.
1008 *Betsy's Wedding*, p. 52.
1009 MHL to L. Demp, 11-2-56.
1010 *Minneapolis Tribune*, 11-30-17.
1011 *Betsy's Wedding*, p. 57.
1012 *Minneapolis Tribune*, 11-29-17.
1013 *Betsy's Wedding*, N.Y. file.
1014 *Betsy's Wedding*, p. 63.
1015 Ibid., p. 59.
1016 *Minneapolis Journal*, 11-29-90.
1017 *Betsy's Wedding*, p. 60.
1018 *Minneapolis Tribune*, 11-29-17.
1019 MHL to J. Tessari, 8-11-73.
1020 *Betsy's Wedding*, p. 70.
1021 Ibid., p. 67.
1022 Richards, ed., *Minnesota Writers*, p. 207.
1023 MHL to J. Tessari, 8-11-73.
1024 *Betsy's Wedding*, p. 72.
1025 *Minneapolis Star Tribune*, 9-2-84.
1026 *Betsy's Wedding*, p. 76.
1027 Ibid., p. 81.
1028 Ibid.
1029 Ibid., p. 82.
1030 MHL to B. Norum, 3-11-74.
1031 MHL to J. Tessari, 8-11-73.
1032 MLK to SSW, 11-15-91.
1033 MHL to J. Tessari, 8-11-73.
1034 *Betsy's Wedding*, p. 79.
1035 Ibid., p. 80.
1036 *Emily of Deep Valley*, p. 8.
1037 *Betsy's Wedding*, p. 85.
1038 *Betsy in Spite of Herself*, p. 238.

[1039] MHL to L. Demp, 11-2-56.
[1040] *Betsy's Wedding*, p. 85.
[1041] Ibid., p. 76.
[1042] Collection of the Minnesota Valley Regional Library.
[1043] *Betsy's Wedding*, p. 117.
[1044] Ibid., p. 93.
[1045] Ibid., p. 102.
[1046] *Betsy and the Great World*, p. 70.
[1047] *Betsy-Tacy and Tib*, p. 49.
[1048] *Betsy's Wedding*, p. 204.
[1049] Ibid., p. 113.
[1050] *Carney's House Party*, p. 91.
[1051] *Betsy and Joe*, p. 254.
[1052] *Betsy's Wedding*, p. 200.
[1053] Ibid., p. 101.
[1054] Interview with L. Crabtree, 2-18-90.
[1055] Interview with L. Crabtree, 4-28-90.
[1056] MLK to SSW, 11-15-91.
[1057] Interview with L. Crabtree, 2-18-90.
[1058] *Heaven to Betsy*, p. 13.
[1059] *Betsy in Spite of Herself*, p. 70.
[1060] *Betsy's Wedding*, p. 214.
[1061] Ibid., p. 101.
[1062] Ray, "Maud Hart Lovelace and Mankato," p. 206.
[1063] *Betsy's Wedding*, p. 76.
[1064] Ibid., p. 113.
[1065] *Mankato Free Press*, 2-4-65.
[1066] M.H. Lovelace, "Borghild's Clothes," *Modern Priscilla*, April 1922.
[1067] Ibid., p. 13.
[1068] *Betsy's Wedding*, p. 119.
[1069] Ibid., p. 138.
[1070] Ibid., p. 142.
[1071] Ibid., p. 111.
[1072] *Minneapolis Star*, 3-15-77.
[1073] *Betsy's Wedding*, p. 186.
[1074] *Minneapolis Star*, 3-15-77.
[1075] Bradley L. Morison, *Sunlight on Your Doorstep* (Minneapolis: Ross & Haines, Inc., 1966), p. 51.

[1076] *Betsy's Wedding,* p. 133.
[1077] MHL to M. Freeman, 5-19-64.
[1078] LWW, p. 11.
[1079] *Betsy's Wedding,* p. 149.
[1080] *Betsy and Joe,* p. 212.
[1081] Ibid., p. 214.
[1082] MLK to SSW, 11-15-91.
[1083] MHL to M. Everett, 5-17-48.
[1084] *Betsy's Wedding,* p. 128.
[1085] Ibid., p. 208.
[1086] *Betsy's Wedding,* p. 70.
[1087] MHL to Hart Family, 1-6-31.
[1088] *Minnesota Journal of Education,* Vol. XIII, No. 3, November 1932.
[1089] *Betsy's Wedding,* p. 155.
[1090] MHL to J. Tessari, 8-11-73.
[1091] *Betsy-Tacy and Tib,* p. 48.
[1092] *Betsy's Wedding,* p. 106.
[1093] Morison, *Sunlight on Your Doorstep,* p. 53.
[1094] *Betsy's Wedding,* p. 171.
[1095] Interview with N. Buell, 9-23-84.
[1096] *Betsy's Wedding,* p. 176.
[1097] Nelson et al., eds., *Minnesota Writes,* p. 1.
[1098] *Betsy's Wedding,* p. 174.
[1099] R/N *Betsy's Wedding,* Ella, pp. 1-2.
[1100] *Minneapolis Star,* 1951.
[1101] *Betsy's Wedding,* p. 214.
[1102] MHL to M. Freeman, 5-19-64.
[1103] *Betsy's Wedding,* p. 211.
[1104] Ibid., p. 229.
[1105] Ray, "Maud Hart Lovelace and Mankato," p. 167.
[1106] *Minneapolis Sunday Tribune,* 6-10-17.
[1107] *Betsy's Wedding,* p. 216.
[1108] *Mankato Free Press,* 2-19-18.
[1109] *Betsy's Wedding,* p. 238.
[1110] Interview with M. Martin, 9-15-90.
[1111] Interview with M. Steiner, 5-6-90.
[1112] *Betsy's Wedding,* p. 241.
[1113] MHL to J. Tessari, 8-11-73.

CHAPTER FOURTEEN
Then What?

Because the chronicle of Betsy's life ends before the First World War, we'll never really know the answers to questions such as "Then what? Did Joe come safely home? Did they have their Bettina?" Maud didn't write another book about these characters, so there is no "after the war" for Betsy and Joe. But since the lives of the Rays and Willards so closely parallel those of the Harts and Lovelaces, the characters derive something of a continuing half-life from our knowledge of the later histories of Maud, Delos, Tom, Stella, Kathleen, etc. From the events in the lives of the real families, we may make educated guesses about what might have become of Betsy and Joe.

After their marriage, Delos reported back to Camp Dodge, twelve miles northwest of Des Moines, Iowa. Maud continued working for Lillian Wakefield that winter. In January 1918, her parents and g went to Florida, and Maud lived at the Gamma Phi house in Minneapolis. She joined Delos in Iowa in the middle of February. Maud took a room with an old Scotch lady in Des Moines. She and Delos had just one night together before a calamity befell them. Delos went back to camp and the next day he planned to be home at six o'clock after being relieved of duty. A friend named Jerry Barry was also going in to town to see a girl. Delos recalled: "*That afternoon a surprise announcement that all officers of the division must report at seven for a lecture. Jerry Barry and I started over with all the other officers of the battalion and as we walked around the corner of a barracks on the way to the lecture hall, we agreed that if we just stopped there and let the rest of them go on, we could turn around and take a train and go to town and so we did.*"

"*He spent the night with me,*" Maud remembered. "*And the next morning got back to the company area about a quarter to six, very punctual.*" But Delos found he had made a fatal error. "*Jerry and I discovered to our horror that the Divisional Commander had added something to the officers' meeting that he hadn't announced earlier, a roll call. The adjutant of the battalion had been compelled to report that two officers were unaccounted for: Lt. Barry and Lt. Lovelace. ...Divisional Headquarters ordered that we be confined to Camp when not with the company. Therefore Jerry and I did all our regular work but after six o'clock either* [he] *or I were left in charge of the company and all the other officers took off to town. That continued for about three months.*"

Maud was able to see Delos on the base only on weekends. "*At the end of about three months, Jerry and I were notified that we had to face a special court martial. We agreed there was nothing to do but tell exactly what happened, without evasion or circumlocution or imaginative adornment. So when specification of charges were read, my council put me on the witness stand and I told the truth.*"

He told them he'd been married Thanksgiving Day, had had three days with his new wife before returning to Camp, that Maud had visited for but two days at Christmas, and that she had just come down to live in Des Moines the evening before the orders for the officers' meeting had come. "*We were not cross examined for the judges could not keep their faces straight. Anyway the judges listened to my story, found me guilty of something but not much, for the decision was sent to Division Headquarters, received, approved, and a week later my confinement was removed and I was free to go in and see my wife.*"

Maud's parents came to see them during this time, and Maud "*invented all sorts of reasons for his being so busy. We went out to camp to visit him, and they never found out* [about his confinement to base]."

After he was free to leave the base, Maud and Delos rendezvoused at the Hotel Chamberlain, where an orchestra played on a balcony overlooking the lobby. And soon after they found "*a lovely room in a sweet house*" where they were able to live together. "*Delossy had to leave about four or five in the morning to get to camp by reveille. I made him powdered coffee over a Sterno and he always had to run to make the train. ...We went canoeing on the Des Moines River and were very very happy.* [Their landlords] *knew we were bride and groom and were so kind to us. When D's orders to go overseas came, we moved in to the Brown Hotel where we said goodbye early in the morning. Katie was there as Gene went too. I remember that she sang at a concert. 'They were all out of step but Jim.' How I cried! I had found a job much earlier, with Lillian Wakefield's help. A very fine job. Director of newspaper and magazine publicity for the United War Work Campaign, State of Iowa. I was really not quite qualified for such a job but did it, and it went very well.*" Maud remained in Des Moines until after Armistice Day (November 11, 1918).

Delos was in France, a second lieutenant in the 339th machine gun battalion. Maud wrote to him: "*Honey, don't be too lonesome.*

Try to keep happy and to look on the bright side of everything. If you aren't happy I can't be, you know, sweetheart. Here are my arms around you all close and my cheek down on your yellow hair. That's how close to you I am. And how close I'm going to stay till you come home to me."[1114]

At the end of the war, the Army sent Delos to Trinity College, Cambridge, for four months of study, while he waited for space on a troopship home. After his return from Europe in 1919, Delos became head of the copy desk at the *Minneapolis Tribune*.

By 1921, the Lovelaces had developed the itch to move to New York. When the two enrolled in an advanced writing course at the University of Minnesota in the fall of that year, it was "*with the understanding that they could drop it at any time to leave for New York*," said professor Anna Phelan.[1115] Maud and Delos made the move to New York before the end of October 1921.

They went without definite prospect of employment, but Delos must have been in one of Joe's mountain-toppling moods, for he landed a job on their first day in New York (just as Joe did on his first day back in Minneapolis in *Betsy's Wedding*). Maud remembered that "*Delos said the city was his oyster and he was going to open it. He did.*"[1116]

According to Delos, "<u>*The Daily News*</u>*, then a young, rambunctious tabloid, put me to work as a reporter, then copy editor, and about a year later I was night editor, but then I had to resign because of illness.*"[1117] In fact, "*a doctor told the young copy reader he was sick enough to make an extremely early death a good possibility.*"[1118]

Delos left *The Daily News* on January 1, 1923. "*We got a room in Yonkers,*" Maud said. "*It's near New York. We could have run down town any evening to go to the theater - if we had had the money. We stopped collaborating* [on short stories] *and Delos began writing short stories in earnest. We lived at Hampton Bays, Long Island, for a time and then moved back to Minnesota.*"[1119]

When Delos and Maud returned to Minneapolis, it was not to the *Tribune*. Delos' short stories had begun to find favor with major magazines. Between 1922 and 1930, he wrote nearly one hundred stories. "*He sold 50 stories in a row to a single large national magazine, and he got up to $1000 apiece for them.*"[1120]

Maud had begun research for her first novel in the summer of 1924. After the loss of their first child in 1925, the Lovelaces did a good deal of traveling. Delos described Maud's writing of *The Black Angels* in 1925-1926 as extremely peripatetic, "*during the days when it lived the curious expectant life of a novel half in the mind of its maker, half in manuscript.*"[1121] Some of the cities they visited were New York, Detroit, Grand Marais (MI), Chicago, and New Orleans (they stayed near Tulane).

The Black Angels was printed in 1926 by the young John Day Company of New York, the first publisher to see it. The story was about a band of traveling singers, based on the Andrews Opera Company of southern Minnesota. Maud loved Mankato's semi-centennial book, *Mankato - Its First Fifty Years*, published in 1902, and "*Maud did not, one feels sure, overlook the following statement in this book: 'The early pioneer hereafter will be the interesting victim of the novelist, as well as the subject of the historian. The literary ferret will hunt their lives for romance, and their exploits will be celebrated in story and song.*'"[1122] *The Black Angels* was only the first of Maud's literary "celebrations" of the history of her home state.

Minneapolis was delighted with *The Black Angels.* The Minnesota Federation of Women's Clubs hosted a concert at the Minneapolis Institute of Arts on January 29, 1927, consisting of ballads from *The Black Angels*, sung by Kathleen Hart Bibb. Surprisingly, the music was arranged by Mrs. Harry B. Wakefield, the fictional Mrs. Hawthorne. A second recital was given by Kathleen at the University Club. Kathleen portrayed two characters from *The Black Angels*, Fanny Angel and Angel John, singing old ballads, as well as selections from Gilbert and Sullivan.

Maud and Delos sold the "Canoe Place" house in October 1926. Since their home at Lake Minnetonka was not fully insulated, they wintered in an apartment at 2900 James Avenue South in Minneapolis. The next autumn, 1927, they moved into a St. Paul hotel to facilitate Maud's research at the Minnesota Historical Society on *Early Candlelight*, her second book.

"*Perhaps the simplest way to give you an idea of the process of writing an historical novel is to tell you how I wrote Early Candlelight. You realize, of course, that no two novelists work just alike. My method is a method I have devised for myself, and it might not work at all for another writer. Each one must find for himself the difficult, circuitous, and often fog-bound road which will lead him to his story. I use my simile advisedly, for the place where stories lie waiting to be told seems to me an actual country into which I must somehow, with each new novel, find a route. In the case of an historical novel, I know that this country is in the past, but that does not make it any easier to find. The idea for* <u>Early Candlelight</u> *came to me when I was doing the research for my first novel,* <u>The Black Angels</u>. *In reading the history of Minnesota, I ran across a description of life at early Fort Snelling, and the situation there - a civilized social life superimposed upon the wilderness - fascinated me. I resolved then to make it the background for a future novel*."[1123]

In the course of Maud's historical research for *Early Candlelight*, "*the story began to come clear; the characters sprang to life and I wrote the opening chapter of the novel. When spring came, we moved back to Minnetonka; but I continued to visit the Historical Society. That summer I turned my rough outline of the novel into a rough draft - not so rough in some spots, for a few chapters came clear enough so that they could be written in finished form. My husband and I, sometimes with my father and mother, drove around southern Minnesota visiting the places mentioned in the novel. It would take too long to tell you about the adventures we had finding the sites of the early trading posts and settlements. I went often to Fort Snelling, and although I had long been familiar with this spot, I now saw it with new eyes. Mendota took on a charm impossible to describe.*"[1124]

After a final summer at the lake, the Lovelaces moved back to New York in the fall of 1928. Maud continued her research for *Early Candlelight* in the New York Public Library. And "*of special help was the American wing of the Metropolitan Museum. My husband used to go there with me and there, together, we furnished M'sieu Page's house. We have often said that no bride and groom ever had more fun furnishing their home than we did furnishing M'sieu Page's house out of the American wing at the Metropolitan Museum. When you go there you can find, if you hunt, the wall paper with hunting scenes which went into the dining room of M'sieu Page's house. You can find the statues of Washington and Lafayette, which stood on his mantel piece, the piano, and the wing chair where he was sitting when he fell in love with Dee. As the book neared the end, I stopped going to museums. Instead of writing four or five hours a day, as is my habit, I wrote from morning till night. For by that time I had found my way into the heart of that sunny country where stories lie waiting to be told.*"[1125]

Meanwhile, late in 1928, Delos had begun work for the *New York Sun*. In the spring of 1929, he took a position as associate editor of *The North American Review*; but by the end of the year, Delos had returned to the *Sun*, where he remained for over twenty years.

They lived in a freshly painted studio apartment with a fireplace, in a house with a garden and a green gate. "*Our street is a slum and so interesting,*"[1126] Maud wrote. The Italians who rented the two-room apartment next door told the superintendent they were a family of three - but sixteen moved in! Maud was a great "people watcher" and she found much to observe in New York. Out her window, she noticed the residents of the adjacent building ... a woman who often brought her baby to look out, an old man who sat all day in another window, a woman with a purple dress who came to consult with her caged canary in a third window.[1127]

New York was an adventure for the Lovelaces, but Maud sometimes found the city frightening. "*I have a curious fear of New York. Feel it especially when passing under the 'L.'*"[1128] The Minnesota girl in her must have found it stifling to see the sky only through the interstices of buildings. In November 1921, Maud was struck by the sight of "*a slim crescent moon with a tiny star beside it, hanging in the evening sky between two rows of tall buildings.*"[1129]

The Lovelaces never resided in Minnesota after 1928, though they remained owners of the Minnetonka house until 1939. For many years, they considered their "stay" in New York temporary. In 1929, Maud told a reporter: "*Of course, we mean to return to Minneapolis. This is our home here* [Minneapolis] *and we wouldn't want to live anywhere else. We still maintain our home at the lake. Our work makes it necessary for us to spend some time in New York. But when I am not working I like to lie down on the grass in the sun and just do nothing -- and I can't do that in New York. Of course, we're very fond of the theater and that is one of the compensations of living in New York. But we'll be glad to come back here.*"[1130]

In 1930, Maud wrote to her family: "*If, as mother says, my letters sometimes sound distressingly definite about staying in New York for quite a while, the only answer is that you can't live always on the verge of a change. You have to feel fairly permanent in one place in order to feel contented.*"[1131]

In 1932: "*When we come back to live in our home at Minnetonka, as we shall surely do some day, I shall again write of the history of the middle west.*"[1132] (Maud had no idea that her further history of the Middle West would take the form of a series of books for children!)

Maud and Delos enjoyed a very active social life in New York. They found the company of fellow authors and journalists stimulating. (The Lovelaces entertained Rose Wilder Lane in 1930. Maud cooked jellied chicken for her.) At functions of literary groups they met prominent writers, agents, publishers. New York was the place to further a writing career. In this respect, the two Minnesotans were "seduced" by the big city. "*The fact remains that I have three novels which are potential movies with many motion picture companies interested, that I have a new book out which is a potential best seller and another one in the course of writing which is an almost certain one. Something is bound to break soon if we just keep on in the way we are going, especially if we use the stay in New York to the very best advantage.*"[1133] No movie rights were ever sold for the novels.

Early Candlelight was published in August 1929 by the John Day Company. A month later, the commandant of Fort Snelling invited Maud to a military parade in her honor. "*We wanted to honor Mrs. Lovelace because of her interest in Fort Snelling, an interest manifested in her novel. We are glad to honor her in the accepted fashion of the post.*"[1134] This was the first time an American regiment accorded such tribute to a civilian woman. The Third Infantry, which paraded, was the oldest regiment in the army.

Maud was very moved by this honor. "*I am so thrilled. I had no idea that modern Fort Snelling would be so interested in my story of pioneer Fort Snelling. I've begun to wonder if I'll be able to go through such an impressive ceremony. They tell me all I have to do is stand beside the colonel. And I think the glorious military music will help me.*"[1135]

For the ceremony, Maud chose "*an ensemble of leaf green tweed with blouse of eggshell satin and a green felt hat and a corsage bouquet of pink roses and gardenias.*"[1136] It was a dramatic day. "*A lowering sky and haze shrouded the parade ground in a gray light as the ceremonies began. Bugles sounded retreat as the evening cannon fired its solitary shot. Slowly the flag was lowered while the regiment stood at*

MHL Archive

Stella and her Eldest Daughters

Stella Hart is flanked by Maud (left side of photo) and Kathleen (right side). Behind them is the back porch of the Hart home, on which Betsy and Joe sat drinking coffee on the morning of their wedding day.

MHL Archive

Mrs. Fowler, Mrs. Foster, and Mrs. Lovelace

Helen, Kathleen, and Maud were at the height of 1920s fashion.

Duplicated in several collections

The Young Novelist

Maud was not fond of this publicity portrait, but she enjoyed her career as a novelist. She said, *"What's life without something you're striving to do or get or be!"* (6-21-31)

MHL Archive

Mr. and Mrs. Delos Lovelace

This photo was taken late in 1924, during Maud's first pregnancy.

MHL Archive

Maud in 1924

MHL Archive

Delos Lovelace in 1924

Duplicated in several collections

Delos and Merian Lovelace

Maud said that Merian "*has so many looks like Delos. She pulls her brows together and they bulge just exactly like his.*" (10-13-31) *attention and the band played the Star Spangled Banner. The parade began. Fifteen companies, led by the band, swung into line and marched before Mrs. Lovelace, banners flying and footfalls treading an even beat on the sod. Mrs. Lovelace stood with Colonel W.C. Sweeney, commandant.... Dressed in green suit and hat, Mrs. Lovelace lent the only contrasting color to the waves of khaki before her.*"[1137] Maud considered this event one of the highlights of her career.

Numerous dramatizations of *Early Candlelight* were devised. Hennepin Avenue Methodist Church, the Minnesota Federation of Women's Clubs, and Carleton College were among the groups to perform scenes from the book, shortly after its release.

Early Candlelight also ran serially in the *St. Paul Dispatch*, beginning in January 1930. The book remained in print until 1944, when wartime paper shortages stopped its production. In 1949, *Early Candlelight* was reprinted by the University of Minnesota Press as part of the celebration marking Minnesota's territorial centennial. *Early Candlelight* was the biggest success among Maud's works of historical fiction, and it was the novel for which she was remembered by many adult readers. The Minnesota Historical Society Press reprinted the book in 1992, a gratifying commemoration of Maud's own centennial.

Maud and Delos became the clients of New York literary agent Nannine Joseph in 1930. Miss Joseph grew to be a close family friend over the forty-five-year period during which she handled the Lovelaces' literary business. One of Miss Joseph's better-known clients was Eleanor Roosevelt.

Maud's third novel, *Petticoat Court*, published in 1930, was a surprise to her following. Not only is *Petticoat Court* set outside Minnesota, it is not even set in America - but in Paris during the time of the Civil War. And although the heroine, Chloe Peyroux, is American, she is a Southerner, trying to enlist the aid of the Emperor for the Confederacy. The book was published by the John Day Company and met with favorable reviews.

Maud finished *Petticoat Court* in February 1930, and on April 1 she began research for *The Charming Sally* (like *The Black Angels*, a story about a group of performers). While researching in Philadelphia, Maud visited a Quaker church. "*She made herself conspicuous by sitting on the men's side of the church. She sat there until a Quaker reminded her that men and women never sat together in Friend's church!*"[1138] During her visit to the church, Maud decided her hero would be a Quaker.

In the spring of 1930, Maud and Delos had some good news for the family. Maud was pregnant. They received the following reaction from Stella: "*Dear Children, Oh so happy around our house since Saturday morning. Congratulations. We are all so happy for your letter with such good news. Everyone will now be giving you advice so I will refrain from that, but only refer to the fact that Minnesota is by far the best place to bring babies into the world. A first class A number 1 baby in Minnesota costs about $100 and in New York about a thou. My three babies cost me about $25 each (and see what we got!). You know 905 is wide open and Lake Minnetonka is waiting for a baby out in that beautiful lawn ... what a place for a youngster to get a good start in life. Anyway we are all tickled to death, especially me.*"[1139]

Maud had completed research on *The Charming Sally* by the time the baby was born, but she had not yet begun to write. "*Having a baby around helped me with the baby in the book,*" she commented.[1140]

The pages of *The Charming Sally* reveal that the author knew the experience of motherhood. But there is a poignancy to some of the passages which reveals the author to have also known the pain of parting from a child, as Maud did when her tiny son died in 1925. "*This child was hers; she had borne it. Why could she not watch the miracle of its growth? Why could she not hold the clinging hands, guide the stumbling feet, feed the little eager mouth, wipe away the tears which must come sometimes if the eyes were so much like her own? She asked these questions fiercely, rebelliously.*"[1141] Meg, the protagonist of *The Charming Sally*, who has been separated from her child, stops mothers on the street to ask the ages of their babies. Meg's heart contracts when she finds a baby the same age as her own child. Maud may have had such thoughts as the months passed after the death of her son. Six months later, when she saw a six-month-old, her heart must have contracted, like Meg's. "*You don't know ... you don't know, until you have a baby. It's closer to you than your own life is. It tears your heart out to think of parting with it.*"[1142]

It was reassuring to Maud that her second baby was so active in utero. "*Tommie sends a kick which is his way of sending a hug,*" she wrote to her family on August 16, 1930. Despite some inevitable anxiety, Maud enjoyed her pregnancy. "*The doctor and I have lots of fun. Today he asked me whether I felt much movement and I said, 'Yes, he's a good lively boy.' The doctor was listening at the stethoscope and in a moment he said, 'Well, she has a good strong heart beat anyway.'* "[1143]

Though she gained little weight, Maud carried the baby very prominently. Friends joked that she was carrying not only little Thomas ... but little Thomasina as well! In a letter written to the Harts, Delos joined in the teasing. "*Come to think of it, maybe you didn't know she has been getting fat. That you shouldn't know is by no means impossible, for now it comes to me I haven't ever told you she is going to have a child (1) or some children (2). The truth is she is. Maud, in a word, is about to become a mother, if you are willing to accept some time in January as about.*"[1144] (Maud did <u>not</u> get fat. She weighed only 145 pounds in the ninth month of her pregnancy.)

"*At least half our Christmas cards from New York people said to Maud and Delos and Tommie. I do feel sure that it's a boy but don't <u>care</u>. I do think baby girls are adorable, and Delos does, too. It would only be nice to have a chance to name him for daddie, since his own three were girls. We keep trying out Stella but don't like it with Lovelace, and I know mother doesn't either. We also try out Josephine for Delossy's mother.*[1145] *... Delossy's suggestion is Thomasina Cooperina Lovelace.*"[1146]

Merian explained: "*They were sure I was going to be a boy and the only name they had in readiness was Thomas! When I turned out to be a girl, they were stumped, and picked Merian because Coop was such a good friend. Maud considered Diana, but thought a girl named Diana Lovelace would have to be <u>awfully</u> pretty, and didn't want to saddle me with it in case I wasn't. (She assured me that I was, of course. But I think I'd rather be Merian.)*"[1147]

Daughter Merian arrived in Manhattan on January 18, 1931. Tom Hart sent a telegram, proclaiming that the family in Minneapolis was "*eating her health in onion sandwiches.*"[1148] Stella took the train to New York to help Maud. "*I don't think I ever appreciated anything more. I was afraid to pick the baby up, almost, at first, and mother was so handy with her.*"[1149] Maud's recuperation from childbirth was gradual. The delivery was not difficult, but she suffered a hemorrhage afterwards.

1931 was a good year for the Lovelaces - in addition to the birth of Merian, Delos' book, *Rockne of Notre Dame,* was published by Putnam. It was a biography for boys of Knute Rockne, legendary coach of the Fighting Irish. Sports enthusiast that he was, Delos describes the advent of the forward pass with obvious relish. *Knute Rockne,* written in just three weeks, was Delos' second book. His first, *Byrd and the Polar Expeditions,* was published under the pen name "Coram Foster."

Maud resumed her regular daily schedule of writing when Merian was two months old. The full-time presence of a German nurse named "Hanni" made this possible. (This was not the Hanni whom Maud had known in Munich in 1914.) In November 1931, Maud wrote to her family to explain why a trip home to Minneapolis would be impossible. They would have had to take Hanni along, and the expense was prohibitive. "*There are so many complications surrounding the trip. First comes the matter of Hanni. I don't suppose any of you have any idea how completely Hanni takes care of the baby. I haven't bathed her in my life. I never change a diaper ... and have no more idea how to prepare and strain her food than Gigi* [her ten-year-old nephew] *has. Understand, I don't like taking so little care of my own baby. I'm so crazy about her I'd like to take all the care of her. It's just been necessary because of my book. I've made the baby absolutely Hanni's job, and she takes full responsibility, and I only play with her the way a visitor might do. I don't even go into the nursery without knocking. After the darned old book is done, I'm going to do more with the baby but for the present this arrangement is ideal, of course, and Hanni is perfect.*"[1150]

By 1933, the Lovelaces had moved to Mount Vernon, New York, where they lived at 590 East Third Street. Maud was now working on *One Stayed at Welcome* (published by John Day), which brought the return to a Minnesota setting. This was her first collaboration with Delos on a novel. *One Stayed at Welcome* is the story of two young men who establish a town in the Bloomington, Minnesota, area. (There really is a Welcome, Minnesota, but Maud didn't discover this until after the publication of the book in 1934.)

Maud and Delos enjoyed working together on *One Stayed at Welcome.* "*Having watched other collaborators getting into each others*

Delos wrote to his in-laws:

"*Had a glass of orange juice and a bag of peanuts today for lunch, in the forlorn hope that such thin fare would lose me a pound. Likely, I should have lost a couple if I'd foregone the peanuts. I'm not gaining. I still weigh my beautiful hundred and eighty. But as I have sadly, and futilely declared before, a hundred and eighty is too much. Every once in a while I get downright ambitious and swear I'll reduce, but nothing much comes of it.*" (10-15-30)

MHL Archive

Maud and Delos

Maud wrote: "*Delos and I are mutually agreed that marrying each other was giving the perfect answer to life.*" (11-28-31)

MHL Archive

Gardening

The Lovelace family spent the summer of 1931 in a rented house in New Rochelle. After years in New York City, backyard trees and gardens had become something of a novelty.

MHL Archive

Maud in the 1930s

Coll. of Edward Palkot

63 Wyatt Road

All but one (*Betsy's Wedding*) of the Betsy-Tacy books were written in this house, which the Lovelaces built in 1938.

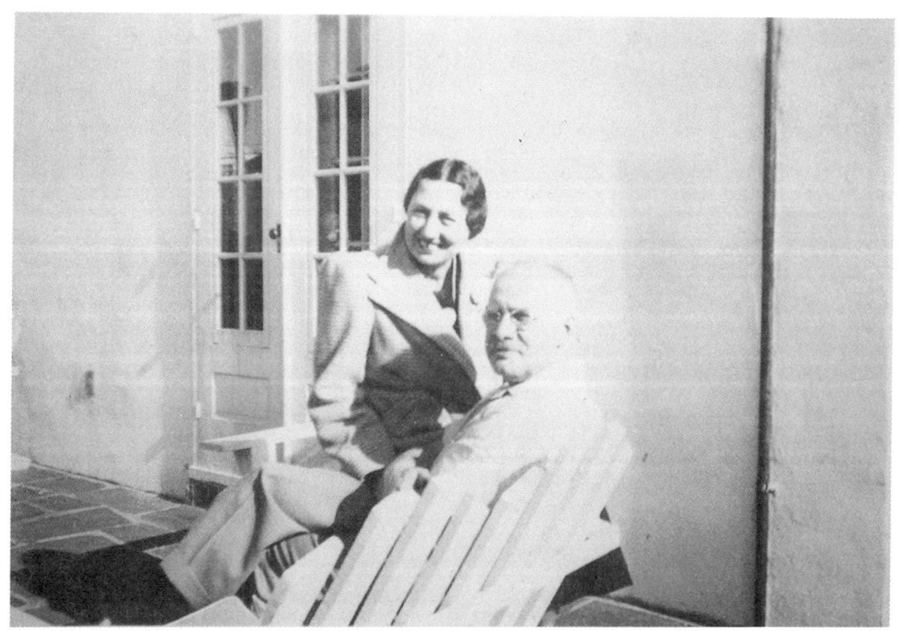

MHL Archive

Maud and Delos

This photo was taken on the patio of the Wyatt Road house.

hair and on each others nerves, we have reached the conclusion that happy collaborations like happy marriages are made in heaven. When we do a book together, we simply share the work. Some instinct tells us which chapters belong to Delos, which belong to me, and which must be tussled with together. Some parts of the work, such as any necessary research, fall naturally to me, and other parts, such as whipping up a plot, fall naturally to him. Collaborations aside, he has a finger in all my literary pies and I in his."[1151]

The next year, Maud and Delos moved to 69 Highbrook Avenue in Pelham, New York, where they remained until the late 1930s. Here they wrote *Gentlemen from England*, another successful collaboration, which was published by Macmillan in 1937. Tom Hart had passed away in 1936, and before long, Stella joined the Lovelaces in Pelham. She was part of their household until she died in 1947.

Maud had a number of ideas for future projects after *Gentlemen from England*. She dabbled again in short stories, and intriguingly, toyed with the idea of publishing under the pen name "Susan Cray."

A Minnesota librarian wrote to Maud to suggest she write a biography of Charlotte Ousiconsin Van Cleve. Maud responded: "*It would be a pleasure to me to write it - I remember her story very well and her own delightful book. I can only put the suggestion, though, into that pocket of books-I-should-like-to-write; a pocket which I frequently turn inside out, somewhat ruefully. There is so much work planned ahead.*"[1152]

Maud's mental pocket didn't yet contain the Betsy-Tacy books, though she had been observing another writer and friend enter the field of children's literature by the same route she herself would eventually take. In 1933, Maud wrote: "*I think that Emma Gelders Sterne is doing beautiful things for children. She lives near us and has two daughters who were originally responsible for her writing for children.*"[1153]

The Lovelaces moved to 63 Wyatt Road in Garden City, New York, in 1938. They were the first owners of this blue-shuttered, white house, and Maud insisted that the builders include recessed bookcases in the 15' x 20' living room. The dining room was 11' x 15', with a bay window which looked out into the side yard. There was a first-floor powder room, as well as two full baths on the second floor. There were four bedrooms. The Lovelaces had a full-time maid until the early 40s, and the fourth bedroom was hers, until it became Delos' study. (Maud's desk was in the bedroom.) The family lived in this house for the next seventeen years, until they sold it to Edward Palkot.

It was in Garden City that Maud began writing the Betsy-Tacy books, inspired by the often-repeated bedtime stories she had been telling about her childhood. "*After we finished Gentlemen from England, I found myself reluctant to start another novel.... Merian was six years old and so interesting, so really fascinating to me, that I could not bear to take the time for any long piece of work. I tried short stories again but without much enthusiasm and no success. Meanwhile, as several happy years passed by, I was telling her stories about my childhood in Mankato. By 1939 I was calling myself Betsy and my best friend Tacy, and they had been put into a book.*"[1154]

On November 17, 1938, Maud noted in her diary that she had an "*idea for a new story.*"[1155] She began writing *Betsy-Tacy* several days later.

Maud was reported to have planned only one Betsy-Tacy book; but *Betsy-Tacy* leads so naturally into *Betsy-Tacy and Tib*, it is difficult to believe that this was the case. A new Betsy-Tacy book arrived each year, with a one-year break between *Downtown* and *Heaven to Betsy*. (At the same time that she was writing *Betsy and Tacy Go Over the Big Hill*, Maud collaborated with Delos on *The Golden Wedge*, a collection of nine Indian legends from pre-Columbian South America, published by Crowell in 1942.)

Maud apparently considered ending the Betsy-Tacy series after the first four titles. Delos and Merian helped change her mind. In about 1944, some boxes which had been stored in Minnesota were sent out to the Lovelaces' home in Garden City. Maud's high school diaries were among the contents. When she first reread them, Maud found them silly, "*full of slang, and boys, boys, boys.*" She initially dismissed the diaries as possible story material. But then, "*I heard my husband laughing in the living room and I went in and there he was reading my diaries. And he said, 'Maudie, these are rich. You must take Betsy through high school.'*"[1156]

As Maud was writing the Betsy-Tacys, Merian was growing up. "*Merian was in Garden City High School while I was writing the books.*

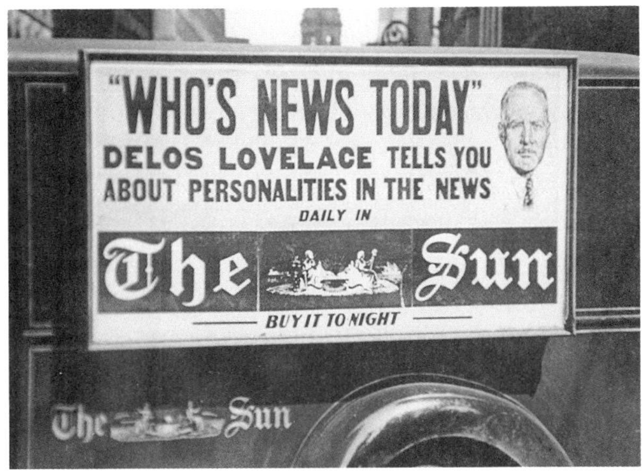

MHL Archive

Who's News

"Who's News Today" was Delos Lovelace's syndicated column for the *New York Sun* from 1943 to 1947.

Coll. of Elizabeth Miller

Celebrating *Betsy-Tacy*

Maud visited Mankato in 1940 when *Betsy-Tacy* was published. She posed in front of the Center Street house with her sister Helen. Behind her (l to r) are Tess Kenney Holden and Bick Kenney Kirch. Maud and Bick had a picnic on the Big Hill together during this visit!

She brought the atmosphere of high school into the house, helping to refresh my memory."[1157] Betsy's excitement over dances, social activities, and clothes must have been given life by the teenager in the Lovelace house. "*I'm meeting Merian for lunch today to buy her graduation dress; the prom dress ... pale green and fluffy, is already bought.*"[1158] Maud was aware of Merian's effect on the series. "*Although the stories are based on my own life, they followed hers, almost from grade to grade, through high school, Europe, and marriage. That accounts partly, I think, for the reality they seem to have.*"[1159]

After writing *Betsy and Joe*, Maud again contemplated discontinuing the series. "*The latest Betsy story* [*Betsy and Joe*] *is the last, said the author, pointing out a letter just received from a young reader who pleaded that Betsy be taken through college.*"[1160] Perhaps part of Maud's hesitation was the idea that Betsy would not make an ideal role model. She (Maud/Betsy) hadn't made a success of university work, and at just this time, Merian was preparing to start Smith College. Maud must have been very proud of Merian and perhaps a bit regretful that she couldn't in good conscience send Betsy through college (since Maud herself hadn't finished college!). But there was someone else she could send to college - Carney! *Carney's House Party* was published in 1949. A non-Betsy-Tacy juvenile title, *The Tune Is in the Tree*, was published in 1950, the same year as *Emily of Deep Valley*. *The Trees Kneel at Christmas* appeared in 1951. Maud was inspired to write this book (about a Syrian family in Brooklyn) by her earlier research on Syrian traditions for *Over the Big Hill*.

Carney's House Party and *Emily of Deep Valley* form a useful link between *Betsy and Joe* and *Betsy and the Great World*, but this was essentially accidental. Even while writing *Carney* and *Emily*, Maud hadn't made up her mind to write another book about Betsy. After *Emily*, she must have felt that an educational trip to Europe was as good as college, and she sent Betsy to the *Great World* in 1952. *Betsy's Wedding*, published in 1955, was an inevitable sequel.

Serendipitously, Merian was married in New York City in August 1954, while *Betsy's Wedding* was in the works. The Lovelaces' new son-in-law was Englebert Kirchner, a young man who had emigrated from Munich. Merian and Bert, both journalists, remained in New York. They had no children.

After *Betsy's Wedding* was published in 1955, Maud was again urged by her readers to write another Betsy-Tacy book. "*Most of the letters I get ask two questions. And I always answer them personally to tell the girls that Joe does come back from the war and they do have a daughter they call Bettina.*"[1161]

Elsewhere Maud remarked: "*In Betsy's Wedding, Betsy's husband went off to the First World War and many letters have begged me to bring him safely home. The letters even offer me titles for another book, obviously in the friendly assumption that when a writer has found a title he is over the hump. Welcome Home, Joe! was suggested by one. Many have asked for Betsy's Baby. And some have even hit upon the title I have selected myself, Betsy's Bettina.*"[1162]

Maud would have liked to satisfy her readers, and she gave serious thought to writing *Betsy's Bettina*. While contemplating plans for another book in 1959, Maud wrote to her agent, "*I wish it were Betsy's Bettina but that won't be written until I feel it, and I want to write it. It isn't stubbornness; I can't write a book any other way.*"[1163] Two years later, it was reported that "*the next Maud Hart Lovelace book will be entitled Betsy's Bettina.* [Maud said,] '*I have done some work on the book but it really hasn't started rolling.*' *The latest in the Betsy-Tacy series will be about the child of Betsy and her husband.*"[1164]

Maud's comments on writing *Betsy's Bettina* became decidedly pessimistic as the years passed. In 1962: "*In the past few years I have tried again and again to write Betsy's Bettina but it didn't come, which means ... with me ... that it isn't meant to.*"[1165] In 1964, Maud commented on the series: "*Although they used to come along so regularly, I never wrote one unless I really wanted to, and Betsy's Bettina has not yet asked to be done.*"[1166] Finally, in 1973, Maud wrote: "*No, I never warmed to Betsy's Bettina. I did a little research on it but didn't care to write it.*"[1167]

Maud always began work on a book with research on the place and period of her setting. For *Betsy's Bettina*, both place and period would have presented stumbling blocks. Maud planned to set *Betsy's Bettina* at Lake Minnetonka ... but her daughter Merian was born in New York, far from kith and kin. If Maud set *Betsy's Bettina* in the Midwest, she would have had to fictionalize relationships between the Willards and characters from the series whom the Lovelaces did not see in these years. On the other hand, if she set the story in the East, Maud would have had to leave behind all the Minnesota Betsy-Tacy characters and settings and introduce new ones (awkward for the last book in a series).

As for the period of *Betsy's Bettina,* Merian was born in 1931; but Maud's readers would have expected Bettina to arrive a decade earlier - a year or two after Joe's return from the war. If Maud set Bettina's birth back to about 1921, she would have had to fictionalize to an extent never before required, inventing a life for the Willard family that bore little resemblance to either the life Maud and Delos lived in the 1920s or the life of the Lovelace family in New York in the 1930s. Maud would not have been willing to depart so drastically from the reality she had captured so faithfully in the previous ten books.

Then, too, there were in those years events which, to borrow Maud's description of the creative process, would have formed quagmires in the country she wished to travel. Maud and Delos lost their firstborn. Kathleen lost her first son, and after her first marriage ended in divorce, she remarried, lost a baby daughter, and moved away. It is understandable that Maud did not "warm" to *Betsy's Bettina*.

Since we know that Maud always did her research before beginning to write, we can be reasonably sure that there are no existing manuscript pages for *Betsy's Bettina*.

During the Betsy-Tacy years, Delos continued to commute into New York City to the paper. From 1943 to 1947, Delos wrote a syndicated column for the *New York Sun* called "Who's News Today." He was the *Sun's* assistant city editor until 1950, when the paper merged with the *World Telegram.* Delos wrote features for the *World Telegram and Sun* until 1952. (He also did a comic strip!) His newspaper colleagues called Delos, "Doc." Delos resigned as staff writer in the fall of 1952. He had written a boys' biography, *Ike Eisenhower*, which came out during World War II (plus an expanded edition released when Eisenhower was running for president). Delos also wrote the juvenile title *That Dodger Horse,* published by Thomas Y. Crowell in 1956, as well as a story about the birth of Jesus called *Journey to Bethlehem*, published in 1953.

In the autumn of 1952, the Lovelaces drove across the country to California. Near Los Angeles in November, they passed through Claremont, a pleasant college town, and were charmed. "*On their way to the home of Maud's sister Kathleen, the Lovelaces went through Claremont. 'Delos declared immediately that this was where he wanted to live,' said Maud. 'He drove to a real estate office, told the man we wanted to buy a home in Claremont and that he should look for a place while we continued on to Kathleen's.' The characteristic speed and decisiveness will seem familiar to those who know the Joe of the Betsy-Tacy books.*"[1168] The Lovelaces obviously made their decision to retire in Claremont then and there, but it was more than a year before they returned.

The Lovelaces sold their Garden City house in June 1953. They spent two months of that summer in Minneapolis (en route to California), renting at 4312 First Avenue South. (Maud was busy gathering material for *Betsy's Wedding*.) Returning to Claremont, they purchased 774 West Eighth Street (a small house with lemon trees in the backyard) early in 1954.

In 1953, Crowell published *Winona's Pony Cart*. This book is a spinoff which departed from the momentum of the Betsy-Tacy series. (After writing about Betsy in *Great World* as a young adult in the months prior to the outbreak of World War I, Maud suddenly jolted us back in time to turn-of-the-century Deep Valley.) In 1955, *Betsy's Wedding* returned readers to the "normal" chronology of the series with a bang. Another book Maud wrote in California was *What Cabrillo Found*, a biography of explorer Juan Rodriguez Cabrillo, who "found" California. *Cabrillo* was published by Crowell in 1958.

Though her other titles were well received, the Betsy-Tacy series remained Lovelace's most popular children's books. *Downtown* was the first Betsy-Tacy book to be issued in paperback. It was published by Scholastic Press in 1962 and illustrated by Lisa Weil. Maud said of these drawings: "*They are very gay, in a cartoonish style*."[1169] *Betsy-Tacy* and *Betsy-Tacy and Tib* were issued in paperback in 1974 with the original Lenski drawings.

Of the California years, Delos wrote: "*Even in my most reluctant moments ... I feel that putting words down, in more or less sense, is preferable to any other work I might find in my semi-retirement; and I plan to go on putting them down as long as I am willing to maintain an acceptable 8 to 1 routine. This 8 to 1 routine is, however, a secret.... In*

Claremont my wife and I have broadcast word that we work until four o'clock every afternoon. For a fact, we sometimes do. If the telephone rings earlier, I, being a City Room veteran - able to interrupt any sentence, take the call and note down all messages for my wife."[1170]

With its numerous colleges, Claremont must have provided a stimulating environment for the Lovelaces. "*We are deeply interested in the civil-rights movement, deeply sympathetic to it. A student group at the College recently sponsored a series of meetings.... Dr. Martin Luther King was not here, which we regretted, but we wish that his leadership would be continued. His non-violent approach to the needed reforms has done so much*."[1171]

Maud's interest in the civil rights movement no doubt gave her the idea for her last book, *The Valentine Box*, published in 1966. The story was adapted from one published in *Jack and Jill* magazine. "*It's something I had been anxious to do ... a book with a Negro child in it, and yet happy, no big problem involved. It's sad how seldom a Negro child can find a book with Negroes in the illustrations. He shouldn't always have to read about white children. I found an old short story of my own which seemed to lend itself to this kind of treatment. Only the illustrations will show that the heroine is a Negro. I loved doing it*."[1172] By a pleasant coincidence, Merian was at this time working on a picture history of the civil-rights movement, published in 1965.

After *The Valentine Box*, Maud planned a story set in late-Victorian California, possibly based on the experiences of the Austin relatives who moved to the San Diego area. Santa Barbara apparently also figured in. *California, an Intimate Guide*, by Aubrey Drury was to provide turn-of-the-century background. Maud never went beyond the note-taking stage on this project.

In 1966, Maud described her work on a book she had begun to write. "*It is for adults, although I think young adults will enjoy it, too. This also is not a Betsy-Tacy book, and it's not fiction, but much of it transpires in Mankato. I'll soon be back at work on it again, and will tell you more later*."[1173] This book, which would have been a memoir of Maud's life as a writer, was never finished.

In the memoir, *Living with Writing*, Maud related a painful incident from her childhood which never appeared in a Betsy-Tacy book. It occurred in the summer of 1905. "*There is a sad story of which memory does not spare me a single detail. It was so awful that I never forgot it. No one in the family ever mentioned it to me after it was over. It never became a subject for joking as so many childish misadventures did. I have never written it down and probably have never told it more than once or twice.*

"My mother had a dear childhood friend with a husband and five children in Minneapolis who used to visit us. On her last visit to Mankato, she invited me to go home with her for a stay of a week or so. Mother gave her permission and I was dancing with joy. To go on a train, to see Minneapolis, to meet Aunt Merrie's children whom I had never seen. Kathleen had gone all the way to California to visit Grandma and Grandpa Austin. Now I was off to see the world. My clothes were washed, starched, and packed. I got a new hat with flowers on it, and I started away with Aunt Merrie, so shining with happiness that I must have glowed like a lamp. The whole family and Bickie saw us off. 'Write to us,' mother called, waving, as we stood on the platform while the train moved out. There was really no need to remind me, for I had packed paper and a clutch of pencils with my most important impedimenta, and papa had given me stamps. Writing letters home would be part of the fun. The whistle blew, the bell tolled, the conductor cried 'All aboard' and the train chuff chuffed away. I loved Aunt Merrie and felt sure that I would not be homesick on this visit, and I wasn't.

"I had a very fine time. Their home was a humble one, near the railroad tracks, but Aunt Merrie and her husband were very kind to me. One morning I delayed going out to play in order to write the promised letter home. There was much to tell and one of the most interesting things to me was that these people were so different from the Harts. The children didn't have good table manners. They grabbed and talked with their mouths full. And they sassed their mother. She was very gentle, not a disciplinarian like Stella. Even now I cannot imagine anyone with temerity enough to sass mother. As Kathleen said one day, mother had implanted in us a conviction that if we did certain things the sky would fall. Aunt Merrie had no such power. The children told each other to shut up and even told their mother to shut up.

"I described all this with a skill of which I was proud and probably, being a fiction writer, colored it up a bit. The girls were calling me to come out and play, so I soon finished the innumerable pages and stuffed them in an envelope. Aunt Merrie said, 'Run along dear. I'll stamp and

mail it for you.' So I put it down and ran outdoors. As we played I began to have a queer sickish feeling which I've had now and again in crises through my life. I knew in the pit of my stomach that something was wrong. I remembered that I had not sealed my letter. But surely Aunt Merrie would not read it. I had been brought up to believe that people did not read other people's letters.

"Finally, through the noise of our play, I heard her sweet voice. 'Maudie, will you come in a minute? Not the others. Just you.' I ran in, still trying to make myself believe that nothing was wrong. Then I saw that she had been crying. She went to her rocking chair and took me on her lap. 'Maud,' she said. 'I read your letter. I thought it was nice that you wrote such a long one and I wanted to see what you said. I wish you wouldn't send it. You know, dear, this is a big family....'"

That is as far as Aunt Merrie got. Maud broke into tears and couldn't control them. She cried over and over that she wanted to go home. The children had come running in, and joined Aunt Merrie in urging Maud to stay (though they didn't know what had happened). They eventually put her to bed and Stella later told Maud that she had been feverish and Aunt Merrie stayed up all night with her. The next morning, Maud was still crying and still wanted to go home, so Aunt Merrie agreed. *"But, I declared, tears breaking out afresh, I could not go home without buying presents. No Hart did. And papa had given me money to buy them. So they all took me downtown and, weeping, I bought presents and, weeping, I was put on the train. Aunt Merrie had telephoned my family that I was coming and had told them the reason why. She also sent the letter.*

"Mother met the train. Back in the safety of home, I told her the whole humiliating, horrible story. She was all protective sympathy and pity. She comforted me in warm loving arms. 'Aunt Merrie should not have read that letter. She got what she deserved.' Papa was sympathetic, too, but before I went to bed that night, he took me on his lap and told me a story. It was about desert chieftains and the loyalty they felt to anyone whose salt they had eaten. 'You had eaten Aunt Merrie's salt,' Papa said. 'So you should not have written that letter. Always remember, Maudie, that when you accept someone's hospitality, you have an obligation to that person.'

"Aunt Merrie is the heroine of this story. She wrote to mother and apologized for having read my letter. She told her children the things I

had written about their behavior. She said it had helped them. She forgave me. Later we moved to Minneapolis and the thought of meeting her after the awful letter made my flesh crawl. Although I was now 19, a student at the University, I felt it was impossible to enter their house again, but I did. Wonderful Aunt Merrie! I was received warmly, lovingly, like a dear friend. In no time I was chattering at their table. The girls and I picked up our friendship where we had left it. My disastrous visit was never mentioned by them or by my family, and it was never put into a book. But an experience so deep and cruel, when it happens to a writer, could not but get into a book sometime. So here it is, in this one."

Of course, the book Maud was referring to was the never-finished *Living with Writing*. For several years, Maud worked periodically on the manuscript. She also considered the idea of a collection of more Betsy-Tacy stories, to be called *Mostly Betsy*. But between answering her ever-arriving fan mail and the many interests she and Delos pursued together, Maud never completed another book.

Maud and Delos returned to the East for frequent visits. "*Delos and I are going to New York for a good visit with our children. We try to go there in October because during the summer they, Merian and Bert, spend such long weekends out at Fire Island. They have a house there which they lease every year. It's right on the ocean and absolutely delightful but a little too primitive for D and me for long stays*."[1174]

In Claremont, Maud and Delos were kept busy by their lively interest in the cultural events of the community, as well as social and intellectual pursuits at home. The following quotations reveal the Lovelaces' varied interests:

"*And wasn't the New York season opened beautifully last night at Lincoln Center? We saw and heard it all on television. And Mrs. Kennedy's gloves to her elbow! What about the long ones we all bought last year?*"[1175]

"*We will hear the Los Angeles Symphony Orchestra under Zubin Mehta. They play here* [Claremont] *four times a year*."[1176]

"*One big event of the summer has been the visit of the Dead Sea Scrolls.... We did finally get in and I found the exhibit most impressive*."[1177]

"*Delos was reading Tielhard de Chardin aloud to me. That went on*

MHL Archive

774 West Eight Street
Claremont, California

Maud and Delos purchased this house in 1954.

Mount San Antonio Gardens

Maud moved into the "Gardens," a retirement community in Claremont, California, about 1970. Maud was happy in this cottage at 884 West Harrison Street.

for months and even years for we are fascinated by his learning and his philosophy."[1178]

The Lovelaces were among the founders of Claremont's first Episcopal church, St. Ambrose. Maud wrote a short essay, "Thoughts on Prayer," for *We Believe in Prayer*, published by T.S. Denison. "*I believe in praying as I believe in breathing,*" she wrote. "*An involuntary procedure, prayer runs along with the day, following the convolutions of work and play, duties, problems, and delights. ...It is my way to turn to God at any hour, with a small joy as well as with a sorrow, with plans, hopes, thanks - even wishes. Not that I expect Him to stay the course of the planets while He grants my often misguided petitions. But since He is love and is everything, 'nearer than hands and feet,' one may share everything with Him, and there is a blessed release in doing so. What He gives, I earnestly believe, in response to such spontaneous prayers, is strength, insight, appreciation, serenity, but above all a continuing reassurance of His presence. As for formal prayers, they differ, naturally according to one's faith. But I love to say upon awaking the opening verses of the greater doxology. They include the whole world and seep away pettiness as the sun is sweeping away shadows, focusing one's thoughts on the glory of the unseen creator, the One who gives us the gift of life.*"[1179]

Maud and Delos had an extraordinarily successful marriage. Delos died in the same year they would have celebrated their 50th wedding anniversary. "*We used to talk so much that we were late in starting to write. When I was writing Early Candlelight we lived at Lake Minnetonka. We would get up as early as five a.m., have breakfast and talk. On the breakfast table was an alarm clock, set for eight a.m. When it rang we quit talking and went to work.*"[1180]

One is not surprised to hear that Maud and Delos always had a lot to talk about. The same was true of Betsy and Joe. "They talked hard and fast.... They never seemed to tire of talking. In fact, they never seemed to tire of each other."[1181]

1114 Fragment from Early Years of Marriage file.

1115 *Minneapolis T.*, 4-19-32.

1116 Maud's notes on New York.

1117 Richards, ed., *Minnesota Writers*, p. 206.

1118 *Nassau Daily Review-Star*, 9-25-41.

1119 *St. Paul Dispatch*, 1-19-28.

1120 *Nassau Daily Review-Star*, 9-25-41.

1121 *Minneapolis Tribune*, 10-10-26.

1122 Ray, "Maud Hart Lovelace and Mankato," p. 158.

1123 Nelson, et al., eds., *Minnesota Writes*, p. 45.

1124 Ibid., p. 46.

1125 Ibid.

1126 Winter Notes, p. 3.

1127 Ibid., p. 4.

1128 Diary excerpts in B.F.

1129 Ibid., 11-14-21.

1130 *Minneapolis Journal*, 9-26-29.

1131 MHL to Hart Family, 8-14-30.

1132 *Minneapolis Journal*, 5-1-32.

1133 MHL to Hart Family, 8-14-30.

1134 *Minneapolis Journal*, 9-28-29.

1135 Ibid.

1136 *Minneapolis T.*, 9-28-29.

1137 *St. Paul Dispatch*, 9-28-29.

1138 Ibid., 9-28-34.

1139 S. Hart to M&D, spring 1930.

1140 MHL to M. Freeman, 5-19-64.

1141 *The Charming Sally*, p. 240.

1142 Ibid., p. 165.

1143 MHL to Hart Family, 9-30.

1144 DWL to Hart Family, 10-15-30.

1145 MHL to Hart Family, 12-26-30.

1146 Ibid., 12-30-30.

1147 MLK to SSW, 11-15-91.

1148 TWH to Lovelaces, 1-19-31.

1149 MHL to T. Edwards, 8-3-55.

1150 MHL to Hart Family, 11-6-31.

1151 MHL mini-bio, 1940. EYM file.

1152 MHL to G. Countryman, 12-6-35.

1153 MHL to D. McGregor, 11-15-33.

1154 MHL to M. Freeman, 5-19-64.

1155 R/N *Betsy's Wedding.*

1156 Lovelace Interview, University of Michigan.

1157 *Newsday,* 9-30-48.

1158 MHL to M. Everett, 5-17-48.

1159 MHL to L. Demp, 11-2-56.

1160 *Newsday,* 9-30-48.

1161 *Minneapolis Tribune,* 8-25-65.

1162 Richards, ed., *Minnesota Writers*, p. 212.

1163 MHL to N. Joseph, 4-16-59.

1164 *Mankato Free Press,* 10-6-61.

1165 MHL to N. Joseph, 9-23-62.

1166 MHL to S. Thiets, 10-31-64.

1167 MHL to J. Tessari, 8-11-73.

1168 Ray, "Maud Hart Lovelace and Mankato," p. 171.

1169 MHL to A. Wiecking, 11-20-62.

1170 Richards, ed., *Minnesota Writers*, p. 207.

1171 MHL to R. Lee, 4-21-64.

1172 Ibid., 7-25-65.

1173 MHL to A. Wiecking, 8-19-66.

1174 MHL to R. Lee, 7-25-65.

1175 MHL to N. Joseph, 9-23-62.

1176 MHL to R. Lee, 4-21-64.

1177 Ibid., 7-25-65.

1178 Ibid.

1179 MHL, "Thoughts on Prayer," draft, *We Believe in Prayer* (Minneapolis: T.S. Denison, 1959).

1180 *St. Paul Dispatch,* 9-28-34.

1181 *Betsy and Joe*, p. 78.

CHAPTER FIFTEEN
"What Ever Happened To ..."
Summaries of the Adult Lives
of Crowd Members

Bick and Charley Kirch (Tacy and Harry Kerr) were transferred from Minneapolis to Buffalo, New York, in 1922 by the Munsingwear Company. Their second son, James Kenney Kirch, was born in Buffalo on Christmas Day, 1924. Their third son, Charles Eugene (called just "Eugene"), was also born in Buffalo. He had a fatal birth defect which could not be remedied, though his parents resorted to a trip to the Mayo Clinic. Eugene died on February 4, 1928.

Charley Kirch started his own paper goods company, which Bick took over after his death in 1961. "*Bickie is so well, so strong, so beautiful, and still carrying on her husband's business with great success*."[1182] Their home in Buffalo was at 103 Larchmont Road.

Midge Gerlach Harris (Tib Muller) did a fair amount of moving around, since her husband, Charles, was a traveling salesman. Charles worked for the Rollins Hosiery Company of Des Moines, Iowa. In the late 1920s, Midge and Charles separated. He moved to Jackson, Mississippi, and she to Chicago. Midge rejoined Charles when ill health confined him to the home of his sister in Winterset, Iowa. He died of diabetes in April 1929.

About this time, Midge's younger sister Dolly was divorced and at loose ends in the Chicago area with her young daughter, Joan. (*Betsy-Tacy and Tib* was dedicated to Midge and Joan.) Midge's mother was by this time a widow in Mankato. The three women joined forces and set up housekeeping together in Chicago. "*Tib is now Mrs. Harris and she lives in Chicago. She has no children but she has a little niece named Joan who looks just exactly as Tib looked in the Betsy-Tacy and Tib book.*"[1183] Dolly remarried and became Mrs. Arthur Mahle. Mrs. Gerlach returned to Minnesota in her old age and lived at the Lutheran Home. Midge never remarried. As Joan's beloved "Aunt Mimi," she lived near the Mahles, watching Joan grow up, marry, and have her own little boy. Midge died after a six-month battle with cancer on December 15, 1964.

Maud wrote of Midge: "*Who can forget her delighted burst of laughter at another's witticism? However, her admiration was always balanced by a salutary frankness. She was an honest, loyal, loving friend.... After her husband's death in 1929, she worked ... as a dress designer. One of her favorite anecdotes concerned the request of a manufacturer during the depression of the 'thirties for an attractive dress which could sell for one dollar. Midge achieved this miracle. She engaged also in prosaic business enterprises which seemed more remote from her dainty femininity. She made a trip around the world, alone, when such tours were not common. She looked helpless but she was independent, practical and courageous and knew how to meet, unaided, both good fortune and bad."*[1184]

Kathleen and Eugene Bibb had remained in Minneapolis until 1921, when Eugene moved his law practice to New York City. In Minneapolis, the Bibbs lived first at the Leamington Hotel (demolished in 1989), then at 1200 Franklin Avenue West, and finally at 2600 Colfax Avenue South. Their son Eugene (called Gene or Gigi) was born in New York on August 7, 1922. (Both Eugenes had red hair.) Kathleen discovered that dishes in New York must be washed immediately after meals, for fear of cockroaches. Even in the Bibbs' elegant apartment, Kathleen scared mice out of the kitchen every night when she got up to heat the baby's bottle. "*She knew the various ones by sight.*"[1185] Kathleen performed several recitals in New York City. In 1925, the *New York Times* reported: "*An attractive stage presence, a charming delivery and a fresh soprano voice assured the success of Kathleen Hart Bibb at Aeolian Hall yesterday afternoon.*"[1186]

Despite financial and personal trials, Kathleen and her second husband, Frohman Foster, enjoyed a happy life. Frohman adopted Kathleen's son from her first marriage. (Her first husband remarried and had a son. In 1931, Bibb was arrested for drunk driving and striking an officer.) Kathleen and Frohman were overseas when the stock market crashed and returned home to find their assets gone. From 1930 to 1934, the Fosters lived in Minneapolis, where Kathleen taught in the music department of the University of Minnesota. The Fosters returned to Minneapolis about the same time Maud left, so Stella Hart had one of her two older daughters nearby (in addition to Helen) until only two years before Tom's death.

The Hart family was surprised and delighted in June 1931 to learn that Katie (as Maud called her) and Froh were expecting a baby in December. Maud wrote to them, "*Well, what have you gone and done anyhow! Delossy and I were simply struck dumb, deaf and blind by your news. Helen tells me that I am not to worry as* [the doctor] *says there isn't a trace of the kidney trouble* [the toxemia which had plagued Kathleen's first two pregnancies] *and that being the case I can't help rejoicing although you should both be spanked. What fun for us to have youngsters so near of an age! And do you want a boy or a girl! I am simply twittering and it seems to me I will explode if I can't get there and talk it over.*"[1187]

The family was expecting a girl, and the Fosters planned to call her Helen Elizabeth. As in the last trimesters of her previous pregnancies, Kathleen, now aged forty-two, developed toxemia (a condition of pregnancy associated with high blood pressure and the presence of protein in the urine). The baby girl did not survive birth at Abbott Hospital in Minneapolis on September 30, 1931. The effects of toxemia also put Kathleen at serious risk.

After the danger had passed, Maud wrote to Kathleen: "*I'm so thankful, dear darling precious, that you're all right. Now do get well fast, just as fast as you can, and we'll all start enjoying life again. Darling, I won't even speak of your terrific disappointment. You know, I know just exactly what it is, and my only consolation in thinking of it is that you have Gigi. I know that I could never bear even to mention or hear mentioned my first baby until Merian came, and now I speak of him quite often. So I feel sure that having Gigi, and him such a sweet dear little boy, will make all the difference to you and Froh between this experience being something just unbearable and something which can be borne. I know too that with my first baby, I was glad just to have* <u>*had*</u> *him, even though I lost him, and I imagine that you and Froh must feel something like that about your little girl, unless your terrible illness makes it different in your case.*"[1188]

Kathleen and Frohman lived at 2315 Irving Avenue South, 2647 Irving Avenue South, and 2530 Dupont Avenue South. They moved to 1880 Grand Avenue in St. Paul in 1934. The Fosters subsequently moved to Los Angeles, where Kathleen continued giving lessons in voice. The Fosters saw a good deal of their grandson in California in the early 1950s. In 1952, Maud wrote, "*Kathleen and her husband are so enjoying little Tommy, their year and a half old grandson, named for my father. And Helen and Frank have a little granddaughter, Cathy, who is the apple of their eye.*"[1189]

MIIL Archive

Helen and Frank Fowler

Helen and Frank are preparing to enjoy a Minnesota winter in the 1920s.

MHL Archive

Kathleen and Frohman Foster

This photo was taken in 1943.

MHL Archive

Gene Foster

The child of Kathleen's first marriage, Gene, was adopted by her second husband. This photo was taken in 1922.

MHL Archive

Two Flutists

Frohman and Gene Foster were both professional musicians. The *Golden Wedge* was dedicated to the two of them.

MHL Archive

Tea on the Terrace
Stella and Maud

Stella Hart lived with the family of her middle daughter for the greater part of the last decade of her life. This photo was taken about 1944.

MHL Archive

Stella Hart and her Grandchildren

Stella was photographed in about 1932 with her two grandchildren - Gene Foster and Merian Lovelace.

The Fosters moved to Salt Lake City in 1953, to be near Gene, who had joined the Utah Symphony. Gene Foster was a flutist, having followed in his stepfather's footsteps in his choice of instrument. Kathleen's second marriage was very happy, and Eugene and his stepfather were as close as father and son. In 1955, Kathleen joined the department of music at the University of Utah. She pursued her career as a vocal instructor at 439 South 11th Street East until her death on June 30, 1957, of a cerebral hemorrhage. Her ashes were spread among the rosebushes at her home.

Eugene Foster died in 1972. He had married four times and left half a dozen talented children. Two of them are aspiring writers, one is a violist, and an adopted daughter is a filmmaker.

Helen Hart married Frank Fowler on November 26, 1924. Like Maud, she was married in front of the fireplace at the Hart home, 905 W. 25th Street. Helen's only attendant was a pregnant Alice Dunnell (Louisa). Helen worked as a librarian at Jefferson Junior High School in Minneapolis and did social service work at the Minneapolis Public Library. Helen and Frank had no children of their own but were involved in the foster care of older children, particularly boys. Frank said: "*All my adult life I have been interested in boys and helping them whenever there is trouble in their homes. We never could have any children, and being a Big Brother meant a lot.*"[1190] The Fowlers took in five boys at different times for long-term care. They adopted one of them, Alfred Fowler (whose daughter Cathy became "the apple of their eye").

Frank bought a theater business in Forest Lake, Minnesota, in about 1937. By 1950, Frank, Helen, and Al had moved to California. Helen battled multiple sclerosis at 900 North Cleveland Street in Oceanside, California, until her death on December 15, 1960. She was buried in Fairhaven Memorial Park in Santa Ana, California.

Marion and Bill Everett moved to Minneapolis after their marriage. They lived at 2949 Portland Avenue for some years. Their three children were born at Abbott Hospital in 1922, 1923, and 1924. Marion's brother Grant (Hunter) lived nearby until 1924, when he returned to Mankato. Later the Everetts lived on Pillsbury Avenue South at 38th Street. In 1932, they built a beautiful home at 306 East Minnehaha Parkway (just east of 35W on the north side of the Parkway). Marion's addition to the floor plan was one closet for each of the children in the upstairs hall.

After the publication of *Heaven to Betsy* in 1945, Marion commented: "*I felt rather foolish at first, having been made a character in the book, but then excited high school girls began to approach me and ask, 'Are you really Carney?' Then I naturally became very proud.*"[1191]

In 1925, Marion Everett traveled to Seattle to be in the wedding of Connie Davis (Bonnie Andrews). Connie married Arthur Houlihan on November 16. She had met him in Seattle, to which she had moved from St. Paul in 1921. She had graduated from the University of Minnesota in 1914. Connie and Arthur had two sons and a daughter.

After high school, Jab Lloyd (Cab Edwards) attended the University of Minnesota's School of Forestry. He worked as a salesman for the Universal Portland Cement Company, then began work for Thompson Yards (Weyerhauser Lumber Company). Jab worked in St. Cloud, Minnesota; Mitchell, South Dakota; and Willmar, Minnesota. Jab and Grace's first son arrived in October 1918. Two more children, a son and a daughter, were born in Minneapolis after the war. In 1929, the family moved to Mankato, where Jab became division manager for Thompson. Jab Lloyd worked for Thompson Yards for thirty-nine years. He retired in 1955 and established Lloyd's Lumber, which his son Bob took over.

Eleanor Johnson (Winona II) attended the State Normal after graduating from high school in 1909. (She played on the basketball team at the Normal, which one can easily envision Winona doing!) Eleanor taught school in southern Minnesota for some years and became engaged - but not to Dennie. Fortunately for him, Eleanor broke off this engagement. Later, she did marry Dennie (Paul Ford). They were wed at the parsonage of St. John's Catholic Church in Mankato on January 22, 1918. It was a very small ceremony, at which Eleanor wore "*a handsome traveling suit of beaver silvertone and a tailored hat of white satin. She wore a coursage* [sic] *bouquet of sweetheart roses and violets. They were unattended.*" A wedding luncheon was held at the Johnson home at 325 Clark (East Pleasant). "*Covers were laid for twenty.*"[1192] Paul and Eleanor

Coll. of Louise King

Mr. and Mrs. William Everett

Marion Willard and Bill Everett (Carney Sibley and Sam Hutchinson) were married after the war on August 27, 1919.

Coll. of Louise King

The Clencher

Bill and Marion pause for an embrace before departing on their honeymoon camping trip.

Coll. of Louise King

Marion Willard Everett

Marion was photographed in her wedding pearls in 1919.

Coll. of Louise King

Marion and Rupe

"Carney" and "Larry" remained friends all their lives.

MHL Archive

Connie Davis Houlihan and Family

Connie (the fictional Bonnie Andrews) had three children. Two of them are shown here with Connie and her husband Arthur.

Coll. of Bonnie Bond

Beulah Hunt IlgenFritz

Beulah (Winona in *Downtown)* was photographed in front of the building of the *Mankato Free Press*, which her father once owned.

remained in Mankato through the early years of their marriage, living at 816 South Broad and later at 317 Hickory. Their two sons were born in Mankato before the Fords moved to Minneapolis in about 1937. They eventually moved to Lake Minnetonka.

Mildred Oleson (Irma Biscay) attended the State Normal after graduating from high school in 1912. Mildred did a great deal of singing at functions in high school, at the Normal, and around town (Maud mentions Irma's "sweet soprano voice" in *Betsy and Joe*[1193]). Mildred taught school in 1914 in Waseca, Minnesota, where she met a young dentist, John F. Cahill. The two were married on August 3, 1917. They lived in Waseca throughout their married lives, but their two sons were born at the hospital in Mankato. With her parents and two married sisters living in her hometown, Mildred no doubt traveled a great deal between Waseca and Mankato through the years.

Ruth Williams (Alice Morrison) also attended the State Normal in Mankato, then studied at the Chicago Art Institute. She eventually received her B.A. from Columbia. Ruth taught at Frostburg, Maryland, and Ann Arbor, Michigan. She met her future husband at a Christian Endeavor meeting in Ann Arbor. William T. Williams was attending medical school at the University of Michigan. The couple married in Pittsburgh in 1924 and had one daughter, born in Montana in 1926.

After high school graduation in 1911, Beulah Hunt (Winona Root I) attended the "aesthetic department of physical culture of the Cumnock school of oratory of Northwestern University." After this one-year course, Beulah attended the University of Wisconsin for a year. She was injured in a bobsled accident there and left the university. She spent the next year traveling in the western states and in Alaska. Beulah married Edwin IlgenFritz in the bay window of the library in the Hunt house on the corner of Byron and Clark (East Pleasant) on November 13, 1914. This was a Friday the 13th, a day chosen because Beulah and Edwin had met on a Friday the 13th at Northwestern. A black cat was pictured on their wedding invitation. Beulah's wedding dress was of "*rich embroidered oriental crepe. It was fashioned with a court train, and a Liege cape of chantilly lace. Her flowers were a shower of bride's roses.*"[1194]

The Hunts' wedding gift to their daughter was a house at 131 Byron in Mankato. Beulah and Edwin later lived at 415 Byron. Edwin was employed in Mankato by the Consumers Power Company. After the birth of their second daughter in Mankato in 1920, the couple moved to Illinois. In 1930, Edwin was offered an executive position with Florida Power, and the family remained in Florida permanently. Beulah was called "Betty" in her adult life.

Robert W. Hughes (Dave Hunt) earned a B.S. degree in mining engineering from the University of Wisconsin in 1915. He moved to Arizona in 1916 to begin work for the Inspiration Consolidated Copper Company. In 1925, he became chief mine engineer for the Miami (Arizona) Copper Company. Bob became vice-president and general manager of the company before his retirement in 1957. He and his wife Verna had a son and a daughter. Bob was said to have "doted" on the Betsy-Tacy books.

James Baker (E. Lloyd Harrington) attended the University of Minnesota and was editor of the *Minnesota Magazine* in 1912, at the time Maud's story "The Three Roses" appeared in it. After graduating in 1914, Jim taught civics and physics at Mankato High School (and acted as debate and athletics coach) for a year. Jim earned a master's degree in journalism from Columbia University before serving as a foreign correspondent in Mexico. He covered General Pershing's chase after Pancho Villa. Before the United States entered the First World War, Jim went overseas to serve in the Norton-Hardjes ambulance corps and later became a lieutenant in the French artillery. Back home in the Twin Cities, Jim was for many years Sunday editor of the *Minneapolis Tribune.* Later he became executive secretary of the Hennepin County Medical Society. Jim married Ada O'Neill of St. Paul in 1922, and they had a daughter and a son. Jim's children verify that, like E. Lloyd, Jim was a photo buff as a young man.[1195] About 1934, Jim gave his daughter a copy of *Early Candlelight* and told her he had known the author, but it does not appear that Jim and Maud maintained contact through the years, though Jim and his wife socialized with Marion and Bill Everett.

Tom Fox (Tom Slade) spent a year at the University of Illinois before his appointment to West Point. He pursued a lifelong military career. His brother George, the character Jerry, had died

Coll. of Ruth Hudgens

Cloche Quarters

Tess Kenney Holden, the character Katie, had one daughter. She opened a chicken restaurant in Minneapolis.

Coll. of Elizabeth Miller

Eleanor Wood Lippert

"Dorothy" was photographed on her wedding day in 1912.

Coll. of Paul Ford

Eleanor Johnson Ford & Son

"Winona" really married "Dennie." They had two sons.

BEC in WWI

Henry Lee

Henry inspired the high school character "Al Larson."

Coll. of Billie Andrews

Helmus Andrews

Helmus, otherwise known as Herbert Humphreys, was holding a cigarette in his right hand when this photo was taken.

Duplicated in several collections

Robert Hughes

Bob Hughes, who inspired the character Dave Hunt, became a mining engineer.

Duplicated in several collections

Mildred and Jack Cahill

Irma married a young dentist from Waseca.

of pneumonia in 1912 at the age of twenty-six. Tom met his future wife while attending West Point. A friend introduced Tom to his five sisters, the Berry girls. Tom went out with one after another, until he came to Lucy, the fourth. Tom and Lucy were married on September 4, 1919. Their son was born in 1921.

Rupert B. Andrews (Larry Humphreys) graduated from Stanford University in 1914. He met his wife Florence in Riverside, California. After their marriage, Rupert and Florence moved to Nevada, where Rupert became head of the Sierra Nevada Power Station. The couple's first son died of meningitis at age one. A daughter and another son came along in the years that followed. One of Rupert's greatest dreams was that his son would play football for Stanford, and this dream came true.

Helmus W. Andrews (Herbert Humphreys) also graduated from Stanford University in 1914. Both Andrews boys spent their first year at Pomona State College. During college, an artist asked Helmus to pose because of his fine physique. Helmus agreed, though he felt shy about posing in tennis shorts for a lady artist. Later the artist sent a snapshot of her finished statues, inscribed to "Mr. Andrews and his knees." The statues were made for Union Station in Washington, D.C. Helmus earned a degree in law but decided he did not want to be an attorney. He set up business as a produce broker in San Diego. Helmus ran the Andrews Brokerage Company profitably for many years. "Hal," as he was then called, met a young lady named Billie Owen at a party. He had been going with the hostess of the party, and Billie said she "*sort of put a stop to that in a hurry.*"[1196] Helmus and Billie married in 1925 and had one daughter. They built a beautiful home overlooking San Diego Bay.

Paolo Conte - Marco Regali in *Betsy and the Great World* - appears to have recovered expeditiously from the rejection of his marriage proposal to Maud in 1914. He accepted an offer to head the conservatory (music department) at the University of North Dakota in August 1914. On August 10, 1915, he married Mary Esther Johnson, his first music student.[1197] The University of North Dakota has a substantial Paolo Conte Collection - consisting of hundreds of musical compositions and other papers. Paolo wrote the score for *Wings*, the first Academy-Award-winning film.

After high school, Marguerite Marsh (Emily Webster of Deep Valley) stayed in Mankato with her grandfather until his death in 1915. She enrolled in a home economics course at the University of Wisconsin for the fall semester in 1916 and completed that academic year. In the autumn of 1917, Marguerite enlisted in the YMCA for canteen work. She went overseas with the 82nd Division to run a YMCA cafe at Tours, France, and later at Gondrecourt. In 1921, Marguerite enrolled at Columbia University's teachers' college. Here she met Myron Wilcox, who most likely inspired the character Jed Wakeman. (Myron had also been at Gondrecourt, so it is possible they met earlier, in France. Myron had also been at the Second Officers Training Camp at Fort Snelling.) Marguerite and Myron were married in New York in 1923. Myron took a teaching position in Cedar Falls, Iowa, where the couple lived until 1925.

Just four days before the arrival of her baby, Marguerite wrote a letter to a friend who had recently become a new mother. "*I want to know such bushels of things. Can you go up and down stairs? How do your clothes fit? Can you bathe the baby yourself? Are you afraid you will drop her? And how about a buggy?*"[1198]

Perhaps Maud felt a special bond with Marguerite after life and death touched each woman in February 1925. Each gave birth to a son. Maud's son died the day he was born. Marguerite's son lived, but she herself died soon after his birth.

Betsy, Tacy, and Tib (Maud, Bick, and Midge) were reunited in Mankato for Betsy-Tacy Day in 1961. The Mankato branch of the American Association of University Women sponsored this event. Mayor Rex Hill officially proclaimed October 7 as "Betsy-Tacy Day." On Friday evening, October 6, Maud had an autographing session and reception. Children met Maud on Saturday morning at Lincoln School. On Saturday afternoon, there was a second autographing session at the old Carnegie Library, along with walking tours of the Center Street neighborhood. The Blue Earth County Historical Society had an exhibit of turn-of-the-century objects, one of which was the steam whistle from the Big Mill!

The chairman of the Betsy-Tacy reunion was Dr. Anna Wiecking. "*I have known the Wieckings since I was a little girl, and*

Duplicated in several collections

Maud and Bick

This photo was taken on a visit to Mankato in October 1940.

Coll. of Peggy Kirch

Bick Kenney Kirch

After a visit with Bick in 1948, Maud wrote: "*Bick looked so pretty and had such pretty clothes!*" (4-14-48)

Coll. of Peggy Kirch

Maud and Bick

Maud and Bick visited back and forth between California and New York on a regular basis.

Coll. of Peggy Kirch

Maud and Bick

Maud and Bick took a trip to Europe together in 1968.

aren't they fine people! I have found Dr. Anna to be such a good friend and I greatly appreciate knowing her and her sisters. My sister Kathleen ... Julia, in the books ... was in Martha's class in school."[1199]

Bick and Maud spent a good deal of time together in the late sixties. Delos died of a heart attack on January 17, 1967, and his ashes were scattered over the Pacific Ocean. After his death, Bick came to spend two months with Maud. A year later, Bick came back for another month when Maud was recovering from surgery. Maud and Bick left on September 1, 1968, for a trip to Ireland (to trace Bick's roots), London, Portugal, Spain (where they visited the castle in Madrid, looking for the king), and Rome. Maud and Bick sailed home on the S.S. *Michelangelo* in November 1968. Bick passed away suddenly, of cardiac arrest, on December 14, 1969. She was buried at Mount Olivet Cemetery in Tonawanda, New York.

In 1970, Maud moved out of her house and into a pleasant cottage at 884 West Harrison in Mount San Antonio Gardens, a retirement community. In December 1974, she moved to an apartment in the Lodge at Mount San Antonio Gardens. Maud passed away quietly on March 11, 1980, from complications of pneumonia, in the medical unit at Mount San Antonio Gardens. Her ashes were interred at Glenwood Cemetery, Mankato.

It is sad to think that all of the Betsy-Tacy characters have ascended to the big Sunday Night Lunch in the sky. Through the Betsy-Tacy books, of course, they have achieved some measure of immortality. But more importantly, these people were full of a joy and spirit which surely could not simply cease to be. This is not only a matter of basic theological truth but also metaphysical imperative - something we need not come to, but simply know. As Maud wrote in *Betsy and Joe*: "You felt a sort of pulse ... which proved that nothing dies, that everything comes back in beauty."[1200]

[1182] MHL to A. Wiecking, 8-13-66.

[1183] MHL to Miss Gilland's Class, 5-22-42.

[1184] *Mankato Free Press*, 2-4-65.

[1185] Winter Notes, p. 16.

[1186] *New York Times*, 2-25-25.

[1187] MHL to Foster Family, 6-31.

[1188] MHL to K. Foster, 10-5-31.

[1189] MHL to T. Edwards, 11-3-52.

[1190] *Register*, 1959.

[1191] *Mankato Free Press*, 12-16-74.

[1192] Ibid., 1-22-18.

[1193] *Betsy and Joe*, p. 150.

[1194] *Mankato Free Press*, 11-14-14.

[1195] Interview with B. Baker, 6-17-90.

[1196] Interview with B. Andrews, 11-3-90.

[1197] Interview with W. Conte, 10-18-94.

[1198] Marguerite Marsh Wilcox, 1-29-25. Sesonske collection.

[1199] MHL to E. Deike, 8-25-66.

[1200] *Betsy and Joe*, p. 203.

ACKNOWLEDGMENTS

Grateful thanks to the descendants and near relatives of the "characters" from the Betsy-Tacy books, without whom this book would have remained a long list of unanswered questions: Merian Lovelace Kirchner, Mary Nankervis, Susan Ryder, Celo Hartman, Romie Van Etten, Louise Lee, Mary Garbutt, Mary Ann Clark, Thom Foster, Anita Exline, Jone Foster, Brent Foster, Louise Foster, Alfred Fowler, Madeline Fowler, Don Freeman, Dorothy Gerretson, and Bill Gerretson. Charles and Eileen Kenney, Jane Kirch, Peggy Kirch, Peter Kirch, Katie Kenney, Jim Hudgens, Ruth Hudgens, Margaret Thuente, Jeanne Fahey, and Edward Murphy. Beverly Schindler, Joan Nichols, Mary Martin, and Lloyd King. Robert Cahill, Helen Benham Day, and Jean Babcock Lander. Louise King, Caroline King, Jim Willard, Nancy Fifield, and Margery Erstgaard. Bill Houlihan, Ruth Faber, and the Chapin family. Bonnie Bond, Beverly Crowe, Paul Ford, Bunny Ford, Mary Harty, Helen Kigin, Colleen Kigin, and Helen Bouilly. Howard Williams and Fallie Beers. Billie Andrews, Peg Barnard, Rupert B. Andrews, and Pat Kresin. Robert Lloyd, Millicent (Mickee) Steiner, Tom Fox, Elizabeth Miller, Jim Allen, Allegra Eldridge, Dorothy Enfield, Mary Vestal, Bart Baker, Sally Ross, Natalie Houdlette, Robert Ahlers, Peggy Brockmeyer, John Hoerr, and Jane Mitchell. Ralph Wilcox and the Sesonske family. William Conte, Brad Morison, Peg Gingerich, Nancy Leussler, Doris Bergman, and Merritt Campbell. Alice Brown, Eva Kenyon, Lucy Crabtree, and Paige Cavanaugh.

Thanks also to Ed Franey, Arthur Tourangeau, Mrs. William TerLouw, Deborah Naffziger, Violet Hoehn, Bernice Harvey, Jill Hile, Mary Black-Rogers, Lyman Wakefield, Esther Hautzig, Elizabeth Riley, Elizabeth Leslie, Norman Brouwer, Phillip Gossett, and Gene Skurupijs.

Many thanks to Betsy-Tacy fans who have shared their Lovelace collections: Libby Moore, the Berg family, Joelie Hicks, Floyd Smith, Betsy Norum, Shirley Lieske, Laurel Erickson, Elaine

Flathers, Donna Mallon, Jacque Cloninger, Carlienne Frisch, Marcia Marshall, Evelyn Mikkelson, Jim Schendel, Kathleen Baxter, Gretchen Wronka, Debbie Hanson, JoAnne Ray, Amy Dolnick, Kelly Reuter, Colleen Timmins, Lona Falenczykowski, Susan Thiets, RuthAnn Green, Anne Whitman, Bonnie Gardner, Mary Atwell, Bill Edwards, Lisa Mayotte, Beth Hudson, Melanie Rigney, Anne Kolibaba, and Helen Dusbabek. Though the Betsy-Tacy fans who have shared copies of nearly four hundred MHL letters are too numerous to name here, their generosity is warmly appreciated.

To librarians and other resource persons who have been great facilitators: the staffs of Nichols Library, Emmaus Library, Blue Earth County Historical Society, Minnesota Historical Society, Iowa State Historical Society, the Kerlan Collection, Minneapolis Public Library, Minnesota Valley Regional Library, Hennepin History Museum, St. Paul Public Library, Claremont Public Library, Milwaukee Public Library, Chicago Public Library, New York Public Library, the British Museum, the Library of Congress, and the former night owl librarians at Arlington Heights. Thanks to Lois Ringquist, Shirley Bradey, Karen Hoyle, Mary Ann Vande Vusse, Shirley Higginbotham, Doris Pagel, Caroline B. Davis, M.E. Ragan, Nicola Southworth, and Betty Peck.

To residents of Mankato, present and former, and other experts on Mankato: Gail Palmer, Tom Hagan, Emma Wiecking, Colleen Smith, Bunny Just, Gordon Kennedy, Ken and Marilyn Berg, Joe Abdo, Leslie Morse, Arthur Johnson, George Scherer, Mary Jane Koehler, Ruth Confer, Mildred Bolstad, Morgan Brandrup, Margaret Druckenbrod, Lillian Leftault, Frank Manning, Sandy Kerkoff, Blanche Barnhart, Irene Kemp, Viola McConnell, Mary Dickmeyer, Kay Frost, and Cora Linder Thro.

Illustrations reproduced from the Betsy-Tacy books, with the permission of HarperCollins, are by Lois Lenski and Vera Neville. Illustrations drawn for this book are by Cheryl Harness.

Thanks to those who have assisted with their remarks on the manuscript: Merian Kirchner, Johanna Hurwitz, JoAnne Ray,

Stephanie Cummings, Margaret Scannell, Suzanne Mosesso, Marcia Marshall, Diane Gonzalez, Susan Stanfield, Michele Franck, and Laura Grieve.

Architectural plans by Nancy Beckner Bastian.
Edited by Laura Vadaj.
Electronic index generation by Shawn Scannell.
Photo credits - where no credit line runs under an image, the photograph was taken by the author.

Sources of photographs which were abbreviated in credit lines:

1895 Atlas:
The Standard Historical and Pictorial Atlas and Gazetteer of Blue Earth County, Minnesota (Minneapolis: Central Publishing Co.), 1895.

History of BEC:
Hughes, Thomas, *The History of Blue Earth County* (Middle West Publishing Co.), 1906.

Mankato, Its First Fifty Years, Containing Addresses, Historic Papers, and Brief Biographies of Early Settlers and Active Upbuilders of the City (Mankato: Free Press Printing Co.), 1902.

Castle, Henry, *History of Minnesota*, Vol. III (Chicago: Lewis Publishing), 1915.

INDEX

CHARACTERS AND COUNTERPARTS

Bonnie Andrews	Constance Emily Davis
Dr. Andrews	Dr. George W. Davis
Mrs. Andrews	Sarah Emily Grinshaw Davis
Dr. Atherton	Dr. Lathan Crandall
Aunt Dolly (Hornik)	Dell Irasek Prescott
Aunt Ruth (Willard)	Josephine Wheeler Lovelace
Mr. Bagshaw	Jack Sickle
Miss Caroline Bangeter	Caroline Fullerton
Bob Barhydt	Bill Brewster/Russell McCord
Miss Benbow	Myrtle Francis
Mrs. Benson	Mrs. Benedict
Irma Biscay	Florence Mildred Oleson
Phil Brandish	Carl George Hoerr et al.
Mr. Burton	Mr. Richmond
Jean Carver	Jean Etty
Mr. Chandler	Mr. Hollis
Miss Clarke	Grace Eleanor Comstock
Jimmy Cliff	Earle Buell
Marbeth Cliff	Marietta (Mett) Buell
Jimmy Jr. Cliff	Bud Buell
Bobby Cobb	Robb Williams
Miss Jessie Cobb	Kate Robb
Leonard Cobb	Walter Williams
Dolly Cohen	Caroline Soloman
Mr. Cook	William Warwick
Clay Dawson	Francis Creighton Fowler
Mamie Dodd	Mamie Skuse
Dorothy Drew	Eleanor Wood
Jack Dunhill	Charles Albert Harris

Cab Edwards	Jabez Alvin Lloyd
Jean Edwards	Grace Cable Reed Lloyd
Effie	Ella Dickenson
Mrs. Ekstrom	Mrs. Asplund
Miss Erickson	Helen Cooper
Dennie Farisy	Paul Gerald Ford
Ferdy	William Prescott
Miss Gwendolyn Fowler	Gwendolyn Fischer
Fred (Julia's beau)	Dick Wood
Mr. Gaston	Dr. E.C. Stakeman
Frau Geiger	Fraulein Kellner
Hanni	Hannie
E. Lloyd Harrington	James H. Baker Jr.
Harry (Julia's beau)	Jay J. Flachsenhar
Mr. Bradford Hawthorne	Harry B. Wakefield
Mrs. Eleanor Hawthorne	Lillian Hammons Wakefield
Sally Day Hawthorne	Lucy Day Wakefield
Mrs. Heaton	Mrs. Brumwell
Louisa Hilton	Alice Dunnell
Judge Hodges	General James H. Baker
Grossmama Hornik	Katherine Irasek
Grosspapa (Alois) Hornik	Alois Irasek
Uncle Rudy Hornik	Jack Irasek
Hugh (Julia's beau)	Alan C. Fleischbein
Herbert Humphreys	Helmus Weddel Andrews
Larry Humphreys	Rubert Burke Andrews
Mr. Humphreys	Charles Nathaniel Andrews
Mrs. Humphreys	Mary Frances Andrews
Dave Hunt	Robert William Hughes
Sam Hutchinson	William Everett
Jerry (Julia's friend)	George Talfourd Fox
Bee Kelly	Ruth Evangeline Kenney
Celia Kelly	Margaret E. Kenney
George Kelly	George E. Kenney
Katie Kelly	Theresa Catherine Kenney
Mr. Kelly	Patrick Kenney
Mrs. Kelly	Rose Kenney
Mary Kelly	Rosemary Kenney
Paul Kelly	Charles Ignatius Kenney

Tacy Kelly	Frances Vivian Kenney
Mr. Kendall	Charles Griebel
Harry Kerr	Charles Eugene Kirch
Baby Kelly Kerr	Robert Charles Kirch
2nd Baby Son Kerr	James Kenney Kirch
Kismet the Cat	Kismet
Cap' Klein	Cap' Keysor
Al Larson	Henry Orlando Lee
Leo (Katie's beau)	Charles Holden
Tony Markham	Clarence Lindon (Mike) Parker
Mr. Maxwell	Donald MacDonald
Mr. Meecham	James Ray Tinkcom
Miss Mix	Amelia Rausch
Stan Moore	Herman Hayward
Alice Morrison	Ruth Fallie Williams
Freddie Muller	Henry Clay Gerlach
Grossmama Muller	Marie Gerlach
Grosspapa (Gerhard) Muller	Max Gerlach
Hobbie Muller	William Dewey Gerlach
Mr. Muller	Henry Christian Gerlach
Mrs. Muller	Wilhelmina (Minnie) Gerlach
Tib Muller	Marjorie Gerlach
Grandma Newton	Albertine Palmer Austin
Grandpa Newton	Chauncey Austin
Mr. O'Farrell	William James O'Hagan
Miss O'Rourke	Emma C. O'Donnell
Paige (Julia's husband)	Frohman Murphy Foster
Patty	Ella Dickenson
Peg	Sybil May
Old Pete	Guy Moore
Pin	Charles Ernest (Pin) Jones
Mr. (Melborn) Poppy	Clarence Saulpaugh
Mrs. Poppy	Roma Saulpaugh/Nettie Snyder
Isobel Porteous	Dorothy Brinsmaid
Q	Darragh Aldrich (Clara Thomas)
Betsy Ray	Maud Palmer Hart
Julia Ray	Kathleen Palmer Hart

Margaret Ray	Helen Palmer Hart
Mr. Bob Ray	Thomas Walden Hart
Mrs. Jule Ray	Stella Palmer Hart
Miss Raymond	Fanny Pitcher
Dick Reed	Claude Anderson
Mr. (Leonard) Reed	Mr. Anderson
Marco Regali	Paolo Conte
Rena	Abby Cragun
Mr. Root	Frank W. Hunt
Mrs. Root	Nellie Hunt
Winona Root I	Beulah Ariel Hunt
Winona Root II	Mary Eleanor Johnson

Bobbie Sibley	John Harrington Willard
Carney Sibley	Marion Willard
Hunter Sibley	Grant Robbins Willard
Jerry Sibley	Harold Sibley Willard
Mr. Sibley	William Dodsworth Willard
Mrs. Sibley	Louise Robbins Willard
Sigrid	Doris Edsten
Grandma Slade	Mary Pitcher
Tom Slade	Thomas Warren Fox
Hazel Smith	Hazel Schoelkopf (?)
Miss Sparrow	Miss McGraw/Miss Van Buren
Squirrelly	Earl Elmer King
Miss Surprise	Miss Siboni
Anna Swenson	Anna (Gustafson?)

Tilda	Else

Mr. & Mrs. Van Blarcum	Jesse & Lucetta Barclay
Helena von Wandersee	Hertha von Einem

Jed Wakeman	Myron Jefferson Wilcox
Washington (the Cat)	General Baker (a cat)
Emily Webster	Marguerite Elizabeth Marsh
Grandpa Cyrus Webster	John Quincy Adams Marsh
Mrs. Wheat	Mrs. Moore
Joe Willard	Delos Wheeler Lovelace
Ben Williams	Warren Yates
Miss Williams	Gertrude Yates
Win	Adeline DeSale
Winkie	Annie Green

BOOKS BY MAUD HART LOVELACE
in order of publication

The Black Angels	1926
Early Candlelight	1929
Petticoat Court	1930
The Charming Sally	1932
One Stayed at Welcome with Delos Lovelace	1934
Gentlemen from England with Delos Lovelace	1937
Betsy-Tacy	1940
Betsy-Tacy and Tib	1941
Betsy and Tacy Go Over the Big Hill	1942
The Golden Wedge with Delos Lovelace	1942
Betsy and Tacy Go Downtown	1943
Heaven to Betsy	1945
Betsy in Spite of Herself	1946
Betsy Was a Junior	1947
Betsy and Joe	1948
Carney's House Party	1949
Emily of Deep Valley	1950
The Tune is in the Tree	1950
The Trees Kneel at Christmas	1951
Betsy and the Great World	1952
Winona's Pony Cart	1953
Betsy's Wedding	1955
What Cabrillo Found	1958
The Golden Pheasant (booklet)	1963
The Valentine Box	1966